DATE DUE

7-10-2020

PRINTED IN U.S.A.

BONANZA WEST

The Story of the Western Mining Rushes, 1848–1900

BONANZA WEST

The Story of the Western Mining Rushes
1848•1900

William S. Greever

UNIVERSITY OF IDAHO PRESS ◆ MOSCOW, IDAHO

LIBRARY OF CONGRESS CATALOG CARD NUMBER: 63-8991
Copyright 1963 by William Greever

TO MY WIFE

IN America before the twentieth century a major factor in our national development was the existence of unoccupied land which steadily drew the settler farther west until finally there were no significantly vacant regions left to occupy. Beyond the frontier line, cutting edge of orderly development, lay the almost untrammeled wilderness. Here, where ordinary men dared not yet tread, ranged the harbingers of civilization—the Indian trader, the trapper, the cattleman, and the miner—eager to exploit the unconquered wilds, to make unusual efforts in the hope of exceptional rewards, to live beyond the restraint of ordinary conventions, perhaps also to seek superb adventure or to find consoling solitude.

The miner cherished the greatest hope, that of making an electrifying discovery which would thrust a real fortune into his hands. Usually he was a young man, with unbounded optimism, with persistence which buoyed him over many a disappointing obstacle in months or years of search, with physical stamina for prolonged strenuous efforts, and with idealistic eagerness for adventure akin to that of a patriot volunteering for army service the first week after a declaration of war. The prospector began with as little technical knowledge of mining, as scant information about the region where he was going, and as slight experience in the living conditions he would face as the average American of 1961 had about outer space. The miner searched for sudden wealth under circumstances much more favorable to the ordinary person than those today in stock markets, gambling, lotteries, or invention. Proud of his independence, alone or with a few partners, he sought a fortune he need share with

no one else. Those who caught his spirit but were too old, too tim-
orous, or too encumbered to leave their established homes shared in
the daring adventure by financing a young man's trip west or by
recklessly braving the dangers of honest failure or intentional fraud
to invest in mining-company stock. Others who took no action still
talked and dreamed about the current mining rush. Only a very few
resolutely put such thoughts completely out of their minds; most notable were the Mormons in the California of 1848 who eagerly left the
possibility of finding a mere fortune to go on to Brigham Young's
Utah and help build there a kingdom of God.

The western mining rushes attracted merchants, saloonkeepers,
entertainers, wagon freighters, steamshipmen, stage coachmen, and
food producers—all expecting to reap considerably higher profits
than in more settled regions, all confident that their more certain
rewards were better than attempting to grasp the gigantic prize won
by only a few lucky miners. The rushes fostered supply points between civilization and the isolated mining communities. They stimulated railroads. They caused permanent settlement of the Trans-
Mississippi West more quickly than would have happened under
normal circumstances and in geographical patterns quite different
from those which would have developed out of a steady, orderly
pushing of the frontier line westward from the Arkansas-Missouri
border of the early 1860's until the gradually engulfed wilderness
eventually brought the pioneers to the waters of the Pacific Ocean.

The saga of how bold men braved great perils, won huge riches,
met tremendous disappointments, sought dubious recreations, flouted
laws, rose up as vigilantes, started to develop areas steadily from wilderness to urban center, abandoned places to sink back into an almost
virgin land—all this and much more is the story of the western mining
rushes. To recapture this epic, to tell what happened in one of the
most colorful and important eras of America's development, to present a well-rounded picture of the many things occurring simultaneously, to gather and cull much scattered information about the
rushes into a single compact, authoritative, and readable synthesis
is the objective of this book. It does not attempt to include or catalog every flurry about all minerals throughout the West, but con-
centrates on the great and significant rushes. It makes no pretense
of being an original contribution to knowledge based upon material

never before examined, but from a variety of highly specialized studies by many researchers performs the necessary and useful service of presenting composite findings.

The book is intended for both the general reader and the scholar. For the reader who knows nothing more about the rushes or western development generally than what was learned in high school history, the book is designed to give a reasonably well-rounded picture of exactly what happened. This is why the discussion of California contains an account of how wagon trains moved westward from Independence, Missouri, to California—a process well known to the expert in western history but not to the general public. For the scholar, the book is intended to supply all the general information necessary for any ordinary pupose. To anyone contemplating intensive study of a particular rush, the text presents a comprehensive overview and the bibliography an accurate guide to the most important books and articles in this field. Anyone interested in a particular topic, such as newspapers or the theater in gold rushes, may follow it by using the index and for further references can consult the footnotes.

Where the necessary information could be unearthed, an important purpose of the book is to be as specific as possible, to put the facts concretely rather than vaguely. Thus the chapters devoted to California go beyond the usual statement that many permanent buildings were made of stone and enumerate the kinds employed; the text tells precisely the kind of paving used on the trail across Panama in Spanish times and describes as faithfully as possible what Lola Montez' famous dance was. Another objective of the book is to discuss the literary figures who took part in the rushes and wrote about them; usually these are mentioned so casually that a reader, to secure any significant information about them, must consult a literary history or a biography.

Much of the work on this book was made possible by a fellowship in 1958–59, gratefully acknowledged, from the John Simon Guggenheim Memorial Foundation. A large portion of the research was done in the excellent collection at the Bancroft Library, University of California, Berkeley, whose staff was both co-operative and cordial. Many helpful suggestions about style were made by my father, Garland Greever, professor emeritus of English at the University of

Southern California, and by my wife, Janet Groff Greever, who holds a doctorate in history. Mrs. Carrol Dozier helped type the final manuscript.

William S. Greever

UNIVERSITY OF IDAHO
JANUARY, 1963

CONTENTS

MAPS

BONANZA WEST

The Story of the Western Mining Rushes, 1848–1900

1

T H E gold rush to California made the name of John Augustus Sutter a byword to most Americans of his day, but it destroyed the agricultural empire and budding industrial enterprise upon which his early fame rested.[1] Born in Switzerland, he had gone bankrupt there and escaped imprisonment for debt only by flight. He quickly came to America, where he began inflating his ego by telling tales of his adventures in the Swiss military, although actually he had never served in any army. In 1838, he went to California by an indirect route: overland with various fur-trading parties until he reached the Hudson's Bay Company post of Fort Vancouver, then by ship, first to Honolulu, next north to Sitka, and finally to San Francisco. Styling himself "Captain Sutter," in August, 1839, he established a ranch at what is now the city of Sacramento. Before long he became a Mexican citizen, received a routine-size land grant of 48,818 acres, secured appointment as the local political and military authority, and, to console himself for the wife he had virtually abandoned in Switzerland, installed two Hawaiian concubines.

Sutter erected a private fort upon a slight elevation. It had an excellent strategic location, directly on the route from the Missouri and Willamette rivers overland to San Francisco Bay, and dominated the northern half of California's great valley. Within the quadrangle of its bastioned, loopholed adobe walls were granaries, stores, workshops, dwellings, and a central headquarters. On the large, well-drained fields adjacent Sutter raised wheat, cattle, and some fruit. Gradually he expanded into pioneering industrial ventures which

[1] James P. Zollinger, *Sutter: The Man and His Empire*, 4–223; Owen C. Coy, *Gold Days*, 23–26; John W. Caughey, *Gold Is the Cornerstone*, 4–5.

3

promised future profits but whose present deficits plunged him ever more deeply into debt. He employed as many whites as were available, a rather unattractive lot, but depended most for labor upon the lazy and inexperienced local Indians. Inept mechanics, inefficient supervision, a heart too kind to refuse any applicant employment, and an openhanded generosity to immigrants made his problems more difficult. His real hope for financial success lay in emigration from the United States, which was increasing but slowly.

When peace was restored at the end of the Mexican War, California became an American possession. Sutter's activities continued much as before but with faster tempo. Aided by increased immigration, especially in getting some trained mechanics, but hampered by his ever more difficult financial situation, he turned more often than he should have to drink. When 150 men from the famous Mormon Battalion of the Mexican War stopped at his fort and commented that Brigham Young had ordered them to remain in California awhile before going on to Utah, Sutter employed many of them.

Some he used on a project important to California's history, his sawmill.[2] His partner in it, apparently an equal one, was James Marshall, thirty-three, a man sensible and skillful, especially in carpentry and farming, but moody. The two placed the mill forty-five miles from the fort in a valley four miles in circumference and close to excellent stands of oak, pine, and balsam. Soon at work at the site were Marshall, Peter L. Wimmer and his wife, who served as cook, eight other whites, including some Mormons, and a number of Indians, ten of whom spoke Spanish. The plan was to build a log-and-brush dam from the south side of the stream to a good-sized bar about the middle of the river. This would divert water into an old dry channel that cut directly across a strip of land around which the main stream now swung wide, approximately in the shape of the letter C. About a third of the way down the unused bed, which would be deepened into a race, the mill would be built. Work progressed according to plan.

When the workmen made the first trial of the mill, they discovered that the tailrace was not deep enough at the lower end. They began digging again, extracting rocks by day and turning in the water at

2 Zollinger, *Sutter*, 226-35; Coy, *Gold Days*, 31-36; Caughey, *Cornerstone*, 6-16, 22; Hubert H. Bancroft, *History of California*, VI, 27-51, and *California Inter Pocula*, 47-50, 65-79.

night to wash away the unencumbered sand and gravel. On the morning of Monday, January 24, 1848, Marshall walked down the tailrace to see what had happened during the night. At the lower end, on the north side about two hundred feet below the mill, his eye caught a glitter about six inches under some water on a riffle of soft granite. He extracted the material, quickly concluded it was not the proper weight for mica, and pounded it on a flat stone until satisfied that it was too malleable to be copper. Could it be gold? He decided it was. Apparently he told his men nothing of the discovery until evening; nobody got excited at the news. The next morning, Marshall again investigated. He picked out perhaps a half-ounce of the metal, placed it in the crown of his hat, and returned, exclaiming, "Boys, by God, I've got it." One of the men, Azariah Smith, drew out a five-dollar gold piece for a crude comparison with Marshall's metal. The likeness seemed convincing; so did the result of biting the ore and pounding it on an anvil. All now went down to the race and extracted tiny pieces of the shiny substance. They poured vinegar on a bit of it and further tested it by boiling in Mrs. Wimmer's soap kettle.

The great discovery was made. True, it was not the first, for in the early 1840's a single mine had been discovered in Southern California, but nothing more developed there. From the gold in the race of the sawmill came the famous rush.

Marshall promptly reported the find to his partner. On a rainy afternoon he entered Sutter's headquarters, dripping water and oozing excitement. He requested that they go into the private office, asked if the door was locked, demanded assurance they were alone, and then said he wished to make some scales. Instead, Sutter unlocked the door and got scales from the apothecary's shop. Marshall had started to show something in a white cotton rag when a clerk passed, causing him to thrust it back in his pocket in hasty alarm. When the clerk was ordered out and the door again locked, Marshall showed Sutter the metal and expressed the belief that it was gold. Sutter carefully examined the tiny pieces, then remarked, "Well, it so looks; we will try it." First they applied aqua fortis. Then they balanced the scales with equal weights of silver dollars and Marshall's gold; under water, the gold outweighed the silver. They consulted a volume of the *American Encyclopedia* about other tests. Sutter concluded that the sample was the finest kind of gold. He was urged by Marshall to return at once to the mill but instead waited until the next morning. His partner, without supper, hastened off in the rain.

Back at the sawmill the next morning, Marshall suggested to his men that they replace their bits of gold in the tailrace. All these Sutter could then supposedly discover for himself and it would doubtless excite him so that he would give all hands a treat from the bottle he habitually carried. The plan misfired, for as Sutter headed toward the water, one of Wimmer's young boys raced ahead, picked up nearly all the gold again, and hurried back to boast of what he said he had just found.

Sutter proposed to the men that they keep the discovery of gold secret for six weeks, until he could complete his mill. All of them willingly agreed, but actually the news could not be suppressed. Sutter's long conference with Marshall that rainy afternoon had led many at the fort to suspect the discovery of a mine, generally supposed to be quicksilver. He aroused further suspicions when he and Marshall secured from the local Indians, the Culumas, a three-year lease on ten or twelve square miles of the area around the sawmill for an annual payment of hats, handkerchiefs, and other items of no special value. He asked the military governor, Colonel R. B. Mason, for title to the land, including pasture and mining privileges, but the Colonel had no authority to make such a grant. The man who carried his application to Mason at Monterey was a Mormon, Charles Bennett, who confided the secret to men boasting of a coal mine near Mount Diablo and to Isaac Humphrey in San Francisco, a man experienced in Georgia gold mines. Sutter himself told John Bidwell, Henry Lienhard, Mariano Vallejo, and perhaps others. Then, toward the end of February, the Captain sent a Swiss teamster up to the sawmill with supplies. The Wimmer boys told him about the gold; he laughed. Their mother defended them by confirming the discovery, and he left with a sample. Back at the fort, he tried to use it to buy whiskey at the store. Its worth doubted, he challenged the clerks to consult Sutter, and the Captain had little choice but to confirm the news.

At the mill itself, the men were not too excited after Sutter's visit. The only one to take immediate steps was Henry W. Bigler. On six days, usually alone, he went looking outside the tailrace and always managed to extract a little gold with the point of his knife. On the night of February 27, three Mormons arrived and picked up some gold. As they were returning, they prospected the river about halfway between the sawmill and Sutter's flour mill and made an excellent find, Mormon Bar, as it came generally to be known, which proved clearly that there was gold to be found in other places besides the famous tailrace. The sawmill was finally completed and the first log was made into boards on March 11. Gradually the men began to drift away; the rush really began when Sutter's former employees began their gold seeking. Incidentally, many of the Mormons followed Brigham Young's orders to band together in June and go to Utah; their obedience in leaving a possible fortune for the grinding tasks of building a desert empire was a remarkable demonstration of religious faith and of how Young could inspire his people.

The great discovery did not bring wealth to either Marshall or Sutter. The carpenter was too moody, too certain that the world owed him a great deal for his find, and so utterly failed to grasp the opportunity a man of action would have seized. Sutter tried to keep his men at work, but of course he could not. He did not apply himself with great vigor to the perhaps impossible task of holding his empire together. He often put his signature on important legal papers without reading them, sometimes signing when considerably under the influence of liquor, and generally he neglected his business. He gave unbounded hospitality to any who sought it and lived in a grandiose style, even after the United States Supreme Court held invalid his major land grant from the Spanish. The net result was that Sutter lost almost everything and as an old man in Pennsylvania lived in ordinary middle-class comfort. His financial difficulties in later years, however, can never obscure the vital role he played in the early history of California and the gold rush.

The year of discovery, 1848, saw generally the start of the rush.[3] At first the news of what Marshall had found made little impression in California. No newspaper mentioned the event until a brief paragraph appeared in the *San Francisco Californian* on March 15. For a while men in the bay town, a place of about eight hundred population, were interested but hesitated to say much openly for fear of ridicule. Then, early in May, Samuel Brannan, a thoroughgoing extrovert, paraded through the streets of San Francisco with a bottle of dust, shouting, "Gold! Gold! Gold from the American River!"

[3] Bancroft, *History*, VI, 53–96; Coy, *Gold Days*, 60–87; Caughey, *Cornerstone*, 20–38.

He precipitated a rush out of San Francisco. By the middle of June, three-fourths of the town's men had left for the mines, the two news-papers stopped publication for want of a staff, and even the meetings of the town council were suspended. Land values in the city fell by half, goods not used in mining became a drug on the market, and many a place of business bore the sign "Gone to the Diggings." Sailors deserted their ships; when one captain found he had no crew left, he, too, departed for the gold fields, leaving his wife and daughter as an anchor watch. The price of a shovel jumped from one dollar to ten, of a rowboat from fifty to four or five hundred. The rush which started in May from San Francisco began in June from San Jose and Monterey and in July from Southern California. The men of these areas were stirred less by the known facts than by the example of San Francisco. Men of Spanish origin were less excited than Anglo-Saxons. From various army posts a large number of American sol-diers deserted. Gradually the news spread beyond California— Ha-waii received two pounds of gold on May 31, but not until July did a substantial exodus begin. From there Hudson's Bay Company men took the word to Oregon, which by fall had lost two-thirds of its male population to California's mines. During the later summer a considerable number of gold seekers began coming from Mexico, especially Sonora. By the end of the year, a few men had arrived from Chile, Australia, and China.

The early gold seekers found that the most direct route from San Francisco lay in going by some kind of boat to Sacramento. Except for this bit of water, all travel was by land. There were no roads, simply trails between the larger settlements and beyond only the sun and the mountain peaks as guides. While some men drove wagons and others simply walked, most rode horses. Gradually the number of miners increased, the estimates placing eight hundred at work in May, two thousand in June, four thousand in July, and between eight and ten thousand by the end of the year. They spread out from Sutter's sawmill until they covered a large area from the Trinity River in the north to the Tuolumne River in the south. They made important finds on the Tuolumne, the Stanislaus, the Feather, the Yuba, and the Mokelumne, as well as on the northern and middle forks of the American, and established such important mining camps as Placerville and Sonora.

Nobody will ever know precisely how much gold was extracted from California's streams in 1848, but the best estimate sets its value at ten million dollars. It is frequently said that the average miner earned an ounce a day. Even in the first year, however, the unfortunate largely outnumbered the lucky. Some simply did not happen to look in the right places; others fell ill from such causes as the mental pressure of excitement and hope, working in moist earth or knee-deep water, sleeping on the bare ground, scurvy, dysentery, unaccustomed hard labor, or prolonged exposure to the broiling sun.

Some of the whites employed Indians to work for them. At first the red men did not properly understand the value of what they were unearthing and naïvely thought a small quantity of their accustomed trade goods a fair exchange. Later in the year they demanded and secured a system of fixed prices, but were often defrauded by such devices as faulty scales. Some Indians worked at established diggings; others simply brought in the gold, and in at least two instances, white men, by trailing them, learned the secret source of their wealth. When the men of San Jose joined the rush, jailer Henry Bee took along with him the ten Indian prisoners in his custody and forced them to work. He netted a considerable sum before other miners persuaded the captives to revolt.

During 1848, the great majority of miners used very primitive methods, sometimes a knife, simply picking gold out of cracks in rocks. There were not yet any rules about ownership of claims, so the men hopped about from place to place like grasshoppers, skimming off what was most readily available. Some found wonderful caches of gold, most commonly where a rock formation or some other irregularity on the bottom of a stream had formed a natural trap. If they dug at all in 1848, they seldom went deeper than two or three feet. Many believed that the gold was washed down from some kind of solid bed, perhaps in the mountains and that whoever found this would really be rich. No matter how much their present site was yielding, the gold seekers were anxious to rush on to another one reported to be still better. Perhaps it was because they were so prosperous that there was no crime in the gold fields of '48, perhaps because it was easier to find gold than to steal it, perhaps because all went so heavily armed, perhaps because so many were Californians they all felt neighborly, but whatever the reason, all testimony agrees

9

that the area was remarkably free of crime. Many at the time were more impressed at the extraordinarily high prices which prevailed in the mine areas.

During the year 1848, news of Marshall's discovery reached the eastern part of the United States, first faintly, then to be mentioned on every lip.[4] Early in August various newspapers in New York City, Philadelphia, and Washington discussed the general mineral resources of California, but not until August 19 did the *New York Herald* print a definite item about Marshall's discovery; nobody paid any attention to it. More important was the long letter from the Reverend Walter Colton of Monterey which the *Philadelphia North American and United States Gazette* published on September 14. The preacher declared: "The farmers have thrown aside their plows, the lawyers their briefs, the doctors their pills, the priests their prayer books, and all are now digging gold."[5] He added that ten thousand men in ten years could not exhaust the supply. Soon letters from other writers were published in various papers.

What really excited easterners was a passage written by President James K. Polk. On December 5, in his annual message to Congress, he declared that the mines, known to exist at the time the United States acquired California from Mexico, were more extensive and valuable than were supposed: "The accounts of the abundance of gold in that territory are of such an extraordinary character as would scarcely command belief were they not corroborated by the authentic reports of officers in the public service, who have visited the mineral district, and derived the facts which they detail from personal observation." Polk was so impressed with the careful, precise report of the military governor, Mason, that he appended it to his message. The officer declared that the surface of the area's wealth had only been scratched, that a laboring man at the mines could earn in a day twice what a private soldier was paid for a month, and that the mineral wealth in the area drained by the Sacramento and San Joaquin river system would pay the cost of the war with Mexico a hundred times over. On December 7, two days after the President sent his message to Congress, a courier from Mason, Lieutenant Lucien

[4] Ralph P. Bieber, *Southern Trails to California in 1849*, 19–27; Bancroft, *History*, VI, 111–25; Caughey, *Cornerstone*, 42–54; Coy, *Gold Days*, 328–32; Oscar Lewis, *Sea Routes to the Gold Fields*, 6–11.

[5] Bieber, *Southern Trails*, 23.

Loeser, arrived in Washington with a tea caddy containing pure gold samples, of the greatest fineness, totaling in weight 230 ounces, 15 pennyweights, and 9 grains.

It was Polk's message which aroused truly remarkable gold excitement in the eastern and middle western United States, much as Sam Brannan's display had done earlier in San Francisco. A fever gripped the nation. Little was actually known of California, for, as John W. Caughey has pointed out, it was as remote and mythical to the people of that generation as the Solomon Islands were to Americans of World War II. It seemed like a fairy story come to life, so certain stories which circulated about it naturally became too good to be true. Some declared nuggets were to be found clustered thickly about grass roots and others alleged the mountains contained so much gold they reflected an amber light.

To capitalize on the excitement, during 1848 and 1849, some twenty-five or thirty guidebooks to the new territory were published; these told how to get there and what conditions the new arrival would find. Most of them were hastily thrown-together concoctions designed to do one thing—sell; however, a few of them were carefully prepared and contained maps having some value.

The excitement was nationwide. It found the country highly prosperous, with a completed war which had made America more of a transcontinental power than ever, with a considerable number of emigrants from Europe, with many war veterans not yet satisfactorily settled back into civilian life, and with the usual supply of young men anxious for adventure. From Maine to Texas it is almost literally true to say that California was in every mind and on every lip. Many prepared to make the trip west: "After a parting knell of exhortation for calm and contentment, even ministers and editors shelved their books and papers to join foremost in the throng." Those who were too old or entrenched to make the trip themselves were often eager to gamble a loan of the necessary $500 to $1,200 to some young man whom a year earlier they would have considered a most unpromising financial risk. (Incidentally, few of these loans were repaid, not because of dishonesty, but from poor luck or improvidence in California.) To outfit so many people going west at the same time made a tremendous demand for many items, almost as if the nation were equipping an army for combat. Even pawnbrokers did the best business within memory. Many machines, invented by those who had never seen the gold fields, suddenly appeared on the market at high prices, but they were seldom of any worth. In the excitement, social distinctions were discarded, as is dramatically illustrated by the physician in a Massachusetts town who abandoned his practice and enrolled in a group going west under the leadership of his own coachman. The gold fever was not confined to America, for by January, 1849, there was scarcely a European port which did not have at least one ship fitting for California and, half a world away, the Chinese were the most severely affected of Asiatic nations because of their strong gambling instincts.

For Americans wanting to go to the golden territory there were various possible routes: overland across the central or southern part of the United States or through northern Mexico, by sea around Cape Horn, or, mostly by ship but with a brief land journey, across the Isthmus at Panama or Nicaragua. Each had its advantages and disadvantages, but more often these were outweighed by the easterner's traditional use of the sea or the middle westerner's habits of wagon travel. There was not a great difference in these trips, whether taken in '49 or at any time in the fifties.

Those who went overland from the Missouri-Iowa frontier usually departed from Independence, St. Joseph, or the Mormon town of Kanesville (later called Council Bluffs).[6] It was quite remarkable that in 1849 the three cities could secure sufficient supplies of wagons, animals, foodstuffs, and mining equipment to meet the demands of the gold seekers. In later years there was enough, of course, except at St. Joseph in 1850.

Many of those who started overland were ignorant of frontier travel and others had only limited experience. They were often a group of three or four men who had banded together to drive a wagon west. However, families and newlyweds made the trip, too, even in '49 and increasingly in later years. Occasionally a poor man would earn his passage and food by serving as a driver and general

[6] Irene D. Paden, *The Wake of the Prairie Schooner*, 2–467; Georgia W. Read and Ruth Gaines (eds.), *Gold Rush: The Journals, Drawings and Other Papers of J. Goldsborough Bruff*, 9, 25, 46, 53, 339, 344, 637; John W. Caughey (ed.), *Rushing for Gold*, 15–21; Owen C. Coy, *The Great Trek*, 104–86; Caughey, *Cornerstone*, 97–120; Bancroft, *History*, VI, 144–48; Walker D. Wyman (ed.), *California Emigrant Letters*, 62, 67, 108–10; Louise A. K. S. Clappe, *The Shirley Letters from the California Mines in 1851–52*, 40; Bayard Taylor, *Eldorado, or Adventures in the Path of Empire*, 166.

assistant to some family. For the amateur, the ideal outfit was a small wagon, well made with seasoned hardwood and pulled by three yoke of medium-sized oxen. For the experienced, mules for heavy hauling and saddle horses for speed were best. Oxen usually traveled twelve or fifteen miles a day, throve on food a horse wouldn't touch, and were comparatively easy to keep in condition. Mules, requiring better care and better forage, could normally go twenty-five miles daily and in favorable flat country sometimes attained forty miles. Many of the travelers obtained their equipment at one of the out-fitting towns. Normally the animals were unbroken, and if the new owner was also inexperienced, all had a lively time until they learned new ways.

A general air of excitement prevailed each spring at Independence, St. Joseph, and Council Bluffs. The gathering from afar of a large, miscellaneous crowd; the incessant gambling; the constant selling; the breaking in of animals; and the accidents bound to occur when almost every man, even a novice, went armed—all added to the anticipation of the trek and of the treasures to be found. Almost all travelers formed themselves into some kind of company or trail organization. The groups generally drew up rules to govern themselves, usually too few or too many; later these would be amended. Sometimes the members of the party faithfully observed these codes, but often, as the leader of one band predicted, they regarded their obligations "about as much as singing psalms to a dead horse." Once the regulations were agreed upon by popular vote, the next task was to select an experienced man to serve as captain: to determine the order of march, to set the time of starting each day, to select the next campsite, to organize protection from storms, to guard against Indian depredations, to look for water in arid areas, and, generally, to assume command of the group. All this he had to do without any legal authority: only by the power of his personality and by the respect he could engender. Since his was certainly a difficult task, it was not always easy to pick a good captain. Most groups were quite instable, making en route a change in leaders, in rules, or in the size of the company, perhaps more than once and perhaps in all three. In any case, government of the caravans was truly democratic.

While most travelers went with wagons in some kind of group, there were inevitably some exceptions. A few had only the packs on their backs or used carts. At least one pushed a wheelbarrow west, refusing all company, and those who observed were impressed that he was making good progress. Probably unique was the man who drove a cow westward—to carry his gear and to provide milk, too.

When to leave the outfitting town for the West was a problem often causing bitter arguments. There was no point in going too early, before the grass had sprouted. Especially those who drove oxen had to be patient, for bovine teeth could not take care of grass as short as could those of mules or horses. But farther west those outfits which came first would have a good chance of getting an adequate supply of forage everywhere, while those who trailed along last might face considerable shortages.

Finally the great day, usually sometime in May, came and the group began its long journey. There was much to learn by experience. Even starting and stopping was a task, for not until well along in the mid-fifties did any animal-drawn conveyances have the newly invented wagon brakes. Before then the cumbersome vehicles rolled and lurched, sometimes with such a violent movement that the occupants were thrown to the ground. They wriggled quickly out of the way of the wheels or had a horrible accident and often met death. Inevitably there were mishaps with axes or firearms in the hands of those unfamiliar with their use. Sometimes a vital part of a wagon broke. Almost every wagon train stopped at least once to look for a missing person; if it were a child, the danger from coyotes and wolves was serious. Cooking was commonly done in a Dutch oven. Men depended mostly on "sowbelly" (bacon), "biscuits" (hot bread), and much coffee, with flapjacks occasionally for a change. If a woman did the cooking, there was more variety and she probably so objected to water with "wiggle-tails" in it that she boiled it for tea or coffee. During a normal stop there was so much washing, mending, baking, cooking, harness repairing, animal doctoring, and wagon mending to do that if there was a spare moment the travelers were glad enough simply to throw themselves down and rest.

When the train moved out in the morning, each wagon fell into its assigned place. Those at the head of the column one day were at the very rear the next and advanced forward again a notch each sunrise. When the group crossed a small stream, it would angle its direction upstream so that the rushing water would not strike the wagons and animals broadside; on a large river, the slant would be with the current. When the party reached a descending slope, it would stop completely and each wagon's rear wheels would be chained to prevent their revolving. This precautionary practice worked well enough if the company realized it was approaching a descent, but hardly helped when a downhill runaway developed. Sometimes a horse-and-mule train might try to pass an ox outfit; under ordinary circumstances the slower-moving group made no effort to aid or resist. Any group had constantly to beware rain, hail, tornadoes, cloudbursts, and lightning. Also to be feared was a stampede at night, with riders tearing along in the dark seeking to overtake or turn the runaways; even worse was one in daylight when a bunch of wagons went whipping along behind their animals like so many five-gallon cans tied to terrified dogs.

Another problem was Indians. As soon as the group entered the prairie country of the Pawnees, the first tribe encountered, guards had to be posted to safeguard the livestock. The first few nights on duty, many could not tell whether the numerous crackling noises they heard were ordinary night sounds or those of Indians. It was a real ordeal. Occasionally a nervous man would give a false alarm; sometimes the danger was genuine. After a raid, the company seldom recovered all the livestock driven off. Indians also visited trains in supposedly friendly fashion, but with an eye to gifts or theft; they usually engaged in horseplay which became rougher by the minute but did not resent such forceful remonstrances as whacking a young Indian over the head with a gun he had tried to purloin. Generally the younger red men were a bit headstrong in their contacts with the whites; the older ones counseled restraint but did not enforce their recommendation. In the Rockies, not until the late fifties did the Indians make any attempt to molest the whites.

There was divided opinion whether dogs should be allowed to accompany wagon trains. Some considered them a useless bother, others a means of alarm in case Indians approached. One diarist, J. Goldsborough Bruff, recorded how his large yellow cur visited various messes in the morning for a snack, watched the mules come in, observed the teams being hitched up, then started out in advance and continued until he found a shady spot to rest. Waiting until the oncoming train nearly reached him, he then jumped up and went farther ahead. If the group made an unusual halt, he would return, watch, know whether the stop was temporary or for a considerable time, and govern himself accordingly.

On the prairie the caravanners were alert for buffalo, a novel sight to most and a possible source of varied diet. If they got meat, they might eat it on the spot, but more often than not they "jerked" it, that is, cut it into thin (sometimes small) strips, placed it on some kind of elevated rectangular frame, and kept a smudge fire going underneath for a day or two until the flesh had been cured enough to keep indefinitely. This was laid away as a reserve stock for a later time when ordinary food supplies might become scarce. Certainly not all buffalo hunts ended in success. Casualties were common as wounded buffalo charged the men, sometimes unhorsing and injuring or even killing them. The hunters frequently lost rifles and pistols, their mounts might run off with the buffalo, and they themselves might face a long, tiresome night walk back to camp. Even if unmolested the buffalo made oxen and mules nervous. A herd on the run was an impressive and literally earth-shaking sight; if it happened to cross a river in its flight, the massive bodies might actually dam the stream. The animals' manure, known as buffalo chips, was highly valued as fuel along two hundred miles of the Platte River where almost nothing else burnable could be found. To secure chips, most families walked beside their wagons, with each person carrying a bag to hold what he might gather; mules would often stop at a good pile by force of habit. The buffalo was useful, but travelers found the prairie dog just as interesting.

Cholera was a dread disease, most likely to strike along the Platte River Valley's crowded campsites and polluted wells. Its worst ravages came in 1849. It struck with such suddenness that in extreme cases a person perfectly well in the morning might be dead by noon. It aroused terror that those tending the stricken might contract the disease. So fearful were the less admirable wagon trains that they abandoned the sick to live or die as chance might dictate, leaving them perhaps with a single friend or utterly alone. Even among the best of the groups there was a great hurry to bury a victim, once it was obvious that he was beyond any earthly help, before somebody else became infected. In the face of cholera and other dangers, quite a few travelers changed their minds and backtracked to civilization before it was too late.

Although spring storms with icy winds occasionally caused discomfort early in the trip, many a day was so heavenly springlike that even those sad at leaving home and friends spoke of it in their diaries.

Another note of cheer was added when the wagons made their first major stop at Fort Kearny. A real test of a caravan's determination, however, came at the South Platte River near Brule, Nebraska, where the very wide crossing had much quicksand. Usually the men raised the beds of their wagons above the water by inserting blocks between the bed and the bolster, attached ten to fifteen yoke of oxen to one vehicle, and drove it off the four-foot drop, so steep the wheelers were held under water until the leaders pulled them free. They kept the team moving quickly, to avoid the quicksand, through a series of high and low spots so intermixed that part of the oxen would be walking and part swimming. The next important obstacle was Windlass Hill. Here the men anchored a big vehicle tightly and wound a long, strong rope around its axle, tying the loose end to a wagon which was to go down the hill. At the top of the hill some men gripped the spokes of the wheel and slowly paid out the rope as others walked down and helped to check the descending conveyance; two animals held up the tongue.

After passing near Courthouse Rock, Chimney Rock, and Scott's Bluff, the train arrived at Fort Laramie. Here the group signed the register book, which listed the companies that had passed through. Beyond lay the Black Hills, a haven of pure water to restore the health of ailing animals and a dumping ground for items once considered invaluable but discarded now as excess weight; often these goods were deliberately damaged so that no one else could use them. At Dry Creek Ferry, or two days upstream at Mormon Ferry, those who had been following the Oregon Trail on the south side of the Platte crossed over to the north bank, where the Mormon Trail ran; the two went farther west as one. From the Platte River to the Sweetwater the train encountered a fifty-mile desert, with only alkali water available (except at Willow Springs) and with billowing, choking dust nearly blinding the animals. At the Sweetwater was Independence Rock, famous for the large number of signatures which travelers inscribed with wagon paint or axle grease. Beyond lay South Pass, a hurdle despite its easy grades, and then Fort Bridger. Here one train in about ten turned south to Salt Lake City, where rumor had it that the Mormons misused California-bound emigrants, but all written evidence remaining points clearly to the contrary. So many emigrants decided to sell their surplus goods there in 1849 that they flooded the market and received about half the wholesale price in an eastern city. After passing Salt Lake City, many of the wagon trains turned northwest until they rejoined the main trail. Some dared to go directly west over ninety miles of waterless desert, but this so-called Hastings Cutoff was so deadly that after 1850 it was totally abandoned.

The majority bypassed Salt Lake City and continued from Fort Bridger on the Oregon Trail into the Bear River Valley. Those who were venturesome avoided Fort Bridger by using Sublette's Cutoff and going directly from South Pass to Green River and the Bear River Valley. They crossed a fifty-two-mile desert from the pass to the Green, safe enough for trains run by experienced leaders but for others an exhausting brush with disaster. When they rejoined the main trail, they usually found coming down it the group which had earlier been just behind them and so they had not saved by their hazardous undertaking. In Bear River Valley the travelers generally rested a day or two, enjoying the game, berries, and good firewood. The traditional way of leaving the valley was to follow the Oregon Trail to Fort Hall and then turn off to California. But in 1849, a leader named Hudspeth had the "colossal imprudence" to take his wagon train west from the valley over uncharted mountains and, surprisingly, was successful; the new route saved twenty-five miles. Increasingly with the years groups drove the Hudspeth Cutoff rather than go by Fort Hall. These two routes and the one northwest from Salt Lake City made a three-way junction near the meeting of the three forks of Raft River.

Soon the trail ran along the Humboldt River for more than three hundred miles, requiring two or three weeks of travel. It furnished only small amounts of water, generally quite impure and growing more unpalatable the farther west the wagons went. The travelers of 1849 brought along enough food to get over this stretch without shortages, but in later years many of the emigrants misjudged and faced short rations. The road was strewn with abandoned wagons and dead animals; to provide proper teams, some wagons had to be consolidated with others. People fell by the wayside and some died from exhaustion; others so despaired that they committed suicide. Finally the struggling wagon train reached the Great Meadow of the Humboldt, where the town of Lovelock now stands; it was a haven eight miles long with ample grass and satisfactory water. Often a company would send an expedition back into the threatening desert to rescue straggling people or animals, but mere property they abandoned. Indians, too, became a problem, partly because the travelers relaxed their vigilance; the theft of livestock in such a desert as this was a major disaster. By 1852, several trading posts had been established at the meadows.

Beyond Great Meadow the trail a wagon train followed depended upon which pass it decided to use. The two basic routes were the Carson River and the Truckee River; for each of them there was a choice of two passes over the Sierras. If the group decided to head first for the Carson River, it had to cross Humboldt Sink, so called, a full day's journey in which the surface water was undrinkable. Farther west was more desert, an area so awful it came to be called Destruction Valley. Here many animals died and others sank to the ground so exhausted that their owners mercifully killed them. Abandoned goods lay strewn about in large quantities, adding to the horror of the struggle to get across. Often a train tried to make as much of this stretch as possible by night; when it abandoned some wagons, it set them afire as beacon lights. To cross was so difficult that it is a literal fact that nobody helped a fallen person unless convinced the victim absolutely could not move. Finally the group reached the Carson River; here it usually sent a relief party back into the desert with water. After that came the Sierra Nevada Mountains. Some groups pushed on with all their possessions; others cut down their wagons into carts; still others, abandoning much remaining equipment, packed what they could on the backs of the animals. The ascent was difficult. At some points the vehicles had to be emptied and lifted over huge logs and boulders. Above the mountain meadows, the men sometimes got fodder for their animals by cutting branches from trees. Once the summit was reached, the descent proved more abrupt than the climb.

From Great Meadow the alternate route was that of the Truckee River. Midway in the desert it had a reliable spring whose water was boiling hot but often a lifesaver. At the western end was Truckee Meadows, where Reno now stands, then the mountains.

Another possible route to California was to follow the Oregon Trail considerably beyond Fort Hall to Goose Lake and then turn south, along the Pit and Feather rivers, into California. This was the so-called Lassen's Cutoff, although from South Pass it was actually long and roundabout.

In the years 1849 and 1850, some travelers started west so late that they encountered particular difficulties as the winter season approached. Many of them would have struck utter disaster had not generous Californians financed relief expeditions. Some groups lost all of their own draft animals, exhausted their provisions, devoured dead livestock they found along the road, and walked across the mountains in a fierce struggle to escape the snowstorms which were closing the passes. Such desperate straits brought out in some people their noblest qualities, but others, casting off the restraints of civilized society, took any step available to insure their own safety and well-being. They stole from the weak and plundered wagons obviously abandoned only temporarily. Their selfishness and hypocrisy contrasted radically with the selfless generosity of some toward total strangers.

With all the hazards facing overland travelers, it is not surprising that an observer in California, Bayard Taylor, wrote of the emigrants, "Such worn, weather-beaten individuals I never before imagined," and of their oxen that the toil and suffering they had encountered had given their countenances a look of almost human wisdom.

There were southern as well as central routes overland to California.[7] These were boosted with exaggerated claims by Missouri, Arkansas, and Texas. To El Paso and thence directly west led two trails from San Antonio and one from Dallas, all characterized by great heat, much dust, and inadequate food supplies. To go to Santa Fe, gold seekers could start from Fort Smith, or travel from Fayetteville, Arkansas, along the Cherokee Trail, or from Independence, Missouri, use the famous and pleasant Santa Fe Trail. From Santa Fe one group of roads led southwest along the Gila River to San Diego or Los Angeles, where the travelers either took a ship for San Francisco or went overland; this general route included two difficult desert crossings. An alternate way from Santa Fe, less popular with travelers but actually requiring less travel time, was to go toward Salt Lake City, perhaps along the Old Spanish Trail, which led somewhat south of the Mormon city to Southern California, perhaps to the city itself and then west either to Los Angeles or San Francisco. Some of a group which got off the main road perished in Death Valley; their tragedy gave the area its name.

7 Bieber, *Southern Trails*, 29–60.

To go through Mexico was another way of getting to California.[8] Travelers using it often started from New Orleans. One route, through northern Mexico to Mazatlán, was the easiest; another northern trail, ending at Tucson, Arizona, was the most difficult; the third possibility was to go through central Mexico to Guadalajara, San Blas, or Mazatlán, thence by ship. Although some Mexicans were still resentful over the outcome of the recent war, most were friendly enough to Americans. The gold-seekers were eager to view a bullfight but shocked at what they saw, were usually amused at mixed bathing in the rivers, and some were hostile to Roman Catholic religious practices.

Most Amercians who lived in the eastern part of the United States found it natural to go by sea to California, perhaps using the all-water route around Cape Horn.[9] They created such a tremendous demand for ships that within six months the American flag had nearly disappeared from the ports of the world; all vessels were headed for California. To supplement those which already had passenger accommodations, cargo carriers were converted and America's whaling fleet was diverted almost en masse. The demand was too strong for anybody to wait long enough for extensive alterations, but cargo space was remodeled into crude living quarters and some arrangement made to get more light and air into the depths. Another source of ships was to patch up those abandoned so long that waterfront observers had considered them beyond reclamation. Those who wished to go to California could not be choosy in the seller's market of 1849 and the early 1850's; they simply paid what was asked and hoped for the best. While the majority of ship agents did not exaggerate their claims unduly, some deliberately sold the same cabin space to several different customers or indulged intentionally in some other dishonest practice.

The number of vessels making the trip westward was impressive. Between December 14, 1848, and January 18, 1849, sixty-one ships with an average of fifty passengers each sailed for California from

8 Caughey, *Rushing*, 33–41.

9 Lewis, *Sea Routes*, 14–155; Bancroft, *History*, VI, 121–23; Garrett W. Low, *Gold Rush by Sea*, 27–30; John E. Pomfret (ed.), *California Gold Rush Voyages, 1848–1849*, 20–65, 102–22; Raymond A. Rydell, *Cape Horn to the Pacific: The Rise and Decline of an Ocean Highway*, 112–25; Octavius T. Howe, *Argonauts of '49*, 83, 159–71; Caughey, *Cornerstone*, 85–90.

New York City, Boston, Salem, Philadelphia, Baltimore, and Norfolk. In the month of February, 1849, sixty ships were announced to sail from New York City alone, seventy from Philadelphia, seventy from Boston, and eleven from New Bedford. Even so, it was unusual indeed when on one day forty-five ships from the East Coast arrived at San Francisco.

In the first few days after leaving port, few had the experience of John N. Stone, who tells in his diary how on a dark, hazy evening the captain suddenly bellowed: "Sail ho! Hard down your helm! Bring a light!" His orders caused such an alarmed, noisy chattering among the passengers that he shouted: "Silence! or we will all go to hell together." He just managed to miss the other ship.

Passengers found it quite a change from the feverishness of preparation to the tedium of the long voyage. The vigorous often made the transition with difficulty, but the lazy or unimaginative had little trouble. Some turned to almost any activity to keep themselves busy —such as keeping a diary. They resorted to practical jokes, perhaps suspending a bucket of water above a doorway so that the next person to pass would be doused; on the *Henry Lee* this practice abruptly ceased when an early victim was the captain himself. Some turned to fishing, on rare occasions landing bonitas, dolphins, or even sharks or turtles, but generally getting only infrequent nibbles. Anglers were occasionally the victims of a practical joke, like the man who thought he had a large fish on his line and after a hard struggle managed to haul out a chamber pot. Other passengers turned to gambling. On such a long trip the law of averages worked; players ended up owning as much as they had started with, but not the same things. Some gold seekers amused themselves by pilfering from the galley or from the supply of sweets, preserved fruits, or liquor which a fellow voyager had. One intended victim, seeing a group of men descending on him to suggest a friendly treat that would have drained his bottle, managed secretly to pour in an emetic with results considerably more amusing to him than to those who took a swig. Other passengers entertained themselves with group singing, drawing, or reading. Sometimes debates were organized, a paper gotten out, or poems written. On Sundays there were usually two sermons but generally attendance fell off as the voyage progressed. If Thanksgiving, Christmas, or the Fourth of July occurred during the trip, there would be quite a celebration. The intimate friendships which formed proved to be unstable; the similarities which at first drew men together were upon closest association outweighed by incompatibility in background or temperament. Toward the end of the voyage, the ordinary passenger became quite tired of the majority of his associates and wanted very much a little privacy.

There was much discussion about food; generally it was coarse and lacking in variety but plentiful. Since the causes of scurvy were well understood, almost all ships tried to keep on hand adequate supplies of fresh fuits and vegtables, but not infrequently they ran out for considerable periods between ports. Some vessels carried live animals to supplement their butchered meat. Water rationing was seldom necessary, although the quality, after being stored for a while, left much to be desired. Voyagers on every vessel welcomed a chance in port to go ashore for really good water and a change of diet. If food, water, or anything else was extremely bad, the passengers might take the unusual step of lodging a complaint with one of the American consuls in South America. He could, and sometimes did, remove incompetent captains, levy fines against owners, send mutinous sailors home in irons, and force ships' officers to provide the services and supplies necessary for the health and safety of the passengers.

Most of the ships carrying passengers to the gold fields were old and comparatively slow. The trip from the East Coast around the Horn and up to San Francisco often took more than six months; the average time was 168 days. Usually the voyage was made as fast as possible, thanks to a veteran captain who had rounded the Horn several times before and to his ability in selecting a crew when he could have his pick of experienced men eager to go to California.

As the ship bore south into the tropics, clothing was shed to the irreducible minimum; many tried to escape the heat at night by sleeping on deck. Metals grew so hot that men shrank from touching them, and tar liquified in the rigging. When the ship reached the equator, King Neptune generally came aboard to conduct ceremonies for those who had never crossed it before. Usually there were no excesses, but sometimes the horseplay got out of hand. On one vessel everybody crowded forward as Neptune came over the bows. "I rule the sea," he proclaimed, "I cause the winds, and when I order it, it rains." At this precise moment two sailors the captain had stationed aloft upset a barrel of water on the assembled group.

The first stop ashore was sometimes St. Catherine, an island off the coast of Brazil where indolent natives were crafty in their trading with Yankees. Much more often the stop was at Rio de Janeiro, a city large enough not to be overrun by Yankees. Often ships tarried as long as ten days, but their passengers enjoyed the stay. Here, as in all foreign ports except in the Panama area, the gold seekers were treated with great kindness and minor infractions of the law were overlooked; in return, the northerners seldom showed unusually bad manners. Those who carelessly failed to get aboard at the time set for sailing were left behind.

Unless water or repairs made a stop at the Falkland Islands necessary, the next important event was the thirty- or forty-day trip around Cape Horn. It was uncomfortable, with the temperature around freezing, no heat, and everything damp; often it was so cold that much of the time passengers kept to their berths. At meals the sudden lurches of the ship sometimes intermixed diners and food in one heap and at night prevented sleep until exhaustion overcame natural protective instincts. It was a difficult time for the crew, especially if hands or arms had been lamed; on some ships the passengers willingly sprang to the men's assistance but on others were reluctant to do so even when urgently needed.

The alternative, a trip through the Strait of Magellan, was less attractive. The prevailing winds there were adverse, williwaws sprang up to blow with intense force for a few moments and then subside, the currents were shifty and erratic, and adequate room to make tacking maneuvers against the unfavorable elements was unavailable in the passage, which was from two to fifteen miles wide. Whether by strait or cape, there was always danger of shipwreck; a few vessels, nobody knows how many, foundered there, yet no ship turned back defeated because of the various difficulties.

Once a ship sailed safely into the Pacific, there were several possible stops. One was Juan Fernández, famous as the castaway island of Alexander Selkirk, whose experiences Daniel Defoe immortalized in the novel *Robinson Crusoe*. The voyagers approached the now sparsely inhabited island, fifteen miles by four, with a storybook anticipation. Here was the best drinking water in the Pacific, available from a mountain spring through a wooden trough at a point where barrels could be filled while still in the rowboat. Here, too, was excellent fruit and, surprisingly, a redheaded Yankee from Maine who monopolized all business. Another stop might be Valparaiso, next to Rio de Janeiro the favorite port of call for gold ships; farther north was Callao, where almost all passengers got off to make the seven-mile trip to Lima. A final difficulty was to find the Golden Gate, often shrouded in fog and with a channel less than a mile wide.

Those who had made the trip entirely by sea inevitably grew soft from months of relative idleness. They were ill prepared to meet a life of extreme physical activity, such as that in the mines, and some who attempted to make the transition too swiftly injured their health.

Less than half the men who sailed all the way to San Francisco came as individuals. The others were members of emigration companies, co-operative associations intending to get their members safely to California, there to keep them all together as a unit while mining and carrying on their other money-making activities.[10] A small group would organize, appoint or elect officers, then solicit more members. Its headquarters became the local center for gossip about California. A share or membership in the group cost a fixed amount; the lowest which scholars know of was fifty dollars and the highest one thousand. Each person paid the unvarying fee, received the same treatment, and was to share equally in the anticipated profits. Sometimes, instead of all members going, there would be a lottery to select the fortunate few, but this was not a general procedure. Each company had a name and a set of bylaws containing such stipulations as no liquor, swearing, or gambling. Generally there was a proviso that by a two-thirds vote of the members the company could expel anybody guilty of bad conduct. The association usually tried to enroll as members only persons of good character. It sought both professional men and mechanics, often took in several sea captains, and tried to include also men of small means. The leaders of the sea companies seldom issued orders which were questioned or indeed were of vital importance.

The members of a company generally came from the same area, which offered reassurance that companionships would be pleasant, that the sick would be well taken care of, and that mutual protection would be available in lawless California. Many of the groups intended to carry on a variety of activities in the new region, with each person working on the specialized task he was best fitted for and all sharing equally in the various profits anticipated. A very common plan was to carry out merchandise for resale either at San Francisco or in the

10 Howe, *Argonauts*, 4–64, 171–80; Lewis, *Sea Routes*, 21–29.

interior. This seemingly practical scheme seldom worked out satisfactorily because some of the goods were unsuitable (such as fur-
lined overcoats and gloves), because some of the items were in great
surplus at the company's destination, because the group, misjudging
the demand, tried to hold for too high a price, because articles were
damaged or spoiled in transit, or because the association bought junk,
long unsalable in the East, at a cheap price, only to find there was no
demand for inferior goods in the west either.

With all these high hopes, the first task obviously was to get to
California. Most companies purchased a ship, at a price from thirty
thousand dollars downward, and either hired a crew or had their
own members work the vessel westward. Of those companies which
originated in Massachusetts, the average cost for the trip to San Francisco Bay was at least four hundred dollars for each gold seeker in
addition to at least a hundred more for spare cash and personal
equipment. This would mean that for Massachusetts alone in 1849
about four million dollars was raised to send men in companies to
California.

If the group departed from New England, it would first observe
an interesting old custom. The members would march in a body to
some church to receive a sermon or admonition and warning.

When the associations arrived in California, they broke up, some
immediately and others more slowly. The members found that company for mutual protection was unnecessary, that trading and other
business ventures were not very successful financially, that their
ships were too slow and sluggish for local freight service, and, by far
the most important, that the possibilities of profit to the fortunate
few at the mines were so great that no man was willing to be tied
down to a socialistic type of organization. Thus the companies failed
in some of their plans but accomplished their major objective of
getting their members west.

The best of these groups, in the opinion of the specialist in their
history, Octavius T. Howe, was the Boston and California Joint
Stock Mining Company, organized in Boston in December, 1848.
Among its 150 members were a clergyman, 4 doctors, a mineralogist,
a geologist, 15 other professional men, 8 whaling captains, 76 mechanics, and a number of merchants, farmers, and manufacturers.
When its vessel arrived in San Francisco, the harbor was so crowded
that the ship sailed on to Benicia the following day. Soon the men

WESTERN MINING RUSHES, 1848–1900

marched to the gold fields at Mokelumne Hill, where with some
members sick and others lazy, the company soon voted to disband.

Cape Horn was important for passengers but invaluable for
freight, since it was the only practical route for Atlantic merchants
to reach the California market.[11] By it sailed clipper ships, a type in
existence since the early forties but with the demand of the gold rush

11 Rydell, *Cape Horn,* 128–42.

era now reaching their greatest development. The clippers, freight haulers rarely carrying passengers, were essentially streamlined and were intended to carry a maximum amount of sail under formidable weather conditions, to be driven to their limit. The boom period for these ships was from 1850 through 1853. The charge for California freight in 1850 was sixty dollars a ton and on their first voyage out to California most of the clippers made enough, or nearly enough, to pay the cost of their construction. From San Francisco they often went on to China, then to London and back to America, thanks to the lucrative opportunities made available by England's throwing open her sea trade to ships of all nations. The clippers' natural speed was increased by following the sailing directives of the United States Navy's Lieutenant Matthew Fontaine Maury, who had compiled from a host of ships' logs a "maritime mosaic of winds and currents" and thus predicted where the fastest sea lanes might be found. His work was probably as influential as that of clipper-ship designers and captains in bringing about the revival of American ocean shipping in the 1850's. Thanks to his advice, to expert construction, and to determined seamanship, the clippers made a few record voyages of ninety days from the East Coast to California.

In 1851, a total of 48 clippers from the East arrived in San Francisco; in 1852, there were 95, and 1853 saw 145. At first a number of their cargoes were damaged by moisture-heated air rising to the cool decks, condensing, and draining back onto the boxed freight; proper ventilation corrected this. The ships' captains were well paid, but ordinary seamen earned only ten dollars a month. By the fall of 1853, it was clear that there was not enough business in California— or indeed anywhere—for all the clippers. A competitor, the Panama Railroad, which spanned the Isthmus, was completed in 1855. By 1857, only 68 clippers arrived in San Francisco; clearly, the picturesque era of these famous ships was nearing an end.

Quicker for passengers than the long haul around the tip of the continent were the Panama and Nicaragua routes.[12] Interest in the Central American shortcut was stimulated in 1846 when the United States secured from England the permanent possession of Oregon Territory. In 1847, the federal government awarded contracts for

[12] John H. Kemble, *The Panama Route, 1848–1869*, 1–195; Pomfret, *California Gold Rush Voyages*, 224; Lewis, *Sea Routes*, 173–272; Bancroft, *Inter Pocula*, 144, 172–73; Caughey, *Cornerstone*, 60–68, and *Rushing*, 45–46.

the first American mail service over the Isthmus to two speculators, who quickly sold them. The United States Mail Steamship Company came to own the one from New York to Chagres, on the east side of Panama, and the Pacific Mail Steamship Company the one from the west side by steamship to San Francisco and beyond by sail to the Pacific Northwest.

As luck had it, the two companies were ready to start their service just as the gold rush was beginning. The Pacific Mail had built three steamers. The first one left the East Coast for the trip around the Horn before the real excitement began. When it arrived at the city of Panama, its normal southern terminal, on January 17, 1849, it found a tremendous crush of potential passengers who had left New York City (after the rush started) on United States Mail ships, crossed the Isthmus, and were now eager to complete their journey. There were 726 of them, whereas the Pacific Mail ship had accommodations designed for about 250. Some of these were occupied by passengers picked up in Peru. At an angry meeting ashore, the Americans, coveting the space, demanded that the Peruvians be transferred to a sailing vessel, but the latter wisely refused to set foot off the steamer. Finally, hastily constructed bunks were thrown up for the foreigners and the staterooms given to North Americans. The ship sailed with 365 passengers, some of whom reportedly paid as high as $1,000 for space in the steerage.

The Pacific Mail was at first unable to handle the horde of people who swarmed across the Isthmus. Sailing ships improvised passenger accommodations and helped carry the surplus, but having to tack out almost to Hawaii, thanks to prevailing winds and currents, before turning to San Francisco made the voyage very slow and a quite unsatisfactory substitute for steamer service. Speculation in accommodations developed on the Pacific Mail ships; something roughly like a stock exchange operated in the city of Panama for the buying and selling of tickets. Normally the price was $50 to $150 more than the company charged. The Pacific Mail moved as quickly as possible to build or buy enough additional ships to handle the heavy traffic.

Competition arose. In December, 1849, the United States Mail and Pacific Mail began operating ships on the "wrong side" of the Isthmus, that is, in each other's territory, but in January, 1851, they agreed to abandon the practice. In 1852 and 1853, a number of short-lived operations sprang up. In 1859, the original mail contract expired, the United States Mail Steamship Company went out of business, and a company headed by railroad capitalist Cornelius Vanderbilt secured the new government agreement for mail steamers on both sides of the Isthmus. The Pacific Mail met the interloper by operating its vessels in both the Atlantic and the Pacific, and not until February, 1860, did the two make peace, each agreeing to confine itself to one ocean.

Rates varied with the competition. In April, 1851, for example, just after the United States Mail and Pacific Mail had agreed to co-operate in maintaining through service, they fixed New York City to San Francisco charges at $330 for a first-class cabin, $290 for a lower-class cabin, and $105 for steerage accommodations. On through freight, 64 per cent of the fee went to Pacific Mail and 36 per cent to United States Mail.

Originally the Pacific Mail planned one departure a month but in 1851 started sailings every two weeks and also ran occasional extra ships. At first its vessels took eighteen to twenty-one days for the trip from the city of Panama to San Francisco, but when it got faster ships, it cut the schedule to fourteen days. From New York to Chagres the voyage at first took eleven days, later seven and one-half. Initially the best voyage time from New York City to San Francisco was thirty-three to thirty-five days, but with the completion of the railroad across the Isthmus, the time normally came to be twenty-three to twenty-six days.

The ocean voyage was much the same, whether taken in 1849 or twenty years later. At sailing time in New York there was much confusion, with people crowding on and off. As quickly as possible after the ship left the dock, the passengers were herded below, their tickets examined, and the few who had none sent ashore with the pilot. At first the ships stopped at Charleston, below Savannah, and at Havana. After 1852, the vessels landed only at Kingston for coal, brought aboard by sturdy Negresses balancing sixty-pound tubs on their heads, and for provisions. When the ships were running through the Tropics, passengers sprawled all over the benches on deck at night, trying to find a cool place to sleep. Of the women passengers on one vessel a man commented that those who at home were so particular they would cover up the legs of a piano, now in their dress seemed to have lost all sense of decency.

There was similar confusion in boarding the Pacific ship at the city of Panama but everybody had to show his ticket at the gang-plank. Native boatmen rowed the passengers out to the vessel, but in 1850, a steam tender went into service. The Pacific Mail ships at first stopped at Acapulco, San Blas, Mazatlán, San Diego, and Monterey but after 1851 usually stopped only at Acapulco, whose excellent harbor made it an ideal supply point, or at Manzanillo, with its profitable shipments of silver bullion. As soon as the steamer was seen approaching San Francisco from the station atop Telegraph Hill, signals were displayed to inform the city. In the earliest days the ships simply anchored in the harbor and the passengers got ashore by paying three dollars each to men in rowboats who quickly surrounded the vessel. There were also other boats—carrying the curious, the agents for auction houses, anxious to learn what merchandise was aboard, and employers who were eager to hire such people as blacksmiths and cooks at a daily wage higher than was offered for a week's work in the East. This picturesque and confusing spectacle was eliminated in 1850 when the Pacific Mail began tying up its steamers at Central Wharf.

The day a ship departed southward from San Francisco was important, too. "Steamer day," as it was called, was a feverish time for settling accounts, taking stock of merchandise, making remittances to the East, and paying bills, both local and distant. The custom gave San Francisco business life a unique kind of periodicity.

The Pacific Mail vessels built after the gold rush began were about 3,800 tons in size, large for that day on any ocean. They had wooden hulls, coal-burning engines, sails for emergencies, and paddle wheels, which made them steadier than propeller-driven ships. They had more cabins on deck and more open space than did the average vessel in transatlantic service. The first-class staterooms usually contained three berths, a cushioned locker on which the fourth person slept, a mirror, toilet stand, washbowl, water bottles, and glasses. The floors were carpeted and the berths made private by curtains. The room opened onto the center of the ship, facing the dining saloon which was used at off-hours for lounging. The second-class cabins were on the same deck but had a larger number of bunks in one room; their occupants ate at the same dining saloon as did the first-class passengers. The steerage was an undivided common compartment, often with no segregation of the sexes. Here a passenger was allotted a space six feet long and thirteen and one-half inches wide in a tier of bunks measuring three across and three high. Breakfast for all patrons was from eight to ten, dinner from one to three, and supper from six to eight. For fresh meat, the ships carried live cattle, sheep, hogs, and poultry. There was often illness aboard the northbound Pacific Mail vessels from diseases contracted in Panama. Judging the Panama route by the standards of the day, historian John H. Kemble has concluded that it was no worse than most others.

To maintain an adequate coal supply was one of the problems facing the Pacific Mail line. It secured fuel from many places: England, the eastern United States, and certain points along the Pacific Coast. The company provided its ships with large storage spaces, but even so, in the earlier days they would occasionally run out. As consumption gradually cut the weight of the remaining coal, a vessel slowly rose in the water until at times the paddle wheel was out of the water. In the boiler rooms the temperature rose as high as 132° F. The ships' officers were usually on leave from the United States Navy, anxious to learn all they could about steam-powered ships during their three years of civilian service. There were occasional difficulties with the engines, causing a delay while repairs were made. The most frequent disaster, however, was running aground at night or in a fog, with the threat of fire or of breaking up under the pounding of the waves. Operating the Pacific Mail ships was always costly; nevertheless, it was profitable, except during the brief periods of the bitterest competition.

An important segment of the trip was that across the Isthmus. Until 1852, all Atlantic passengers landed at Chagres, sometimes with difficulty when the rough surf held them aboard for several days. They found the Americanized town of hotels and saloons so unhealthy that they were especially anxious to leave quickly. Several of them would form a group and bargain with a boatman to carry them up the Chagres River in a native canoe, called a bungo, hollowed out of a single log perhaps twenty-five feet long and two and one-half or three feet wide. Poled by three or four natives, it carried two to four passengers and their baggage. The rate per person quickly rose in 1849 from ten to fifty dollars but by 1851 was back to about ten and the next year fell to five or four. Often the whites tried to cheat the natives, and as frequently the natives attempted to gyp the whites, so a common arrangement was to pay half the fare at the outset and the other half upon arrival at the final destination. In these negotiations the Americans sometimes tried to intimidate the boat-men with a pistol, but this had been done so many times before that the natives no longer had any fear of such threats.

The trip up river was enlivened by the bungomen singing such songs as "Yankee Doodle" and "Oh! Susanna," even though they didn't understand the meaning of the words. The travelers slept at native villages. The trip upstream generally took three or three and one-half days, depending upon the skill of the boatmen in keeping their bungo close enough to the bank to use their poles effectively.

The transfer from river to trail was made during the dry season at Gorgona, 39½ miles from Chagres and 20 to the city of Panama; in the wet season at Cruces, 44 miles upriver and 18 to Panama. From Gorgona the path was easier and more pleasant but not usable during the rainy season. From Cruces part of the trail had been paved with cobblestones in Spanish colonial times, but now there were some badly storm-damaged portions. In one spot the path degenerated into so narrow a defile that animals could not ordinarily pass, so groups approached the spot with much shouting to warn those coming from the opposite direction; if, despite all precautions, two parties met in the narrow passage, the animals could barely squeeze past each other when the riders lifted their legs out of the way. The trip by mule was made in one very long and exhausting day; natives toted the baggage. For the journey overland some women wore trousers, but others insisted on keeping the protection long skirts gave their ankles in a region where the Indians felt those who wore the least clothing were the most fashionable. The trip from the river to Panama usually cost somewhere between fifteen and thirty dollars for each person, with extra fees for baggage.

At the city of Panama passengers often had to wait three or four months to get space on a northbound ship; a few therefore went into business temporarily. Others were interested in seeing the sights of a foreign town two centuries old; more often, drunken Americans caused near riots by entering the cathedral with hats on and showing the utmost disrespect for everything there. To most the delay was an expense they could ill afford. Room and board at a hotel or pension cost about eight dollars a week, but in the earliest period neither these nor the restaurants had enough space to care for everybody. During the first half of 1849, Panama was so badly crowded that a large number of men camped out. Their utter indifference to sanitation, crowding, and exposure and their overindulgence in food and liquor made for considerable illness. Not until 1851 was there an American hospital with doctors to care for the stricken. Although Panama had a reputation as being a very unhealthy place, the statistics suggest it could not have been as bad as was generally supposed at the time.

Bungo and mule were not a permanent solution to Isthmus travel. In 1849, the Panama Railroad secured a concession from the government of New Granada, which owned Panama. The company chose as its Atlantic terminal Aspinwall, now known as Colón, four miles northeast of the port of Chagres. By 1852, the line opened for service the first seven miles west, reaching Gatún, on the Chagres River, where travelers could transfer to bungos. The chief railroad-construction problem was to secure an adequate labor supply and to keep the men healthy. However, the old tradition that the line cost a life for every tie is so false that each person ever employed would have had to die six times to convert legend into reality. The railroad, passing over the Continental Divide at three hundred feet, was finished in 1855 and cost $6,546,552.95. Its trains, carrying passengers at $25.00 each, made the run in four hours; travelers could leave in the morning and be certain of being aboard another ship on another ocean by evening.

It was not long before eastbound travel on the Panama route from San Francisco to New York City came to equal that going west. There was more demand for steerage space to the East than to the West. Steerage was patronized by those who could afford no other way, by those who preferred to economize, having become accustomed to rough conditions, and by the ineffectuals, shipped west by relatives to make a fresh start, who now must be hauled east to prevent their utter destruction. Often miners going steerage had plenty of gold dust; they traveled in groups of two or three, went armed to the teeth, and never left their common treasure unguarded for one instant.

Of the gold seekers who in 1849 arrived in San Francisco by ship, 15,597 came via Cape Horn and 6,489 by way of Panama; in 1852 and later, about fifteen or twenty thousand a year came by Panama as the popularity of the Cape route sharply declined.

A rival to Panama was the route across the Isthmus of Nicaragua. Over it Cornelius Vanderbilt launched through service from New

York to San Francisco in 1851. His claims that in Nicaragua the climate was cool and that his route was disease free were strongly denied by his patrons. He began operations before being adequately prepared but eventually built a twelve-mile plank road, used adequate steamers for his lake or river service, erected acceptable but not luxurious hotels at overnight stops, and improved his landing facilities. Following the opening of the Panama Railroad in 1855, shipwrecks, cholera, and unstable political conditions hit the Nicaragua route so severely that in 1857 Vanderbilt ceased operations.

2

CALIFORNIA MINES

OCEAN-borne gold seekers ended their journey at San Francisco,[1] a city whose real awakening came with the arrival of the first Pacific Mail steamship, followed by so many vessels that by the middle of November, 1849, a total of six hundred had entered the harbor. Among the passengers of that year was Bayard Taylor, a journalist whose description of the conditions he saw on his trip is a very valuable contemporary report. When he landed, found no space at the first hotel where he applied, secured accommodations at a second, and asked there for a porter to pick up his bags at the first, he was told that in San Francisco each man carried his own. He saw many of his fellow passengers start speculations almost the moment they landed, and, catching the fever, he himself sold some newspapers he had used to fill up crevices in his bags at a 4,000 per cent profit. He commented that every newcomer in San Francisco in 1849 was at first completely bewildered. It took time to get used to a place where there was a shortage of all kinds of workmen, where there was such a demand for goods that shopkeepers were generally indifferent whether a person bought or not, where all debts were punctually paid, where laundry was sent to China or the Hawaiian Islands to be done for eight dollars a dozen pieces, and where change was so rapid that when Taylor went away for six weeks, he had difficulty recognizing the city upon his return.

San Francisco early in 1849 had a population of about three thousand and by the end of the year had grown to about twenty thousand.

1 Bancroft, *History*, VI, 166–218, 758–60; Coy, *Gold Days*, 250–75; Bancroft, *Inter Pocula*, 261–85; Taylor, *Eldorado*, 43–46, 85–87, 226–30; Valeaka Bari, editor, *The Course of Empire*, 43–46.

It was a city of tents, rising in a crescent incline from the shores of the bay. The most striking landmark was Telegraph Hill. Montgomery was the most important street, lined with major importing firms and many auction houses. Several special sections arose in the city: Little Chile for any Spanish-American, Little Germany, Little France, Little Chinatown, and, quite unusual, Sydney Town for the British convict class, coming mostly from their exile in Australia. All of these areas were respectable except the last, whose occupants were likely to sandbag the unwary and to go on thieving raids into other neighborhoods.

In the early days of San Francisco, any old shed served as a lodging-house, with bunks costing $6 to $20 a week without bedding. A room at an ordinary hotel was $25 to $100 a week and at the best perhaps $250. In 1850, about one thousand people lived on ships abandoned by their crews. The cheapest food was to be found at places run by Chinese, marked with triangular yellow flags, where a substantial meal cost $1.00; at the best place in town, the Delmonico, a small meal was at least $5.00. Among the luxury items at deluxe eating places were eggs at seventy-five cents or a dollar each and salads at $1.50 or $2.00.

There was much speculation in city real estate, even though questions about validity of titles plagued water-front lots until 1851 and interior lots until 1861. It became common for a lot to command ten to a thousand times its original cost in 1848. The eager buyers were simply speculators, seldom foreseeing any future greatness for San Francisco because they thought the interior, once the mines were exhausted, would never be very useful for anything but grazing. In the last half of 1849, about one thousand flimsy sheds and homes were built, reportedly at a cost five times greater than would have been paid on the Atlantic Coast.

As the city grew, some of the hills were leveled down in order that the business district might expand; the soil was dumped into the shallow portions of the bay, forming new solid land. As the filling process became systematized, hundreds of piles, twelve to eighteen inches in diameter and thirty to forty feet long, were driven into the earth fill. The expansion made major changes in the appearance of the city; thus in 1849, Montgomery Street skirted the water but in little more than a year it ran through the heart of the city. Except for such a special development, the thoroughfares were at first neglected because most people thought their stay in the city would be brief. They failed to reckon with the unusually wet winter of 1849–50, which flooded buildings and turned ordinary streets into swamps. It mired down animals so badly that the only one in town able to pull a good load was a huge London dray horse which earned its master a hundred dollars a day. Signs began to appear, such as "Head of navigation; no bottom" or "Horse and dray lost; look out for soundings." Merchants began making sidewalks out of whatever excess supplies were cheap: boxes or barrels of tobacco, iron, cement, beans, salt, beef, wire sieves, gold-washing machines, and sheet lead. When spring came, the city government started improvements and by the following winter the avenues of the central district were planked. In the middle fifties, the city adopted a new system of grading which left some buildings sitting atop banks fifty feet high and others in deep hollows with the street on an embankment. Eventually the structures were raised or lowered.

San Francisco suffered a series of disastrous fires. The first one, on Christmas Eve, 1849, was blocked only by pulling down some buildings in its path after it had burned fifty homes. So threatening was it that one merchant paid a dollar a bucket for water. On May 4, 1850, a seven-hour conflagration consumed four million dollars' worth of property and three hundred homes. Beyond doubt it was started by certain criminals who made it an opportunity for theft. Many of the spectators refused to help fight the fire until hired at three dollars an hour; water sold for sixty dollars a cartload. Another fire, starting in June from a defective stovepipe, caused over three million dollars' worth of damage and a third on September 17 fed on a half-million dollars' worth of property. Then came the really great fire of May 3, 1851. Incendiary in origin, it eliminated between one and two thousand buildings, did destruction of about twelve million dollars in all, and afforded robber gangs the opportunity to carry off a huge quantity of goods. It crept under the funnel-like planking of sidewalks and streets, suddenly breaking out at points thought secure. It grew so hot that it expanded iron shutters before melting them and prevented the escape of people in buildings who thought they could simply shut out the fire. On the following June 22, still another fire caused two and one-half million dollars' worth of damage.

These disasters caused a gradual increase in well-constructed, comparatively fireproof buildings using granite from China, lava from

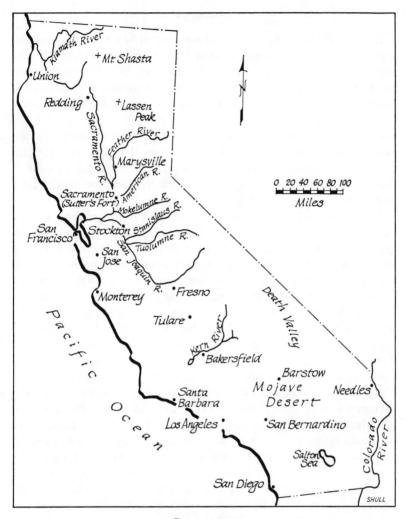

CALIFORNIA

the Hawaiian Islands, or bricks from eastern cities. These materials transformed San Francisco in appearance from a temporary gold-rush port into a permanent city. Additional protection came from the increasing number of volunteer fire companies; not until 1869 were they merged into a paid, professional department. City government, suspended in the rush of 1848, resumed in December of that year.

In the early days one of the major events in San Francisco was the arrival of the mail steamer. As soon as the signals on Telegraph Hill were raised, a line started to form at the post office. Each newcomer went to the end of the line, for the group prevented any unfairness, unless he paid as much as twenty dollars for the place of somebody who had occupied it as a business venture. The crowd waited until the mail was all sorted, which took usually twelve to twenty hours. When distribution began, it was from two windows, one for the "navy and army, the French, Spanish, Chinese, clergy, and the ladies," the other for everybody else. Californians, like soldiers in wartime, were very anxious for mail.

Although other cities rose in California, San Francisco remained by far the greatest.[2] Sacramento, at the site of Sutter's Fort, came to have real estate values exceeded only by San Francisco. This major city of the interior was built in what was a forest of oaks and sycamores, often six feet in diameter, which were soon destroyed by camping miners setting their fires against them. In 1849, Sacramento was so unhealthy, Bayard Taylor estimated, that three-fourths of the settlers had such diseases as ague and diarrhea. He described the place as a furnace in summer and a swamp in winter. Certainly at night the danger of falling off a platform into the mud, striking a stray beam, tumbling over the guy wire of a tent, running into a stump, or stumbling across a picket line into the hoofs of a mule was such that most Sacramentans of 1849 simply took to their blankets after dark. A neighboring town which hoped to become great was Benicia, at whose deep-water port on an arm of San Francisco Bay the Pacific Mail Steamship Company constructed docks and built its major repair shop; even so, it did not prosper, for San Francisco was at the mouth of the river system and Sacramento was nearer the mines. In contrast, Marysville, established in 1849, grew because it was at the head of navigation on the Feather River.

Between 1849 and 1855, the chief mining towns to emerge were Downieville, Nevada City, Grass Valley, Coloma, Placerville, Jackson, Mokelumne Hill, and Sonora. Some set up a city government only to find, like Nevada City, that it was too expensive; they simply

2 Taylor, *Eldorado*, 164–65, 204–205; Charles H. Shinn, *Mining Camps: A Study in American Frontier Government*, 199–202; Oscar O. Winther, *Express and Stagecoach Days in California*, 78; Coy, *Gold Days*, 200, 232–33; Rodman W. Paul, *California Gold: The Beginning of Mining in the Far West*, 71, 79–80.

eliminated it. An exceptional case was Sonora, which in November of 1849 organized itself municipally, surveyed the town, laid out streets, declared that all lots belonged to the town, and with the money from their sale operated an expensive hospital, devoted mostly to treating cases of scurvy. In some mining towns, permanent and comparatively fireproof buildings and fine residences were erected. Others never prospered greatly or endured long. At the bottom of a steep ravine or gulch, they frequently had only a main street, perhaps following the windings of the canyon floor and usually rutty and strewn with debris. About the average mining town there was, by deliberate intent, almost nothing beautiful, comfortable, or convenient. Speculation in townsites was a favorite method of trying to make money.

Transportation between settlements gradually became easier and better.[3] At first those who arrived on steamers at San Francisco simply purchased oxen and carts for the journey to the mines. The demand outran the supply and soon most newcomers went as far as possible by river. Steamers quickly appeared on the major streams, sometimes coming around the Horn under their own power. One of these was under attachment for nonpayment of debt in an eastern port, with deputies aboard to guard it. The owner-captain got up steam, sailed (despite the protests of the officers), and, when safely away, set the deputies off in a small boat to row back. Some of the river ships were dismantled and carried to California in other vessels. In one unusual case, a sailing ship was sunk and a smaller steamer put inside her. The sunken ship was then raised, sent around the Horn, sunk again, and the steamer removed. The sailing ship was then raised again and placed anew in service.

By 1850, there were twenty-eight steamships on the Sacramento-Feather River and others on the San Joaquin, many of them owned by their captains. With so much competition, the day of quick fortunes from river transportation speedily ended. Rate wars plunged the fare from San Francisco to Sacramento as low as ten cents a per-

3 Winther, *Express and Stagecoach*, 10–166; Shinn, *Mining Camps*, 202; Wyman, *California Letters*, 140; Jerry MacMullen, *Paddle-Wheel Days in California*, 6–27, 41–63; Bancroft, *Inter Pocula*, 332; Caughey, *Cornerstone*, 206–208; Joseph H. Jackson, *Anybody's Gold: The Story of California's Mining Towns*, 142, 146, 151–55; Oscar O. Winther, "The Southern Overland Mail and Stagecoach Line, 1857–1861," *New Mexico Historical Review*, Vol. XXXII (1957), 81–106.

son. Another form of competition, and sport, too, was racing. Many a ship thus courted disaster, but the passengers almost invariably urged the crew on. Occasionally racing vessels ran aground, burst their boilers, or caught fire; sometimes they exploded at the dock because the crew had built up a big head of steam and then failed to release the safety valve on the boiler when they shut off the engine.

The river steamers were side-wheelers with lead hulls. At their prows were the so-called China holds for Oriental passengers; next came the machinery; to the stern was a main deck for cargo, atop it a cabin used as a social hall, and then a third deck with the main cabin. There was sometimes competition between ships on the quality, quantity, or price of their food and liquor. The duties of the captain were largely administrative and social; the pilot did more work and got more pay.

In 1854, all the ships in service on the Sacramento and San Joaquin rivers were merged into the California Steam Navigation Company. It eliminated racing, cut down on the number of runs (thus scheduling two ships daily in each direction between San Francisco and Sacramento), and established a higher system of rates than had prevailed earlier (for example, between the two cities the line charged ten dollars each for passengers and eight dollars a ton for freight). The new company gave good service, but occasionally rival lines arose and disrupted the orderly monopoly until they were bought out.

Freight service to the interior was at first by pack trains of mules, American owned but Mexican driven. Four or five men could handle an average-size train of forty or fifty mules for an ordinary day's travel of twenty-five miles. The cargo was of every conceivable kind, even pianos and iron safes, loaded about three hundred pounds on each animal. The mule carefully guarded his load, avoided knocking it against obstacles, skirted any projection which might throw him off the trail if hit by his pack, and with each step carefully set his feet firmly on the ground. If his load slipped, he was lassoed, a hood put over his eyes, and the cargo refastened. If the pack rubbed a sore on his back, it was promptly daubed with a good and convenient remedy, horse manure. The size of these pack-train operations is illustrated by statistics on the traffic between Marysville and Downieville; they required twenty-five hundred mules and employed between three and four hundred men.

Wagons replaced mules as soon as trails became roads, sometimes toll roads. The standard freight conveyance became a large wagon, trailed by a small one and powered by six or eight mules. In a typical week of the early fifties, 794 wagons with more than 2,000 animals left Marysville for various destinations.

As early as 1849, express companies were formed to serve the miners by carrying special packages and gold. They also picked up mail at the San Francisco post office for the patrons on their list and carried it at an extra charge—sometimes as high as four dollars a letter, but considered well worth it because the federal government at first provided no such service and later gave only exceedingly slow delivery. The field came to be dominated by two concerns, Adams and Wells Fargo. Adams and Company, an eastern organization, established a California branch in 1849, which in 1854 became a firm of the same name but independent of its parent. Its high charges attracted a rival, Wells Fargo and Company, established in 1852 as a separate corporation by the leaders of the East's American Express Company.

Both California companies quickly built up service into the hinterland, Adams at first by connections and Wells Fargo by purchasing existing organizations. From New York the two companies brought such staples as clothing and such perishables as fruit trees out over the Isthmus to San Francisco in thirty-four days, compared with ordinary freight service that took three to six months around the Horn. Often the quick return the owner secured on his investment more than repaid the high cost of transportation. Charges were initially seventy-five cents a pound, but competition eventually lowered them to forty cents. The two companies handled C.O.D. shipments to either coast. In the West they carried the mail extensively. The two not only hauled gold dust but bought it, in 1849 for ten dollars an ounce at the mines and in 1852 for sixteen; usually they sold it at the federal mint for eighteen. Both companies expanded this activity into general banking. In the California business panic of 1855, Adams and Company failed; Wells Fargo, weathering the storm, emerged to dominate the state's express business and eventually to play a major role elsewhere.

Stagecoach service began in California, during the fall of 1849, with runs from Sacramento to towns along the American River and from San Francisco to San Jose. To some of the coach companies the United States awarded mail contracts in 1851. Sacramento, not San Francisco, emerged as the center of staging operations and held its pre-eminence during the 1850's. In the fall of 1851, for example, six stages daily left Sacramento for Marysville, two for Coloma, and one each for Nevada City, Placerville, Auburn, Stockton, Drytown, and Jackson. At first service was expanded through the establishment of many small, independent units, but about five-sixths of these were merged in 1854 to form the California Stage Company. This combination did not succeed in stifling competition, for in 1856, about half of California's three thousand miles of stage-line routes were operated by independent concerns.

For mountain travel the lines used the so-called mud wagons, built low to the ground, and for ordinary service the celebrated Concord coach. The body of the latter rested on stout leather straps, called thorough braces, which rocked the stage body back and forth in a motion more pleasant to passengers than the ordinary jars of a wagon. The thorough braces' chief function, however, was to act as shock absorber for the team, diminishing the violence of jolts transmitted from the coach to the animals. A stage's driver was sober, dependable, young, swaggering, profane, rough mannered, and pronounced in his opinions but usually gentlemanly and accommodating to passengers; on his coach he was second to none of his passengers, no matter how distinguished they might be elsewhere. Often the stage started its run at daybreak from some hotel, where the innkeeper roused travelers to breakfast by candlelight.

In 1858, the Overland Mail Company, headed by John Butterfield, began carrying passengers and United States mail along a transcontinental "oxbow" route 2,630 miles long from the railhead at Tipton, Missouri, through El Paso, Tucson, and Los Angeles to San Francisco. With the mail tucked into a space under the driver's seat, its stages made the trip in an average twenty-one days and fifteen hours. The rate for a through letter was ten cents and for a through passenger usually two hundred dollars. The company used 800 men, 1,000 horses, 500 mules, and approximately 250 stagecoaches and wagons. Few of its riders were through passengers, but it developed a considerable volume of local, short-haul patrons. It continued service on its original route until March, 1861, when the Civil War forced the adoption of a more central one.

Spectacular was the Pony Express, organized by men famous for their frontier freight-wagon service—William H. Russell, Alexander Majors, and William B. Waddell—to run from the railhead at St.

Joseph, Missouri, to San Francisco, a distance of two thousand miles covered in ten days. The rate for letters varied from one to five dollars per half-ounce, yet there were not enough of them to pay one-tenth the cost of operation. The first westbound rider left St. Joseph on April 3, 1860, and eighteen months later the completion of the first transcontinental telegraph line sealed the doom of the enterprise. The Pony Express was short lived, a major economic disaster for its owners, but its picturesque and romantic aspects are a major part of the present-day America's concept of the western frontier.

The California gold fields, which all these transportation facilities served, may best be classified, as Rodman W. Paul has written, into three geographical districts.[4] The southern area included Calaveras, Tuolumne, Mariposa, Stanislaus, and San Joaquin counties. In 1849 and 1850, it seemed as rich as any region in the state, with attention concentrated on placer mines rather than quartz, but later proved less productive under other types of development. The southern area especially attracted men from Mexico.

The central region, embracing El Dorado, Amador, Placer, Nevada, Yuba, Sierra, Butte, Plumas, Sacramento, and Sutter counties, was rich in placer. It contained almost all of the state's so-called deep-gravel mines, where thick layers of debris covered the gold-bearing gravel. It also had quartz deposits. In the early days the central region's mines, like most in the state, were at an altitude of between one and two thousand feet, but later, good ones were discovered at higher elevations, which afforded better rainfall and more easily tapped drainage from the Sierras. The better mines of the central area were more accessible than those of equal quality elsewhere. The region also had the largest population—in 1852 twice that of the southern area and fourteen times that of the northwestern area. Initially most Americans came to it as the terminus of most overland trails and the place where Sutter had his fort.

The northwestern region was strung along the Trinity, Klamath, and Scott rivers and their tributaries. This rugged, remote, inaccessible region had a comparatively severe climate and Indian inhabitants more vigorous than those elsewhere in the state. There was no rush to the area until 1850; even then development was so slow that in 1856 a man could still find virgin territory in it when in other areas

---

[4] Paul, *California Gold*, 39–43, 92–114; Coy, *Gold Days*, 104–107; T. A. Rickard, *A History of American Mining*, 31–32; Bancroft, *History*, VI, 351–52, 373–79.

miners were reworking the same diggings for the fifth or sixth time. Simple placer operations continued in the northwest long after they were virtually abandoned elsewhere.

Another important geographical classification, aside from the three regions just described, was the so-called Mother Lode country, located in both the central and southern areas. It was a region of quartz deposits about 120 miles long, in width from a few hundred feet to two miles, in altitude from 1,000 to 2,700 feet, extending approximately from Mariposa to Coloma (its precise limits are a matter of disputed definition).

The first task of a miner was obviously to find a deposit worth developing.[5] This search in areas sometimes nearly unexplored involved travel over considerable distances and much backbreaking work. It might leave the prospector poorer than when he started, but meanwhile the possibility of finding riches was a safety valve for men discontent and discouraged at the hardships and monotony of ordinary mining life. Good training served the searcher well, but some discoveries were made by accident. That gold is where you find it was dramatically illustrated at a California funeral. The minister's prayer was so long that some of the mourners began idly to finger the dirt thrown up from the grave; they grew so obviously excited that the preacher stopped, looked himself, and bellowed that it was the richest kind of diggings. The dead miner was taken from his grave and hastily buried elsewhere; then the minister led the rush of the mourners to prospect and stake claims.

Good luck or bad was still in the hands of fate once the development of a claim began. Thus near Massachusetts Hill, Michael Brennan was superintendent and probably chief owner of a quartz mine. At first it was quite successful, but as his men dug deeper they found nothing further; he borrowed all the money he could to continue searching and was still unrewarded. In despair he killed himself, his wife, and his three children. A few days later, others resumed the work and a few feet deeper found a vein which produced millions of dollars' worth of gold.

No matter how successful a miner might be, there were always rumors of richer deposits elsewhere. Especially in the early days, when men still believed that gold in the rivers had all come down in the

5 Coy, *Gold Days*, 115, 150; Jackson, *Anybody's Gold*, 83; Bancroft, *History*, VI, 385–92.

erosion of a fabulously rich solid bed hidden somewhere up in the mountains, the miners tended to abandon work wherever they were and try at a spot they believed was more promising. Many of them jumped about like grasshoppers, usually gaining little or no advantage and sometimes losing sharply.

The earliest mines of California were all placer, which involved extracting loose bits of gold from the intermixed sand, gravel, and boulders in a stream bed or hillside.[6] The methods, comparatively simple, were taught Californians of 1848 by such men as Isaac Humphrey, a San Franciscan experienced earlier in the gold mines of Georgia. In 1849, tyros learned from veterans of the previous year and from professional miners who came from Cornwall, Wales, Germany, Spain, France, Italy, Chile, Mexico, the coal and iron districts of Pennsylvania, and the lead regions of the upper Mississippi Valley. Many of the men in 1848 preferred simply to pick out gold with a knife from cracks in the rocks, a process known as "crevicing." More effective was the use of a pan made of sheet iron or stiff tin, with a flat bottom ten to fourteen inches across and sides four to six inches high. A miner partly filled it with dirt, put it in the water, shook it with a sidewise rotary motion, creating a whirlpool, to float out the soil and sand, then raked out the stones and gravel; what was left was gold, sunk to the bottom by its higher specific gravity. Thus to wash a pan took ten to twelve minutes, and fifty of them were regarded as a good day's work. The method was profitably used only on a very rich strike and required a strong back.

Faster than this was the rocker, or cradle. Looking somewhat like a child's cradle, with similar rockers and a perpendicular handle to set it in motion, it was basically a wooden box or trough perhaps twenty inches wide, forty long, and four high. At the upper end was a hopper, twenty inches square, whose bottom sieve had holes one-half inch in diameter. Under this sloped a canvas or wooden apron from the lower end of the hopper back to the upper end of the cradle; sometimes there was a second stretch of canvas, underneath the first, down, again, to the hopper's lower end. Two or three so-called riffle bars were on the bottom in the lower half of the rocker. When the device was set in a good location and the hopper filled, the operator

6 Coy, *Gold Days*, 85–87, 115, 122–24, 132; Rickard, *American Mining*, 30–32; Clappe, *Shirley Letters*, 214; Bancroft, *History*, VI, 84–89, 409, 413; Caughey, *Rushing*, 25–28; Taylor, *Eldorado*, 65–66.

seated himself, kept the machine rocking with one hand and poured in water from a half-gallon dipper with the other until all that remained in the hopper were rocks too large to pass through the sieve. The resulting mixture of dirt and water ran along the apron to the upper end of the cradle, then, at a lower level, back to the lower end and out. On the canvas apron, especially at the riffle bars, was deposited its gold. A rocker could be put together in a few hours' time and was portable, but it lost the finer particles of gold.

Better than a cradle was a long tom, essentially a rocker immobilized and extended until perhaps ten to thirty feet long. The lower end, called the riddle, replaced the hopper; here a heavily perforated sheet-iron bottom allowed the mass of earth and water to drop through to a riffle box, similar to but longer than the bottom of a rocker, where the riffles caught the gold particles. The raw material was put in at the upper end of the long tom and the liquid added by a hose from a tiny dam.

The long tom was improved by adding a series of riffle boxes at the end to act again on the dirt and extract additional gold. When thus remodeled the long tom was called a sluice. At first these were \/-shaped but soon came to be three-sided. The sluice was often lined with rock, in part to save the expense of timber, which sometimes had to be renewed as often as every twenty days, in part because a rock sluice retained more gold than did a wooden one. The long tom and the sluice were improved by putting quicksilver at the riffles to help catch the gold. To separate out the precious mineral, the quicksilver, upon removal from the riffle, was first placed in a buckskin bag and as much of it squeezed out as possible, then heated to secure the rest. Unless worried about theft, miners made it their common practice to let a sluice run for a week and then, usually on a Sunday, clean out the accumulated gold.

To operate a pan required one man; a rocker, two or three; a long tom, three to six; and a sluice, five to twenty. To put a large quantity of gold-bearing dirt through a rocker cost only one-fourth the expense of panning; through a long tom, only one-fourth of a rocker's cost; and through a sluice, only one-third of a long tom's expenses. The typical California miner was slow to adopt these innovations because he was a novice who learned by imitation, because his enterprises were small, and because he hesitated to use big-business methods for fear his deposit would either become so quickly exhausted that it would bankrupt a company formed to exploit it or else prove so valuable that he would have to share with many others the great wealth he had initially uncovered.

By 1851, the deposits easily worked by the methods just described were beginning to be exhausted, and there began a transition to new techniques, heavy investments, corporations, and hired hands.[7] Gradually the ordinary miner could no longer find opportunity to extract his own gold; he had to become either a mine employee or a hired prospector, and by 1858, many miners needed work.

One of the new methods, called river mining, was to divert a stream temporarily and secure the gold in the dry, exposed bed. Such a project, undertaken only in the summer during the low-water season, had available a maximum working period of five months. Always there was the danger of early rains to bring disaster on structures never intended to withstand a flood. Work turning aside the river began in late June or early July and was completed by September. Mining the exposed bed quickly began and continued as long as possible. The diversion dam was built of heavy logs and turned the water into a flume of planks and canvas for sometimes a hundred yards, sometimes as much as a mile, before it was put back into its accustomed course. It was cheaper to build a flume than to dig a ditch because the soil was so rocky; by 1854, preference for it was almost universal. There were in 1855 an estimated 4,493 miles of such flumes and canals. Often the enterprises were undertaken by joint-stock companies of miners, who contributed their services for a period of months, and perhaps also money, in return for stock. The company had such a limited time in which to work that everybody labored at top speed.

The total return from all of California's river mining, historian Owen C. Coy concluded, was little more than the investment required to secure it. Sometimes a number of companies were working at various points on the same stream, so that of the American River it could once be said it hardly touched its original bed for many miles, yet the various enterprises never united in one great effort. A problem sometimes encountered was that a layer of clay seemed to be the bed of the stream but actually was not and farther down on bedrock would be the true natural bottom to which the gold had descended.

7 Paul, *California Gold,* 64, 117, 125–30, 147–69, 172–78; Taylor, *Eldorado,* 65; Shinn, *Mining Camps,* 191, 250; Caughey, *Cornerstone,* 175, 258, 261–65; Coy, *Gold Days,* 105, 129, 130, 133–35.

River mining began with an initial boom in 1849–50, encountered some bad years, then reached its highly successful peak in 1855–56, and by 1863 had sunk so low in the opinion of the Americans that they allowed it to become the almost exclusive province of the Chinese. A variant was so-called booming, collecting a large mass of water behind a dam and then turning it loose all at once on a desired area. Such wasteful flooding often carried the finer gold so far downstream that it was lost.

Not all of the placer deposits were in existing streams, but at earlier periods in geological history the rivers had sometimes run in quite different places. In these old beds, often now in such unlikely locations as high on the side of a present hill, were sometimes rich deposits. Occasionally a bit could be scratched away from the surface and the deposit exposed, but much more often the expense of removing the accumulated debris was too great. The alternative was a method termed "coyoting" but sometimes called deep mining or tunnel mining; it was simply to dig a hole into the hillside, extract the rich gravel, carry it to the nearest stream, and wash out the gold. The practice began in California with some Cornishmen of Nevada County in 1850, and what was at first a small-scale enterprise gradually became more complicated: simple holes gave way to tunnels, quite commonly one to two thousand feet long. These were dug by joint-stock companies, owned chiefly by the miners who were doing the work. The task was not as difficult as boring through rock in quartz mining, but the danger of cave-ins was greater.

Another way to get rich gravel out of an old stream bed was ground sluicing. The miners dug a small gully on a hillside, sent water cascading steadily down it, shoveled in dirt, and expected the rocks and natural obstacles in their artificial stream to catch some of the gold.

A great improvement on this method was hydraulic mining, which came to be used wherever profitable, even if it destroyed growing crops, uprooted orchards, undermined houses, or moved an entire town. It began in Nevada County in 1852 when a Frenchman named Chabot, using a short length of hose, turned the water in a flume he had built toward a hillside. A year later, Edward E. Matteson attached a nozzle to a hose, but not until several years after this innovation did hydraulicking become a general practice. At first the hose was simply of canvas, later was reinforced with iron rings, rope binding, or strong netting, and finally was replaced by iron pipe, first made of sheet iron and then of wrought iron. Initially the nozzles were wooden but later were of iron. In some easy spots the hydraulic blasts from the hose seemed simply to melt away the gravel, but at more difficult ones the miners sometimes burrowed into the side of the hill and exploded a charge of powder. Occasionally they ran a tunnel in at a sharp, upward angle, so that it would also serve as a sluice, then forced the water up nearly vertically to bring down the gravel.

The gravel flooding off hillsides was run through a series of sluices on nearly level ground. As late as 1858, however, these were still losing a quarter to a half of the gold they processed. To correct this, miners lengthened them to perhaps several thousand feet, but thus extended, great boulders tore along them, causing much damage. The small riffles were replaced with loose planks and either wooden or granite blocks. Another improvement was the so-called undercurrent sluice, in which a grating in the bottom of the regular sluice allowed fine debris to fall down into a second sluice, where a much quieter current extracted more of the gold. These improved methods were so effective that sometimes the debris from earlier operations was reprocessed with a greater yield than was originally secured. The cost of thus working one cubic yard of gravel was as low as one-half cent, compared to several dollars had the rocker method been used. Hydraulic pressure was often inadequate when directed at the bottom stratum of a deposit, where the gravel was likely to be so compacted into heavy chunks that it was called cement. Sometimes these blocks were simply set aside to weather away, but by 1857, stamp mills were constructed to break them up.

When gold was separated from ordinary gravel in the sluices, a considerable quantity of debris remained. This was dumped in the nearest creek to wash downstream, burying many of the famous river bars which had yielded such wealth in 1849, interfering with traditional placer mining by older methods, hindering or preventing navigation, inundating arable land, and creating the ominous danger of floods. Despite increasingly strong objections, it was not until a court decision in 1884 that hydraulic operators were restricted, and sharply, too, with regard to where they could dump.

To obtain an ample supply of water at sufficient pressure for hydraulic mining was a major problem. Sometimes a mining company got its own, but more often, and increasingly as time went on, it purchased from one of the special water companies. These often went long distances to reach a source of supply, erected reservoirs, dug tunnels through ridges, and put up aqueducts over canyons. In normal terrain, they at first built wooden flumes but in later years saved money by using pick and shovel to dig ditches with an ideal downgrade of thirteen feet per mile, although from six to twenty-five was practicable. Their construction costs, averaging perhaps one thousand dollars per mile in the uncomplicated stretches, frequently exceeded the original estimate.

Virtually every company found a ready market for the water, which it sold by the so-called miner's inch, generally defined as the amount of water that would flow through a hole one inch square in a period of ten hours. Occasionally resistance to the rate set arose, but since everybody recognized the financial damage inflicted when buyers suspended purchases until this was lowered, disputes were generally compromised. The great increase in hydraulic mining and the consequent demand for water came in the middle 1850's during one of California's dry cycles, causing much complaint about a drought when actually steady progress was made in obtaining additional supplies. By 1856, the largest system in the state was the Eureka Canal in El Dorado County, whose dams, reservoirs, and 247 miles of canals had cost $700,000.

The methods discussed so far were for placer deposits, but California also had quartz mines.[8] In these, veins of gold were so imbedded in rock that they could not be separated from it by any easy or simple process. A man discovering such a claim could not hope to do more than a little preliminary work himself before selling it to financiers or a company which could expend the large sums necessary to insure proper development. The first California quartz mine began operation near Mariposa in 1849; the first mill to process ore was founded at Grass Valley in 1850 by G. W. Wright. A speculative frenzy in quartz mining began in 1850, swept to dizzy heights, then crashed in 1853. When assays seemed to indicate that many California ledges were ten to one hundred times more valuable than those in foreign countries which quartz miners were working profitably, the excitement began. Hopeful financiers organized many a company. These bore heavy transportation costs on all supplies or equipment they

[8] Coy, *Gold Days*, 139; Bancroft, *History*, VI, 415–18; Caughey, *Cornerstone*, 252–57; Paul, *California Gold*, 131–44.

shipped in, of necessity paid exceedingly high wages, and had much trouble in finding skilled labor. Often they built a mill at the site of a rich outcropping without learning its extent, only to find it a pocket not nearly large enough to warrant the expenditures made. Often the machinery they installed in their mills was costly and elaborate, but of untried design and so ineffective that about nine-tenths of it had to be sold as junk. Such mistakes bankrupted perhaps 90 per cent of the companies, but the others owned rich ledges and by employing careful methods continued successful operation. After the 1853 crash, confidence was gradually restored and the quartz-mining industry continued to develop, using saner methods.

During the 1850's, the deepest shafts in California quartz mining went down only about three hundred feet; often a deposit was worked by a tunnel into a hillside or even an open cut. The men used picks, hand drills, sledges, and a little black powder to extract the ore, installed hand windlasses or a simple steam engine for hoisting, employed moderate-sized steam pumps for drainage, and faced no serious problems of timbering.

To separate the gold from the ore was a difficult process. One well-known way, surviving for centuries throughout mining areas of the world, was the arrastra method. In its pure form this was a circular, stone-paved basin of considerable size with a low retaining wall. At the center was a strong post; from it jutted a horizontal shaft which dragged, by chains or ropes, heavy abrasive stones. A mule pulled the shaft around the circle, causing the boulders to grind the ore into a fine sand or powder from which the gold could be washed by pan, rocker, or sluice. A variant of the arrastra was called a Chile mill and instead of heavy abrasive stones used a large stone wheel or roller. Another important device, utilized as early as the sixteenth century, was the stamp mill, which is quite comparable to a pharmacist's mortar and pestle. As first used in California, it had a shallow wooden basin to hold the ore. Over this was the stamp, a long piece of wood with a heavy, square iron head, which was repeatedly pulled up into position and then dropped to crumble solid rocks into powder. A simple but major improvement, first made in 1851, was the so-called California stamp, all iron, rounded instead of square, and revolving freely rather than being held rigidly in place. Later the head came to be fashioned of heavy cast iron rather than soft iron, the mortar to be deep and made of cast iron. In 1856, a complete stamp mill could be built for between six and ten thousand dollars, but it would extract only one-fifth to one-third of the gold. Quite commonly the debris from the mill was ground in an arrastra and quicksilver also applied, perhaps in the mortar but more likely in some kind of sluice, to secure more of the riches. Another process, after pulverizing the rock, was to have water carry the powder over coarse blankets, which caught some of the gold. No other methods were used until after 1860, when a chlorination process was introduced to separate sulphides from metallic gold. Quartz mines and these refining devices produced only a very small fraction of California's total gold production in the 1850's, perhaps as little as 1 per cent.

The total value of gold produced in California in 1848 was $245,-301; in 1849, $10,151,360; in 1850, $41,273,106; in 1851, $75,938,232; in 1852, $81,294,700; in 1853, $67,613,487; in 1854, $69,433,931; in 1855, $55,485,395; in 1856, $57,509,411; in 1857, $43,628,172; in 1858, $46,591,140; and in 1859, $45,846,599; or a total of $595,010,834 from 1848 through 1859. A sweeping generalization would be to say that the first half-billion dollars of California's all-time gold yield came almost entirely from placer mining, the second half-billion mostly from hydraulic operations, and the second billion chiefly from quartz mining. The largest nugget ever found was at Calaveras in November, 1854; it weighed 161 pounds, of which 20 were quartz and the rest gold, and was valued at more than $30,000.

3

CALIFORNIA MINERS

CERTAINLY there was gold to be found in California, but there was great variety in the luck of those seeking it.[1] Thus in September, 1849, one middle westerner wrote back to a newspaper near his old home that he had been extremely fortunate on the Feather River, taking out $16,000 worth of gold in eight working days. In contrast, another middle westerner in a different area wrote back to a second paper only a month later that he did not intend to remain in California under any circumstances, that a great many gold seekers were sick and dying, that thousands were leaving daily, and that all of his old neighbors should stay home.

Forty-niners generally tended to feel sorry for themselves and bemoan their fate. Some quickly changed from mining to a different task, but others, in the prime of life, full of optimism, strong in pride, were determined to secure the riches they said they would get when they left for California. Some who met with great success made ostentatious display, like the young man around Sutter's Fort early in 1849 who wiped the mud off his boots with a fine silk handkerchief, replying to remonstrances that it made no difference if he spoiled the one for he always carried another for his nose. Much more common was the miner who was secretive, not wanting to admit it if his fortunes were poor and having good reason to keep any spectacular success hidden.

How much did the average self-employed gold seeker make? One measure might be the prevailing wage, because it was supposedly fixed at how much an ordinary individual could earn for himself as an in-

[1] Paul, *California Gold*, 119–22; Caughey, *Cornerstone*, 169–73; Taylor, *Eldorado*, 196; Bancroft, *History*, VI, 424; Wyman, *California Letters*, 27, 78–80.

dependent miner. In 1848, daily pay was twenty dollars; in 1849, sixteen; in 1850, ten; in 1851, a little less than eight; in 1852, six; in 1853, five; and from 1856 through 1859, three or a little more. Perhaps such a yardstick exaggerates, for historian Hubert H. Bancroft estimated that if in 1852 the total amount of gold extracted were divided among all the miners then working, the average daily income would be two dollars; yet wages were six. At first glance such earnings seem high when compared with an average daily pay of less than $1.25 for employees of eastern coal and iron mines, but the 1849 cost of living in California mining camps was 300 or 400 per cent more than it was elsewhere, even in expensive San Francisco. As late as 1861, despite a heavy decline, it was still twice as high as in the eastern states.

When early-day miners borrowed money, they pledged their honor without offering further security and usually repaid on the date promised. Most gold seekers were kind; generosity, openhandedness, and largeheartedness were characteristics they especially admired. For example, at one diggings a sixteen-year-old boy wandered in, obviously out of luck, and looked about at the busy miners with so much dejection that they decided they would all work an hour for him. Soon he was handed the one hundred dollars thus collected, along with a list of equipment he should buy, and was promised that upon his return the men would pick out a good claim for him to work. Another attribute of most miners was their great pride in their expert profanity, even if in the East they had hardly ever uttered an oath. Some men specialized in the alliteration of their curse words, others liked unusual combinations of rather familiar phrases, and still others preferred such grotesque comments as "Only let me get hold of your beggarly carcass once, and I will use you up so small that God Almighty himself cannot see your ghost."[2] Another characteristic was youth, for about 80 per cent of the miners were between eighteen and thirty-five years of age.

Some gold seekers wore the red flannel shirts so generally thought of today as being typical, but more often it was gray or blue flannel or red calico. Their trousers were usually of wool but sometimes of white duck. Those who waded in mud and water all day wore high boots, much like those of some present-day fishermen, and their hats,

2 Coy, *Gold Days*, 146–47; Bancroft, *Inter Pocula*, 318–19; Clappe, *Shirley Letters*, 79–80.

more often than not, were low crowned, broad brimmed, black, and made of felt. Clothing was usually washed by the bearded owners themselves on a Sunday and generally they did a poor job of it. Their careless work made the louse a familiar pest, although they sometimes had trouble with fleas, too.

Some miners wore their camp clothes when visiting San Francisco; others dressed considerably better. Indeed, it is said that in the city was to be seen every varied style of dress that had prevailed anywhere in the world in the previous quarter-century. Early Californians did not regard clothes as a gauge of respectability nor did they think that any honest occupation, however menial, affected a man's social standing. Theirs was a very democratic country where strokes of fortune often placed many in far different positions than they had previously occupied. Some who had once held exalted posts came to saw wood or drive teams while others who had been day laborers rose to be heads of important business enterprises.[3]

The miners' diet in camp had little variety.[4] Chiefly it was bread and salt pork or jerked beef, occasionally supplemented with beans, rice, and wild game, but only rarely enriched by such novelties as potatoes, onions, dried apples, and dried peaches. Complaints were made mostly about the monotony of the same dish too often repeated and the uninspired bungling of those to whom cooking was an unwelcome burden dispatched as quickly as possible.

Some men suffered from scurvy in 1849 but recovered as soon as they got enough green things to eat. They all knew the cause to be a lack of vegetables, but only in later years were adequate supplies of these grown locally or imported. It is a fact that some gold seekers starved to death because they had no funds to buy food, they were too proud to ask aid, and their plight went undetected in a mining community where charity was "emotional and demonstrative rather than reflective and organized."

In the winter of 1849–50 there was much illness; often the victims, isolated, lacked doctors, money, and sometimes even friends.[5] A middle westerner writing to his home-town newspaper in January,

3 Jackson, *Anybody's Gold*, 80–81; Clappe, *Shirley Letters*, 61; Geoffrey Bret Harte, *The Letters of Bret Harte*, 352; Caughey, *Cornerstone*, 182–84; Bancroft, *Inter Pocula*, 295–97; Taylor, *Eldorado*, 236; Bancroft, *History*, VI 224.

4 Caughey, *Cornerstone*, 178–79.

5 Caughey, *Rushing*, 97–108; Bancroft, *Inter Pocula*, 351; Wyman, *California Letters*, 157–58.

1850, estimated that at least one-third of those who came to California lost their health, sometimes for months. The next summer, cholera struck heavily in the cities; the cause, now known but then undetected, was impure water and poor sewage disposal. Cholera, typhoid fever (also from unsanitary conditions), malaria (contracted in Panama but breaking out later), meningitis, and rheumatic fever were rampant in California before 1856. Cholera, typhoid fever, and dysentery were all characterized by diarrhea, with its chills, headaches, gas on the stomach, violent purging, and burning fever. In mining areas poison oak was troublesome, eye troubles came from the evaporation of mercury in open pans, and rheumatism was common. San Franciscans frequently had coughs and sore eyes in the early years from the dust storm of almost every afternoon; in the bay area generally there were many throat and lung difficulties. Everywhere overwork and exhaustion were factors complicating other illnesses.

Although some patients recovered satisfactorily, others were left weakened for life. To treat them, patent-medicine shysters abounded and advertised extensively. In the mining areas they were not very subtle, but in San Francisco they resorted to a variety of tricks to simulate the respectability they lacked, sometimes even going so far as to purchase from a doctor's unscrupulous widow her husband's diploma of graduation from a medical school of recognized excellence. Capable, genuine doctors were at first very scarce but by the middle 1850's became more numerous. In San Francisco their fees were standardized at $32 for an ordinary visit and $100 for a night visit, with operations from $500 to $1,000. California patients needing special care often found no good hospital available, but fraternal organizations and religious groups operated some of high quality. San Francisco's general health problems were increased by its large number of rats, brought in by ships from five continents, and not until 1853 were there enough cats and terriers to reduce the rodent population to normal proportions.

Housing in the mining areas was at first quite inadequate and only gradually improved.[6] When a settlement first developed, usually in the summer, few of the men had wagons or tents in which to sleep. During the fall the wiser of them dug caves or put up log cabins with

[6] Olaf P. Jenkins (ed.), *The Mother Lode Country*, 92–93; Caughey, *Cornerstone*, 182; Clappe, *Shirley Letters*, 48–49, 96; Paul, *California Gold*, 75; Bancroft, *Inter Pocula*, 666.

canvas roofs and mud-and-stone chimneys. The more careless did nothing until the onslaught of winter forced them to leave or else endure much discomfort from cold, rain, and sometimes snow. If the camp showed signs of permanence, houses were eventually built. The majority of these, until the late 1850's, were of light, frame exterior walls with tightly stretched cotton cloth for interior dividers, ceilings, and the inside covering of the outer shell. Sometimes merchants and their employees simply slept scattered about in their store building. The reason for such makeshifts was that most men would not turn aside from making money long enough to provide anything better and doubted whether they would stay in the camp long enough to justify more. Their shelters were often a prey to fire, for a minor accident in one of them might easily develop into a serious conflagration of many. The obvious remedy, less timber in the structures, came to be provided much more for business houses than for homes. Mexicans, native Californians, and the frugal Chinese favored adobe walls, most Americans preferred brick, and New Englanders and Italians liked stone. All covered the heavily raftered roofs with metal, topped by a thick layer of sand, and protected doors and windows with close-fitting sheet-iron shutters. Townspeople almost always used the kind of stone available in their immediate area, generally rhyolite tuff, locally known as lava. It was durable, strong enough to provide long, narrow lintels over doors and windows, yet soft enough for masons to cut all six sides to fit the adjacent stones snugly with a minimum of mortar.

Hotels in the less developed mining camps were usually one story high, a barroom in front, a dining room with long, clothless tables and wooden benches, and one or more bunk rooms.[7] The bunks were often canvas stretched over wooden frames, equipped with a hay pillow and a pair of blankets to rent for a dollar a night. At the outside rear were a barrel of water, three or four tin basins for washing, a piece of looking glass, and, chained near by, a well-worn brush and comb. In the more stable communities the quarters were considerably better. The best of California sleeping accommodations were usually kept by Americans and the best eating places by Germans, French, or Italians.

[7] Bancroft, *Inter Pocula*, 661, 666–68, 674–78; Caughey, *Rushing*, 102; Clappe, *Shirley Letters*, 165–70; Jackson, *Anybody's Gold*, 252–54; Franklin A. Buck, *A Yankee Trader in the Gold Rush*, 135.

To some gold seekers, drinking liquor seemed as necessary as sleeping and eating. A holiday, any kind of news, a hanging, the death of a friend, and almost any other occasion were all used to justify taking a nip; perhaps life so dull that nothing could be found as an excuse was also a cause for imbibing. Occasionally, especially in isolated areas, a whole camp might suddenly go on a drunken spree. Thus the widely known letter writer Dame Shirley of Indian Bar, a small snowed-in settlement, observed a celebration of Christmas turn into a four-day drunk, then taper off, only to break out again worse than ever on New Year's Day.

Under normal conditions in many a small camp, the saloon was the only center available for companionship, relaxation, and sociability. A typical one was built sometimes of logs but more usually of boards to a height of one or two stories; it spread over considerable ground and was made as conspicuous as possible in appearance. Its owner certainly installed a bar and card tables, where the play was for money with fellow miners or professional gamblers or else for drinks among friends. If his establishment was large, he added a tobacco stand and served an elaborate free luncheon once or twice a day. If he was in a rather lawless district, he put bags of sand inside his counters so that his employees could duck down behind them when shooting started; but happily in any saloon, comedy was the rule and tragedy the exception. Although the barkeeper could provide various mixed drinks, most of his sales were liquor straight. An invitation to drink from one patron to another was almost a command.

Enough San Franciscans of 1853 liked to drink for the populace to support 537 places selling liquor and employing 743 bartenders in all. In both city and mine there were men afflicted with alcoholism and delirium tremens, causing Californians genuine concern. San Francisco built an Inebriates' Home, and Californians joined branches of eastern temperance organizations and in 1859 organized a new group called the Dashaways because its members would "dash away" the use of liquor.

Not all men were impressed with antiliquor activities. A merchant named Buck wrote his New England relatives that when a certain Miss Pellet came to his town, mounted a dry-goods box, and commenced giving a temperance lecture, she emptied the saloons and stores quicker than any dogfight had ever done. She had a fine voice and such a torrent of language that she talked for an hour, seemingly without stopping for breath. When she was finally finished, the group dispersed and "thanked our stars we were not tied to her for life."

Gambling at cards was a popular form of recreation, in part because mining itself was also a gamble.[8] The most common place for it was a saloon or a special gambling establishment. Men generally played for small stakes unless they happened to hit a streak of luck, when they would continue doubling until they had taken all their opponent's money or, by the turn of a card, lost everything. Most players were the ordinary run of people trying their luck; there were also gentlemen gambling mainly for recreation but occasionally acting as amateur dealers. Some of the professionals had a specific table at an establishment, bought licenses, paid rent, and ran an account at the bar. Others moved about from place to place, seeking the largest crowds or the best mining centers. They all accustomed themselves to going without sleep or rest for several nights and days while their luck was holding well. These professionals were better dressed than any other class in California; temperate in liquor drinking; supremely self-controlled; prompt to act with coolness, cunning, and courage; reticent; expressionless, whether winning or losing; generous in philanthropy, but not by any code; and supremely confident that in the long run the mathematical laws of chance were on their side. They met financial adversity with equilibrium, even when they borrowed to pay their debts.

In the larger cities the gamblers fitted up extensive establishments with such splendors as mirrors from floor to ceiling and large paintings of female nudes. Some of these businesses ran day and night. The El Dorado in San Francisco was so prosperous that it could well afford its $6,000-a-month rent. For those who wished to gamble the larger places offered quite a variety—the pure chance of faro, monte, and dice; the chance and skill combined in whist, euchre, poker, and backgammon; and skill alone in chess, checkers, and billiards. Generally games requiring much exercise of skill or thought were never very popular, for they were slow and required considerable effort; the average patron of a gambling hall wanted instead something quick and "soul stirring." How many professionals and their patrons attempted to cheat each other is a matter on which historians have no statistics, but it did happen. Among the more common methods were

[8] Bancroft, *Inter Pocula*, 687–712; Taylor, *Eldorado*, 90–91; Jackson, *Anybody's Gold*, 122–28.

waxing the cards, using an imperfect deck, and marking the cards with tiny punctures imperceptible to the touch—unless one's fingers had been sensitized with a bit of acid. Considerably less subtle was simply robbing a professional gambler at work with his stack of money in front of him; few attempted such boldness in the face of almost certain interference from bystanders.

California miners expected professional gamblers to be men. The only successful exception was Eleanore Dumont, who abruptly appeared in Nevada City, opened a card palace, dealt twenty-one like a veteran, drank whiskey wisely, rolled her own cigarettes with charm, and knew just the right degree of friendliness to keep patrons happy but at the proper distance.

Women of any kind were such a novelty in the mining area that men sometimes traveled a considerable distance just to see a newly arrived one.[9] Even in 1860 there was only one woman in the camps for every eight or ten men. As early as 1849 some women came overland with their families; by sea almost none arrived except those planning to take commercial advantage of the woman shortage. Beginning in 1850, the number of respectable ladies and their children using ships started to increase. In some instances a wife came with her husband on the initial trip west; in others she was sent for as soon as good fortune permitted. To live in early-day California put a woman's love, pride, health, strength, honor, and religion to a crucial test.

The state in the 1850's had a severe shortage of unmarried but respectable and suitable women. Eastern spinsters who came to visit relatives were often surprised to find themselves getting married, and quickly. Sometimes a man sent a letter to a female acquaintance he had known casually in his old home town, or perhaps in a community where all the best younger man had gone west, the woman took the initiative in writing. In either event it was not unusual for the second or third letter from California to contain a proposal. If accepted, the man sent money for the trip, and as soon as the ship docked at San Francisco, he rushed aboard to greet his bride and take her to a preacher. Comparatively few grooms learned, on the ship's arrival, that the girl had died during the trip or that she had decided instead to marry a fellow traveler. So great was the shortage that Mrs. Eliza

9 Bancroft, *History*, VI, 233; Caughey, *Cornerstone*, 189; Paul, *California Gold*, 317; Lewis, *Sea Routes*, 35–40; Bancroft, *Inter Pocula*, 311–13; Howe, *Argonauts*, 11.

Farnham announced that she was going to bring out from the East a group of educated, cultured, and respectable females. More than two hundred young women expressed interest in joining her group but for some reason Mrs. Farnham arrived with only three eligible young ladies.

With such a shortage of women, dances were always a problem—but they were held.[10] In San Francisco at least one masquerade ball had not a single female to grace it. In some parts of California the miners attended the fandangos of the native-born Californians. Sometimes they amused themselves by singing songs of the day popular in the East and also those peculiar to the regions, such as "Crossing the Plains," "Coming Round the Horn," "The Fools of Forty-Nine," and the one about "Hangtown Gals," who thought themselves too good to associate with miners. Other forms of recreation included whittling, bull-bear fights, bear-jackass fights, wrestling, prize fights, watching magicians, and celebrating such great holidays as the Fourth of July. National fraternal organizations, such as the Masons and Odd Fellows, early active in the mines, had a considerable membership. The most popular by far was one unique to California, the E Clampus Vitus, with chapters in virtually every town. Its stated purpose was benevolence but perhaps it devoted more effort to conviviality and sometimes raucous fun. The better-established mining towns gradually developed literary societies, libraries, debating clubs, lyceums, and glee clubs. North San Juan even had a soda fountain.

Another diversion was going to the theater.[11] The first structure built for strictly dramatic performances was the Eagle, in Sacramento, which opened in the fall of 1849. The seats in its "dress circle" were reached from outside the building by a stepladder with canvas nailed to the underside "in deference to the ladies." On wet nights those seated on the ground floor had difficulties with water, but never so severe that they had to stand on their chairs. San Francisco's first, over a saloon, was Washington Hall, opened January 16, 1850; various others were soon built there. The opening night of the American was the most distinctive—the foundations of the building were so poor that it sank two inches!

10 Buck, *Yankee Trader*, 96–97; Coy, *Gold Days*, 283; Jackson, *Anybody's Gold*, 99; Paul, *California Gold*, 311–16; Caughey, Rushing, 186–92.

11 Jackson, *Anybody's Gold*, 183–98; Coy, *Gold Days*, 282; Bancroft, *History*, VI, 244–45; George R. MacMinn, *The Theater of the Golden Era in California*, 28–496.

The greatest variety of attractions was, of course, in San Francisco. There during the 1850's some 907 plays, 48 operas, 84 extravaganzas, ballets, and pantomimes, and 66 minstrel shows were presented. Some of these required a big-city stage, but most of the dramas needed only the simplest arrangements and were played in the mining towns. Probably the crudest stage of all was the stump of a giant tree, once used by the George Chapman company.

Typical of the touring groups was McKean Buchanan's, which in six weeks of 1856 played in forty different towns and traveled about seven hundred miles. It once suffered disaster when a runaway team dumped all the costumes over a mile and a half of downgrade, but it still gave a performance that evening. After the show, Buchanan won enough at poker to make good all the damage. Mining-town audiences, in the opinion of veteran actor Walter Leman, were as intelligent as those in San Francisco or Sacramento. As for money, he recalled that when on tour with Julia Dean, they never took in less than three hundred dollars a night, even in the roughest camp. While actors of genuine ability with a good play seldom failed to receive proper appreciation, poor plays and players might suffer bombardment or even expulsion. In the early 1850's, the miners did not like tragedy, apparently because they saw so much of it in real life.

Of the stars, the most talented were Alexina Fisher Baker, Catherine Sinclair, Matilda Heron, Laura Keene, Junius Brutus Booth, Edwin Booth, and James Kirby. Among the lesser ones were Sarah Kirby Stark, Charles Chapman, Catherine Caroline Chapman, Frank Cahnfrau, and C. E. Bingham. The great Edwin Booth, who appeared first in California at the age of nineteen, played such major Shakespearean roles as Iago, Shylock, and even Lear, along with a great variety of other parts in many other plays.

One San Francisco custom was, on the opening night of a popular play or at a special performance, not to sell tickets but, rather, auction them off. Another was to hold a benefit night for a popular actor or actress at which presents were given, sometimes even diamonds of considerable value. It was quite common to follow a Shakespearean play, sometimes considerably abridged, with something much lighter, such as *Macbeth* relieved by *Slasher and Crasher* or *Romeo and Juliet* succeeded by *Cool as a Cucumber*. San Franciscans could see women playing men's roles, such as Romeo, and children taking adult parts, such as Shylock. One July when Mrs. Baker and Mrs. Sinclair appeared together in Dion Boucicault's *London Assurance,* each played a role one night, exchanged parts the second, and on the third alternated roles with each new act.

A lower level than this was the burlesque of current events given in San Francisco by D. G. Robinson, a raucous and unsubtle but for a time amusing comic. There were also bit and two-bit theaters which catered to men only with much that was ribald and bawdy.

Minstrel shows were popular. Billy Birch and Charley Backus headed the chief San Francisco group with such success that they later went to New York City. Their shows were more refined than most and tried to keep as much as possible to real plantation models, using "simple settings, beautiful ballads and real Negro comedy for their success." Such competition was very difficult for the visiting eastern companies to meet. In mining camps, however, minstrel shows were often amateur. One opening night at Grass Valley, the man leading the group on stage at the start of the performance tripped nervously, fell, and three who followed sprawled over him. This mishap the audience took to be a well-calculated joke and "no more ice need be broken that night."

Various singers appeared in both the San Francisco Bay area and in the mining communities. Anna Bishop had the most vocal ability, but Elisa Bisaccianti and Kate Hayes were quite popular. Most performers gave operatic selections mixed with popular ballads. Some good bands, usually French or German, were to be heard in the best of the gambling halls. The first opera company, a group from Italy, appeared in San Francisco during 1851. As early as 1849 a circus came to the city, with acrobats, clowns, and horsemen the chief attractions.

Of all the entertainers, probably the most discussed was Lola Montez and her famous dance about a woman fighting off an attack by spiders. What made men flock at first to see Lola was her notorious past. She originally married an army officer but deserted him to become a dancing girl and then found even better opportunities as mistress to Ludwig of Bavaria. Lola was one of the factors contributing to a revolution there. Going back to England, she married a second time without the formality of a divorce, stood trial for bigamy, shortly came to New York City as a dancer, and, when attendance fell off, wandered on until she came to California. In San Francisco her popularity did not last too long because she lacked unusual talent, despite her colorful background and her great beauty. For several years she rusticated in Grass Valley, where one of the neighboring children was Lotta Crabtree. Lola gave the girl lessons, but how much of Lotta's success came from these and how much from natural ability is not clear. Lotta's real debut came in 1855 at Rabbit Creek. Actually eight but in appearance only six, she was a great success. Going on tour that summer, she became a very celebrated child performer. Lotta had a way of laughing while she danced and was seemingly tireless. Eventually she grew up, went east, and continued her success.

Another pastime for the miners was reading newspapers.[12] The chief ones were in San Francisco, where in 1853 a total of nine morning dailies, three afternoon dailies, two triweeklies, and three weeklies were published. The *Alta California*, which became a daily on January 22, 1850, was for two decades the town's leading journal. To issue such a paper required about a thousand pounds of type, a hand press, and perhaps six printers. The relatively small amount of capital required to start publication accounted for the number of journals in San Francisco. In 1856, the largest of them had a circulation of 3,600 and the total for all was 15,000, which was small considering San Francisco's size. It was difficult to make them pay and many went bankrupt. These papers of the 1850's, not strong in news coverage, simply printed what they could conveniently gather without too much effort. They were reticent in reporting local crime. In their dramatic criticism most of the discussion centered on the content of the play rather than how well it was acted. For events outside California they depended upon condensing portions of the eastern newspapers brought in by steamer, publishing the most important items as quickly as possible after the ship docked and the remainder in the next issue. Their editors thought all this should be subordinate to the editorial column, presenting the views of the paper's sponsors, often in scathing language. Comments on local affairs, such as municipal corruption, were held to the minimum, while much was written about national affairs. Writers did not temper their views in news or editorial columns to appease advertisers, even those who paid to appear on the front page. In questions of format and make-up, the printers were usually more influential than the editor. They used small type generally in both news and advertising columns.

How much the early miners read books, even those they brought

12 John P. Young, *Journalism in California*, 9–56.

with them, is a question.[13] Bayard Taylor commented that many preferred simply to lie at ease, turning over in their minds all the possible maneuvers of some speculation in order to make sure they had left no possibility uncalculated. No doubt interest in reading increased after the first frenzy of '49 and '50. By December, 1852, there was enough to greet the founding of the *Golden Era,* a four-page literary weekly, with immediate and sustained popularity. Its editors were Rollin M. Daggett, who toured the camps in miner's boots and flannel shirt securing subscriptions, and J. Macdonough Foard. Some critics complained that the paper catered to tastes too low and that once a writer earned a reputation in its pages he would turn elsewhere, but certainly every contemporary California author of any importance contributed to it at one time or another. The *Golden Era* paid not over five dollars a page for prose and nothing for poetry. *Hutchings' California Magazine Illustrated* started in 1856 and lasted five years; the *Pioneer,* a literary magazine founded in 1854, survived only four months.

One writer about California was Mrs. Louise Clappe, who in 1851–52 as "Dame Shirley" sent twenty-three letters to her sister in the East describing life in Rich Bar and Indian Bar on the Feather River. She undertook to give a true picture; her observation, objectivity, and lively style made the version of these letters published in the later 1850's a minor classic. Alonzo Delano, a leading businessman of Grass Valley who used the pen name "Old Block," pictured the unfortunates who had found little success in California, only hard work, suffering, and mishaps. Much of his writing depended upon familiarity with the mines and quickly became dated. The humorist "John Phoenix" was actually an army officer, a West Pointer named George Horatio Derby. He was one of the first who tried to amuse without illiteracy or bad grammar, but conservatives thought him too fond of horseplay. Among his take-offs was one on the *Pacific Railway Reports,* poking fun at both the procedures and the literary styles of the explorers. Much of his California reputation depended upon puns, unamusing without the proper build-up, and upon stories attributed to him but never printed because they were off color. An English immigrant, J. M. Hutchings, wrote the "Miner's Ten

[13] Taylor, *Eldorado,* 205; John W. Caughey, "Shaping a Literary Tradition," *Pacific Historical Review,* Vol. VIII (1939), 210–14; Franklin Walker, *San Francisco's Literary Frontier,* 22–52.

Commandments," which began "Thou shalt have no other claim than one" and was so popular that nearly one hundred thousand copies of the sheet were sold in one year. *The Annals of San Francisco*, by Frank Soulé, James Nesbit, and John H. Gihon, published in 1854, was an eight-hundred-page survey of the area's history written in breezy and interesting fashion. John Rollin Ridge, whose pen name was Yellow Bird, was a half-Cherokee, half-white writer best known for his book about the bandit Joaquín Murieta. He supposedly based the book on fact but actually imagined part, thinking of the revenge he would like to have taken himself against those who killed his Indian father. The book contained every important event that has now become part of the Murieta legend.

The average American today thinks of none of these writers on California but rather of Bret Harte.[14] Actually, Harte did not enter the state until 1854, and then he was hardly more than a schoolboy. He taught school for a while at La Grange, a mining camp on the Tuolumne River, and his experiences may have formed the basis of his short story "M'liss." The next summer, 1855, he and some congenial, youthful companions did enough amateur mining at Robinson's Ferry (now Melones) on the Stanislaus River to pay their food bill. By the time Harte reached the area, many of the mines had declined in productiveness and the towns were starting to decay, though yet far from ruined. This was the type of community Harte later portrayed in his fiction, certainly not the California of '49 or '50. He usually imagined geography to fit the needs of his story, but about the Stanislaus River region he showed accurate, personal knowledge. By the end of 1855, Harte had probably experienced all he was to know firsthand of California mining. He worked a short time in a drugstore, served briefly as a tutor, and for a few weeks was a Wells Fargo expressman on stagecoaches. In the summer of 1857, at the age of twenty-one, he went as a tutor to Union (now Arcata), a coastal point for reshipment of goods to the interior mines. Harte found time to write constantly but achieved little success. He came to understand the local Indians and later in his writings pictured red men sympathetically although not romantically.

Harte's fortune began to change late in 1858 when he became printer's devil on a newspaper just being established at Union. At first his duties were entirely on the mechanical side, but as early as the

14 George R. Stewart, Jr., *Bret Harte: Argonaut and Exile*, 29–88, 165–79.

next February he wrote a little. Previously, Harte's writing had shown almost no promise; having nothing really significant to say, he simply tried to sound literary and important, but now that he had definite subject matter, a known audience, only brief space, and compulsion to be clear enough that people would read him, his worst faults as an author disappeared. In February, 1860, the editor was absent, with Harte left in charge. One night a group of whites, hating all red men and wanting their lands, attacked the camp of the local peaceful Indians while most of the bucks were away and slew sixty women and children. Harte's courageous, scorching editorial against those unknown men who had perpetrated the massacre ended with these words: "We can conceive of no wrong that a babe's blood can atone for."

Within a month after the editorial appeared, Harte left Union by request, but the precise circumstances are unknown. Eight years later he scored a tremendous success with a short story then boldly original, "The Luck of Roaring Camp." When he published his poem "Plain Language from Truthful James" in 1870, it quickly spread, like a popular song or vaudeville joke, to become the property of the man in the street. Harte's position in American literature is not that of the great writer his contemporaries thought him to be, but his pen picture of slightly decaying California gold mining towns in the middle fifties will long endure.

In the field of art the most notable figure was Charles Christian Nahl.[15] Trained as an artist in Europe by his father, he came to California in 1850, mined for a bit, painted in Marysville and Sacramento, and in 1852 established himself permanently in San Francisco. He was tremendously industrious, turning out a large number of paintings, lithographs, and etchings on a variety of subjects. As a painter he had a smooth, highly sophisticated, self-conscious technique, made effective and positive use of color to give a sense of actuality, and showed to perfection many small objects and details. He is remembered for his lively and romantic interpretations of rough-and-ready mining camps. His best-known work, "Sunday Morning at the Mines," showed quite a variety—four horses being raced; a brawl in front of a saloon; two older prospectors restraining a youth from throwing away his money in a drunken frenzy; two miners listening

[15] Eugen Nuhaus, "Charles Christian Nahl: The Painter of California Pioneer Life," *California Historical Society Quarterly*, Vol. XV (1936), 295–305.

to a third read a book; two men washing clothes; one writing a letter; and one simply smoking a cigar in relaxation.

Educational facilities were slow to develop in California.[16] A private school opened in San Francisco in 1847 and was succeeded the next year by a public one at which all students who could afford it paid tuition. It was abandoned when everybody rushed off to look for gold. Before too long a determined eastern idealist, John C. Pelton, appeared in San Francisco without funds but with many donated educational supplies. He began teaching on December 26, 1849, and the following April, the city decided to make his enterprise a free, tax-supported institution. By July, 1854, San Francisco had seven public schools with an enrollment of 1,740, and if the city could have secured suitable additional buildings, this would have risen to about 2,500. That year it paid its principals an annual salary of two thousand dollars, not in cash, but city scrip that circulated at a discount of 5 to 40 per cent. Elsewhere, few of the state's leading towns had public grammar schools before 1854. San Francisco established its first high school in 1856, and there was none elsewhere for six years more. In California generally, there was considerable opposition to free public schools, for many considered education to be the sole responsibility of parents.

The College of California, originally started at Oakland in 1855 but soon moved to Berkeley, graduated its first class in 1864 and eventually evolved into the University of California. The Methodists established California Wesleyan College at San Jose in 1851, and at length it became the College of the Pacific at Stockton. At Santa Clara College, begun by Catholics in 1851, students for many years could not use tobacco and had to deposit all pocket money with the treasurer, to be doled out to them at not more than twenty-five cents a week. St. Ignatius College rose in San Francisco in 1859.

Religion was not a very strong institution in the days of gold.[17] Some of the pioneer preachers who came to California turned to more worldly pursuits, but most of them remained so faithful, hard working, devout, and self-sacrificing that they were held in high esteem.

---

16 William W. Ferrier, *Ninety Years of Education in California, 1846–1936*, 4–210.

17 Caughey, *Rushing*, 85–96; Bari, *Course of Empire*, 257–58; Bancroft, *Inter Pocula*, 799–800; Buck, *Yankee Trader*, 136.

Early ministers represented the Baptist, Catholic, Congregational, Episcopal, Methodist, and Presbyterian churches. One of the real pioneers was Timothy Dwight Hunt, who followed his congregation from the Hawaiian Islands, arriving in San Francisco on October 29, 1848, and for a year served as municipal chaplain to provide union religious services for all Protestants. Another notable figure was William Taylor, a street preacher who in seven years delivered to San Franciscans almost six hundred sermons. His method was to mount a goods box or whiskey barrel, start singing a hymn in a high key, and when a crowd collected, begin his talk. His audience often numbered several thousand.

The Christian principle of brotherly love was not always observed among the various races who flocked to California.[18] Lowest in esteem were the Indians. In 1848, the whites allowed them to work in the mines for hire, but the next year, they were ordered out. Enmity developed on both sides; many whites felt none too friendly to any Indians after their troubles with other tribes to the east on their overland journey, and the California red men regarded the Americans as trespassers. Each race attacked any convenient group of the other, not bothering to seek out any individual or band guilty of misconduct but simply starting a fight. The better-armed whites, with no families to protect, slaughtered the Indians.

There were many Mexicans in the mining area, especially in the southern portion, and almost one out of every five miners in California was Chinese. Aiming at these two racial elements, the state legislature passed a discriminatory law called the Foreign Miners Tax. While in theory it applied to all foreign citizens, in practice it was enforced only against these two groups. In 1850, the tax was twenty dollars a month, heavy enough to be virtually prohibitive, and was collected at most places, despite talk of resistance, but in some remote camps it met complete and successful defiance. The next year, the legislature repealed the law, in 1852 it restored the tax at three dollars a month, and in 1853 changed it to four dollars a year. Mexicans in the central and northwestern areas were few enough in num-

18 Charles M. Shinn, *Land Laws of Mining Districts*, 147, and *Mining Camps*, 134, 203–207, 264, 278; Bancroft, *History*, VI, 403–407, and *Inter Pocula*, 437; Taylor, *Eldorado*, 79, 185; Caughey, *Cornerstone*, 192–200, 294–95; Paul, *California Gold*, 26.

ber for whites sometimes simply to eject them from desirable claims; they could offer no effective resistance. In the south they were numerous and less likely to be imposed upon. The Mexicans usually did not stay in California for an indefinite period, but came north to the gold fields in the spring and went back to their homeland in the fall. A good many of them brought wife and children along. The Chinese, with their pigtails, shapeless dress, and singsong language, would have amused the whites more had they not been such hard workers. To offset their tireless industry the Americans totally excluded them from a few areas, at others restricted them to working for hire, and at most camps permitted them only to own claims or rework tailings that no white man considered profitable enough to waste his time on. At Weaverville, two Chinese groups became so enraged at each other, for obscure reasons, that they threatened war and, incited by whites, actually did battle. Their armament was long spears and squirt guns containing unpleasant liquid; their protection was sheet-iron helmets and tin shields. In the fight, eight Chinese and one Dutchman, who couldn't mind his own business, were killed.

There was a fair number of Frenchmen in the California mines, thanks to their famous lotteries for passage to the gold fields. They were considered clannish and somewhat impractical, working together like a swarm of bees. Their impatient phrase to their interpreter, "Qu'est que ce dit?" earned them the nickname of "Keskydees." There was some discrimination against them. Germans and Irishmen encountered only slight difficulties. Old-time Californians, Englishmen, and Australians mixed in well with the Americans.

One of the Australians, E. H. Hargraves, was forcibly struck with the similarity between the California region where he was mining and a spot he remembered in New South Wales. He returned to Australia and in February, 1851, discovered gold there in a dry creek bed. He continued his investigations until he was satisfied the deposit was extensive and rich. Instead of trying to keep it a secret, he informed his government, proclaimed the news widely, received an appointment as commissioner of crown lands, went to the diggings to teach others proper mining techniques, and collected a government reward of £10,000. He was followed to Australia by many Californians.

The vast influx of gold seekers into California created considerable business opportunity, but certainly under conditions different from those known elsewhere.[19] Many a newcomer merely observed at first, then sprang into vigorous action, often casting aside his accustomed prudence for reckless daring. Thus one man brought with him on shipboard to San Francisco fifteen hundred dozen eggs. He feared he might not sell them, but finally unloaded them on a broker for thirty-seven and one-half cents a dozen. He promptly observed in shocked surprise how they were being resold for four dollars, then recovered himself sufficiently to repurchase what remained, take them to Sacramento, and sell them for six. Sometimes unusual items sold well, such as an 1851 cargo of cats from Mexico which readily brought eight to ten dollars each.

California's supplies came from many places, such as Peru, Tahiti, China, the Pacific Northwest, and the eastern United States. In the early days the market was generally a scarcity one, but sometimes serious miscalculations resulted in San Francisco's accumulating such surpluses as a sixty-five-year supply of tobacco. Businessmen throve by operating stores, wagon factories, tanneries, textile mills, lumber mills, powder mills, sugar refineries, and iron works. Some, who were so shrewd and farsighted that they came to be merchant princes, later overreached themselves and went bankrupt. Not one man in ten who had his own business in 1849 was still operating in 1855.

In a new mining camp some merchant would arrive quickly. He laid in a stock of necessities and such other items as he could secure. He charged high prices because of heavy transportation costs, shortages, and the reckless habit of the miners to pay without stint for anything they really wanted. If by any miscalculation he carried an item the men did not desire, by no reduction or bargain prices could he persuade them to purchase it. His limited stocks, inferior quality of goods, and refusal to extend credit the miners willingly accepted, but his certain profits irritated them.

Merchants neither accepted nor gave in change anything smaller than a fifty-cent piece. They took in gold dust as if it were so much sand; indeed, sometimes part of it was, for adulteration was not al-

[19] Jenkins, *Mother Lode Country*, 99; Bancroft, *History*, VI, 226; Taylor, *Eldorado*, 233–34; Bancroft, *Inter Pocula*, 325, 338–49, 693; Caughey, *Cornerstone*, 34–38, 204–205, 215–18, 291; Buck, *Yankee Trader*, 56–59, 90, 112, 150; Winther, *Express and Stagecoach*, 106–10, 139–41; Evelyn Wells and Harry C. Peterson, *The 49ers*, 140–42.

ways easy to detect. To help remedy the situation the United States government authorized the coinage of private money, under government inspection, in 1849. At least a dozen concerns actively responded. The first apparently was the Pacific Company in San Francisco, but the largest was Moffatt and Company, whose mint was in the Mother Lode country at Mt. Ophir. Generally the companies produced fifty-dollar slugs, actually putting a trifle more than fifty dollars' worth of gold into each and still making a profit because they paid only sixteen or eighteen dollars an ounce for raw gold whose actual assayed value was twenty. In 1854, the federal government opened its first mint in California. For those who did not have money but had to borrow it, the usual banker's rate (until well into the 1850's) was 3 to 5 per cent a month; the pawnbroker's was 10 per cent a month or any part of it, with the right to sell unredeemed pledges at the end of the month.

California's gold rush was unique among those of the world in that it formed a springboard for the area's rapid and gratifyingly consistent economic development. Thus the demands of the forty-niners for food did much to launch the great agricultural expansion.[20] At first the long-established California ranchers made a great deal of money selling meat to gold seekers but could not supply the demand. This left a gap to be filled by long drives, earlier than those to become so famous on the Great Plains, of cattle from Texas and of sheep from Chihuahua and New Mexico.

In 1849, there were American farmers scattered along the Sacramento Valley almost as far north as Redding, in the San Joaquin Valley as far south as the Stanislaus River, and in the Suisun, Berryessa, Chiles, Pope, Napa, Alexander, Russian River, Santa Clara, and Livermore valleys. They used American-type plows, but otherwise their equipment and procedures were crude. Their Indian employees harvested for weeks with sickles, butcher knives, pieces of hoop iron, and dry willow sticks. To thresh, they drove a huge herd of wild horses at full speed back and forth through the straw for perhaps an hour. Winnowing might take another month, for they had to wait until the wind was strong enough for them to throw the shovelfuls into the air, with the heavier grain sinking into a separate heap from the straw and chaff.

[20] Caughey, *Cornerstone*, 208–209, 291; Claude B. Hutchinson (ed.), *California Agriculture*, 31–44.

As the gold-rush fever waned, many Americans turned to agriculture and by 1852 there was a large increase in all types of production. Breeds of cattle were improved, and the number of sheep rose sharply until by 1860 there were over a million head in the state, yielding annually more than two million pounds of wool. Horses, in great demand for various uses, increased from 62,000 in 1852 to 160,000 in 1860. As for crops, farmers at first concentrated on barley but later shifted to wheat. In 1860, they grew nearly six million bushels of the latter, cultivating fields so large that their operations came to be known as bonanza-style farming. Some farmers raised oats, which they cut mostly for hay, and there was some fruit growing, small in relation to other agricultural products in the fifties but influential on future developments. At the time, emphasis was on grapes, in demand locally and exported for wine and brandy making; orchard fruits were just being introduced. By 1860, California irrigation was still on a small scale.

To preserve law and order the pioneer miners had to take action themselves with little assistance from either state or national officials.[21] When lawlessness in an area forced the miners to take action, they first held a meeting to determine how they wished to conduct trials. Sometimes they decided there should be a jury of six, twelve, or twenty to hear cases, sometimes that all who attended the hearing, whether residents of the district or not, could vote. Such miners' courts never tried to collect debts or settle minor personal difficulties, but concentrated on such crimes as theft, assault, and murder. These tribunals listened to testimony, but not for very long would they abide arguments. They were often swayed by prejudice, passion, or the honeyed words of a smooth talker. They acted in haste and mistakenly punished more innocent people than regularly established eastern law courts would have done. Seeing such a miners' group in action, storekeeper Buck commented that if circumstances were adverse, an innocent person would stand no chance before an excited people and were he ever charged with a crime, he would prefer "all the police of New York first." In the absence of jails, the tribunals punished by banishment, whipping, or hanging. Occasionally a mob would arise, not wait for a trial, but immediately mete out what it

---

[21] Shinn, *Mining Camps*, 103–19, 159–217; Caughey, *Cornerstone*, 233–38; Buck, *Yankee Trader*, 111; Clappe, *Shirley Letters*, 154–57; Bancroft, *Inter Pocula*, 586–610; Bancroft, *History*, VI, 231; Taylor, *Eldorado*, 77–78.

thought was justice. Thus on one occasion a murderer caught red-handed did not get one hundred yards from the scene of his crime before spectators seized pick handles from a barrel in front of a store and beat him to death.

Instead of the miners' courts, some communities elected a single person, the alcalde, a time-honored official in Spanish-American practices, to exercise all government authority. Perhaps the camp might also select a sheriff and a mine recorder to help him. Its alcalde did not conform to any law, follow the example of what anybody was doing elsewhere, or report to any higher official. When he heard a law case, criminal or civil, his judgment was final; there was no right of appeal. His methods were simple and direct; often he was an ignorant man yet made decisions whose essential justice earned him the loyal support of his community. A few were well trained, like Stephen J. Field, who held office in Marysville and later served on the supreme courts of both California and the United States. Typical of an alcalde's methods was one of Field's first cases. As he was walking along the street he noticed two men arguing. A well-known citizen, riding a newly bought horse, had been halted by a pedestrian, who asserted that the animal belonged to him. The two saw Field listening and appealed to him in his official capacity; he swore them as witnesses, heard their testimony, made a decision favoring the pedestrian, took his fee of an ounce of gold, and all three adjourned to the neighboring saloon for a drink.

In San Francisco some men virtually appointed themselves judges, before city government was effectively organized, served successfully because people came to them for decisions, and supported themselves by their fees. One of them, untrained in the law, turned from peanut vending to holding court. He had an ability to get at the root of a matter, heard discussion only until he felt he fully understood all that was involved, and then rendered his decision quickly, courageously, and righteously. He was popular with those who came before him, since nobody in 1849 wanted to waste much time in a law court. A tale told of another judge concerned the case of a prostitute; when the justice asked her in routine fashion who she was and where she lived, she, with an arch smile, replied, "Ah! Judge you know all about it!" In 1850, however, the informal judges of San Francisco and the alcaldes of the mining communities gave way to justices of the peace, whom a new state law said should be elected for terms of one year in every township.

When justice generally functioned to the dissatisfaction of most people, vigilantes sometimes arose.[22] They sprang up when the people felt that the regular courts were too slow, too weak, or too corrupt, when they were inflamed with racial hatred, or when they suspected that smooth-tongued lawyers were befuddling the judges. These self-appointed enforcers of law and order certainly acted more quickly than regular officials, but whether their justice was wiser and more certain is a matter of dispute. Even under the best of circumstances the accused had no right to challenge the jury, no way to compel a witness to attend or force him to testify, no method to secure a change of venue, no device for appealing to a higher court, no power to resist if the vigilantes sought to secure his confession by torture, and no protection against the prosecution's running the trial because the presiding official had so little power. That the vigilantes were good was a discreet thing to say at the time and most historians have echoed the sentiment, but some recent students have cast serious doubts, pointing to miscarriages of justice and punishments which did not fit the crime. The vigilantes' defenders have emphasized the undeniably evil conditions existing and the successful short-run elimination of a great deal of crime.

The vigilantes were always local groups, were not run by outsiders, nor were they allied to similar organizations elsewhere. During the 1850's, standing committees of them sprang up in San Francisco, Sacramento, Stockton, Marysville, Sonora, San Jose, and Los Angeles, while in smaller mining towns committees simply arose when some lawless deed prompted men to take action. Thus at Downieville on July 4, 1851, Jack Cannon got so drunk that he staggered into a house occupied by a young Spanish-American woman and her paramour, a Mexican; his companions pulled him back out. The next morning Cannon undertook to apologize, but he and the two Mexicans got into a very excited conversation in Spanish which ended abruptly when the girl drew a knife and killed him. A vigilante committee, com-

22 William H. Ellison, *A Self-Governing Dominion: California, 1849–1860*, 195–266; Caughey, *Cornerstone*, 245–48; John W. Caughey, "Their Majesties the Mob," *Pacific Historical Review*, Vol. XXVI (1957), 217–34; Bancroft, *History*, VI, 742–70.

posed of men angry that a "foreigner" should "murder" an American, held a brief trial at which they were unimpressed by the Mexicans' testimony about Cannon's insulting language the morning after, brushed aside protests that a pregnant woman should be spared, and hanged her. These vigilantes were nearly a lynch mob. In rural areas in the later 1850's this was the increasing tendency.

The most important of the vigilante organizations were those in San Francisco. The first was organized in 1849 to oppose a group calling themselves officially the San Francisco Society of Regulators but generally known as the Hounds. On July 14, these lawbreakers invaded Little Chile, chasing the Spanish-Americans out of their homes, robbing, beating, and shooting them. This outrage caused respectable elements in the city to take up a subscription to aid the victims. A committee of 230 men, organized to dispose of the Hounds, established a court with a judge, prosecuting attorney, and defense lawyers. It convicted eight or nine men and banished them; the other Hounds scattered.

By 1851, San Franciscans were aroused about their city's poor law enforcement and weak courts. Their excitement increased when in broad daylight two men beat merchant C. J. Jansen and robbed him of nearly two thousand dollars. At a trial in a regular court he identified two suspects as his assailants. While it was proceeding in regular fashion, a mob of six or eight thousand men formed and seized the men from a defense force too weak to resist and almost hanged them. With much difficulty the mob was persuaded instead to appoint a special court to hear the case. At this impromptu proceeding the informal jury could not agree; the mob at first wanted to hang them, too, but finally dispersed. It gave the men back to the civil authorities, the regular trial continued, and the court convicted the two suspects, on flimsy evidence, because of popular pressure. Almost immediately one of the men escaped and went home to Australia. The other was shortly cleared by the confession of a notorious criminal, captured in another connection, that he and another man, not the Australian, actually had attacked Jansen. Obviously, two innocent suspects had been falsely convicted and had nearly been hanged.

Too excited by the whole episode to reflect on the serious error almost made and angered further by the great fire of May 4, a group of San Franciscans formed a voluntary patrol to assist policemen in preventing looting and other lawlessness in the conflagration's wake.

On June 9, the men reorganized as a vigilante committee to enforce the law themselves rather than simply aid the regular officials. It was this moment that John Jenkins chose to steal the portable safe of George Virgin; his timing was poor, for the vigilantes captured him one evening shortly afterward, tried him that night, and hanged him at two o'clock the next morning. When the city coroner published the names of nine committee members involved, the vigilantes replied by publishing the first 180 names on their roster. The group eventually had 707 members, but much of the work was done by a twenty-member executive committee.

Dissatisfaction finally arose in the whole group over a criminal named Samuel Whittaker. He was being returned to San Francisco police by a sheriff from Santa Barbara when the vigilantes kidnaped him, then yielded him up when served with a warrant by the governor of California and the mayor of San Francisco, only to seize him again and hang him. This unorthodox and vacillating procedure caused such dissension that the general committee adjourned, leaving the executive committee technically in charge but actually dormant. In the period of about three months in which the vigilantes were active, they hanged four persons, whipped one, deported twenty-eight, delivered fifteen to the regular authorities, and released forty-one. They frightened robbers, thieves, and murderers, but not those guilty of political and economic exploitation; in other words they simply scooped "a little scum off the surface of the social cesspool."

In May, 1856, two murders revived the vigilantes. Gambler Charles H. Cora killed federal marshal William H. Richardson because of a quarrel, at a theater, between Cora's rich mistress and Richardson's wife. At his trial the gambler was freed when the jury disagreed. The second murderer, city politician James P. Casey, shot crusading newspaper editor James King of William. In discussing city politics, King took "a cruel and unnecessary thrust" at Casey by revealing that Casey was a former convict. On the afternoon the editorial appeared, Casey came to the *Bulletin*'s office, only to be stonily ordered out. He waited on the street until King walked by, then killed him.

The two murders and one acquittal aroused such an outburst of anger against all lawlessness that the executive committee of the vigilantes of 1851 called for action. Another group, much like the old, was formed, with a new executive committee of thirty-nine and a total membership of eight thousand. It held very careful trials on Casey and Cora, found them guilty, and hanged them. Organizing itself in military fashion and holding drills, it established headquarters at a fortified spot called Fort Gunnybags. The new group encountered heavy criticism from the so-called Law and Order party, which included many prominent citizens and took the position that the proper solution to poor law enforcement was to vote poor officials out and replace them with honest, efficient ones.

The vigilantes at first received the reluctant approval of state governor John Neely Johnson, but he soon changed his mind, calling, without much success, for aid from the state militia and the United States. Finally, General John W. Wool discovered six cases of muskets which he felt federal regulations would allow him to release to the Law and Order party. When he did, the vigilantes seized the weapons. They at first arrested the two messengers accompanying the shipment, then released them, then sought to detain them again. The second time, when a fight developed, Judge David S. Terry of the California Supreme Court aided one of the messengers and sank a bowie knife into the neck of vigilante Sterling A. Hopkins. The committee promptly arrested Terry, then began to wonder how it could possibly try such a high state official. With Hopkins fortunately recovering rapidly, it thankfully turned Judge Terry loose in the middle of the night and he shortly left for Sacramento. Terry's arrest was a fatal blow to the vigilantes; they soon adjourned. In slightly over three months they had hanged six, deported twenty-five, and driven about eight hundred out of the city. Their conduct was as careful and high minded as that of any such group could be, but by their secrecy, hate, and disregard of the rights of the individual, they had done harm as well as good.

Despite the traditional fame the vigilantes have subsequently acquired, it was no such group that captured the best known of California's outlaws, Joaquín Murieta; in reality, Murieta himself is mostly a legend. The facts are simply told.[23] There were in the state a number of criminals, some Mexican, and of these several were named Joaquín, including Joaquín Carillo, Joaquín Valenzuela, and Joaquín Murieta. In 1853, the state legislature authorized Harry Love to organize a body of state rangers to serve three months, each being paid $150 a month. The rangers were to capture "the five

23 Jackson, *Anybody's Gold,* 112–16.

Joaquíns" and were entitled collectively to a reward of $1,000, apparently if they got any Joaquín they could prove was an habitual lawbreaker. Near the end of their three months the rangers attacked a band, killed one man, preserved his head in a jar of spirits, and sent it to the governor, demanding the reward. They swore they had shot Joaquín Murieta, but others said it was Joaquín Valenzuela; however, the rangers collected the money and the legislature later voted Love $5,000 extra. These simple and few facts bear little relation to the traditional Murieta, a kind of Robin Hood whose marvelous feats were indeed too good to be true.

The excitement over the Joaquíns was more than matched at the time by the discussion of a duel between two politicians.[24] The trouble started when David C. Broderick, United States senator, led a wing of the Democratic party at the state convention which defeated the renomination of David S. Terry to his post as chief justice of the state supreme court. The disappointed judge made insulting comments about the clique. When these were repeated to Senator Broderick, they goaded him in his first fit of anger to disrespectful personal remarks about Terry. Two months later, and one day after the election was over, Terry resigned his post and challenged Broderick to a duel. Their first encounter was stopped by law officials, but the secret that a second meeting was intended was better kept; Terry killed Broderick.

More important than duels were mining regulations.[25] Because there were no federal or territorial statutes on the subject, the pioneers had to work out effective measures. There were no problems when the first few miners came into an area; when more arrived, they held a meeting and agreed orally about regulations; if still others poured in, they formalized their understanding in writing. The group called itself a district, likely including the claims of all miners present at the organizational meeting and such adjoining areas, easy of access, as seemed likely to be valuable. Typical of the written regulations were those of the Tuolumne County district known officially as Jackass Gulch. It limited a claim by right of original occupancy to "not more than a hundred feet square." It defined as valid a bill of

24 Bancroft, *Inter Pocula*, 763–73.
25 Shinn, *Land Laws*, 10–37, and *Mining Camps*, 103–19, 159–69, 174, 225, 259–67; Paul, *California Gold*, 213–22; Ellison, *Self-Governing Dominion*, 126–219; Caughey, *Cornerstone*, 228–30.

sale for a claim if two disinterested parties certified on it that the signature was genuine and that the prescribed payment was actually made. If dispute arose over it, a jury of five people was to settle any question. If water for mining became exhausted, a renewal notice every ten days would hold a claim; but while the water was flowing, the claim had to be worked once every five days or become forfeit, except in case of sickness, accident, or "reasonable excuse."

The codes of the different districts naturally varied. Many of them contained regulations similar to those in Mexico, Spain, or England. Some allowed several individuals, each owning a claim, to concentrate all their work on one of them. Some authorized a person to hold two claims, one worked mostly during the winter and another chiefly in the summer. Some, in a very narrow gulch, authorized a claim to run the entire width of the defile. Some granted the original discoverer of a placer diggings a double-sized claim. Some required those who destroyed a path or road in their operations to replace it. Some authorized digging on any farm, provided the agriculturist was fully compensated for damages. Almost all prevented, either directly or indirectly, absentee ownership. None approved large enough claims to make monopoly a possibility. None allowed the owner of one at the mouth of a gulch or canyon to forbid others a right of way. Almost all provided an official with whom the claim had to be registered. Almost all had means for settling disputes, usually by arbitration before an individual or committee appointed by the district to handle such matters. Such arbitration, simple and final, required no lawyers and could not be appealed to county or state officials. Sometimes, when a district had been pretty well mined over, the district authorized an increase in the size of a claim.

In general the codes were concise, well worded, and clear. Regulations originally drawn for an area where operations were placer were adapted, with only a few changes, to new conditions when any other types of mining began in the region. Increasingly during the 1850's, local California regulations tended to become standardized. Their terms came to be copied, with little modification, in Nevada, Oregon, Idaho, Arizona, New Mexico, and Montana.

In 1851, the California legislature voted that if cases involving ownership of mine claims should reach the courts, local customs should prevail. Soon the state supreme court began hearing such appeals. In its decisions it respected local regulations if they were clearly what miners had agreed to in a public meeting and then observed. The court gave preference to a reasonable custom generally observed over a written regulation generally disregarded. It did not expect a person to do more work in maintaining title to a claim than local codes required, but it enforced forfeiture if this minimum had not been met. The court, prior to 1860, approved oral transfer of title if locally customary. It recognized special rights given discoverers and first locators. Its decisions helped gradually to standardize such terms as "claim," "forfeiture," "ditch," and "water right" in their usage throughout the state.

While the miners were working out their own local regulations, the federal government considered taking action. After much discussion from 1851 to 1854, Congress followed the recommendation of President Fillmore and adopted a policy of *laissez faire*.

Another problem in the relationship between the United States and the gold area was California's government.[26] After federal troops conquered the region during the Mexican War, it was placed under a military governor, Colonel R. B. Mason. He was in a difficult position, with no laws for the area, with towns housing few able-bodied men once the 1848 gold rush started, with forts so emptied by deserting soldiers that there weren't enough left to maintain the guns, and with very few communications from his Washington superiors. To make matters worse, Congress talked of establishing the usual form of territorial government in California but took no action before it adjourned, leaving Washington officials, Mason, and the people to improvise as best they could. The first serious complications arose in the fall of 1848 over a San Francisco election for town council. The citizens removed all of the old members and voted in a completely new slate. The incumbents cried fraud so loudly that another election was held, at which the people chose a third and entirely different group. For a time the three rival sets of officials all tried to serve, but by February, 1849, the people of San Francisco became so irritated with the situation that they called a meeting, eliminated all three groups, and elected instead a so-called legislature of fifteen men.

The next important development was the presidential appointment of a new California governor, General Bennett Riley, who took office on April 13, 1849. He was described by some contemporaries

26 Ellison, *Self-Governing Dominion*, 21–101; Bancroft, *History*, VI, 265–79; Taylor, *Eldorado*, 114.

as a "grim old fellow" and a "fine, free swearer"; despite his military background, he filled his post well. Riley issued a proclamation on June 3 calling for a convention to organize a civil government. The delegates, elected to the convention by the people, assembled in September, 1849, at Monterey. Three-quarters of them were American citizens by birth, thirty-two of them were under forty years of age, and the other sixteen were between forty-three and fifty-three. Those who were native Californians were expected to co-operate in making a constitution which would conform to American political theories, not Mexican or Spanish, and they did.

The delegates faced the task of creating a government where none existed. Although they had copies of the constitutions of Iowa and New York to serve as models, much more important were the knowledge and unexpectedly good mental equipment of this unusual group of men. It is significant that the first thing they did was to adopt a bill of rights. After much discussion they gave the vote to all white male citizens of the United States and also those of Mexico who chose to become American citizens under the terms of the peace treaty which ended the Mexican War. They did not extend the franchise to any Indians at the time, but said that a legislature by a two-thirds vote could do so later.

The men were generally agreed that slaves should be kept out but were quite divided over whether to exclude free Negroes; finally they didn't. They forbade duels, divorce, and lotteries. Most delegates wanted a real estate tax, but those from the area of the Spanish grants objected to it because most people owned no land; the final compromise was to retain the tax but to have assessors and boards of supervisors elected by the voters of the town or county in which the property was situated.

The convention gave women property rights separate from those of men and instructed the legislature to pass laws clearly defining the rights of a wife in property held in common with her husband. It provided in the constitution for an elected judiciary. It debated extensively how far east to extend California's boundaries, perhaps to include all the area acquired from Mexico by the Treaty of Guadalupe Hidalgo, but finally settled on the present limits as those most likely to secure prompt admission of the proposed state into the Union.

The convention delegates did excellent work in drawing up their constitution, showing clearly a capacity for self-government. They certainly earned their expense money of sixteen dollars a day plus sixteen dollars a mile. At the end of the session it was paid to them in silver, so hard to carry that the little Irish boy who acted as page was nearly pressed down by the weight of his wages.

At a referendum the public approved the constitution by a vote of 12,061 to 811. At the same time they elected a governor (Peter H. Burnett) and the members of a legislature. At its session the legislature made laws on the theory that until the admission of California as a state was accomplished, the region was a self-governing dominion. It passed 146 acts and 19 joint resolutions, completing the body of government whose framework had been erected in the constitution. Its members, concluded historian William H. Ellison, were almost all indefatigable workers who showed in most matters "consummate good judgment." Their excellent work was somewhat obscured by the unfortunate nickname the group acquired: "Legislature of a Thousand Drinks," which referred, not to general tippling, but to one particular wealthy member.

California's admission into the Union was not as easy as people there supposed it would be. They thought they were a rich gift, one the United States would promptly welcome. They failed to realize how strong the dissension over slavery had become. The question was whether or not involuntary servitude should exist in any of the territory captured from Mexico. Californians became alarmed at the great discussion and indignant at the thought of delay or rejection. This is not the place to tell how Henry Clay finally proposed the Compromise of 1850, how John C. Calhoun attacked it, how Daniel Webster upheld it in his famous "Seventh of March" speech, and how it was finally adopted as a supposedly permanent solution to the national dispute. One of its terms was the admission of California as a state without slavery. The news reached San Francisco on the mail steamer *Oregon,* which entered the harbor bearing two huge banners inscribed "California is a State." Practically the entire population of the city gathered in Portsmouth Square for a celebration.

California was the first region of the United States to have a gold rush of any consequence. Just acquired from Mexico, it was an area remote and generally unknown. To reach it required a difficult journey, whether by wagon train overland, by sailing ship around Cape Horn, or by vessels principally on the Panama route. In the early days an air of excitement and speculation prevailed as miners and businessmen sought to make their fortunes quickly. Gradually supply shortages disappeared and local transportation improved. Skimming off the surface by panning gold gave way to more careful placer and quartz mining, sharply limiting the opportunities of the individual, relegating many men to the status of employees, and emphasizing the need for corporate activity. Living conditions slowly improved, better entertainment became available, and the cost of living decreased. The pioneers, by their regulations about mining and conduct, generally showed a good capacity for self-government. The activities of the gold-rush era laid the solid foundation for California's extensive, continuous economic development from that day to this.

4

THE DISCOVERY OF THE COMSTOCK LODE

"CALIFORNIA drew to her golden shores the pick of the world. Nevada drew to herself the pick of California."[1] For this statement by C. C. Goodwin, veteran Nevada newspaperman, there was some justification, based on the number and roughhewn competence of those attracted. In 1873, the Virginia City chapter of the Society of Pacific Coast Pioneers, who had arrived in California during 1849 or 1850, was as large as that in San Francisco.

The earliest miners who came to Nevada thought of gold, only to realize considerably later that the silver there was more important. By far the richest area was the Comstock Lode, or "Washoe region," located about twenty miles south of present-day Reno, particularly on Mt. Davidson in the Washoe Range. It was in this area that the first mineral discoveries in Nevada were made in 1849, not of silver, but gold.[2]

Down from Mt. Davidson to the Carson River ran several ravines; the five-mile one came to be known as Gold Canyon. Something there must have attracted Abner Blackburn, for, disregarding the immediate neighborhood of his small trading post, he went forty miles to the canyon and unearthed a small amount of gold dust. Another man who extracted a little gold in the ravine that same year was William Prouse, who did not take his find seriously. When snow momentarily blocked the mountain passes ahead, his group returned to Gold Canyon. Another member of the party, John Orr, pried loose

---

[1] Grant H. Smith, *The History of the Comstock Lode, 1850–1920,* 30.
[2] Effie M. Mack, *Nevada: A History of the State from the Earliest Times Through the Civil War,* 197; Smith, *History,* 3; George D. Lyman, *The Saga of the Comstock Lode: Boom Days in Virginia City,* 13.

a slab of slate and found a nugget. The men continued on to California as soon as they could, but Orr always retained this lump of gold as one of his prized possessions. All three of these discoveries were from the many little veins abounding in the vicinity of present-day Silver City and were not erosion from the Comstock Lode. The next year, 1850, several more groups tarried at the mouth of Gold Canyon, but they soon hurried across the Sierras toward the reportedly greater opportunities of California.

More permanent were the Mormon farmers, who in 1851 selected adjacent Eagle Valley as the site for an irrigation project and hired one hundred Chinese to help dig the ditches. As the work of others in the placer-type mining of Gold Canyon began generally yielding richer returns, the farmers and their hired hands turned from agriculture to exploiting the gravel of the ravine. If one of the yellow men tried to trespass on the rights of a white man, he was strung up by his pigtail to the nearest cottonwood tree.

At the mouth of Gold Canyon a small settlement, first known as Chinatown and later as Dayton, arose; farther up the gulch the village of Johntown developed. As the miners worked their way up the mountain, increasingly they found their gold mixed with annoying "blue stuff." They did not bother to identify this, but cursed it for reducing the market value of their dust from fifteen dollars an ounce to eleven. They disregarded the inarticulate protests of two Mexican peons, familiar with silver, as they cast the unidentified material aside.

Among the miners in the canyon were the Grosch brothers, Allen and Hosea.[3] The Pennsylvania-bred sons of a Universalist minister, they sailed from Philadelphia in 1849 to make their fortunes and then return to aid their father. In California their good luck at some times was matched by ill at others, so that when they crossed the Sierras to Gold Canyon in 1853, they had little but experience to show for all their work. From several books on mining and chemistry they had with them the brothers had learned a great deal about metallurgy and assaying. As early as 1856 they knew they had discovered silver in the ravine but decided not to tell the other miners until they had a more secure hold on their own fortune. With their savings exhausted, they began looking for a well-financed partner.

[3] Mack, *Nevada*, 201; Smith, *History*, 4; Rickard, *American Mining*, 88; Lyman, *Saga*, 233–36.

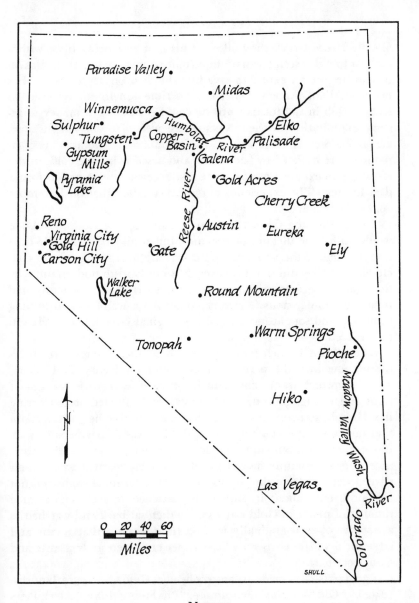

NEVADA

Shortly Hosea struck the hollow of his foot a glancing blow with a pick; at first this seemed an unimportant annoyance but erysipelas set in and despite all efforts to save him, he died on September 2. His brother Allen, though confessing horrible loneliness, resolved to secure a job in California until he could earn enough money to resume exploitation of their Nevada discovery. He delayed his start across the Sierras until so late in November that he and his companion were buffeted by bad storms and beset by intense cold. In the last stages of exhaustion, they were finally rescued by some California deer hunters. The experience so overtaxed Allen that on December 19, he, too, died.

To say that the Grosch brothers uncovered the Comstock Lode would fulfill the dictates of romance, but would be false. Old-time mining men of the area and the more careful historians have concluded that they did not. However, it is not hard to understand why their father became convinced in later years that they really had found the now famous Comstock, organized a well-financed mining company, and sought recovery of the original Grosch claim. He did not succeed.

When Allen Grosch failed to return in the spring of 1858, his cabin came into the permanent possession of Henry T. P. Comstock. Comstock was a man with few virtues, with little concept of right and wrong, good natured, liberal, and talented at concocting lies. He told so many conflicting stories about how he got the cabin that nobody will ever know the truth.[4] He was in partnership with the brothers, or promised to protect the property whenever they were absent, or else simply moved in. He probably learned where their silver ledge was from the papers left in their cabin. If so, he did not tell his friends about it; instead he hastened to stake claims at a number of places in Gold Canyon. He then sat back and watched as a number of men gradually worked their way up that ravine and adjacent Six-Mile Canyon, whose upper ends were only a mile and a quarter apart.

A gold strike was made at the very head of Gold Canyon in January, 1859, by "Old Virginny" Fennimore, "Big French John," Aleck Henderson, and Jack Yount; almost at once Comstock also staked a claim. The discovery was made on a Saturday and the next day most of Johntown inspected it, pronouncing it less valuable than their own

4 Mack, *Nevada*, 204–205; Lyman, *Saga*, 12.

workings. But the richness of its yield soon proved them wrong and they moved up to the new area, calling the town they threw together Gold Hill.[5] The new diggings were a great mass of decomposed croppings, and not for three years did the miners realize that beneath these lay a part of the Comstock Lode.

Early Gold Hillers were at first quite casual in recording their claims with the blacksmith who kept the book of records. It lay unprotected on a shelf in a saloon and was sometimes used by loungers to bang a neighbor over the head, sometimes inspected by the curious, and sometimes altered by the dishonest. Its notices were often intentionally vague, masking greed or fraud. In later years this practice led to a number of lawsuits about exact locations. In one case the point at issue was "this stump." To enable the witnesses to locate it precisely, the court adjourned to the site—in vain, for the night before it had been dug out and the ground leveled so that not even the spot where it had been was discernible.

To preserve law and order, in June, 1859, the miners of Gold Hill drew up a code much like the earlier ones of California's gold rush. It forbade gambling games. For killing a person, the penalty was fixed at death; for robbery or theft, it was whipping or banishment; for assault, battery, or exhibition of deadly weapons, it was fine or banishment; and for wounding somebody, the punishment was left for the jury to determine.

Among the prospectors working in June, 1859, near Gold Hill, at the top of Six-Mile Canyon, were Peter O'Riley and Pat McLaughlin, who discovered what was to be the celebrated Ophir mine.[6] When they had dug down four feet, they uncovered a rich decomposed ore which was actually part of the Comstock Lode. That day, Comstock himself happened by. He pointed out to the two that all the land was his because he had posted a notice claiming 160 acres for grazing—but he neglected to add that he had never recorded this in any official place. He also declared that he, Emmanuel Penrod, and Old Virginny Fennimore owned the spring from which the two prospectors were taking water. That either of his statements was true or was believed is exceedingly doubtful, but no investigator has been able positively to prove them false. He blustered and threat-

5 Dan DeQuille, *The Big Bonanza*, 24–25, 40–41; Eliot Lord, *Comstock Mining and Miners*, 49; Lyman, *Saga*, 32.
6 DeQuille, *Big Bonanza*, 24–29, 42–43; Lyman, *Saga*, 73.

ened so much that O'Riley and McLaughlin accepted his declarations. They ceded to him and to his friend Penrod, as he demanded, a substantial share of the claim's fifteen hundred feet. For the water from the springs, they gave the alleged owners a separate, distinct one hundred feet out of the original fifteen hundred. Comstock hastened to purchase Fennimore's share for forty dollars and an old blind horse. When these one hundred feet became known as the valuable Mexican or Spanish mine, Old Virginny went about complaining that he had a "$60,000 horse" but was too poor to buy a saddle.

Those who were the original owners of the rich Ophir mine sold out early. Penrod received $3,000; McLaughlin, $3,500; J. A. Osborne, who virtually at the first had secured a share, $3,000; Comstock, $11,000; and O'Riley, $44,000 or $45,000. These men did not realize the true nature of their mine, they feared it would soon become exhausted, and they believed they had secured a big price for their holdings. Indeed, from what was known in 1859, it was generally considered that they had been fairly treated. For the Mexican mine Penrod secured $3,000 and Comstock two jackasses. Based on subsequent yield, these two animals cost $1,500,000 each.

About a month after the discovery of the Ophir, that annoying "blue stuff" intermixed with gold of the whole area was finally analyzed. Precisely who did what is in dispute among reliable historians, but from conflicting details emerges clearly a broad outline.[7] Rancher B. A. Harrison and trader J. F. Stone became so curious about the strike at the Ophir that they sent ore samples to the Grass Valley area of California. There, J. J. Ott and Melville Atwood, independently of each other, made an analysis and reached the same conclusion. They both found the "useless blue stuff" to be silver of considerable value, precisely how much is now obscure. One of those who helped arrange for the analysis was Judge James Walsh of Grass Valley. He learned the results quickly and by daylight the next morning was on his way across the Sierras with Joseph Woodward. In two days they arrived on Mt. Davidson and purchased an interest in the Ophir mine. When they returned to their California homes, they spread the news that the Nevada diggings were "fabulously rich" and, such was their reputation as experienced miners, thereby

---

[7] Mack, *Nevada*, 208–209; DeQuille, *Big Bonanza*, 33; Smith, *History*, 9; Lyman, *Saga*, 38–41; Rickard, *American Mining*, 95.

touched off a rush. It was intensified in August when Walsh and Comstock brought 3,151 pounds of ore across the mountains and sold it for $1.50 a pound. Equally impressive to the Californians were the 80 loads of silver ore brought from Nevada to San Francisco by mule in October. When refined, it yielded about $3,000 per ton.[8]

The rush led to the founding of a town immediately at the site of the Ophir mine, a mile from Gold Hill. An entertaining tradition affirms that in October, 1859, the town was christened when Old Virginny Fennimore was returning with some friends from a drunken party. He stumbled over a boulder, fell, and broke the bottle he was clutching; Old Virginny rose unsteadily, poured the few remaining drops of liquor on the ground, and proclaimed, with as much dignity as possible, "I baptize this spot Virginia Town." However this may be, a month earlier a town meeting had officially voted the name to be Virginia City.[9]

By the fall of 1859, Virginia City and Gold Hill were final destinations for many prospectors hustling in from California, mostly through Placerville and over the old immigrant route. They quickly threw up at Virginia City a town of canvas houses, mud-covered huts, and cave-homes. Those who did not build their own dwellings patronized instead crude lodginghouses, which charged a dollar a night for a bunk and half that for sitting room on the floor. The miners faced a rugged winter, for snow first fell on November 22. Soon it had piled up five or six feet, cutting off all communication with neighboring Gold Hill. Equally serious was the condition of the passes in the High Sierras, which were drifted as much as sixty feet deep. These adverse conditions caused a food shortage. Relief finally came late in March with the first mule train, but to everybody's shocked surprise the load was liquor and bar fixtures. Shortly flour arrived and other needed supplies quickly followed.[10]

Soon the great 1860 rush to the Comstock area began.[11] The first prospectors to get over the Sierras to the Washoe region came afoot, with their baggage loaded on donkeys; the next rode saddle horses;

8 Rickard, *American Mining*, 97; Lyman, *Saga*, 46.

9 Lyman, *Saga*, 37; Mack, *Nevada*, 207.

10 DeQuille, *Big Bonanza*, 65; Lyman, *Saga*, 87, 93–95.

11 DeQuille, *Big Bonanza*, 70–71, 76; Lord, *Comstock Mining*, 79; C. B. Glasscock, *The Big Bonanza: The Story of the Comstock Lode*, 47; Mack, *Nevada*, 212; Works Progress Administration, *Nevada: A Guide to the Silver State*, 273.

and finally the passes were clear enough to permit stage service. Perhaps three-quarters of the California miners who came to Nevada in 1859 and 1860 used donkeys. As it grew warm enough to camp out that spring of 1860, groups of five to twelve men spread over the area as much as fifty miles from the Comstock Lode. They prospected so energetically that during that year some four thousand claims were staked within a radius of thirty miles of Virginia City. The great majority of these, utterly worthless, would not have tempted the wildest spectator to purchase them, yet were held in high regard by their owners.

The Californians, so expert at gold, were quite ignorant of silver mining. Gradually the prospectors came to use tests, rather than guesses, to determine the value of what they found. They pulverized some of the quartz, then washed it out in a small, canoe-shaped horn; if there was any gold, it would remain in the bottom, a yellow streak as fine as flour. To seek silver, they placed quartz in the horn, washed out the lighter material, placed the residue in a flask, added nitric acid, boiled it until the fumes came off, first red in color and then white, cooled it, poured it into a test tube, and added salt. If the material at once became milky in hue, it was silver. In case of doubt, they added muriatic acid, held the tube in strong sunshine for a few moments, and looked for a rich purple color to proclaim the presence of that mineral.

Not all of those who flocked into the Washoe area that summer were prospectors. Some came to purchase an interest in already proved mines. One of the most fortunate was George Hearst, whose $450 investment in what became the famous Gould and Curry property paid him back an enormous return. It did much to make his fortune, later used to help his son William Randolph start his career as a chain-newspaper publisher. Other men came to get jobs. Those Mexicans who had had experience in silver mining south of the border were at first in great demand, when most Americans knew so little about its techniques. This situation afforded a golden opportunity to other Mexicans, actually ignorant of the specialty but appreciative of the great advantage in keeping silent. In later years a considerable group of miners from Germany and Cornwall settled on the Washoe. At all times a number of Chinese were in the area, never really welcome but performing essential services as laundry-men, farm hands, cooks, household servants, and wood choppers.

When living as servants in white homes, they were obedient, patient, imitative, and quick to learn. As wood peddlers, especially active in winter, they loaded the fuel on their donkeys to make it look like a really imposing pile from the front; if viewed from the rear, however, it was quite ordinary. The Chinese were peaceful, quiet, tractable, industrious, free from drunkenness, seldom disorderly, and likely to ignore the worst insults or injuries. By law, they could not testify in a Virginia City court, and they were discriminated against when the state constitution was adopted. They maintained a few opium dens in Virginia City, but these were also patronized by a fair number of white men and a few white women.[12]

There were no streets when the crowds first deluged Virginia City, and new buildings arose informally at random.[13] As order came, first A and B streets became clearly established, then C; the business area concentrated initially on B, but later the best of it was on C. These three streets, each running on a terrace along the mountainside, were soon filled to a depth of one yard with such flinty material as waste quartz and became hard, smooth, dry thoroughfares. Despite this, the dust lay heavy enough on them to invade the abutting shops and impair the accuracy of delicate scales which assayers kept in supposedly airtight cases. At first there were no streets linking the three terraces and pedestrians clambered down as best they could. Eventually crossroads developed, so steep they were like toboggan slides in winter and even in summer runaway wagons were a routine event. C Street had an elevation of 6,205 feet; the summit of Mt. Davidson lay at 7,775 feet—enough higher that in winter the sun sank behind it at about three o'clock and immediately the city would start to grow cold. The constant sliding and slumping of the surface soil broke windows and rendered doors incapable of remaining closed. Often there was an extremely strong wind, called a Washoe Zephyr, which in the early days blew down scores of canvas buildings.

12 Hubert H. Bancroft, *History of Nevada, Colorado and Wyoming, 1540–1888,* 292; Mark Twain, *Roughing It,* II, 128–30; DeQuille, *Big Bonanza,* 85–86, 291–96; Dan DeQuille, *A History of the Comstock Silver Lode and Mines,* 42; Wells Drury, *An Editor on the Comstock Lode,* 70.

13 Drury, *Editor,* 18; DeQuille, *Big Bonanza,* 106, and *History,* 46–51; Mack, *Nevada,* 420; Twain, *Roughing It,* II, 11; Lyman, *Saga,* 87–89, 91, 93–95, 196; Lord, *Comstock Mining,* 94; Glasscock, *Big Bonanza,* 72; Charles H. Shinn, *The Story of the Mine, as Illustrated by the Great Comstock Lode of Nevada,* 74; Duncan Emrich (ed.), *Comstock Bonanza,* 44–45.

Early settlers obtained legal title to their city real estate under the terms of the federal government's Townsite Act of 1860. This authorized them to settle on a lot and then claim it as pioneers by right of pre-emption, paying the United States the same price as for 160 acres of farm land, namely, two hundred dollars.

So great was the rush to the Washoe region that by October, 1860, the following 154 business establishments had been set up in Virginia City: 4 cigar stores; 3 drugstores; 2 stationery shops; 2 fruit markets; 1 hotel; 4 butchers; 9 bakeries; 7 blacksmiths; 3 tinsmiths; 1 gunsmith; 7 shoemakers; 1 saddler; 2 carpenters; 1 painter; 1 tailor; 3 watchmakers; 2 barbers; 6 physicians; 1 dentist; 8 lawyers; 2 express offices; 2 assayers; 1 surveyor; 5 brokers; 1 auction house; 1 dressmaker; 4 machine-sewers; 10 livery stables; 25 saloons; 9 restaurants; 7 boardinghouses; 10 laundries; 1 bathhouse; 1 theater; 1 music hall; 1 post office; and 5 lumber yards. At the time, masons earned eight dollars a day, carpenters six, tinsmiths five, and common laborers four; cooks secured a hundred dollars a month and waiters sixty. To match these wages were equally high prices, judged by the standards in the East of that day.

The people of Virginia City had very bad water to drink, for it contained arsenic, graphite, copperas, potable gold, and liquified silver. Practically every man became sick from it at one time or another in 1859 and 1860; hundreds died from it. Those who fell ill from any cause were fortunate if there was somebody to care for them; recovery was mostly a matter of luck.

People concentrated in Virginia City with justification, for all the major discoveries were made at the heart of the region and none at the outskirts.[14] The Comstock Lode, as the miners eventually discovered, cropped out twelve hundred feet below the summit of Mt. Davidson, running along it and smaller peaks of the Washoe Range. For the first four to five hundred feet it dipped west at an angle of forty-five degrees, then became perpendicular and reversed itself, dipping eastward at an average of forty-five degrees. Up to January, 1881, it yielded 45.22 per cent gold and 54.78 per cent silver. In all the history of the Comstock, only sixteen really large and rich bodies of ore, called bonanzas, were found. Most of them were within six

14 DeQuille, *History*, 83; Smith, *History*, 19, 76–80; Bancroft, *Nevada*, 121; George F. Becker, *Geology of the Comstock Lode and the Washoe District*, 5; Richard G. Lillard, *Desert Challenge: An Interpretation of Nevada*, 210.

hundred feet of the surface, were concentrated in form, and had the richest ore toward the center. Five of them—the Ophir, the Gould and Curry, the Savage, the Chollar-Potosi, and the Yellow Jacket— were found during the first five years of the Washoe rush and gave the region its fame. Since the location of the remaining wealth was obviously hidden, the miners spread out their workings in every direction and at many levels to seek it and often found nothing of value. Their trial-and-error method inevitably took considerable time and so prolonged the life of Virginia City.

The first mines were simply round holes in the ground, like a well, each with a windlass and a bucket.[15] When production increased, the owners replaced the initial arrangement with a square shaft and a horse-drawn or steam-powered hoist. As a protection against falling earth and stone, the miners early used round logs as buttresses along the one or more levels dug roughly parallel with the surface of the ground. They were placed vertically as posts or horizontally as caps to the uprights. If height was needed, one log was put atop another and the two spliced together with iron bolts and bands. These mines gave employment, by late 1861, to about one-third of the entire Washoe population. If one proved unsuccessful, it was simply deserted and the abandoned shaft lay open and unprotected. On one occasion a teamster, too far distant to do anything but stare, looked on in despair as his eight yoke of oxen, unhitched from the wagon but held together by a logging chain, disappeared down an old shaft when a middle yoke fell into it and dragged the rest down with them.

Among the first to retain a profitable claim from the initial discovery onward and the first to garner real wealth were Sandy Bowers and his wife, known as Eilly Orrum.[16] Coming to Johntown in 1851, Eilly had scrubbed, mended, and pressed for the miners; for her third husband, she took Sandy. Their claim yielded not more than $1,200,000 gross, and perhaps half of that was net profit. The Bowerses were simple, kindly, unlettered people, well respected on the Comstock. Sandy, in his good fortune, was very hospitable and freehanded, but modest and a natural gentleman. The $300,000 mansion of stone they built in the Washoe Valley was a showplace in its day, with doorknobs and hinges of silver bullion and a bronze piano adorned by mother-of-pearl keys. The two took a splendid

15 DeQuille, *Big Bonanza,* 89–90, 103–104; Lyman, *Saga,* 194.
16 Smith, *History,* 96–97; Drury, *Editor,* 25–28; Lyman, *Saga,* 11–12, 251–54.

eight-month European trip, but whether Eilly actually met Queen Victoria is a matter of dispute. When Sandy died in 1868 at the age of thirty-five, his entire estate was appraised at only $88,998. Eilly opened the mansion as a resort, and when she lost this, she earned a meager living as a "clairvoyant," patronized by the wealthy who could afford it. Those who in later years dubbed her "Queen of the Comstock" have tried to create a legend which would have made veterans of the Washoe smile.

Next to the Bowers claim, Joe Plato owned a ten-foot ledge.[17] When Sandy's property showed signs of value, Joe thought hard enough about his own to realize, with a shock, that he had given half of it to a San Francisco prostitute in a drunken night's spree. To recapture those five feet, he performed the herculean task of crossing the Sierras in the middle of winter and finally managed to find the woman. With an inkling of the claim's true worth, she refused Plato's demand to surrender his gift. In desperation, he proposed marriage; she accepted. Their honeymoon was a race back over the mountains in hot haste to make sure no claim jumper was trying to tamper with their property. When Joe died in the 1870's, he left his wife a considerable fortune. She then married "one of the richest and most prominent businessmen of San Francisco and became an ancestress of note."

The Platos had very properly been worried about claim jumpers, for these were one of the several types of lawbreakers active on the Comstock in the spring of 1860.[18] Men called on their friends to come and help them, armed either to repel an attempted invasion or to regain stolen property "by authority of Judge Colt." Almost everybody carried a revolver or other weapon. This practice was a great equalizer of men, making for much politeness when each was the judge of another's conduct and quick to resent the slightest insult. Men fought to the death for almost any trivial reason, even the rumor of unpleasant remarks never really made. That the first thirty graves in Virginia City were filled by violent deaths was a contemporary saying, untrue in literal fact but representing the spirit of the times. Over one of these, an entertaining legend has it, was a headboard reading:

17 Lyman, *Saga*, 254–55, 386.
18 Drury, *Editor*, 17, 158–63; DeQuille, *Big Bonanza*, 67–68, 99–101; Glasscock, *Big Bonanza*, 58.

He had sand in his craw,
But was slow on the draw,
So we planted him under the daisies.

The first real bad man and killer on the Comstock was Sam Brown, who came from California with sixteen notches on his gun belt.[19] Big, thick witted, and with red whiskers, he was careful never to raise his booming voice insolently to those with friends or weapons; to the unprotected, however, he and his gang were a scourge. When a member of his gang was finally brought to trial and Brown publicly boasted how he would force the court to free him, he failed to reckon with lawyer William Stewart. As Brown took the witness stand, the attorney covered him with a derringer, forced him to admit he knew nothing of the case, and finally asked him if he was being intimidated. Brown denied it and, still on the stand, handed Stewart five hundred dollars in cash as a retainer to be his defense counsel in a California case. Brown then suggested that the court adjourn while he treated everybody at the adjoining bar. This was promptly done. Smarting from this defeat as he rode away, Brown unsuccessfully tried to shoot up the wayside inn of Henry Van Sickles. The frightened but determined innkeeper killed him.

Gradually law and order were established on the Comstock.[20] When county courts began to function effectively in Virginia City in 1863, the sheriff impaneled for the first jury only squint-eyed men; for the second, the fattest he could find; for the third, the tallest and thinnest. For the fourth he intended to secure the handsomest, but the judge interfered and spoiled the sport. Washoe juries were strongly disliked by at least one resident of the Comstock, Mark Twain, who in later years declared the requirement that a person must be so ignorant he had not heard of or discussed certain famous cases led to foolish and ill-advised decisions. Those whom the juries cast into prison for their misdeeds found the jails far from escape proof. The buildings should be strengthened, Comstock humorists insisted, by a new coat of whitewash. Only twice did vigilance committees, such as sprang up earlier in California, materialize on the

[19] Lyman, *Saga*, 54, 76, 146–47, 156–62.
[20] Mack, *Nevada*, 177; DeQuille, *Big Bonanza*, 181–85; Twain, *Roughing It*, II, 75–76; Lyman, *Saga*, 237.

Washoe. In 1858, a committee functioned briefly in Carson County. In 1871, a law-enforcement group called the 601 organized so secretly in Virginia City that it seemed to arise by sheer spontaneity on the night of March 24 and hang Arthur Perkins Heffernan, who had just shot a man down in a saloon. It avoided the excesses of which committees in other states were guilty, indulged in little violence, but managed to discourage a good many lawbreakers.

Various criminals lurked on the roads leading to Virginia City and sometimes they robbed the stagecoach in traditionally western fashion.[21] No others had the style of Jack Davis, who once served the passengers champagne and hors d'oeuvers while his confederates blew open the express box. To discourage such delays to their schedule, the stage companies employed shotgun messengers to ride their coaches. To be sure the guards were not asleep, for a time they ordered them to carry their loaded guns with the muzzle resting on their toes. To protect shipments further, the mines in the middle 1870's began sending out their gold and silver in bars so heavy a man could hardly lift them.

Such precautions did not discourage all bandits, especially the most famous on the Comstock, Nicanor Rodrigues, generally called Nickanora. When he finally grew tired of being chased, he agreed to help protect the express company from other bandits. But he wearied of being on the side of the law, resumed his thefts, got caught, received a jail sentence, broke out of prison, and then wisely retired, reportedly to a rancho in Old Mexico.

An important legal question in 1859 and 1860 was which court had jurisdiction over the Virginia City area.[22] At first the region was served by Carson County, Utah Territory, but the official status of the county court was so confused that it functioned little and commanded no respect. Utah tried to solve the problem by sending one of its United States district court judges, John Cradlebaugh, to the Comstock. Of the suits which might come before him, the most important and the most difficult to decide impartially would be those over conflicts in mining claims. Some problems arose out of the hap-

21 Drury, *Editor*, 143–55; Lyman, *Saga*, 211.

22 Lyman, *Saga*, 48–52, 77, 151–55, 163–68, 179–81, 186–93, 235; Smith, *History*, 67; Harry M. Gorham, *My Memories of the Comstock*, 32; Drury, *Editor*, 22–23; Bancroft, *Nevada*, 126–217; Mack, *Nevada*, 182–90, 258–64; Lord, *Comstock Mining*, 133–35, 155, 164, 167–68, 173; Glasscock, *Big Bonanza*, 99–107.

hazard system used, before the fall of 1859, to record claims. The most fundamental question, however, was whether the Comstock Lode was one ledge or many; on this hinged the question of whether adjacent mines were trespassing on each other. Over these various matters a dozen major mines of the Washoe area became involved in 245 suits; for example, the Ophir was plaintiff in 28 and defendant in 9. All of these actions at law were pretty well settled by 1877 at a total estimated cost of ten million dollars.

The chief legal advocate of the one-ledge theory, who became the leading Virginia City attorney, was William Stewart. From the law classrooms of Yale, he went directly to the California mines and then in 1860 moved to Nevada. It was a profitable shift, for in the years of the major legal warfare on the Comstock Lode he collected in fees between one and two hundred thousand dollars annually. He mastered the details of his cases thoroughly and then spoke to the juries without notes, simply and clearly, using much broad sarcasm and ridicule. Some of his cases were spectacular. In one he suspected that the president of a mining company who had hired him to fight a case had subsequently turned traitor to the concern while still its head. Stewart finished his work on the lawsuit at his own expense, proved in court the president's duplicity, and won a complete victory. In another trial he proved that a witness had been bribed; when a crooked juror opposed the decision of the majority in favor of Stewart's client, the others threatened to hang him and with "a well-grounded faith in this assurance" he yielded instantly. Occasionally Stewart met his match. He once said to an opposing attorney, "You little shrimp, if you interrupt me again I'll eat you." The reply was: "If you do you'll have more brains in your belly than you ever had in your head."

The chief legal advocate of the many-ledges theory was David S. Terry. A southerner by birth, he went to California in the gold-rush days and rose to be the state's chief justice. He lost his party's renomination, fought a duel, and before long moved to Nevada.

Terry and Stewart tried to resolve the knotty problem of which court had jurisdiction in the Comstock area by agreeing to try their cases before Judge Cradlebaugh. He held court on the first one, the so-called McCall suit, in the loft of a livery stable at the Washoe town of Genoa. As soon as each day's session began, the bailiff closed the makeshift court room to further spectators; he simply pulled up the ladder. The key point of argument in the trial was whether the Comstock was one ledge or many. When Terry's witnesses swore that a certain spot in a mine was solid granite, Stewart had his experts take ore samples every six inches to demonstrate that the mineralized ledge was undivided and continuous. His proof seemed incontestable, but it did not win him the case. His opponent had managed to get a few secessionist friends on the jury and they divided it, eight to four, making a decision impossible.

The problem of which court had jurisdiction was no sooner solved informally than another arose—which judge had the legal right to preside over it? This question came up when President Buchanan removed Cradlebaugh in October, 1860, and appointed H. P. Flenniken, former minister to The Hague, as the new magistrate. When Flenniken arrived on the Washoe that fall, Cradlebaugh refused to yield his post and asserted that the President lacked the power to remove any territorial judge. To break the stalemate, Stewart appealed a criminal case to the Utah Supreme Court. The following February, it ruled that the incumbent should retain the post and that the new appointment was invalid. Flenniken was indecisive and Stewart forced him to telegraph his resignation.

In 1861, when Nevada became a territory, there was naturally a corresponding change in the courts. President Lincoln appointed George Turner as chief justice of the newly established Supreme Court of Nevada Territory and chose as associate justices Horatio M. Jones and Gordon N. Mott. Each received from the federal government an annual salary of $1,500, which was doubtless adequate in some parts of the United States but literally would not provide them with the bare necessities of life for a single month at Washoe prices. The judges solved their financial problems in a style most generous to their pocketbooks when they followed the example of sheriffs, juries, and witnesses by accepting bribes. Certainly the three discarded the one-ledge theory, and many observers felt that the judges would recognize as many ledges as they were paid for. To do so was easy when there was no federal or territorial law or precedent to bind them. When Judge Turner set his price at $10,000 for a favorable decision in a certain case, his bribers were hard put to locate the sum, for the banks had closed, but they finally managed to secure it all by one in the morning and knocked at the Judge's hotel room. Mrs. Turner answered, holding out her nightgown like an apron to receive the money. When dumped in, the coins were so heavy that they pulled her gown completely off and left her standing naked among the scattered gold pieces.[23]

As corrupt as the judges were the witnesses, often so-called experts from neighboring states, who usually visited the mine in dispute under "the eye-opening influences of liquor and a per diem allowance." They stood ready unequivocally to swear whatever would best serve their employers.

Such wholesale corruption in the courts left the litigants little choice but to "fight fire with fire." When the Potosí mine thought that both Judges Turner and Mott were prejudiced in favor of its opponent in a suit, it took action. It saw Judge Mott resign permanently and in his place John W. North appointed. For stepping down, Mott received $25,000, a fact which the decision of referees in a libel suit confirmed.[24] Public pressure against the crooked judges, led by the newspapers, became increasingly strong and the petition circulated against them gained a huge number of signatures. In August, 1864, all three resigned.

President Lincoln did not appoint any replacements to the territorial court, but, rather, allowed justice to lie dormant until Nevada became a state and, the next November, selected her own judges. While it would be considerably too much to say that Nevadans wanted statehood just to escape the territorial court, certainly after that November the fierce excitement of the mining suits greatly abated. Another quelling factor was the huge expense. An excellent legal proof of the one-ledge theory was made in August, 1864; the following year, a conclusive scientific proof was published by that eminent geologist, Baron Ferdinand von Richthofen.

The Comstock area was originally under the government of Utah Territory, established in 1850.[25] When the so-called Mormon War broke out in 1857, most of the churchmen went to help in what might have been the armed defense of their religious headquarters. With their exodus, little government remained in Nevada. The non-Mormons half-admitted and half-denied the authority of Utah

[23] Lyman, *Saga*, 235.

[24] Lord, *Comstock Mining*, 155; Glasscock, *Big Bonanza*, 105; Miriam Michelson, *The Wonderlode of Silver and Gold*, 153.

[25] Mack, *Nevada*, 169–84, 218–23, 228–30; DeQuille, *Big Bonanza*, 86; Drury, *Editor*, 196; Lillard, *Desert Challenge*, 211–12; Lyman, *Saga*, 177–83.

Territory. Then came the rush of 1860, forcing a decision, and early in 1861, the federal authorities established Nevada as a territory. To the governorship Abraham Lincoln appointed James W. Nye, a Republican politician of New York State who was to become the original for "Bill Nye" in Bret Harte's famous poem "Plain Language from Truthful James" about the "heathen Chinee" card sharper.

Once when Nye was addressing a group outdoors, he was vigorously interrupted by a braying donkey. He promptly declared: "Ladies and gentlemen, that does not disturb me in the least. I have never tried to make a Republican speech in Nevada that the opposition has not trotted out their best speakers to try and down me." He secured an appropriation of $75,000 for a dam and sawmill to manufacture lumber for the Paiutes, but spent the money in a quite unsatisfactory fashion. His mishandling of the funds led to a famous newspaper comment of the day that Nye had "a dam by a mill site, but no mill by a damn site."

The government held elections to the territorial legislature on August 31. The solons located the capital at Carson City. The legislature held a forty-nine-day session and passed 107 laws, most of them modeled on or copied from the California statutes. Included among its measures was the important adoption of time-tested California mining regulations.

The territory was scarcely established before discussion of statehood began.[26] The drafting of a proposed constitution, as authorized by Congress, was undertaken by a convention in November, 1863. The document contained the directive that when the people voted on its adoption, they should also elect the various officials whose posts it would create. This involved the ambitions of the thirty-four delegates to the convention, each of whom apparently hungered for a federal or state office. They determined to thwart lawyer Stewart's great ambition to become a United States senator, which by their combined efforts they might well do, and to support instead Judge John Cradlebaugh. As soon as he learned of their decision, Stewart launched, with great vigor, a public attack on that clause in the proposed constitution which authorized a tax on the shafts, drafts, and bedrock tunnels of mines, whether productive or not. He proclaimed, with much display of virtue, that he was simply protecting "the honest

26 Mack, *Nevada*, 247–66; Lyman, *Saga*, 263–69, 313–25.

miner" from unfair taxation; this is doubtful. Be that as it may, his efforts defeated the first proposed constitution at the election of January 19, 1864.

Only twenty days later, pressure for a second draft began. It resulted from four factors: the emergency of the Civil War, the ambitions of politicians thirsting for the offices to be created, the corruption of the territorial judiciary, and the fear instilled in the mine owners because of suggestions that the federal government would sell the Nevada mineral lands at a price high enough to pay off the North's Civil War debt. To encourage fast action, a bill was introduced in Congress in February, 1864, authorizing Nevada to enter the Union as a state. Opposition arose, but strong support came from President Lincoln. He held hopes for an amendment to the federal constitution which would abolish slavery, and he wanted Nevada's vote to help secure the two-thirds majority necessary for ratification. He promised that the New York delegation could name the collector of customs at the port of New York City. He had the New Jersey congressmen informed that they could pick two internal-revenue collectors for their state. His support helped enough for Congress to pass the measure. Encouraged, the Nevadans drew up a second proposed constitution, which omitted the controversial mine tax and avoided election complications by providing that officials should be selected at a later time than the vote on accepting the constitution. It was adopted overwhelmingly in September, 1864. To be sure that Nevada would become a state in time for its citizens to vote in the national election that fall, the provisions of the document were wired to Washigton—in the longest telegram ever sent up to that time—at a cost of $3,416.77.

State officials were elected in November and the new legislature promptly met. One of its first tasks was to select two United States senators, and as soon as balloting began, William Stewart clearly secured one of the posts; the other was in doubt. Stewart offered to support Judge Cradlebaugh at the price of exclusive control over the state's federal patronage, but the Judge replied, with an inexact paraphrase from Shakespeare, "Tell Stewart that I had rather be a dog and bay the moon than be such a senator." The attorney then threw his weight behind Nye and got him elected.

A major problem under both territorial and state government was what laws of ownership and of taxation should be established for the mines. At first the prospectors drew up local rules and regulations in the informal fashion of the earlier California gold rush.[27] On the Comstock they formed two major districts, one at Virginia City and the other at Gold Hill. At Virginia City they provided that a claim should be for a length of three hundred feet, later reduced to two hundred feet, on the vein, following it into the earth "with all of its dips, spurs and angles." This major qualifying phrase caused almost unbelievable technicalities and complexities, for the vein was often most irregular. The width of the claim was the full width of the vein, which on the Comstock might be as much as one thousand feet. Each claim had to be worked monthly for three days in time or ten dollars in value of labor done.

These regulations remained in effect throughout the territorial days, but some kind of change seemed certain upon statehood.[28] As Senators Stewart and Nye set out for the East on January 5, 1865, they were worried about two proposals: the Secretary of the Interior was advocating a 1 per cent tax on what each Nevada mine produced, and the Secretary of the Treasury was recommending the sale of all mineral lands there at a high price. Stewart did not wait long after his arrival in Washington to take action. Ten days after he was sworn in, he asked the Senate to create a mines and mining committee; on March 8, it did. When a law about Nevada courts was being passed, he inserted two amendments of vital importance to his constituents. One said that the local miners' customs and regulations about the right to exploit a claim should be enforced by the federal courts as though they were law; the second stipulated that in suits over title to mines, no case should be dismissed because the United States owned all the area but, rather, should be decided on the grounds of "possessory mining rights."

Stewart's amendments to the court bill satisfied the needs of placer miners but failed to protect adequately those who made heavy investments in such extensive quartz as the Comstock. The idea of a sale appealed especially to Senator John Sherman and Representative George W. Julian, who envisaged enrichment for the federal treasury. When Sherman introduced a bill authorizing it, Stewart

27 Lord, *Comstock Mining*, 43–44, 91–92; Smith, *History*, 64–65.
28 Beulah Hershiser, "The Influence of Nevada on the National Mining Legislation of 1866," Nevada Historical Society, *Third Biennial Report* (1911–12), 147–48, 151–63; Mack, *Nevada*, 429–30, 432–35.

got the proposal referred to the Committee on Mines and Mining, stifled the measure, and persuaded the group to recommend adoption of a substitute he drew up; this the Senate subsequently approved.

What the upper house enacted was quite unsatisfactory to Representative Julian, who wielded sufficient influence to make sure that it was referred to his Committee on Public Lands. Stewart then seized a routine measure the House passed concerning ditches and canals in the public domain when it came up for consideration before the Senate and persuaded his colleagues to strike out everything after the enacting clause and substitute instead all the provisos of his previous bill about the sale of Nevada mineral land. Stewart's device of the Senate's amending a measure originating in the House meant that the altered draft could not go back to Julian's Committee on Public Lands without the vote of the lower chamber. While this maneuver was going on in the Senate, Julian showed his intentions by introducing to the representatives a bill confiscating the mines. To thwart him, Stewart personally undertook to visit each member of the House and discuss western mining conditions. When the time came for them to consider the Senate's amendment of the bill about ditches and canals, more than two-thirds of them approved and the President signed it into law.

What Stewart had secured was an enactment stating that the federal mineral lands were open for exploitation by any American citizen and that when the claimant had spent a thousand dollars on improvements and labor, according to the mining customs of his locality, the United States would issue him a free title, called a land patent, to his claim. Stewart had achieved a great victory for Nevada and the West; he avoided confiscation and made it possible for the Comstockers to secure ownership from the federal government without charge. His actions were quite in accord with the view of most westerners, and a considerable number of easterners, of his own generation that America's natural resources should be rapidly exploited, sometimes without ownership, by those venturesome enough to undertake the task.

Although threat of federal confiscation or heavy taxation worried mine owners the most, they inevitably faced the possibility of state or territorial levies.[29] The second territorial legislature collected twelve cents on each one hundred dollars of valuation, as contrasted with the

[29] Romanzo Adams, *Taxation in Nevada: A History,* 69–90.

general property tax of fifty cents on each hundred. This mild levy was much weakened by interpreting it to mean the value of untreated ore at the mouth of the mine and so allowing about 60 per cent of the bullion to escape any payment. When Nevada became a state, its constitution forbade a tax on the mines themselves but sanctioned a levy on the proceeds. This phrase the legislature, dominated by mineral interests, interpreted to be the value of unrefined ore and not the smelted bullion. It granted a specific exemption for the expense of milling and laid its tax on three-quarters of the remaining value of the raw ore. This resulted, in 1865 and 1866, in the state's actual revenue amounting to 0.1 per cent of the value of the bullion extracted. The amount was further decreased when, late in 1866, the legislature agreed to accept federal paper money, the greenbacks, at face value for payment of taxes, although these were commonly accepted only at less than face value. In 1871, the legislature made major changes which cut the state's revenue. When Romanzo Adams published his 1918 monograph on Nevada taxation, he observed that at the time, the mines were paying about as much as could be expected.

A related problem was county taxes, especially in Storey County, which included both Virginia City and Gold Hill. The county rate, fixed in 1867 by the state legislature, was a levy of twenty-five cents on each one hundred dollars of valuation in the mines and $1.50 on the same amount of any other type of property; in 1875, the mine rate was increased to thirty-five cents and the other lowered to $1.35. In 1869, the state passed a law forbidding cities to tax the Comstock mines.

War might not be as inevitable as death and taxes, but it did come to the Comstock. Trouble with the neighboring Indians resulted in the Paiute War of 1860,[30] which began when several white men abused two young Paiute women and then imprisoned them at a trader's store. Word of the impending Indian attack was brought to Virginia City by a Pony Express rider. That evening, more than a thousand men proclaimed their eagerness to defend the Comstock, but when the military company was organized the next morning, only a little over a hundred actually appeared. They seized the initiative, marched eastward, and on the afternoon of May 12 entered a narrow pass in a deep valley. It was an ambush; the Paiutes fired

30 DeQuille, *Big Bonanza,* 77–82.

on them from the heights. Many of the whites broke and ran at the first volley. Of those who stood firm, many were killed.

The defeat threw Virginia City into such a panic that martial law was declared. One Dutchman who remained grew so alarmed that he had his partner lower him to the bottom of a fifty-foot shaft, but then his friend ran away; the Dutchman was not discovered by another man until three days and nights had passed. Other defenders of the Comstock thought they were more practical when they bored out a pine log as a cannon and filled it with scrap iron. They did not have a chance to use their weapon in battle, which was fortunate, for when fired later, it simply scattered material in every direction. The local militia was joined by United States Army infantrymen; they fought and decisively defeated the Indians at Pyramid Lake. This ended the Paiute War.

5

THE DEVELOPMENT OF THE COMSTOCK LODE

NEVADA soon became concerned about a more serious conflict, for in 1861 the quarrel over slavery and states' rights finally erupted into the Civil War.[1] The most rabid of the Secessionists on the Comstock was the lawyer David S. Terry. Even before the war broke out he was telling how he would seize the mines to help provide money for the South, and he actually erected forts at three prominent places on the Comstock. When the fighting began in the Confederacy, it was commonly believed on the Washoe that Terry held a commission, signed by Jefferson Davis, appointing him governor of Nevada Territory and that he had a list of proposed subordinate officials. Those sympathetic with the South talked of seizing Fort Churchill, Federal Army headquarters for the area. On June 5, 1861, two hundred heavily armed "Knights of the Golden Circle," the most enthusiastic of the pro-Confederates, established their headquarters in Virginia City at Johnny Newman's saloon. When Yankee troops arrived in town the same day, Southern enthusiasm for military exploits declined sharply.

During the war years in Nevada, funds were raised on the Comstock to aid the United States Sanitary Commission, a private group that performed many services which were the responsibility of the Red Cross and the U. S. Army Medical Corps in World War II. A novel scheme to secure money was originated by Reuel Gridley of Austin, Nevada. He auctioned off a flour sack, the purchaser donated it back, and the cycle was repeated again and again. After he had secured as much as possible from his home town, Gridley brought his flour sack to the Comstock and in a series of auctions raised about

1.Mack, *Nevada*, 187, 270–87; Lyman, *Saga*, 57, 79–80, 171–72, 285–92.

forty thousand dollars in greenbacks; he then went elsewhere in the cause of charity. In all, he raised about a quarter of a million dollars for the Sanitary Commission.

The war years were prosperous ones on the Comstock.[2] Gold Canyon's sawmills, quartz mills, tunnels, and shanties made it practically a continuation of Virginia City. Over the whole area hung a cloud of smoke and alkali, making everything gritty to the touch. In Virginia City proper, the business part of C street was lighted at night by gas jets. It was walled by substantial brick buildings four to six stories high, with iron stands for flowers often jutting from the second story and with wide balconies which formed an irregular arcade underneath. In the middle of the day the street was often blocked with wagons and animals. Advertisements seemed to be posted everywhere. The rich mines were wastefully skimming off the most obvious wealth. Their stockholders cried, not for economy or care, but for higher dividends. They expected their mine superintendent to make a display of wealth, to live in a fine brick mansion and to drive snappy horses. The only obvious shortage in Virginia City was women. Men paid such extravagant homage to them that it was not unique for a nun from the Sisters of Mercy, walking down the street, to have someone fall on his knees and press the hem of her robe to his lips as she passed.

Population continued to increase; by 1875, about 20,000 people were in Virginia City and 10,000 in Gold Hill.[3] The two towns, once a mile apart, gradually grew together. As the good fortune of the area waned, Virginia City shrank to about 9,000 in 1889 and 2,700 in 1900. The streets were not as full of people as an ordinary town of the same population would have been because at any given time perhaps a quarter of the men were working underground.

The Comstock did not have a steady increase in prosperity, followed by a consistent decline, but, rather, suffered vicissitudes.[4] Those who had believed the Washoe contained limitless wealth got a rude

[2] Lyman, Saga, 198, 217–25.

[3] DeQuille, Big Bonanza, xxv, 155, and History, 55.

[4] DeQuille, History, 84–91, and Big Bonanza, xxiv–xxv, 359–76; Rickard, American Mining, 106; WPA, Nevada, 275; Shinn, Story of the Mine, 159; Drury, Editor, 232–34, 269, 289; Gorham, My Memories, 33, 114–17, 159–72; Oscar Lewis, Silver Kings: The Lives and Times of Mackay, Fair, Flood, and O'Brien, Lords of the Nevada Comstock Lode, 277; Mack, Nevada, 450; Smith, History, 59, 141, 199, 250–52, 269; Lucius Beebe and Charles Clegg, Legends of the Comstock Lode, 76.

awakening in 1865 when all of the early bonanzas, from the Ophir to the Belcher, were simultaneously exhausted at the five-hundred-foot level; before long, however, larger and richer ore bodies were uncovered. The original location of the major mine works could not be permanent because the vein dipped away; a thousand feet to the east a second line of works was eventually built. Between 1859 and 1872, twelve ore bodies of such exceptional richness that they were called bonanzas were uncovered; there were to be four more. In October, 1873, came the grand prize, the renowned Big Bonanza, lying at 1,167 feet, mostly in the Consolidated Virginia and the California mines and a bit in the Ophir. The tiny richest part contained minerals worth $1,000 to $10,000 per ton of ore. From the whole discovery the Consolidated Virginia and the California secured $150,000,000 in metals and in twenty-two years paid out $78,148,000 in dividends.

The success of the two mines caused other mine owners to sink shafts to the 1,500-foot level, and the fortunate ones were richly rewarded. In the year 1875, the total mineral yield of the Comstock was worth twenty-six million dollars, in 1876, thirty-two million, and in 1877, the maximum in the history of the area, thirty-six million. The bonanzas in the Ophir, Gould and Curry, Savage, and Hale and Norcross mines returned in gross income twice as much from the silver as the gold, but in the Consolidated Virginia the yield from the two metals was about equal.

Not all stockholders realized as much on their investment as those of the Consolidated Virginia. For example, by the time the Ophir had produced minerals worth $15,000,000, it had paid out only $1,-400,000 in dividends, $500,000 for a smelter, and perhaps $1,000,000 for machinery; the rest had gone for salaries, labor, and what were elastically defined as "supplies."

By 1878, only a few of the bonanza mines were able to continue paying dividends, and on the Washoe mining conditions generally had settled into the doldrums. Although it had not been so apparent at the time, a larger part of Virginia City's prosperity during the 1870's actually came from the expenditure of money in seeking new ore bodies rather than from minerals extracted from proved veins. At a time when many people were discouraged, the Sierra Nevada mine suddenly discovered ore truly Comstock in character and of much value. The company's stock, which had been practically worthless, zoomed to $275 a share; the mine eventually produced over a million dollars' worth of ore. Immediately adjacent to it lay another property, the Union, which appealed to James Fair as perhaps having as bright a future as the Sierra Nevada. He paid one million dollars for major stock control of the property, but alas, his theory was wrong and he found virtually nothing of value.

Search for additional wealth continued in the various Comstock mines, in some which had been great producers at one time and in others which were never more than promising. The exploration was financed by assessments on the stockholders, who could either pay or forfeit their shares. Sometimes there were mishaps. On February 13, 1882, the Exchequer mine struck such a huge quantity of water that it and its nine neighbors were flooded. The various companies, unable to agree about how to divide the cost of further pumping, abandoned operations below the 1,650-foot level. Other miners became discouraged at such deep operations, what with expenses increasing in geometrical ratio to the depth. A few continued such explorations, the Union Consolidated Company doing considerable work at 3,350 feet, but most concerns abandoned them.

Compared to the total mineral yield of the Comstock in the mid-seventies, that of about $1,000,000 in 1881 and almost $1,750,000 in 1882 was small. The outlook was so discouraging that the miners volunteered to suspend their rigid eight-hour shift rule and work ten hours at the same pay. This experiment did not produce much more per man-day.

A revival began in the middle 1880's, based on new methods pioneered by J. P. Jones. He leased the upper part of the Consolidated Virginia mine, that is, all that above 1,550 feet, and reworked it. He searched for any small sources of mineral overlooked in the first hasty exploitation and remilled the so-called fillings, the low-grade quartz and waste material used to fill the space left by the extraction of the rich ore. Between May, 1884, and November, 1885, he mined 18,487 tons, yielding at the smelter an average gross return of $16.70 per ton. Jones's great success so impressed the Consolidated Virginia that it decided to do its own reworking and persuaded him to surrender his lease in return for a one-third interest in the smelter that would mill the additional ore. The mining company, following Jones's methods, did well. From 1884 to 1895, it extracted $16,477,221 worth of minerals and made enough profit to pay $3,898,000 in dividends.

Other companies followed Consolidated Virginia's lead in the careful, painstaking, penny-scrimping but profitable reworking of their property. The venture was so successful that in 1888 the entire production of the Comstock revived to a total value in ore mined of $7,600,-000. Not all of the undertakings, however, proved rewarding. The Belcher, Crown Point, and Yellow Jacket mines produced 750,000 tons of ore between 1882 and 1890 but did not earn enough from all of it to pay even one dividend.

After 1890, the Comstock began to decline rapidly. Some of the companies had no justification for continued operations, but were kept alive to continue paying the salaries of their officials and to fulfill the machinations of stock manipulators.

To operate all the Washoe mines, prosperous or not, required from the earliest years the solution of many problems. The Comstockers, the first to be faced with really deep mining, were excellent in designing machinery and in adapting European methods of timbering to new conditions. They were much less adept at the science of geology and made no important contribution to underground practices.[5]

When the Ophir mine's roof showed signs of sinking, it called in Philip Deidesheimer.[6] He was at first greatly puzzled over the proper solution, but finally received an inspiration when looking at a bee's honeycomb. He devised the so-called square-set method, a series of timber cribs four by six feet square. These were placed atop another to reach any desired height and put parallel to each other to span any width. The series of them, if sketched, would look like the steel supports of a modern skyscraper or the myriad walls of a honeycomb. The hollow, timbered cribs were filled with waste ore, making them practically solid pillars and greatly increasing their supporting strength. They bore such great weights that pieces of pine fourteen inches square were frequently compressed to six (and if removed, this pine would take a polish like mahogany or ironwood). The grinding, squeezing pressure on the wood often produced an acrid, penetrating odor, and some thought it to be a cause of mine fires. The square-set method was a very important contribution and came to be universal in the Comstock mines, for the larger the ore body, the greater the expense of keeping the encroaching elements out. In some situations, the sooner the minerals could be removed, the better.

5 Rickard, *American Mining*, 110.
6 DeQuille, *Big Bonanza*, 91; Gorham, *My Memories*, 178–79; Mack, *Nevada*, 446–47; Bancroft, *Nevada*, 139.

Dynamite, then called "giant powder," was invented in 1863, patented in 1867, and first tried on the Comstock in 1868.[7] It was introduced initially at the Gould and Curry mine as a substitute for black powder and proved unsatisfactory, but within two years further experience so reversed first appearances that it came to be generally used on the Washoe. Drilling was originally by hand. Much cheaper and more effective was the Burleigh mechanical drill, powered by compressed air, which was first installed in 1872. Without it, deep mining would have been impossible.

Proper ventilation was one of the constant problems in Washoe operations, for lack of it in the early days sometimes caused death.[8] The early solution was Root blowers, first used in 1865. With the introduction of the Burleigh drills, compressed-air systems had to be installed to power them, and while they were about it, the mining companies built systems large enough to handle the ventilation, too. They also connected the fresh air in one shaft with that of another. Although eventually electricity was used to light the mines, during most of the Washoe's great era, candles and lamps prevailed; only a few little-used spots were utterly dark.

Heat was another constant problem, made more difficult by variations in the intensity of warmth from time to time at any given spot. At the three-thousand-foot level, for example, temperatures as hot as 130 degrees might be encountered. At depths of fifteen hundred to two thousand feet it was common to strike 110-degree heat and feel rock so hot it was painful to the bare hand. One of the worst spots was a level of the Crown Point mine which had a constant temperature of 150 degrees. In such places as these the miners were drenched, as though in a regular Turkish bath, with perspiration which removed their bodily impurities and gave them a white appearance. They were usually naked to the waist and from the middle of the thighs to the feet. They found the heat in many places too intense to allow them to labor steadily, and, by the so-called double-gang system of relieving each other, two men did the work of one. In their moments of respite, a fixed period varying from fifteen minutes to one hour, they retreated to areas designated as cooling stations, where they drank from barrels of ice water and dipped the towels they used

[7] Smith, *History*, 47, 246; Lord, *Comstock Mining*, 366.
[8] Smith, *History*, 46–47, 246; Becker, *Geology*, 3–5; DeQuille, *Big Bonanza*, 223–51, 386; Shinn, *Story of the Mine*, 217; Lewis, *Silver Kings*, 17–18.

to rub themselves. Surprisingly few of them died of the heat, partly because they were such a picked group physically and also because they were assigned only a week in the torrid zone before being shifted to a more comfortable part of the mine. In the worst area it was literally more than a strong man could do to swing a pick, and only the use of the Burleigh drill made production possible.

Each man was specifically assigned to a certain level of the mine and was forbidden to go elsewhere. Below ground, he was not to fight anybody for any reason. He sometimes made a pet of one of the many rats infesting the mines, for it might well give him the first warning of a cave-in when it was squeezed out of its hiding place by the preliminary shiftings. The miner reported for work on one of the eight-hour shifts—starting at 7:00 A.M., 3:00 P.M., and 11:00 P.M.—by going to the hoisting works and awaiting his turn to descend.

In the shaft of a large mine there were three compartments for hoisting and one for the pumps. The cage in the former might have one, two, or three decks for men or carts; it was suspended by a hemp rope in the early days, but in 1864, A. S. Hallidie of San Francisco devised a woven-wire cable which soon became standard. By the middle 1870's, if the cage's cable broke, a newly perfected safety device halted the descent. In routine operation the cage could be stopped at any number of main levels of the mine, called drifts, from which branched out the crosscuts, where most of the ore was extracted. Occasionally two levels were connected by a sloped passageway, known as a winze. The total length of the Comstock's shafts and subterranean tunnels was estimated in January, 1884, as being between 180 and 190 miles. Along the drifts and crosscuts the ore was generally cut so that it would fall down, facilitating its placement in carts to be wheeled on rails to the shaft.

To solve major problems of heat, ventilation, safety, and easy access to the mines was the ambition of Adolph H. J. Sutro.[9] Arriving on the Comstock in 1860 at the age of thirty, he quickly conceived a plan

9 Lord, *Comstock Mining*, 235–41; Lewis, *Silver Kings*, 19; Lillard, *Desert Challenge*, 78; Smith, *History*, 107–15; Beebe and Clegg, *Legends*, 62; WPA, *Nevada*, 270; DeQuille, *History*, 69; Bancroft, *Nevada*, 144–47; Lyman, *Saga*, 83; George D. Lyman, *Ralston's Ring*, 70, 91–95 116–17, 168–89, 240, 270; Glasscock, *Big Bonanza*, 156–57, 182, 206–209, 230–35, 255–56, 297, 313–14, 351; Gilbert H. Kneiss, *Bonanza Railroads*, 54.

which he was to struggle for years to finance and which was to make him one of the most discussed men on the Washoe. This idea was for a tunnel, thrust into Mt. Davidson from Eagle Valley so that it would hit the Comstock Lode at 1,650 feet. Below the level any of the mines had reached in 1860, the tunnel would solve the difficult water problem by draining all the shafts. It would enable companies to work upward from it to their ore body as well as downward from the surface. It would facilitate ventilation considerably; it would provide a means of escape when disaster struck; it would be a cheap route for hauling ore from the mines to the mills on the Carson River—a feature especially attractive to Sutro because he had visions of owning all the smelters to be built at the tunnel's mouth. Throughout the long years he pressed the plan, he alienated a great many people with his reiteration of how the mills at his city would eclipse those elsewhere and how everybody would move to his town. To many, his vanity, his aggressiveness, and his "insufferable egotism" made him personally offensive. In some way a man with more diplomacy might have accomplished his end more easily, but considering the difficulties he was to face, his dogged determination considerably outweighed any defects in personality.

At first Sutro seemed to have success easily within his grasp. Various mining companies began to approve his plan and to promise him, when his tunnel connected with their operations, a royalty of two dollars per ton on all ore they produced. The state of Nevada and the federal government authorized his tunnel, and he secured subscriptions for a considerable amount of money, those associated with the Bank of California, a financial power on the Comstock which will be discussed later, promising him $600,000.

Sutro's good fortune quickly turned to ill luck. His continued remarks about his own mills at the mouth of his tunnel aroused not a little discomfort among the Bank of California people, especially William C. Ralston and William Sharon; they themselves controlled a considerable number of smelters. They and others, partly through their influence, repudiated their pledges of aid. When Sutro turned to New York City for financial support, he had much difficulty in explaining why experienced Washoe mining interests were withdrawing their support and especially why the Bank of California had circularized important eastern financiers to warn them of its action.

Unsuccessful on the Atlantic seaboard, he went on to Paris, only to have interest in his project evaporate as the threat of a war with Prussia arose.

Returning to Nevada, Sutro continued to do what he could. When the House Ways and Means Committee visited the Comstock in 1868, Sharon tried to monopolize its members, but despite the banker's plans, Sutro managed to sneak in a word, to take the congressmen briefly to the roof of the International Hotel and explain his views on the proper development of the region. The next year, he seized on the disastrous Crown Point–Yellow Jacket–Kentuck fire as an opportunity to issue a striking poster. It contained two views, one depicting miners struggling upward through the flames to certain death and another showing them quietly descending into the safe exit of his tunnel.

The year 1870 was an eventful one for Sutro. A Nevada member of the U. S. House of Representatives introduced a bill revoking Sutro's authority to collect his two-dollar royalty from tunnel users. The Ways and Means Committee reported the measure to the House unfavorably. It failed there of passage, 124 to 42. Sutro himself was busy negotiating in Paris and was just on the verge of finally arranging with Erlanger and Company for a fifteen-million-franc loan when the Franco-Prussian War began and blasted his hopes. Turning to the United States Congress, he persuaded it to send out a commission to examine the Comstock and report on the desirability of his tunnel. He hurried off to England, where success attended his efforts and McCalmont's Bank pledged $2,500,000 toward the completion of his project.

In 1872, the three-man congressional commission published its findings. The trio of engineers declared that the tunnel was feasible but said they thought the estimated cost of $4,418,329.50 was disproportionate to the advantages to be gained from it. Their opinion stunned Sutro, who quickly concluded that their arguments were actually those of mine superintendents known to be dominated by the Bank of California. He persuaded the House Committee on Mines and Mining to hold a hearing on the whole question of his tunnel. At the meeting he acted as his own counsel and the Bank of California sent as its representative one of its best attorneys. In his cross-examination, Sutro sent the bank and its lawyer down to defeat. He proved that he knew more about the ventilation and drainage of the mines than anybody else. He so impressed the committee that it sustained him, not merely in its report, but also by introducing a bill authorizing for him a federal loan of two million dollars; its measure failed to pass the House. However, the committee's confidence so encouraged McCalmont's Bank that it promised to loan Sutro more money. Just as Sutro thought he had secured it, Robert McCalmont was stricken with paralysis and others members of the firm refused then or later to pay out the funds. Again Sutro conducted a vigorous campaign to raise money from any individuals he could persuade and finally did secure enough to complete his project. While his determined surmounting of every financial obstacle is admirable, it is a fact that every one of the fancy claims he made in a prospectus to support his bond issue proved false.[10]

Sutro launched construction of his tunnel on faith, before he was at all sure where funds to complete it would some from. In the initial work he used horses, but, unfortunately, whenever their ears touched an overhanging rock, they instinctively jerked their heads upward and cracked their necks or their skulls. As substitutes he secured mules, whose habit was automatically to pull their heads down to safety when their ears felt a rock. As work progressed, the heat became increasingly severe until it was almost more than man or animal could stand, even when air was continually pumped in. To add to the difficulties, some of the mules would thrust their noses into the air vents and would not move; they had to be forcibly pulled away.

The tunnel was completed on July 8, 1878. It was four miles long, sixteen feet wide, and twelve feet high. Along its floor ran drainage flumes, surmounted by two tracks for horse-drawn cars. Its cost is a matter of dispute; Sutro's brother Theodore insisted the amount was $3,500,000, but when Eliot Lord made his careful investigation of the Comstock area, he set the figure at $2,096,556.

Useful as the tunnel might have been when Sutro first envisaged it in the early 1860's, the project was finished too late. The completed tunnel never had any real bearing on the development of the Comstock, never transported ore to any mill at its mouth, never provided an escape avenue from disaster for any miner, and contributed little to the system of ventilation already perfected. It did provide ample drainage, in 1880 disposing of two billion gallons of water. Had the

10 Smith, *History*, 111.

119

project been pushed through by the middle 1860's, it would have bene-
fited the whole area greatly. That it was not was a reflection on Sutro,
who dreamed too hard of owning mills at the tunnel mouth, mills that
would enable him to "squeeze" the whole Washoe, and upon such
mining interests as the Bank of California group, who feared to share
even a small bit of their Comstock profits. Had all these people been
willing to compromise a little, to be reasonable, great benefits might
have resulted.

When Sutro finally saw the day his tunnel was completely dug, his
contracts with the mine owners had all been repudiated by them long
since. But the Hale and Norcross mine encountered such a sudden
rise of water that its owners could not handle it, so without asking
permission or hinting at a payment, they began pumping it into
Sutro's tunnel. He promptly built two immense, watertight doors
of solid oak and threatened to seal them shut in such a way as really
to flood the Hale and Norcross. Its owners and those of other mines
then came to terms with Sutro, compromising and signing a contract.
Two years later, he had a severe quarrel with his board of directors,
resigned, sold his stock without too much delay, and departed from
the Comstock a millionaire; he went to San Francisco and was very
successful as a developer of urban real estate tracts. His tunnel continued in operation until the 1940's, but it was not successful financially. The market value of its stock gradually sank from six and one-
half dollars a share to six cents, and in 1889, the mortgage holders
foreclosed.

How to refine ore efficiently was a problem long faced on the Comstock.[11] Shipment to mills in Swansea, Wales, or Freiberg, Saxony,
was too expensive, even in the early days. At first the Comstockers
used the so-called patio process. On an area paved with flat stones,
the ore was spread out and a drove of mules driven round and round
in it, stamping the material into pulp. This slow, expensive process
the Washoers replaced with the arrastra, a device much used in California. Arrastras could not handle the large volume of ore the Comstock began producing, however, and after two years of experimenta-
tion, Almarin B. Paul devised the Washoe process for reducing ore,

11 Lyman, Saga, 135–39; DeQuille, History, 71–72, and Big Bonanza, 92–93,
257–65; Smith, History, 41–42, 253–54; Lord, Comstock Mining, 124–25, 248; Rickard, American Mining, 102; Gorham, My Memories, 59–60; Lillard, Desert Challenge, 222.

which, with improvements, was used throughout the boom days of the area. It owed much to methods used in California previously. The basic idea was to settle out some impurities, to use quicksilver for separating the valuable metal from the remaining waste, and finally to detach the mercury from the pure bars of ore. Along with the quicksilver, a little salt and sulphate of copper were mixed in. In the early days, when so little was known of the proper process, other minor ingredients were added in vain attempts to improve it. Potash, borax, saltpeter, alum, cedar tea, sagebrush tea, and Australian sheep-dip were tried unsuccessfully. The idea for using some of these unusual elements originated with the mill superintendents themselves, but others came from "process peddlers," who alleged they knew the key to unusual success and would reveal it for a suitable price.

A large number of small mills early sprang up on the Washoe, but later smelting was consolidated into large units. Some of the early plants were successful from the start, but others were not. The first mill for the Gould and Curry mine was, according to Eliot Lord, "the most conspicuous monument of inexperience and extravagance ever erected in a mining district." On the exterior, it resembled the mansion of a wealthy landowner and was built in the form of a Greek cross, 250 feet long and with arms 75 feet in length and 50 feet in breadth. When an addition was first discussed, some of the directors demurred because it would ruin the symmetry of the cross. The initial plant cost nearly $900,000, but a short trial revealed the machinery for smelting the ore to be so unsatisfactory that the whole mill had to be reconstructed "almost from the foundation" at the additional expense of $560,893.

The cost of refining, fifty dollars a ton as late as 1867, was reduced in the 1870's to eleven or twelve. The silver and gold recovered from the ore was at first only 65 per cent of the actual content, but later, by use of better methods, this was improved to 85 per cent. The additional bullion saved went to the milling company, however, and not to its customer, the mining corporation. Eventually the use of electricity, cyanide, and flotation methods made possible recovery as much as 95 per cent.

Typical of the Comstock in its bonanza days was the smelting process which Dan DeQuille described in 1876. After preliminary crushing, the ore was pulverized under huge stamping machines (whose din was tremendous), atomized further by grinding, and placed in a pan of quicksilver and heated to fuse the silver and mercury into an amalgam. It was then placed in a second pan, where the valueless rock was separated from the amalgam, drawn through a hydraulic strainer to pull out part of the quicksilver, and gradually subjected to intense heat, which separated the rest of the mercury from the pure silver bullion.

Usually the mills were corporations entirely independent from the companies owning the mines. In slack times much competition arose between the various smelters for the available business. They sought it by persuasive salesmanship, by attempting to capitalize on personal friendship, and by offering what was not too uncommon in the business world of that generation but is now considered unethical, a bribe in the form of a percentage kickback to certain mining-company officials on the fees paid. Often the smelters were owned as a private investment by those capitalists dominating a mining company, and the general public came to accept this practice. Another unorthodox method used by "insiders" to swell their bank accounts called for gathering up discarded, supposedly worthless rock left over from the smelting and reworking it as a private venture to squeeze out the last remaining minerals. Still another profitable device was to own a lumber company or a concern furnishing other vital supplies to the mine.

Stock ownership in most mines was spread among a wide variety of people.[12] To facilitate sales in Nevada shares, the San Francisco Stock and Exchange Board was established in September, 1862. It started with thirty-seven member brokers, who in their dealings in stock spoke not of "per share" but rather "per foot," as was the custom in selling a portion of a mining claim. The exchange enjoyed a large volume of sales, for speculation was so widespread that sometimes the number of shares in a particular mine which changed hands would twice a week equal the total number issued by the company. With such lively activity, it is no wonder that brokers and speculators watched each other like hawks! They knew that there were always some mines in *borrasca,* a streak of bad luck, perhaps temporary, and others in bonanza; shortly the status might be exactly reversed. They

12 Lyman, *Saga,* 219; Smith, *History,* 19, 174–79, 199, 209–10, 282; Lord, *Comstock Mining,* 290–91; Bancroft, *Nevada,* 129; DeQuille, *Big Bonanza,* 115, 301–308, 345–46, 381–82; Glasscock, *Big Bonanza,* 293, 301–304; Lillard, *Desert Challenge,* 223; Rickard, *American Mining,* 110.

were stimulated by visions of a sudden shift from *borrasca* to bonanza, putting into their eager hands great and sudden wealth. The speculators and managers kept many an unproductive mine working in the hope a discovery would bring just such an abrupt shift to rich ore. They paid expenses by levying an assessment on each share of stock.

Obviously, when a mine was in *borrasca,* its stock plunged to a low price; if there were a hint of bonanza, it quickly rose. Managers and other insiders sought to keep any discovery a secret among themselves and to buy as many shares as possible at a bargain price. Sometimes, when faced with a good prospect, they levied an additional assessment, stiff enough to discourage many stockholders into selling cheaply. The directors of the mining company usually employed a secret shift of their oldest and most reliable men at the point where they were exploiting a discovery or unusual new development. They assisted these employees to buy a little stock at a low price and purchased considerably more for themselves. To insure as much silence as possible, they sometimes kept these men underground for a week or two, with fancy foods and liquors, at company expense, to while away off-duty hours. If these miners somehow revealed the secret before the time set, each man was discharged; he could not secure work on the secret shift of another mine until the guilty person was found. In any event, the excellent spy system maintained on the Comstock by interested persons prevented any good discovery from remaining unknown for very long. When the news was out, everybody wanted to buy stock in the bonanza mine; the price would soar, usually too high, and shares in adjacent mines would rise in sympathy. Then perhaps the public would grow restive if a yield uniformly rich was not immediately produced and the price would fall again, usually too low. Often a series of swings alternating the value of shares would develop. These shifts were made greater by the actions of the bears (the pessimists) or the bulls (the optimists).

In one famous instance when the stock of a particular company obviously had just become much more valuable and news was released first at Virginia City, a broker monopolized the telegraph line from there for two hours; at a cost of only three hundred dollars he thus bought enough time and continued ignorance of the development to enable his San Francisco associates to buy up a large portion of the stock.

There was a great variety of Nevada mining stock available to suit the tastes of every kind of purchaser. Some of it was in famous bonanza mines, some in long-established ones now in *borrasca,* and some in relatively unestablished ones, either wildly speculative or downright frauds. Most buyers diversified their holdings in shares and were firmly convinced that at least one of these would make their fortunes, but generally they were wrong. They lived, mostly, in one of two areas —Virginia City or San Francisco; on the Comstock, even Chinese who could not read participated enthusiastically in stock speculation.

An excellent example of the kind of excitement that could arise is that occasioned by the discovery of the Big Bonanza in the Consolidated Virginia and California mines. Before it was announced, the market value of all Comstock securities listed on the San Francisco Stock and Exchange Board was (on November 22, 1874) about $93,000,000. Within the thirty days following the release of the news, the total price rose to $175,147,200 and on January 7, 1875, stood at $300,000,000. This was far above the total assessed value of all San Francisco real estate of the time, $190,000,000.

In contrast to this boom, there were several crashes in the market. The worst, in 1877, literally made beggars out of many Californians and Nevadans; at its depth in San Francisco, some twenty thousand people a day were being fed by charity.

In the 1880's, "bucket sales," a common but undesirable practice, arose. When a customer bought a stock on margin, he usually made a cash deposit of half the price and for the rest gave his broker an I.O.U., with interest at the rate of at least 2 per cent a month. The purchaser now assumed that he owned the stock but did not ask the dealer actually to deliver a stock certificate. The broker in fact did not have or purchase the stock for his customer but assumed that he could do so later if necessary at the price his patron had paid, or lower.

Of the major financiers whose names came to be linked with Comstock mining stocks, one of the most well known was a San Franciscan, William C. Ralston.[13] In 1864, he organized, with D. O. Mills, the Bank of California, which almost immediately became the leading financial institution of the Far West. As its guiding figure, although officially only a cashier, he faced a difficult problem when the bank's

13 Lyman, *Ralston's Ring,* 9–351; Julian Dana, *The Man Who Built San Francisco: A Study of Ralston's Journey with Banners,* 117–386; Smith, *History,* 51; Lewis, *Silver Kings,* 215–52; Drury, *Editor,* 118–20; Mack, *Nevada,* 455; Gorham, *My Memories,* 25, 82–84; Glasscock, *Big Bonanza,* 151–75, 211–13, 231, 270, 348–50.

agents on the Comstock, Stateler and Arrington, badly overdrew their account. To retrieve the money, he sent to Virginia City one William Sharon, a California speculator long on experience but, for the moment, short in personal funds. While Sharon was successfully recovering the overdraft, he became convinced that the most profitable policy for the Bank of California would be to monopolize the Comstock, both above ground and below. He argued so persuasively that Ralston sent more bank money to bolster up mines already heavily in debt to the bank in the hope that they would surely discover new bodies of ore. To attract the business of mines obtaining funds elsewhere, they cut interest charges from the usual 3.0 to 3.5 per cent a month to 1.25 or even 1.0 per cent. When a company could not meet a payment which fell due, the bank ruthlessly foreclosed in its determination to monopolize the area.

Not only mines but smelters, too, fell into the hands of the Bank of California. These mills were then transferred to the private ownership of Sharon, Ralston, Mills, and others in the privy councils of the bank, who organized the Union Mill and Mining Company. There were risks, to be sure, but there were also possibilities of large profits, and these were to be channeled, not into the bank, but into the pockets of the few insiders. The new company sometimes persuaded a mine deliberately to mix worthless ore with the valuable, to obtain plenty of profit for the mill even if there was none for the mine's stockholders. It pressured those companies in debt to the Bank of California to patronize its smelters. Within a short time, Mills netted more than two million dollars from his stock; Ralston and Sharon got more than over four million each. In two years' time the company obtained ownership of seventeen mills and the few independents had a starvation diet indeed. Ralston, Sharon, Mills, and their friends augmented their virtual monopoly of the mills by building the Virginia and Truckee Railroad and securing a strangle hold on the supplying of timber to the Comstock.

The millions Ralston wrung from his Comstock investments were fed into the insatiable maw of his magnificent but quixotic concept of a greater San Francisco. Without adequately appraising the immediate difficulties and by looking to what might be the distant future as if it were tomorrow's reality, he expected to make the city into a strong industrial center serving the entire coast and to create also a great cultural center that would rival his model, New Orleans.

To say that he gave San Francisco a lover's devotion would be romanticizing only slightly. He correctly believed there would be a place for each of his undertakings in the economy of the city and the West, but he badly underestimated the length of time and the necessary general development of the whole area. He was right that San Francisco would become great, but it has never been as dominant of the whole Far West as he dreamed it would be.

Real trouble first arose for Ralston's undertakings when the completion of the transcontinental railroad in 1869 deluged San Francisco with all sorts of goods made in the East and delivered to the bay area cheaper than Ralston's companies could manufacture them locally. His empire would have collapsed promptly had he not sustained it with dividends on his stock in the Union Mill and Mining Company and the Virginia and Truckee Railroad. To aid further, he turned to his own bank for loans.

Ralston was still in serious difficulties, needing every cent he could squeeze from his Washoe holdings, when he and his associates lost the Crown Point mine in 1871. Things had not been going well with the property and it was not highly regarded. When a rich discovery was made there unexpectedly, John P. Jones, its superintendent, and Alvinza Hayward resolved not to inform their superior and instead secretly secured almost all of the company's stock. For Ralston and his group to lose the mine was bad enough, but for the banker himself to forfeit the dividends at the time he so badly needed the money was much worse.

Further financial adversity struck Ralston in 1872 when he and his group backed their associate, William Sharon, for United States senator against their new enemy, John P. Jones. In unsuccessfully trying to destroy Jones financially, Sharon unintentionally precipitated in the market a crash which trimmed $48,834,000 from the value of Comstock securities. When he next sought unsuccessfully to bribe a mine foreman into saying that Jones himself had set the disastrous Yellow Jacket–Crown Point–Kentuck fire of 1869, Sharon caused another crash. His actions hurt Ralston, even though dividends continued unabated. The banker's position continued to deteriorate until in February, 1873, his various companies had on loan two-thirds of the Bank of California's total assets.

In 1874, Ralston undertook to buy control of the Ophir mine, located right next to the Big Bonanza of the Consolidated Virginia, but others got the same idea and the upward swing of prices put him to much additional expense; he spent at least three million dollars on this venture. When Sharon learned that the bonanza did not extend into the Ophir after all and started selling his shares rapidly, his large transactions quickly drove the quotation on the mine's securities downward, despite Ralston's frantic efforts to sustain the price. The net result was that the banker was left holding much of the company's stock, for which he had paid more than he could now resell it. Ralston began selling his private property at bargain prices. Two San Francisco newspapers and the wire services of the Associated Press began spreading discreditable stories about him. A further tumble in the stock market caused so many people in a panic to withdraw their deposits from the Bank of California that, closing its doors, it suspended all operations. Ralston, with debts of nine and one-half million dollars and assets he appraised at four and one-half million, turned over absolutely all of his personal property for the benefit of his creditors. His resignation from the bank was forced. That afternoon, Ralston went for a swim in the Pacific and drowned. Some said it was suicide, others declared it a horrible accident, but which it was will never be known.

What San Francisco thought of Ralston was demonstrated by the length of his funeral procession—six miles. Beyond debate he was an unusually generous man. He had a vision of San Francisco's ultimate greatness more correct than that of most of his contemporaries, and he exerted himself to the utmost to turn dream into reality. As a financier who lent his bank's money heavily to his own corporations and who sometimes purchased the bank's assets when he knew they would increase mightily in value, he fell considerably below the standards of conduct required for a banker today. Judged by the criteria of his own era, however, he only did on a larger scale what many another man was doing and the chief complaint against him was not the actions themselves but their extensiveness and their final lack of success.

While Ralston and his associates were still powerful on the Comstock, another group arose to an eminent position, the Bonanza Four: John W. Mackay, James G. Fair, James C. Flood, and William S. O'Brien.[14] Mackay and Fair were long experienced in the mines;

[14] Lewis, *Silver Kings*, 43–268; Drury, *Editor*, 63–65; Smith, *History*, 103–105, 148, 157, 220–21, 262, 267.

Flood and O'Brien ran a San Francisco saloon and began following the advice of those customers who were proved by results to be real experts on the stock market. When Mackay and Fair decided it would be wise to buy up the stock of the Hale and Norcross mine, they added to their partnership Flood and O'Brien as specialists in the purchase of securities. Eventually the four undertook a definite campaign to search for further minerals by gaining control of some unproductive mines between the Ophir on the north and the Best and Belcher on the south. They followed a slender clay seam from the bottom of the Gould and Curry shaft through the Best and Belcher into the Consolidated Virginia, where they found the Big Bonanza. In later years Fair liked to say that the whole idea of where to make the find was his own and that once he saw the vein, knife thin, he doggedly followed it until he made the great discovery. In reality, he probably got the idea of where to look from Pat McKay of the Gould and Curry, and certainly the mine superintendent in charge when the discovery was actually made was T. F. Smith. The vein itself was hardly knife thin, for "a blind man driving a four-horse team could have followed it in a snowstorm."[15]

The Bonanza Four, in the opinion of that careful historian Grant H. Smith, played a fairer game than any other group which controlled mines on the Comstock. They never bought a property except to look for ore, and if they were unsuccessful, they promptly sold it. They never manipulated the operations in a mine to depress the market price of its stock. They never sent ore to be processed at their private smelters unless it was of high enough grade to give a mine's stockholders no loss at the very least. They saw to it that each company they controlled paid dividends whenever possible; in all, these amounted to about eighty million dollars. They did more extensive deep development than anybody else. For themselves, the total in profits from their enterprises was about sixty-two million dollars. This they divided approximately as follows: ten million to O'Brien, twelve million to Flood, fifteen million to Fair, and twenty-five million to Mackay.

The Bonanza Four were vigorously attacked by Squire P. Dewey. He was angry because he thought at the time of the great surface fire in Virginia City in 1875 that all indications showed he should sell his stock in their mines; he did so and shortly the market price

15 Lewis, *Silver Kings*, 156.

went up instead of down. He issued against the partners a pamphlet which lawyer-historian Smith has characterized as "a clever piece of evasion and misrepresentation." At the time, his charges attracted much attention. Four suits were brought against the Bonanza Four; they defeated three and the fourth they compromised rather than appeal it to a higher court.

At first the partners kept their funds deposited in Ralston's Bank of California, but in 1875 established their own institution, the Nevada Bank. Their venture naturally inconvenienced Ralston. Aside from the legitimate withdrawal of their money from the Bank of California to launch their own enterprise, however, they did nothing which could be described as a cause contributing to the disastrous run on Ralston's institution.

John W. Mackay distributed about one-fifth of his twenty-five million Comstock dollars as charity, sometimes under the guise of a loan and frequently with the stipulation that the donor remain secret. He had secured only a slight formal education as a youth, and this made him overmodest. Actually he developed into a person of distinction—well read, widely traveled, a lover of good music, a patron of the drama, and a judicious observer of good paintings. In business, his years of handling great affairs gained him much experience. His wife was highly ambitious socially; he, without cavil, supplied the necessary funds. For well over twenty years they lived apart, he attending to business in such places as Virginia City, she creating a considerable stir in fashionable Paris and London society. When he visited her, he liked to shock the European wellborn by telling them greatly exaggerated stories of how humble his origins were and how uncivilized his early life had been. In 1883, Mackay sold out his remaining Comstock holdings. Thereafter he devoted himself to a transatlantic cable business and to upbuilding the Postal Telegraph Company, a mighty rival to Western Union until the two merged in 1943.

James G. Fair was one of the ablest practical miners ever to develop in the West. Less admirable were his unshakable faith in his own judgment and his conviction that everybody else was a knave, a fool, or both. He got elected to the United States Senate, only to find the post tiresome and dull. When he withdrew from the Comstock, he invested his fortune so wisely in San Francisco real estate that it increased about threefold in twelve years. When his wife won a divorce in 1883 on the ground of "habitual adultery," it caused a great sensation. She was supported in the litigation by her husband's three partners, and this ended his friendship with them.

William S. O'Brien was a man of plebeian tastes who had no wish to raise himself socially or culturally. He contributed a mild-mannered diplomacy to the group but never carried his quarter of its responsibilities. He himself said he simply caught hold of the tail of an ascending kite and hung on.

James C. Flood was the expert on stock-exchange operations for the partnership. He placed great emphasis upon unity among the four of them.

6

LIFE IN THE NEVADA MINES

THE operations of the Bonanza Four, the Bank of California group, and many others did not greatly affect the men who actually worked underground extracting the ore.[1] These were ordinary laborers, raised above the average lot of workers by the kind of task they were set at and by the need to use their intelligence more. Their jobs were likely enough to undermine their health, so many believed in a short life and a merry one. Some 1,996 of them were employed underground, a survey made in 1880 showed; their average age was thirty-five, average weight 165 pounds, and average height five feet, nine inches; most of them were married. In the earliest times they had worked underground ten hours a shift, but they began asking for an eight-hour day. They secured it gradually; it did not become standard on the Comstock until John P. Jones, to bolster his campaign for the post of United States senator, ordered it established in his mine after April 1, 1872, and most other owners promptly followed his example. Later in the 1870's, the state legislature enacted the eight-hour day into law for certain types of labor in the mining industry.

The miners were at first paid between $3.50 and $4.00 a day, but by 1867, the Miners Union enforced a universal scale of $4.00. The same remuneration went to a novice as was paid to an experienced, veteran worker. The cost of labor was high enough for the mining companies to make vigorous efforts at mechanization. Wages were paid out in cash to the men, who lined up for the purpose on the first to the third of each month. The Miners Union required that

[1] DeQuille, *Big Bonanza*, 340–43; Smith, *History*, 241–43; Lord, *Comstock Mining*, 182–90, 209–14, 262–68, 357–81.

none but its men should be employed. It tried to discourage the emigration of any workers to the Washoe in times of *borrasca,* but never to the extent of prohibiting the entry of white laborers. Its membership dues were $2.00 a month. The union would provide not over $80.00 a year toward the care of a sick member and would provide not over $80.00 in funeral expenses. The payments for illness were usually supplemented by a gift from the mining company. In times of *borrasca,* when employment dropped, the first to be discharged were the married men, for as a class they were considered less vigorous, energetic, and daring than the single men.

Miners generally wore coarse, cheap clothing, which they mended and patched themselves. They used leather belts and were not very particular about buttons.[2] Many a miner lived in his own cheaply constructed wooden shack. Typically it was never painted, was plainly furnished, had interior walls of cloth or paper, and lacked any type of garden. If the owner cooked his own food, he probably specialized in flapjacks, beans, bacon, and coffee; if he didn't, he boarded at a restaurant for eight to twelve dollars a week. Bachelors often lived in a small cubicle in one of the many boxlike boarding-houses. These were heated by cast-iron stoves, lighted by candles or kerosene, and had their toilets in the back yard. They charged forty to sixty dollars a month for board and lodging in good times, but less in bad. The professional people, the mine administrators, and the merchants lived in ornate, well-kept houses.

There were always accidents in the mines, even with more emphasis upon carefulness and increasing installations of safety devices.[3] Mishaps occurred to old-timers more commonly than to greenhorns, nervously on the lookout for trouble. One source of constant danger was the ascent from the torrid heat in the lower workings to the much cooler surface temperature. The men had to guard against fainting and falling out of the cage. Another dangerous possibility, especially if the miners were sweaty and half-dressed, was that of contracting pneumonia. No formal record was kept of the accidents in mines, but by reading through the newspapers from October 16, 1863, to June 19, 1880, Eliot Lord tallied 295 fatal and 608 nonfatal accidents.

2 Lewis, *Silver Kings,* 25–26; Lord, *Comstock Mining,* 200; DeQuille, *Big Bonanza,* 72; Shinn, *Story of the Mine,* 63.

3 Lord, *Comstock Mining,* 374, 404; DeQuille, *Big Bonanza,* 145, 150.

A few real disasters struck the Comstock.[4] For example, the entire workings of the Mexican mine to a depth of 225 feet simply collapsed and dropped, in the summer of 1863, with such a force that rock and timber were swept into the adjacent Ophir mine, obliterating 50 feet of its drift. This brought such pressure on the Ophir's second and third levels that they fell, dragging down shaft house, machinery and all surface workings into the pit.

Worse than such a collapse to the mind of the average miner was fire. In illustrating how much fear this possibility caused, Dan DeQuille observed: "Let but a splinter of pine be held in a candle, and soon the smell of burning wood is detected by the miners, above and around, and there is a commotion such as is seen when a hive of bees is disturbed . . . ."[5] The most serious fire in a Comstock mine struck the adjoining Yellow Jacket, Crown Point, and Kentuck mines in 1869. It burned, smothered, and caused to be crushed to death at least thirty-five miners, perhaps forty-nine. First attempts to fight it by pouring water down the shaft had the horrible result of reversing the air flow downward and carrying the flames back onto the entombed miners. After five days, with no hope that anybody remained alive, the fire fighters sealed off the mine and forced down steam. In two more days it was reopened, only to have the fresh air start the blaze anew and force resealing. Fourteen days later another attempt brought the same result. Finally, thirty-nine days after the fire started, some drifts could be reopened and used but others could not. Three years later the temporarily abandoned parts of the mine were reopened and pronounced usable, although in spots the rocks were still red hot.

Above ground a major fire hit Virginia City on October 26, 1875, at six o'clock in the morning. It roared uncontrolled through two thousand of the town's three thousand buildings, destroying more than ten million dollars' worth of property. So intense was the heat that it fused a pile of car wheels into one solid mass. So rapid were the flames that the later, more famous earthquake and fire which ravaged San Francisco for three days "must have been an orderly and unexciting affair compared with it." Within sixty days of the disaster

[4] Glasscock, *Big Bonanza*, 131, 193–94, 278–79; Lillard, *Desert Challenge*, 229; DeQuille, *History*, 53–56, and *Big Bonanza*, 125–31.

[5] *Big Bonanza*, 143.

the business district of Virginia City was rebuilt with larger, finer structures, and full reconstruction in the residential areas quickly followed.

Water adequate in quantity and quality was at first a problem.[6] The initial supply came from tunnels driven into the mountain. When these proved inadequate, new ones were drilled, which for a few days produced a great flood and after that only a very moderate flow. Still, Virginia City frequently suffered from shortage. To relieve the situation, capitalists turned to the Sierra Nevada Mountains, twenty-five miles away, and built a pipeline. A careful survey of the precise route was made and specifications were drawn up for the special manufacturing of the pipe, which was to be made in unusual forms in order to conform exactly to the variation in topography. Water flowed through the line with great pressure, thanks to the intake's being 465 feet higher than the outlet. In 1875, three independent sets of water mains were completed in the city: one for ordinary use, one for the mines, and one for fire fighting only.

In the neighborhood of the Washoe, other necessities—salt, soda, and copper—were secured, but coal had to be imported. Gas manufacture began in Virginia City in 1863.[7]

The first public school on the Comstock began as a result of a wild escapade.[8] Theater patrons were startled one night when two important miners, armed with six-shooters and bowie knives, marched down the aisle and ordered the curtain lowered. Disobeyed, they charged the stage, the actors fled, and the curtain slammed down. The two later grew so ashamed of what they had done to win a barroom wager that they launched a drive for a school, in penance contributing one thousand dollars. This was christened the "Rowdy Fund," and eventually it came to contain enough to pay a year's salary for a teacher. The post went to Harry Floty, an instructor trained in the East who had found two years of western prospecting enough.

The first day at the new school, Floty began class by laying his bowie knife and three six-shooters on his desk. When the first student whispered, Floty covered him with a revolver and cautioned him never to do it again, for there would be no second warning. When

6 *Ibid.*, 168–73.
7 Lord, *Comstock Mining*, 202–205.
8 Lyman, *Saga*, 227–29; Becker, *Geology*, 5.

recess came and a student threw a ball into the air, the teacher seized the opportunity to put a bullet into it before it started to descend. From this unorthodox beginning, a school system gradually evolved. Its attendance was never as great as a town the size of Virginia City would ordinarily have because more than the usual number of men were either unmarried or maintained their families elsewhere. An 1889 survey of children between the ages of six and eighteen revealed that 763 were not enrolled anywhere, 543 were in private institutions, and 2,565 were in public schools.

On the Comstock, decent people far outnumbered the nondecent types.[9] The two classes did not interfere with each other, except when some of the lower element had difficulties with the laxly enforced laws. A common saying of both groups was that "every man has a right to go to hell in his own way." These were a robust and free-living people, such as Shakespeare had written for, and that is one reason why his plays were so popular on the Comstock. Individualists, the people took a friendly interest in each other. They had pride in keeping their word and despised a liar. Humor was regarded as the spice of life, but in front of women a suggestive joke or even mild profanity was taboo. On the Washoe there was liberality with money and a spirit of helpfulness. Because no formal charitable facilities ever arose, every man about town was supposed, as a part of his civic duty, to support or at least to aid somebody who needed it. The habit of spending freely was reflected in the high-quality goods which most merchants carried because there was a brisk demand; inferior products they found difficult to move from their shelves. The diamonds available in Virginia City would have commanded a good market in Paris, and the best-quality food would have distinguished New York's finest restaurants.

As social distinctions arose, the elite began to erect their homes on the higher land above C Street and to furnish them with the best that money could buy. The various upper class groups periodically sponsored a ball, which they prided themselves in making in every respect "high-toned." On one occasion the Ivy Social Club borrowed every canary in town (they were numerous at the time) and kept them for several days in a darkened cellar. On the night of the dance the

9 Smith, *History*, 29–31, 234–35; Drury, *Editor*, 99; Lewis, *Silver Kings*, 6; Lillard, *Desert Challenge*, 228; Glasscock, *Big Bonanza*, 113; WPA, *Nevada*, 278; Max Miller, *Reno*, 69.

cages were suspended from the ceiling in rows and there was little indeed for the orchestra to do.

High society and low took much interest in a variety of recreations.[10] One form of relaxation was to bet at the horse races, for there were frequent competitions and a number of animals to choose from. At one time interest in the abilities of two newly arrived horses rose to such a pitch that the handler was liberally plied with liquor and a trial heat, unbeknown to the owner, was run. The gray won over the bay, but later at the official race the victory went to the bay. Much loud talk of double-crossing arose until the handler finally disclosed had he had deceived the clandestine clockers by loading the shoes of the bay with plates of lead until the great day came.

Other recreations included wrestling, prize fighting, cockfighting, badger contests, chasing coyotes with greyhounds, rifle or pistol shooting, bear fights, bear-bull fights, and bear-dog fights. At one of the competitions a bear broke loose and chased his manager twice around the hall, sending the audience on the main floor swarming up the pillars to safety while the gallery loudly cheered the bear.

For music, there were always plenty of fiddlers available. "All frontiers are alive with fiddlers, because the fiddle is the only complete orchestra that can be carried in a green flannel bag under your arm." To perform on it successfully was a gift given only to the few and was usually alien to those who became expert violinists in the formal sense. Most fiddlers could not read music and often, instead of playing well-known tunes of the day, simply improvised.

Music was frequently heard in the Comstock theaters.[11] Many professionals appeared at Walter's Music Hall, a favorite if rather low-class place of entertainment. Its manager paid high prices for his performers, but unfortunately, his sole standard of their artistic merit was how much they demanded for an appearance. One of his choices that proved less than wise was a singer from Boston, Antoinette Adams. She had the appearance of a New England spinster, with a crooked mouth, faded blond hair, stooped shoulders, and a long neck, and she was old enough to be the aunt of most of her Virginia City audience. Worst of all, whatever singing ability she might once have had, had by now completely disappeared, and the

10 Gorham, My Memories, 181; Drury, Editor, 82–91; 106–108.

11 Gorham, My Memories, 134; Drury, Editor, 35, 41–47, 54–60; Lyman, Saga, 199–201, 239, 271–82.

way she cracked on the high notes was painful to even an untrained ear. That she had reached the age of retirement, when she should be living on a pension, was so obvious to some Gold Hill men that they undertook to provide her with one in a unique fashion. They all came to one of her performances and repeatedly called her back for encores, each time she appeared showering the stage with silver half-dollars. When "her bellows would not work" any longer, she smiled and bowed until she could not totter out again. With enough money pitched onto the stage to last her the rest of her life, she wisely left town the next day.

A caliber of performer better than those at Walter's Music Hall appeared at Maguire's New Opera House, opened on July 2, 1863. At the time there was no handsomer theater in San Francisco. Its stage was quite large and the curtain depicted Lake Tahoe as seen from the summit of the Sierras. The auditorium itself contained a double tier of boxes and had crystal chandeliers. For those who might find the chief attraction a bit dull, there was a billiard parlor, a smoking room, a mahogany bar inlaid with ivory, and green-covered gambling tables.

A noted American performer came to Maguire's in December, 1863—the humorist Artemus Ward. In preliminary negotiations Maguire had wired him "What will you take for a hundred nights?" and received the answer "Brandy and Soda." Ward was a tremendous success with the miners and they with him, for he found the Comstock so interesting that instead of staying a few days, as planned, he remained three weeks. Much of his spare time he spent with the staff of that well-known newspaper, the *Territorial Enterprise*.

Another tremendously popular attraction at Maguire's was The Menken, born Dolores McCord, who appeared in a dramatization of Byron's *Mazeppa*. Her audiences particularly liked the climax of the play, when she was stripped to a bit of gauze, bound to the back of a stallion, and carried dashing up the scenery's mountain.

Maguire's time yielded its predominance to a new rival, Piper's Opera House. Here the audience sat on a level, so the stage was tilted from rear to front and thus avoided cutting off the performers' feet from the gaze of those at the rear of the theater. In the orchestra the premier violinist was William Withers, Jr., who had been director of the musicians at Ford's Theater in Washington the night Lincoln was shot. Piper offered a variety of attractions over the years; some were of high quality. Of plays, Shakespeare's were the most popular and *Hamlet* the most often presented—by Edwin Booth, Lawrence Barrett, John McCullough, and Tom Keene. Piper maintained a small stock company which supported visiting stars, and when he could book nothing better, it presented plays. Its leading lady for years was Annie Adams and in 1877 her "Baby Maude," later to become one of America's truly great actresses, made her stage debut. Among the theatricals presented were a number of Drury Lane melodramas and Irish plays; among the stars, Joe Jefferson and James A. Hearne. Several groups playing *Uncle Tom's Cabin* appeared at Piper's, minstrel shows were well liked, Buffalo Bill spoke, and the Red Stocking Blondes attracted a full house. Among the serious lecturers Piper engaged were Henry Ward Beecher, Robert Ingersoll, and Henry George.

Gambling prevailed less in Virginia City than in most frontier towns, perhaps because so many played the stock market.[12] For those who wished, there were faro, roulette, euchre, keno, poker, and pedro. These activities had to be carried on behind closed doors, thanks to a law the women secured, but the ladies' many attempts to make gambling illegal all failed.

To say that enough liquor was drunk on the Comstock to float a battleship is probably literally true.[13] Many a man downed a quart of whiskey a day, year after year, by taking innumerable small drinks. His favorite saloon often served as a club. Most saloons were "bit houses," charging one bit (twelve and one-half cents) for each drink of any description; some were "two bit houses," collecting two bits (twenty-five cents) for each serving, even if exactly the same thing was available for half-price at the cheaper places. Every establishment had a free lunch; the proper etiquette for a patron was never to appear hungry or hurried, but gradually to eat a generous quantity. Most Comstockers prided themselves on drinking like gentlemen. A count made in 1876 disclosed one hundred retail liquor dealers in Virginia City and thirty-seven more in Gold Hill, not to mention the ten wholesalers and the five breweries. Once in a suit over a defective sidewalk in Virginia City, the defense tried to protect themselves by vigorously complaining that the plaintiff had been intox-

12 Drury, *Editor*, 128–37; Smith, *History*, 234.
13 Smith, *History*, 29; DeQuille, *Big Bonanza*, 268; Drury, *Editor*, 122–25.

icated. The judge ruled against them, pointing out that a drunk was as entitled to a satisfactory surface as a sober man and a great deal more in need of it.

Some men found excitement and recreation, as well as useful service, in joining one of the volunteer fire companies; these not only fought blazes but were a kind of club.[14] The most famous was Virginia Engine Company Number One, whose foreman, Tom Peasley, served Mark Twain as a model in the latter's creation Buck Fanshaw. Peasley divided the town into four wards and built a fire tower, with a watchman constantly on duty. He appointed to honorary membership the noted Julia Bulette, who often lent a hand at the pumps and was always ready to nurse back to health any member stricken while performing his duty. When the various rival organizations were consolidated into the Virginia City Volunteer Fire Department, its chief engineer was James Brown, usually called "K. B." but on more formal occasions referred to by his full nickname, "Kettle Belly." To watch the fire fighters at work was a bit of excitement which attracted most Comstockers; so, too, did civic processions, street fights, murders, inquests, and brass bands.

For those who enjoyed the company of women, there were the hurdy-gurdy houses.[15] They had a number of girls, not necessarily of bad character, who would dance with a man. In return, after each number he would lead her to the bar and she could choose whether he should buy her a drink or give her its money value, two bits. By consistently shunning the liquor, a girl could make a good living.

Much less innocent were the women of the town, for whom the law set apart a distinctive quarter located near the Chinese section. Here were "two rows of white cabins with gaudily-furnished rooms, at whose uncurtained windows the inmates sat, spider-like, waiting for flies." They dressed as close to the Paris mode as did anybody in New York City. In their rooms, so glamorous in appearance to a man straight from the mines, they enforced a strict, punctilious code of behavior; no matter how tough a male prided himself on being else-

---

[14] Drury, *Editor*, 24–25; Lyman, *Saga*, 119–21.

[15] Lord, *Comstock Mining*, 199; Twain, *Roughing It*, II, 27–28; Glasscock, *Big Bonanza*, 218–21; Ivan Benson, *Mark Twain's Western Years*, 65; Mrs. Fanny G. Hazlett and Gertrude Hazlett Randall, "Historical Sketch and Reminiscences of Dayton, Nevada," Nevada Historical Society *Papers*, Vol. III (1921–22), 53.

where, here he must be a gentleman. The most famous of Virginia City's women of the moment was Julia Bulette, a beauty of French extraction who exercised indirectly a considerable influence on the town. When she was robbed and murdered, Tom Peasley's Virginia Engine Company Number One gave her a tremendous funeral.

Religion was not as strong as some other institutions on the Comstock.[16] In the early days one of the most influential preachers was the Episcopalian Franklin S. Rising, who held his first Washoe services in his brother's courthouse. When the Methodists built their first church, of brick, it blew down; their second, also of brick, burned down; their third, wooden, blew down; their fourth, a tent, blew down; but their fifth remained permanent. The Virginia City of 1878 had six churches.

Many newspapers and newspapermen graced the Comstock at one time or another.[17] "Licking the editor" was considered a respectable Washoe sport; therefore, any reporter had to be willing to defend himself in a manly way or else he was useless to his paper. Few had the experience of the boy Wells Drury the first day he worked in Nevada. Left alone to read some proof while the men of the *Gold Hill News* staff refreshed themselves at a neighboring saloon, he suddenly found himself faced by an irate citizen demanding an apology at once for a fancied affront or else he was going to beat up the nearest staffer handy. When Drury nervously picked up the editor's pistol as the man became increasingly threatening, he barely touched its hair trigger and it fired. The complainer implored the youngster not to kill him, then dashed out and slammed the door so hard that all the glass broke. Back rushed the rest of the staff, and they refused to believe the shot an accident. Then everybody, men and boy, went over to the bar.

The most famous of the Comstock newspapers was the *Territorial Enterprise,* founded in 1858 and discontinued in 1893. Its guiding light was talented, courageous, honest Joseph Goodman. His paper always showed a spirit of exaggeration and aggressiveness. He allowed

---

[16] Lyman, *Saga,* 79, 230–31; Lord, *Comstock Mining,* 406; WPA, *Nevada,* 278; Alice F. Trout, "Religious Development in Nevada," *Nevada Historical Society Papers,* Vol. I (1913–16), 143–67.

[17] Drury, *Editor,* 3–7, 169–209; Benson, *Mark Twain's Western Years,* 69–70; Lyman, *Saga,* 208–10.

his staff to perpetrate hoaxes, to assault one another with abuse, and to direct vitriolic comments at individuals—as long as they would defend themselves if challenged. Over the years his most outstanding reporter in the area was William Wright, best known by his pen name of Dan DeQuille. Dan was the first outsider to guess the existence of the Big Bonanza in the Consolidated Virginia and California mines. When it was a tightly kept secret, he greatly startled the managers by telling them its exact position; from his knowledge of developments on either side, he had deduced the spot and the richness correctly. In 1876, he published his major book about the Comstock, *The Big Bonanza,* fundamental to all study of the region. For sixty dollars a week DeQuille worked for the *Territorial Enterprise* from 1861 to 1893. He fell on hard times when the paper was discontinued, until the Washoe millionaire John W. Mackay heard of his plight and donated him a pension of sixty dollars a week until death. Editor Goodman once commented that if in 1863 anybody had asked him who would make the lasting reputation, DeQuille or Mark Twain, he would unhesitatingly have named DeQuille. But Dan shrank back from the world while Twain audaciously braved it.

When there was a shortage of news, DeQuille was a master of that common Comstock practice to fill space, a fabricated story written in great seriousness to entertain the miners. One of Dan's best-known ones was about an inventor of a special cooling suit who set out to test it in torrid Death Valley. When he failed to return, friends searched for him. They discovered that he had not been able to turn off the compressor of his suit and had frozen to death, with an icicle eighteen inches long hanging from his nose—despite a temperature of 117 degrees in the shade! This hoax deceived the *London Times,* which seriously commented that the British government ought to buy the suits for its soldiers in India.

Another DeQuille yarn concerned the stones of Pahranagat Valley, alternately drawn together and hurled apart by a magnetic center. When Dan refused to give some literal-minded scientific groups in Germany further details, they were outraged. Two of his other imaginative reports were about a perpetual-motion pump powered by a Washoe Zephyr and a luminous shrub, gray as sage by day but phosphorescent by night.

The Comstock newspaperman to become most famous internationally was Samuel L. Clemens, best known by his pen name of Mark Twain.[18] Printer, reporter, and Mississippi River steamboat pilot, he came to Nevada as secretary to the secretary of state, his brother Orion, only to discover that there was no provision for his salary. He turned to mining, twice uncovering what he thought were rich claims, only to have his hopes blasted. In the summer of 1862, greatly discouraged about prospecting, he sent some crude burlesque sketches, written in the frontier style of humor, to the *Territorial Enterprise*. The one which particularly interested the paper's readers was "Professor Personal Pronoun," an unsubtle take-off on the vainglorious public speeches of a notorious Comstock judge. The burlesque won Twain a post as reporter on the paper at a weekly salary of twenty-five dollars. At first he signed his articles Josh, but soon substituted the Mississippi River steamboat phrase meaning "two fathoms deep," Mark Twain. Of his flights of pure fancy, akin to those of Dan DeQuille, the best was "The Petrified Man." This spoof so fooled a medical journal, *Lancet*, that in its August, 1862 issue it ran a serious commentary on the article.

As Twain gradually developed a number of sources for news, he relied less and less on imagination and more on facts. He covered two sessions of the territorial legislature for his paper. His reports were generally in a humorous vein, especially when ridiculing Bill Stewart's self-seeking talk about taxation on "the honest miner," but almost always he also commented critically on some political or social problem of importance to the community. These articles made him a notable to the Comstockers, enough that his opinions had influence on whether or not a bill passed the legislature. Both to show their genuine appreciation and play a joke, his friends gave him a party and, with an elaborate complimentary speech, presented him with a pipe. They thought he would surely recognize instantly the difference between their cheap clay and a genuine meerschaum. He didn't, and was greatly touched. When later he learned the truth, he was so crushed that his friends were chagrined. To make amends,

[18] Benson, *Mark Twain's Western Years*, 3, 22, 28, 37–50, 80–93, 101, 113; Twain, *Roughing It*, II, 19–23; Drury, *Editor*, 221–22; Miller, *Reno*, 145; Lyman, *Saga*, 202–14, 246–50, 258, 293–304; Henry Nash Smith (ed.), *Mark Twain of the Enterprise*, 24–29; Van Wyck Brooks, *The Ordeal of Mark Twain*, 64, 99–113; Bernard DeVoto, *Mark Twain's America*, 127–59; Jeanne E. Wier, "Mark Twain's Relation to Nevada and to the West," Nevada Historical Society *Papers*, Vol. I (1913–16), 100–101.

when he gave his first public lecture in Virginia City, they presented him with a bar of silver on which they inscribed "Mark Twain—Matthew V, 41—Pilgrim." Their Bible reference read: "And whosoever shall compel thee to go a mile, go with him twain." Mark was not appeased.

Twain's most discussed exploit as a Washoe journalist was the story he wrote to satisfy the anger of the board of directors of the Gould and Curry mine. In October, 1863, when they declared a monthly dividend of $150 per share, they were incensed at the false statements of the *San Francisco Bulletin* that the payment was unjustified, that it was designed to inflate the market price of the stock, and that they intended to sell out their own holdings at an excessive profit. The directors asked the *Territorial Enterprise* to do something about it and the assignment fell to Mark. He named a noted local saloon owner as having unloaded his valuable Gould and Curry holdings to purchase securities of the Spring Valley Water Company of San Francisco, which in actual fact was well known just to have been "cooked" in outrageous fashion. Twain declared that the barkeeper had lost all his money, murdered his faithful, redheaded wife and their nine children, and then committed suicide. Readers of the paper forgot that the liquor dealer was a notorious bachelor, forgot that no redheaded female on the Washoe was married at the time, forgot that no family as large as nine children could be found in the area, and they became greatly angered. So much discussion arose that on the following day Twain had to admit it was all a hoax.

When the humorist Artemus Ward visited Virginia City, he detected something of Mark's budding powers and strongly urged him to find a broader field of endeavor than the *Territorial Enterprise*. In May, 1864, Twain discovered that the ladies who had held a masquerade ball to benefit the United States Sanitary Commission, thereby raising three thousand dollars, now proposed to use the money for another purpose. He wrote a long article about their donation of the funds to an eastern miscegenation society, ending with the admission that it was a hoax about the recipient but not about the diversion. He earned a vigorous denunciation, in which he was called a liar and poltroon, from editor James Laird in the columns of the *Virginia Daily Union*. That he challenged Laird to a duel and that the editor appeared but refused to fight has been a fact generally accepted by scholars, but the most recent expert to study Twain's

Nevada years, Henry Nash Smith, does not think such an episode took place. At any rate, Twain departed from the state in haste. Mark Twain's subsequent rise to greatness as an American writer lies outside the field of this discussion. One of his major books, *Roughing It,* was to describe his Comstock experiences. Exactly what effect his Nevada life had on him as a creative writer became years later a matter of dispute between two literary critics, Van Wyck Brooks and Bernard DeVoto.

Brooks saw Twain as an artist who was constantly thwarted in his earlier years. First his father's death threw over him for many years an unnatural pall, and then his mother's disapproval of his youthful conduct inhibited him. Mark finally found the first expression of his artistic yearnings in his mastery of the difficult tasks of a Mississippi River pilot; he felt free to do as his spirit urged him. Before long he again lost his true guideline, broke down, and by going to Nevada, Brooks argued, dejectedly accepted the stamp of his environment. Here, no longer free to dress like a river dandy, he grew so frustrated that his clothing was in greater disarray than was usual on the untidy Comstock. This shift to a typical western costume, the critic insisted, was not the normal action of a healthy young man entering the region but, rather, a symbol of degradation. Twain repressed his individuality and suffered from the nasty practical jokes played on him. He failed as a miner, not because he did not happen to look at the right little spot of ground, but because he could not use as a prospector those qualities which had served him so well as a pilot—concentration, perseverance, and judgment. As a reporter for the *Territorial Enterprise,* he had no pride in his work but took refuge in a pen name because he feared public opinion and recoiled at having to compromise his artistic soul by being merely a humorist.

These theories proposed by Brooks were flatly and vigorously rejected by western-born critic Bernard DeVoto. In reading the collection of Twain's letters from the Washoe, he saw reflected a boundless contentment unmarred by any kind of frustration. Mark was raised in a frontier community, DeVoto pointed out, and found the drama of Nevada infinitely absorbing. On the *Territorial Enterprise* he was at the nerve center of the spectacle, privy to many a secret, enjoying the power of a respected reporter on an influential newspaper, and basking in a wide circle of friends. His Washoe articles contained the embryo of the fantasy, the burlesque, the satire, and the irony which were to be the hallmarks of his famous books. His experience in Nevada, DeVoto concluded, was far from a thwarting of Mark Twain; it contributed much that was to make him great. With this opinion most specialists in western history would agree.

Beyond dispute, certain frontier characteristics, acquired partly from the Washoe, were with Mark Twain in all his later life: individualism, almost to the point of being antisocial; a bit of lawlessness; an antipathy to direct control; a keen sense of justice; a strong hatred of those who betrayed their trust; a lively sympathy for the debtor and the laborer; a love of democracy in government; a buoyancy in outlook; and restlessness.

Indeed, this restlessness was typical of frontiersmen everywhere, but especially of those who were miners. Their desire to be on the move themselves or to have supplies brought to them raised many a problem.[19] At first in the Comstock area the freight could come up the slopes of Mt. Davidson only on the backs of mules and, especially, donkeys. The jackasses became accomplished thieves of food, going into action as soon as their owner left camp but calmly, innocently wandering on an adjacent hillside when he returned. In 1859, the building of the first of the toll roads on the mountain foretold that soon the donkey would be replaced by the freight wagon. Such heavy traffic arose that when a roadblock developed, it might last for hours. In February, 1867, in the Gold Hill area, an accident created a jam of 65 loaded ore wagons drawn by 325 horses.

Moving freight in quantity over the Sierras proved to be a formidable task.[20] In 1861 and 1862, the three major toll roads were built: the Big Trees route through Sonora Pass, the route from Nevada City and Grass Valley over Henness Pass, and the road from Placerville. The Placerville route was the most important; 101 miles long from California to Virginia City, it was, though partly new in construction, mostly a great improvement upon the existing road. It was everywhere wide enough for wagons going in opposite directions to pass without difficulty and had turning points where an eight-horse team could swing its load around without slacking the traces, and

[19] DeQuille, *Big Bonanza*, 38, 72–73, 99; Smith, *History*, 102.
[20] Emrich, *Comstock Bonanza*, 17; DeQuille, *Big Bonanza*, 161–62; Glasscock, *Big Bonanza*, 62, 113–36; Lord, *Comstock Mining*, 191–95; Mack, *Nevada*, 353–54; Shinn, *Story of the Mine*, 111–12; Lillard, *Desert Challenge*, 150–51; Lyman, *Saga*, 219–21.

it was macadamized the entire distance, at a cost of $500,000. This highway carried hikers, sheep, hogs, cattle, stagecoaches, and freight wagons in a volume heavier in the early 1860's than was to be found on any other American road. On the ten-mile stretch from Strawberry Valley to West Summit, the owners of the segment, Swan and Company, spent $2,000 to $3,000 annually in maintenance but collected in tolls $40,000 to $50,000. Over the length of the road, in the first few years after the discovery of the Comstock Lode, the entire amount collected from freight teams alone averaged $639,000 a year. The fee for the complete trip was $15.00 for a four-horse team and $1.50 for each additional team on the same wagon and its trailers.

For this service the so-called Washoe wagon was manufactured in Stockton and Placerville by John M. Studebaker, later to become nationally famous for his vehicles, as well as by others. Built of hickory, ash, and wrought iron and equipped with very powerful brakes, it had a stronger and heavier frame and a deeper bed than were customary in the East. Three of the wagons, hooked together and pulled by sixteen mules, could carry twenty-four tons of freight. In handling the animals, no rein was used; they were started, stopped, and turned by the pop of a twenty-foot whip attached to a three-foot handle. It was almost never used on them, but they knew it could be; its crack was inevitably accompanied by a string of oaths. Each mule wore a small brass bell, to warn of approaching wagons; afar this tinkling sounded pleasant but with proximity the charm vanished. That the animals were very well taken care of explains their vigor and their ability to haul such heavy loads. Their driver either walked, rode the swing mule, or sat in the wagon box. Usually he owned his own outfit and belonged to the Teamsters Association. He and his fellows were an honest lot, carting thousands of dollars' worth of goods with no more security to the shipper than the receipt they gave. In summer, the wagons on the Placerville–Virginia City route stretched in an almost unbroken line, and if somebody had to turn aside, he might wait for hours before he had a chance to get back into the procession.

Every few miles on the main toll roads was a lodging station, with stable, saloon, sleeping quarters, and general-merchandise store. On the Placerville–Virginia City highway there were about a hundred of these establishments. The animals, fed barley and hay, were often tied to the tongues or sides of their wagon for the night rather than being put under shelter; the drivers spent the early evening swapping yarns. The most famous overnight stop was the Strawberry Hotel at Strawberry Flat. A large log house with an immense fireplace, it had rough board benches for seats and commonly served eight or ten sittings at meals. The hotel could sleep 340 men, packed close together in their blankets on the floor.

Frequent stagecoaches carried passengers from California to the Comstock.[21] So heavy was the traffic, before the advent of the railroad, that these coaches would sometimes leave in a string of five or six together. Traveling day and night, their schedule called for an eighteen-hour trip between Virginia City and Sacramento. A coach with a capacity of nine passengers cost $1,000, delivered from Concord, New Hampshire, and the harness for its six horses cost $225. Its team was matched with great care for size, color, and endurance; the horses hitched next to the coach were larger than the leaders. It was in charge of a conductor or express messenger, whose run was about two hundred miles, and a driver, whose stint was about fifty miles. To pilot a stage down the Sierras, in the opinion of U.S. Vice-President Schuyler Colfax, took "much more" talent than to serve in Congress.

The most renowned coachman was Hank Monk and his most famous exploit involved the noted New York newspaper editor Horace Greeley. Via the Virginia City–Placerville road, he undertook to get the easterner to California in time for a scheduled speech. He dashed along at great speed, badly frightening the editor, disregarding all demands to stop, and frequently yelling, "Keep your seat, Horace, I'll have you there on time!" He did, but Greeley was not in a very composed frame of mind. Monk's habit of mending his clothes with copper harness rivets instead of buttons is alleged to have given Levi Strauss the idea for his famous men's pants.

Not all drivers were as skillful as Monk, and occasionally there were accidents. In a spectacular one, a stage went over a one-thousand-foot precipice and landed on a tough Sierra pine. The horses plunged on through, but the coach remained atop the tree and the passengers climbed down, limb by limb, to safety.

Almost all stages carried express, a business for years virtually a monopoly in the hands of Wells Fargo and Company, whose specialty was the transportation of treasure. In 1863, for example, it carried

21 Mack, *Nevada*, 349, 356; Drury, *Editor*, 138–41; DeQuille, *History*, 62–63; Lyman, *Saga*, 219–21.

twelve million dollars' worth for its Nevada patrons. It also carted the mail to outlying camps.

When the Civil War broke out, the Overland Mail Company, the so-called Butterfield Stage, moved its passenger and mail service from the southern to the central route, adding the Comstock to the points it served. Important, too, was the Pony Express, the spectacular but unprofitable extra-fast postal service from the Middle West to San Francisco. With the coming of the transcontinental railroad, completed in May, 1869, stagecoach and wagon continued locally to serve many Nevada camps far from the steam tracks. As late as 1880 there were thirty regularly scheduled stage lines active in the state.

To supplement horses and mules, some use was made of camels in Nevada.[22] The inspiration came from an experiment, abandoned at the time of the Civil War, by the United States Army in providing transport to its remote western outposts. This led a San Francisco merchant, Otto Esche, to buy thirty-two camels in Mongolia; fifteen survived the trip to California and soon were busy on the Comstock. They chiefly carried 250-pound loads of salt from the Esmeralda marshes at Leeteville on the Carson River to the smelters of Virginia City. They liked the deep warm sand at the base of Mt. Davidson and enjoyed looking around from a lofty spot at a commanding view. They hated the alkali of the area, which burned their noses, reddened their eyes, and irritated their raw spots. Thanks largely to bad treatment, the camels grew increasingly ill natured until they kicked and bit worse than an army mule. Eventually, regular use of the animals ceased to be made and they mostly roamed about. The last newspaper reference to them appeared in 1876.

How to transport large quantities of lumber from the Sierras to the mines was another problem.[23] The question was a pressing one, for in the middle 1870's, about eighty million board feet were consumed annually on the Comstock. The solution came to J. W. Haines of Genoa, who invented the V-shaped flumes. From such a high spot as Lake Tahoe these carried the finished timber from the mountainside mills to the floor of the Washoe Valley, where other means lifted it to its Comstock destination. The steep-sided flumes were on a steadily descending grade, twisting around the mountainside and crossing

22 Mack, *Nevada*, 353–62; Lyman, *Saga*, 141–43.
23 DeQuille, *Big Bonanza*, 174–78; Mack, *Nevada*, 442–43.

ravines on high trestles. They could accommodate timbers as large as sixteen inches square and thirty feet long. They needed only a small quantity of water to convoy down a whole procession of finished lumber; indeed, a few were so steep they did not need or use water. Some terminated in a small lake, which was a challenge to daredevils who would ride a timber down and make a wild leap just as it hit the pond. To reach these troughs, some of the timber was rafted across Lake Tahoe.

In the very early days the Washoe area was dependent upon a winter postman, John A. Thompson, and his spectacular service.[24] Impressed by the great difficulty in getting the mail over the Sierras to the Eagle Valley region in the wintry fall of 1855, Thompson made a pair of skis such as he had seen as a boy in his native Norway. After practicing in secret, he astounded all Placerville in a public appearance. He undertook to carry the mail from Placerville to the Eagle Valley area for four winters, making as many as thirty-one round trips a season while carrying sixty to eighty pounds of mail. As roads improved over this important route, he turned to winter postal transport elsewhere in Nevada for seventeen years more. Thompson's trips from Placerville to Eagle Valley usually took three days, but he returned in two. Carrying no blankets or overcoat, he camped where night chanced to overtake him. For warmth, he relied upon a fire kindled, if possible, in a dead pine stump; he slept with his feet to the blaze and his head on the mail. He carried only light provisions, requiring no cooking, and for water depended upon a handful of snow. Always setting out on the scheduled day, regardless of the weather, Thompson followed no regular path but kept to his general course by the rocks and trees in the daylight, by the stars at night. When soft snow clogged his shoes, he simply waited a few hours until the crust froze again.

A later Comstock development than Thompson's service was the telegraph.[25] By the spring of 1859 a line extended from Placerville to Carson City and the next year reached Virginia City. One of its financiers, and manager of the Virginia City office, was Fred A. Bee, and it quickly gained the nickname of "Bee's Grapevine Line," especially since the company attached the wires to trees wherever possible. When the wind blew, the wire would stretch enough to lie

24 Emrich, *Comstock Bonanza*, 188–211; Miller, *Reno*, 206; Smith, *History*, 12.
25 Bancroft, *Nevada*, 230; Lyman, *Saga*, 91; Mack, Nevada, 348–49.

in loops on the ground, there to become a mighty temptation to those with a broken-down stagecoach or freight wagon, for a bit of it was most convenient. In 1860, Congress authorized the Overland Telegraph Company to build a line from the Missouri River to San Francisco via the Comstock; by the next year it was completed. Over it messages could not be sent long distance by a single operator but rather had to be relayed, for example sent from Placerville to Carson City and then retelegraphed by a second man to a point farther east.

The story of the first transcontinental railroad, the Union Pacific to the east and the Central Pacific (now called the Southern Pacific) in Utah, Nevada, and California, is too well known to need retelling here.[26] The first through train ran from Sacramento to Reno on June 18, 1868. For years there was much controversy, not only the usual complaints of the period everywhere about excessive rates, but, more important, about discriminatory ones. In 1877, for example, the Central Pacific charged $300 to haul a carload of coal oil from New York City all the way to San Francisco, but from the East to Reno, nearer, the rate was $536 and to Elko, still nearer, $800. Comstockers strongly suspected, but could never have proved in a court of law, that the real reason for the practice was to keep any industry from developing in Nevada as competition for California-made products. This discrimination betwen coastal and inland points was characteristic of the whole Far West, in the earlier days of the railroads. It did not cease until the Interstate Commerce Commission took effective action in the 1910's.

To connect the Comstock itself with the main line at Reno was a much-discussed project.[27] Finally, financier William Sharon and some associates in the Bank of California undertook the task. At an interview later to become famous for its brevity, Sharon asked I. E. James, the leading mine surveyor of the Comstock, as he entered the former's private office, "Can you run a railroad from Virginia to the Carson River?" "Yes." "Do so, then, at once." James turned on his heel and departed. Thus Sharon launched the Virginia and Truckee Railroad. He persuaded Ormsby and Storey counties to give it a subsidy of one-half million dollars. He also secured money from the

26 Mack, *Nevada*, 379; Lillard, *Desert Challenge*, 27–31.

27 Kneiss, *Bonanza Railroads*, 52–70; Beebe and Clegg, *Legends*, 31; Gorham, *My Memories*, 22–23; Lord, *Comstock Mining*, 250–56; DeQuille, *Big Bonanza*, 165–67.

mines, some as a gift and some to be repaid by receipted freight bills. His construction crews started work in February, 1869, and by November completed the line from Gold Hill to Carson City; he promptly pushed through extensions to Virginia City and to Reno. When his tracks reached Carson City, there was a monster railroad ball, with trains hauling participants down from the Comstock. It became such a celebration that the last special didn't start back until nine the next morning.

The steep part of the line between Virginia City and the Carson River, thirteen and one-half miles, had a grade averaging a little more than 2 per cent and curvature equaling seventeen full circles— about one and one-half circles per mile. The total distance by rail from Virginia City to Reno was fifty-two miles, approximately going around three sides of a square. Short stub lines were run to all the leading mines. The total cost of the Virginia and Truckee Railroad was three million dollars. It was built by Chinese labor, imported by Sharon. His action roused the Miners Union of Virginia City and Gold Hill, whose members invaded the construction camp and sent the Orientals flying to the hills for safety. Sharon promised that the Chinese would never be employed in his various enterprises within the two cities and the miners allowed the building to resume.

When completed, the railroad cut the cost of transporting ore from the mines to the Carson River mills from $3.50 per ton to $2.00. A few teamsters, running several wagons hooked together, tried to compete with this lower rate and one of them actually managed to haul down 73,050 pounds in one trip before the uneven contest ended. Some Comstockers maintained that the railroad charged excessively and therefore vigorously attacked its monthly dividend rate of $100,000. The line was kept so busy that rails on its main track lasted only nine months. For years the company ran fifty-two trains daily, often powered by two engines, over its road. Its train crews, on duty eighteen hours out of twenty-four, made four round trips a day between the mines and the river. It avoided any considerable hauling of empties by devising a car which could handle ten tons of ore downgrade and eight cords of wood upgrade.

Over the years the Washoe was a mighty mineral producer. Between 1859 and 1882, the Comstock mines produced a total of $320,-000,000 in valuable ores. The companies that owned them paid out $147,000,000 in dividends to their stockholders and in smelter profits to the insiders. They collected $92,000,000 in assessments for exploratory work. This left, taking the Comstock area as a whole, a net profit of $55,000,000.[28]

Such a vast outpouring of minerals had effects on monetary policy in the United States and abroad.[29] In 1864, Emperor Louis Napoleon of France sent M. E. Guillemin Tarayre on an investigation to the mines of California and Nevada, where he saw vigorous production. This disquieted both France and England, which in their own monetary systems were on the gold standard and were already nervous because of the decline in the world production of gold. They feared the injection of so much silver into the American monetary system, especially since many of their citizens had purchased a considerable quantity of Federal bonds during the American Civil War; they wanted to be certain these would be paid off in gold. Their anxiety led to the calling, in 1867, of the first international monetary conference. As a preliminary, Germany asked Philip Deidesheimer, at this time superintendent of the Hale and Norcross mine, to report on the Comstock. With an overoptimism which was almost magnificent, he sincerely declared that there was one and one-half billion dollars worth of silver "in sight." The net result was to bring about a demonetization of that mineral. Shortly after the conference adjourned, Germany, France, Belgium, Switzerland, Holland, Italy, and Greece stopped making silver coins entirely and the Scandinavian countries greatly curtailed their output. In February, 1873, eight months before the discovery of the Big Bonanza in the Consolidated Virginia, the United States dropped silver from the coins it would mint. This congressional action was simply a routine money reform, passed almost without debate in Senate or House, for at the price the federal government was paying for silver, in terms of gold, nobody had sold to the United States for a long time.

In later years, as the vast quantity of silver produced on the Comstock, in the West generally, and also in South America pressed down its monetary value in terms of gold, many a westerner would have liked to sell his bullion to the federal government. The market was no longer available. Western miners, who previously had been so indifferent, now trumpeted about the "Crime of '73." They and their

28 Smith, *History*, 230.

29 Lillard, *Desert Challenge*, 49; Mack, *Nevada*, 455–60; Gorham, *My Memories*, 173–74.

allies, the western farmers, tried to persuade the American people that splendid economic results would follow for the entire nation if the Treasury were compelled to purchase silver at a higher price than private enterprise would pay. The issue became involved in whether or not the federal government should deliberately cause inflation and came to be, for over a decade, a major political issue. The net result was that America did buy some silver. The Treasury, however, stood ready to give a person a gold dollar for a silver dollar any time he might ask for it; in other words, it made the silver simply a token or convenient substitute for the gold and without value otherwise in our monetary system. The westerners were disappointed, but they could not exert sufficient pressure to obtain the "free and unlimited coinage of silver" they so ardently advocated. While the battle was on, such a large world production of silver continued that its value per ounce, in terms of gold, slid from over a dollar in 1873 to only fifty cents in 1895.

Although the Comstock was the most famous mining region in Nevada, there were others. The rush to the next best known, the Tonopah-Goldfield area, came after the turn of the century and so lies beyond the scope of this study. In the 1860's, the Reese River, White Pine, Eureka, Candelaria, Pioche, and Esmeralda regions each had rushes. These were not nearly so significant to the nation's development as the Comstock area, and historians have not yet published detailed studies about them. Their impact was cumulative; from 1859 through 1937, the total value of mineral production in Nevada was $1,560,127,621.[30]

Developments in the Reese River region began in 1862 when former Pony Express rider William M. Talcott gathered from the stream some ore samples which resembled those he had seen on the Comstock.[31] He and three friends—James Jacobs, Wash Jacobs, and a man named O'Neill—staked out claims. An assay of minerals taken from one of these was so sensational that in 1863 prospectors rushed to the area. Some settled in the valley at Clifton, but most preferred to live a mile up the slope at Austin. Miners continued to press into the area, and in 1864 came the crest, with Austin's population being somewhere between six and ten thousand people. As the town

---

30 WPA, *Nevada*, 58.

31 Oscar Lewis, *The Town That Died Laughing*, 4–198; WPA, *Nevada*, 259–60; Bancroft, *Nevada*, 264–69; Kneiss, *Bonanza Railroads*, 102–29.

boomed, large quantities of stock in its mines were sold on San Francisco steet corners. Its ore was mostly silver, with a small percentage of gold, found in veins narrow but rich. The value of this ore was commonly seven hundred dollars a ton, and the record for a ton was five thousand dollars. Austin, on the route of the overland stage, was connected in 1880 with the main line of the Central Pacific at Battle Mountain by a narrow-gauge railroad line, the Nevada Central. The town continued in prosperity until the mines gradually became exhausted and closed in the middle 1890's. Before 1900, the Reese River mining area produced fifty million dollars' worth of ore.

The White Pine mining district centered at Hamilton and Treasure City.[32] The initial discovery was made in 1865 by prospectors from Austin, especially Robert Morrill and Thomas J. Murphy; in 1868, another one of exceptional promise followed. The area seemed on the verge of becoming another Comstock, and people flocked in until the population of the area rose to perhaps ten thousand. Speculators hastened to buy stock in White Pine mines until the total face value of the securities issued was fifty million dollars. Lawyers struck a bonanza over a unique legal situation arising from the layers of limestone which separated the ore bodies, one underneath another. The net result, however, was that the mines remained in the hands of their original owners. In many of the companies the Bank of California secured an interest.

All of these promising beginnings did not result in the area's becoming another Comstock because the best of the deposits were within one hundred feet of the surface; at deeper levels their value rapidly declined. Although silver was by far the most important mineral, there were also some lead and copper. Production in the district began to fall off in 1873 but did not stop entirely until 1887. The total value of the ore extracted was twenty-two million dollars.

One of the chief recreations at Treasure City was to wager on the regular race between the two express riders, one Wells Fargo and the other Pacific Union, both carrying a share of the mail and both striving to get into town first. On the Fourth of July in 1868, the men of the town and its neighbor, Hamilton, had a dance, enlivened by the presence of two women and four Mormon girls. The festivities con-

[32] Emrich, *Comstock Bonanza*, 75–83; WPA, *Nevada*, 252; Lillard, *Desert Challenge*, 192–93; Bancroft, *Nevada*, 277–80. Not consulted was a study, nearing completion, by W. T. Jackson.

tinued until the one fiddler, carefully guarded to insure sobriety, fell backward through the cloth wall of the hall and, though unhurt, could not be awakened.

In 1864, at Eureka on the Base Range, about fifty miles by wagon road from Hamilton, the first important discovery in the United States of ore containing major proportions of both lead and silver was made.[33] This unusual combination was difficult to smelter, holding back development of the region. In fourteen years at Eureka, were extracted forty million dollars' worth of silver, ten million of lead, and twenty million of gold. Then the mines struck more water than could be pumped out profitably.

The smelters, belching dense clouds of black smoke, sulphur fumes, and arsenic odors, made Eureka quite as unattractive as a Pennsylvania coal town. At first they produced only partially refined ore, which had to be sent to the mills at Salt Lake City for conversion into pure metals. In 1875, the Richmond Consolidated mine patented a new, improved process which was much cheaper and was capable of recovering the silver completely without shipment elsewhere. That same year, the mining center was connected with the Central Pacific Railroad by the narrow-gauge Eureka and Palisade. One of the better-known episodes in the town was unusual because it involved women: "Hog-eyed Mary" Irwin settled her grudge with "Bulldog Kate" Miller in the Tiger Saloon by unladylike means—a knife in the ribs.

Cherry Creek was an active community between 1872 and 1883, with a maximum population of about six thousand. In gold, copper, and lead it produced somewhere between six and twenty million dollars' worth of mineral.[34] Considerably to the south was Pioche, where operations began about 1868; the area reached its height in 1872–73. Up to the later 1930's, Pioche produced forty million dollars' worth of ore.[35] It is said that in the early days of the town a newly arrived eastern bride saw a law officer kill three men on three street corners while she walked from the stage office to the hotel; she left the next day. At Candelaria, silver was first discovered in 1864, and the Northern Belle yielded about three-fourths of the twenty million dollars secured in the mines of the area.

[33] Lillard, *Desert Challenge*, 292; WPA, *Nevada*, 254–55; Kneiss, *Bonanza Railroads*, 79–101; Bancroft, *Nevada*, 281–83.

[34] WPA, *Nevada*, 246.

[35] WPA, *Nevada*, 173; Bancroft, *Nevada*, 272–73.

The Esmeralda mining district, in what is now Mineral and Nye counties, opened up with a discovery made in 1860 at Aurora.[36] In 1864, when the town had a population of about ten thousand people, a vigilance committee arose to improve the city's record of a violent death about every six weeks for the previous three years. It ordered a miscellaneous group of bad men out of town and condemned to death the murderers of W. R. Johnson. News of this action vaguely reached the ears of Governor Nye, who wired for information. To him the United States marshal replied: "Everything quiet in Aurora; four men to be hung in fifteen minutes."

The mineral rushes and developments in Nevada were unusual because they were so much concentrated in the Comstock area. Instead of being widespread, as in California, the operations centered in one spot. Thus in Virginia City a more stabilized mining community, comparable to Butte, grew up. Its lawyer Stewart induced Congress to pass laws giving the mine owners title to their properties, actually on federal land, without charge. Its miners were well paid by the standards of the day and their achievement of the eight-hour day was well in advance of general recognition of such a standard in American labor practice. Its newspapers were notable for their hoaxes, but they also contained much solid material. Its amusements were more varied than could be found in the average eastern town of comparable population. It yielded so much silver that many European nations, alarmed at the large output, took strong measures to preserve gold as their monetary standard. Its wealth did much more to develop the San Francisco area than Nevada. By 1900, the great days of Virginia City and other Nevada mining centers were over, except for the rich new discoveries to come at another locality, Goldfield and Tonopah.

[36] Mack, *Nevada*, 214–15; Lillard, *Desert Challenge*, 203–204; WPA, *Nevada*, 220.

7

EARLY DAYS IN COLORADO

THE first discovery of gold in Colorado aroused almost no interest until eight years after it was made.[1] It was an accidental by-product of the rush to California in 1849–50. On June 21, 1850, a group of 120 whites, Cherokees, and Negro servants traveling through Colorado camped in the general vicinity of future Denver at Ralston Creek. Here they found two or three dollars' worth of gold, but hustled on to California.

When the financial panic of 1857 spread economic difficulties throughout the nation, five different groups of men decided it was time to investigate Colorado's mineral possibilities further. One party, headed by Green Russell, a veteran of the rush to California, came from the Cherokee and gold region of Georgia; another from the area of that tribe in the Great Plains; a third from Bates County, Missouri; and a fourth from Ray County in the same state. By June 24, 1858, the 104 men in these four expeditions were at the mouth of Cherry Creek, Colorado, near Denver, united into a single group in their search for gold. They found only small quantities, not worth mining. On July 7, they were so discouraged that all left for home except Green Russell and a dozen others. Finally, on the South Platte River, one of the thirteen, James H. Pierce, made the first promising find. From a small pocket in the stream the men took out a hundred dollars' worth of gold before exhausting it; shortly they made two similar discoveries. All of these were scale gold, about as coarse as

1 LeRoy R. Hafen (ed.), *Pike's Peak Gold Rush Guidebooks of 1859*, 21–77; LeRoy R. Hafen (ed.), *Colorado and Its People*, I, 145–46; Wilbur F. Stone (ed.), *History of Colorado*, I, 232–34; Charles W. Henderson, *Mining in Colorado: A History of Discovery, Development and Production*, 2–3.

wheat bran, which had evidently floated down from somewhere else. To track down its origin would require a trip into the mountains, impossible with the group's wagons. Instead they prospected further in the foothills and also took a trip to Wyoming, mostly to hunt game.

Meanwhile, a fifth group of twenty-eight men set out for Colorado late in May from Lawrence, Kansas. The previous autumn, Fall Leaf, a Delaware Indian on the near-by reservation, showed a Lawrence butcher some gold nuggets he had obtained from the area of the Cheyenne Indians. Several men organized an expedition which Fall Leaf promised to lead to treasure, but at the last minute he refused to go. Pushing west without him, the whites fixed their objective as Pike's Peak, about eighty miles south of Denver. Not far from there they met the returning contingent of the other four groups and did some joint prospecting, but without favorable results. Separating, the Lawrence men went farther south to Fort Garland, where they heard of Pierce's find and headed north.

Already news of the discovery had spread outside Colorado. A visitor to Russell's little band, John Cantrell, took some gold back to Kansas City, and his account of the area spread a fever of excitement along the Missouri River. Precisely how much gold had been discovered became greatly exaggerated as people and newspapers told and retold the story. They would have been shocked had they known that many of Russell's remaining party were starting for Georgia with a total of about five hundred dollars to show for their efforts.

Ignorant of the true facts, gold seekers began heading west.[2] When they reached Cherry Creek, they found on opposite banks the townsites of Auraria and Denver, not merged into the one city of Denver until April, 1860. They saw no mines in operation; they learned how completely false was the widely circulated story about a man named Robinson, who was supposed to have collected a kettle of gold, worth between six and seven thousand dollars, from the labor of three

2 Hafen, *Pike's Peak*, 77–80; Leroy R. Hafen (ed.), *Colorado Gold Rush: Contemporary Letters and Reports 1858–1859*, 93–322; George F. Willison, *Here They Dug Gold*, 27, 48–49; Hafen, *Colorado and Its People*, I, 159–77; LeRoy R. Hafen (ed.), *Overland Routes to the Gold Fields, 1859, from Contemporary Diaries*, 119, 124–25, 265–81; James H. Baker and LeRoy R. Hafen (eds.), *History of Colorado*, 436; Hubert H. Bancroft, *History of Nevada, Colorado and Wyoming, 1540–1888*, 365–76; James F. Willard, "Sidelights on the Pike's Peak Gold Rush, 1858–59," *Colorado Magazine*, Vol. XII (1935), 3–13.

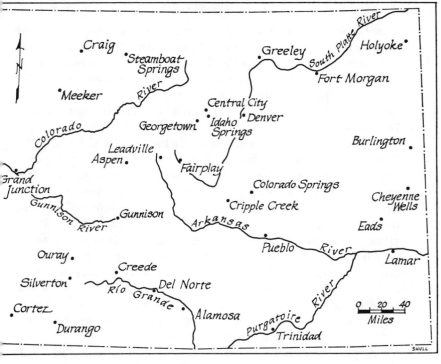

people for two months. Some newcomers began to prospect a little, but by November the ground was frozen very hard and by December snow blocked the canyons and ravines. Most of the men simply built winter quarters on Cherry Creek and idled away their time until spring. They sent back enthusiastic letters, predicting the area would become a second California and making such absurd statements as the one that nobody who had prospected for a single day in Colorado was dissatisfied or discouraged.

Such words as these from the West helped to fan the optimism of people along the Missouri River. Hit by unemployment and business failures during 1857, many of them seized hopefully upon the news. Certain merchants were proficient at broadcasting false and misleading information, cynically hopeful that it would increase their business. Newspapers filled columns with optimistic items, and only a few editors added words of caution. Men who gave favorable reports, especially if they exhibited samples of gold dust reputedly from Colorado, were heard with respect, but those who made adverse comments were considered fools or ignoramuses. Merchants in towns like Kansas City, Leavenworth, Atchison, and Omaha began to lay in extra supplies. Enterprising authors, uninhibited by their lack of knowledge, found publishers for their guidebooks to the Pike's Peak area. Perhaps the most widely distributed of the seventeen was by D. C. Oakes.

As early as February, 1859, men started for the Colorado gold fields, in much the same fashion as those who had been going overland to California for ten years. Some were well financed, but others sold most of their worldly goods to pay for the trip and still others simply told their families to take care of themselves for a while until father had made a fortune. A few went alone; most gathered into groups. Some men had well-equipped wagons; others used a single pack horse, pulled a handcart, pushed a wheelbarrow, or hiked along carrying a carpetbag. A fair number of the men had a good idea of how to travel; many, however, were ignorant of how great the distance was (about six hundred miles from the Missouri River) or what supplies to take. To get accurate information was difficult, but much advice of dubious worth was easily available.

The possible routes west were three: along the main and South Platte rivers, used by far the most; over the well-known Santa Fe Trail and then north; or beside the Kansas River and one of its major branches, the Republican, or Smoky Hill. The Smoky Hill route was the shortest from the Missouri River to the gold region; however, for long stretches it so lacked water and grass that everybody who used it suffered greatly and some perished. There were towns eager to publicize each of these trails unrestrainedly and thereby create more business for their merchants. The flow of Colorado travelers increased until by March at Omaha not a day passed but some group left for the mines and in a certain week in May at Council Bluffs a total of 584 teams headed west. Some of the wagons bore inscriptions, such as the famous "Pike's Peak or Bust." The majority of the emigrants were farmers; most were young men, inexperienced at mining, who found in a gold rush a welcome change from the ordinary routine of life.

Those who arrived in Denver during March or early April found discouraging conditions. The placer miners along the South Platte were taking in only about a quarter of their operating expenses and as yet only meager discoveries had been made in the mountains. To many, this was a great shock. They grew bitterly angry and circulated such rhymes as

Hang Byers and D. C. Oakes
For starting this damned Pike's Peak Hoax.

Many men who had gone west with such high hopes now retreated in panic back to civilization. They had good reasons, for not enough gold had been found to justify any excitement, rank amateurs could not learn prospecting until there was something for them to see or practice on, prices were higher than they could afford, and the supplies they brought with them ran out. As they stampeded east from Denver, they sold equipment, wagons, and tools, but not food, for perhaps a tenth of their original cost or else left them strewn along the trails. These disillusioned men told tales of misfortune which soon became as exaggerated as the guidebooks they so condemned. Their discouraging words turned back other emigrants. A few talked of burning towns like Omaha in retaliation for deceptions practiced. A few put on their wagons such signs as "Oh Yes! Pike's Peak in H—l and Da–n nation!" Of the one hundred thousand gold seekers who probably started west from the Missouri River in the spring of 1859, perhaps fifty thousand reached Denver and twenty-five thousand of these shortly went back east. One who did not turn back was the author of a guidebook, D. C. Oakes, although he was enough shaken by the sight of himself hanged in effigy to bypass the city.

What prevented the rush of 1859 from being the utter failure it was proclaimed to be at the time was three discoveries, each about forty miles from Denver, which became generally known late in May.[3] The genesis of one of them was a prospecting trip begun on December 31, 1858, by George Jackson, James Sanders, and Tom Golden. The last two men shortly turned aside to hunt elk but Jackson continued alone up Clear Creek through snow two or three feet deep. When he came to hot mineral springs, now called Idaho

3 Hafen, *Colorado and Its People*, I, 177–78, 192, II, 485–88; David Lavender, *The Big Divide*, 62–63; Stone, *History*, I, 236–38; Willison, *Dug Gold*, 53–54; Frank Hall, *History of the State of Colorado*, I, 189; Bancroft, *Colorado*, 377–78; Henderson, *Mining in Colorado*, 7; Caroline Bancroft, "The Elusive Figure of John H. Gregory, Discoverer of the First Gold Lode in Colorado," *Colorado Magazine*, Vol. XX (1943), 121–35; Muriel S. Wolle, *Stampede to Timberline: The Ghost Towns and Mining Camps of Colorado*, 483–89.

Springs, he found a good placer prospect on the third day. The ground was frozen so hard that he had to build a big fire to thaw it, but he took out about $10 worth of gold. He next dumped considerable charcoal in his discovery hole, topped it with dirt, built another large fire over it to help conceal his operations, marked a large fir tree near by with his ax, cut the top off a small pine seventy-six steps in a westerly direction from his find, and then retreated to civilization. On the next April 17, he and a group of twenty-two friends set out to relocate the spot. They agreed in advance to a few simple rules about claims and that Jackson should have a double-sized one for his discovery. They had great difficulty forcing their way through the wilderness with wagons, but on May 1, the party arrived at Idaho Springs. They converted their wagon boxes into sluices and during the first seven days of work netted $1,900.

A second major discovery was that by John H. Gregory at the future Black Hawk; it was the first lode of any importance in Colorado. Gregory made his find in the middle of January, but lack of supplies drove him out. In April, he arranged for Wilkes DeFrees to furnish him with needed supplies in return for a stipulated share of what he might develop during the time he was using the food given him. This widespread practice was known as grubstaking, and the man furnishing the necessary items was usually a storekeeper or other townsman who thus speculated in mineral discoveries while remaining at other tasks himself. Contrary to the custom, DeFrees went along with Gregory into the mountains; so did two others. On May 6, the four arrived in the area of Black Hawk. While the other men were looking for gold that might have floated loose from the lode, Gregory gave DeFrees a thrill. The discoverer took his grubstaker to a point about three hundred feet away, pointed to a spot, and told him to dig. With the first shovelful, Gregory himself panned a half-ounce of gold, and the four immediately staked claims. Before long, Gregory sold his share for $22,000. It is not correct to say, as some have, that he was mentally unbalanced or lazy. Gregory may have been moody, but he was also friendly, enthusiastic, very active, and often took the initiative. He disliked routine or continual physical labor. He did scarcely anything alone, but always had some kind of a partner. He bought and sold claims, both placer and lode, ran a smelter mill for a while, and prospected. Although he had little education, Gregory could not only read and write but, as old records show, was extremely shrewd in the specific provisions he inserted into any contract he signed.

The third major discovery, January, 1859, was of placer deposits on Gold Run, where the settlement of Gold Hill quickly arose. Later in the spring a lode deposit was uncovered. Although the Gold Hill area over the years was not nearly as productive as the region of the other two discoveries, it aroused much enthusiasm initially.

These three discoveries saved the rush from collapse.[4] Many went to the sites of Gregory's and of Jackson's discoveries. In June, the renowned editor Horace Greeley of the *New York Tribune* visited Gregory Diggings, a spot uninhabited six weeks before and now having at least four thousand people. Greeley addressed what was the first mass meeting of miners in the Rocky Mountains, talking on temperance, right living, and how to make Colorado a state promptly. More important, he and two other newspapermen issued a joint report which glowingly pictured the diggings. True, they also warned about the dangers of another gold seekers' rush through the difficult plains west of the Missouri River, but their admonition was lost in their optimistic words. By July, there were a hundred sluices operating within a short distance along Gregory Gulch, soon a crude stamp mill was at work, and by August, a newspaper, the *Rocky Mountain Gold Reporter and Mountain City Herald,* was appearing. The towns of Black Hawk, Central City, and Nevadaville arose. Prices for supplies were about a third higher than in Denver; day laborers' pay was $1.50 to $2.50 a day.

People flocked in from all parts of the world except California, whence they went instead to the Frazier River in British Columbia. Most of them were men, joined by a few women and families. Almost everybody was young; one woman said it was several years before she saw in Colorado a man with gray hair. The miners ate mostly flapjacks, bacon, and beans, with coffee to drink; their cooking equipment was reduced to the fundamentals: frying pan, coffee pot, tin cup, tin plate, butcher knife, and iron spoon. Their beds were of pine boughs, with blankets and buffalo robes for cover. Many of them drank heavily, which made for quarrels and even a few duels. They

[4] Hafen, *Colorado and Its People,* I, 179–80, 237–52, and *Overland Routes,* 185–92, 196–97; Baker and Hafen, *History,* 530; Willison, *Dug Gold,* 67; Robert H. Bahmer, "The Colorado Gold Rush and California," *Colorado Magazine,* Vol. VII (1930), 222–29.

used Sunday as their day of relaxation. Some of them went by two or more names, not necessarily because they lacked moral standards; democratic leveling to the contrary, men of some distinction in the East would never want it known that they had worked as common laborers in Colorado.

As the pioneers in California had done earlier, the Coloradans in an area perhaps sixteen to thirty-five miles square formed themselves into a mining district, held a mass meeting to adopt a code, and functioned as a local government where previously there had been no regulation by any agency.[5] The code generally named officials— usually a president, a recorder, and a constable or sheriff—defined their duties, and prescribed how they were to be elected. It established regulations about the making and retaining of claims. Nine different kinds of these were differentiated in the various Colorado districts, although probably no single area had all varieties. The various claims were: lode, sometimes called a mountain; placer, occasionally known as a gulch; water, for a definite quantity from a stream to be used for mining purposes and then returned to the creek; millsite, for building a stamp mill, whether powered by water or steam; timber, for lumbering or fuel; patch, for loose quartz not attached to any rock or embedded in any stream; cabin, for building a dwelling; ranch, for agricultural purposes; and tunnel, for digging along a second lode discovered while running a tunnel into a first one. To the finder of the first mineral in the district, the code usually authorized either a double-sized claim or a second ordinary one.

When disputes over mining rights arose, they could be tried before the president of the district or by a special board of arbitrators, if each side would agree to accept the decision as final, or before a jury of three to twelve men, with the right of appeal to a general assembly of all the miners in the area acting as a so-called miners' court. The code often contained a clause saying that no technicalities should defeat the ends of justice and frequently one prohibited lawyers from appearing in any trial. Moreover, the code frequently governed civil offenses, heard usually by a jury but with the right of appeal to the whole district. Punishments generally authorized were forfeiture of property, whipping, banishment, or hanging.

5 Hafen, *Colorado and Its People*, I, 210–14, II, 488–92; Baker and Haten, *History*, 483; Percy S. Fritz, *Colorado: The Centennial State*, 127–29; Elmer Ellis, *Henry Moore Teller, Defender of the West*, 38.

When Colorado became a territory, separate from Kansas, in 1860, all claims established under these local codes were declared fully valid and the courts concurred. The unique contribution of Colorado's codes was their recognition of tunnel claims. Often these extended two hundred feet along the length of the lode for each member of a mining partnership or association, provided this series of claims was marked in advance on the surface from mouth to termination before the digging of the tunnel began; obviously, to establish such marks was to gamble on where the gold might be deposited. These basic ideas, modified in details, were made part of United States mining law by Congress in 1872.

The methods of mining were much like those of California.[6] On placers, the gold in streams or in gravel, the fifty-niners used picks, shovels, pans, rockers, long toms, sluice boxes, ground sluices, and hydraulic procedures; they dug ditches to bring down additional supplies of water for large-scale operations. At first such placer methods could also be used on what was really a gold lode; near the surface was partially disintegrated quartz. Deeper down the rock was hard; the Coloradans extracted it, ran it through an arrastra and a crude stamp mill to crush it into powder, added mercury to pick out the gold from the waste rock, and then applied heat to separate the two.

That summer of 1859, prospectors looked successfully for gold in other places besides those of the three sensational early discoveries.[7] Several important finds were made in the geographical area called the South Park, roughly ninety miles southwest of Denver. One was at Tarryall Creek, so monopolized that some late-comers thought the name should be "Grab-All"; they moved on to make a discovery elsewhere at a town they pointedly named Fairplay. Years later one of its longest-lived occupants was honored in death by a large stone block with a bronze plaque containing his portrait and the inscription "Prunes, A Burro. 1867–1930. Fairplay, Alma, All Mines in This District."

[6] Hafen, *Colorado and Its People*, I, 181–82, II, 493–94; Francis S. Williams, "The Influence of California Upon the Placer Mining Methods of Colorado," *Colorado Magazine*, Vol. XXVI (1949), 127–43; Hafen, *Overland Routes*, 192–94.

[7] Hafen, *Colorado and Its People*, I 180–81; Henderson, *Mining in Colorado*, 7–8; Works Progress Administration, *Colorado: A Guide to the Highest State*, 405; Wolle, *Stampede*, 74, 86; Stone, *History*, I, 265; Bayard Taylor, *Colorado: A Summer Trip*, 112.

Adjacent to Fairplay another important mining town which soon arose was Alma. Here one of the dance-hall girls was such a favorite that an admirer gave her a pair of silver heels for her slippers. Dancing away the riotous nights, men called her "Silver Heels" until nobody could recall her real name. When a smallpox epidemic struck the settlement, most women fled. Silver Heels, who was a brave girl if not a good one, remained to nurse the ill and comfort the dying. When her task was done, she suddenly disappeared, just as the miners were taking up a large collection for her. Nobody knows what happened to her, but the commonest surmise is that she had caught the disease herself and did not want her admirers to see her with her beauty destroyed. The camp, unable to give her the money, honored her by naming one of the peaks in the area "Mount Silverheels."

Other important discoveries made in the South Park in 1859 were at Montgomery, Buckskin Joe, Mosquito, Hamilton, Jefferson, Negro Gulch, French Gulch, and Breckenridge (originally called Spaulding Diggings). These settlements were often short lived. In 1859, prospectors made several finds outside the South Park along the Arkansas River and also in the general area of the town of Boulder.

The rush of 1860 probably brought as many people to Colorado as that of the previous year, but there was less excitement, more determination, and the new group as a whole was of a higher type.[8] More men brought their families with them to find a new and permanent home. At the maximum in the spring, perhaps five thousand persons a week arrived; it is almost correct to say that for a full month there was a continuous wagon train extending from Omaha to Denver.

The most exciting discovery in 1860, the richest placer ever found in Colorado, was at California Gulch, slightly below the present city of Leadville.[9] Early in April, three small groups of men on the Arkansas River decided to pool their efforts and to share any favorable results. The party of Georgians was led by Abe Lee, who on April 26 reportedly shouted, "By God, I've got all of California in this here pan." His men built a bonfire that night and fired off their

[8] Bancroft, *Colorado*, 398; Hafen, *Colorado and Its People*, I, 193–95.

[9] Stone, *History*, I, 267–68; Don L. and Jean H. Griswold, *The Carbonate Camp Called Leadville*, 3–14; Hafen, *Colorado and Its People*, I, 195–196, 283, 290; Hall, *History*, I, 195, 251; Bancroft, *Colorado*, 483; Mrs. H. A. W. Tabor, "Cabin Life in Colorado," *Colorado Magazine*, Vol. IV (1927), 71–75.

guns; the next morning, the other prospectors joined them. By the end of the summer, ten thousand people thronged six miles of the gulch. The first woman to arrive was the wife of a storekeeper, H. A. W. Tabor, who established himself in the new town of Oro City. The miners found the placer diggings uneven, the barren spots closely intermixed with the unusually rich, but a few of the best claims yielded fifty to sixty thousand dollars' worth of gold each. The pay dirt was under a layer of cemented gravel and scoria, a type of hardpan, six to eighteen inches thick. By 1865, the diggings were generally exhausted and most men drifted away. They did not become very excited over the discovery of a fair lode mine in 1868, but kept on looking for a better one. As we shall see, it was found eventually and the rush to Leadville resulted.

Other men in 1860 prospected in the San Juan Mountains in southwestern Colorado. Led by Charles Baker, an expedition of some size explored the area but missed the gold others were to find later. It encountered much difficulty with heavy snows. The following year, false rumors of fabulous discoveries by this group sent others into the region; winter found hundreds scattered throughout the area and while some struggled out, others undoubtedly died.

A territorial census in 1861 showed 25,331 people in Colorado; of these, 3,000 were in the chief town, Denver. Adverse factors soon slowed the area's growth. The placer deposits were generally exhausted and lode mining became increasingly difficult. The Civil War prompted many a man to go east to fight and immigration declined sharply.

There was a frenzy of speculation in Colorado mines, especially those in the Black Hawk–Central City area, during the fall of 1863 and the next spring.[10] New Yorkers led the way in buying properties at extravagant figures. Coloradans were much interested in selling, especially if their claims were already exhausted or if their ore could not be profitably smelted by methods then known or if the water in their mines was more than the best pumps then available in Colorado would remove. Some of the properties sold were so fraudulent that the buyers could not even find their location. During 1864, the speculative boom was so great that Central City's recorder had to work his force day and night on the many changes of title; his earnings were

10 Hall, *History*, I, 307–308; Bancroft, *Colorado*, 488; Lavender, *Big Divide*, 66; Hafen, *Colorado and Its People*, I, 290; Ellis, *Teller*, 53–54.

estimated at forty thousand dollars. There was so much dishonesty at this time that Colorado mines earned a bad reputation among the investing public, who became reluctant to put funds into any of the area's mineral enterprises, even those clearly legitimate. In the boom period properties potentially valuable were mismanaged by eastern purchasers, who sent out inexperienced men to take charge, bought machinery that was of little use, paid high sums for alleged secrets of smelting which were worthless or fraudulent, and erected expensive buildings before they knew whether they could operate a mine profitably. These same mistakes were made earlier in California's lode mines.

At first miners in Colorado sought only gold; gradually they came to realize that they should also look for silver.[11] In 1864, a careful assay of ore by Frank Dibdin was the first to impress men generally that Colorado had a future in silver. The first paying lode, the Belmont, was discovered on September 14, 1864, not far from Georgetown, about sixty miles west of Denver. To the area, the so-called Argentine District, there was a rush in the middle sixties; its richest lode proved to be the Anglo-Saxon, assaying $23,000 to the ton. In Laramie, Wyoming, Sam Conger noticed a carload of silver ore from Nevada's Comstock Lode being shipped over the Union Pacific and remembered seeing a similar substance in the mountains west of Boulder. Returning to Colorado, he found the Caribou silver mine in 1869, which caused a rush, other discoveries, and the boom town of Caribou.

These mineral developments in the interior made business for the foothill towns, the chief of which was Denver.[12] Almost treeless, in 1859 its best homes were rude log cabins with dirt floors, canvas or earth roofs, stool tables, pole bedsteads, and chimneys of sticks plastered over with mud. The next year, some houses were built with board floors, glass windows, and shingle roofs, painted buildings became common, and brick was used for a few structures. By 1860, Denver had a circulating library, a debating club, a chess group, river-cut ice sold in summer from two wagons, an ample supply of dirty water distributed in barrels, a brick kiln, and enough stores that peddlers were required to have a license. By 1866, it seemed as well built to vis-

11 Wolle, *Stampede*, 116–17; Bancroft, *Colorado*, 492; Hafen, *Colorado and Its People*, I, 336–37, II, 496.
12 Taylor, *Colorado*, 37; Hafen, *Colorado and Its People*, I, 231–35.

itor Bayard Taylor as any town of equal size in the Mississippi Valley.

Denver's first newspaper was the *Rocky Mountain News*, founded on April 23, 1859, by William N. Byers.[13] During the early years those persons just arriving in Denver were urged to register at its office and obtain a number of free handbills introducing them to business houses of the community. Editor Byers always kept a weapon handy at his desk, for he waged vigorous warfare against the pioneer underworld. When in July, 1860, he again attacked the Criterion Saloon, a number of men there raided the *News*. They captured the editor, whose staff seized their weapons, but Byers said he would go quietly to the saloon. At the Criterion the proprietor suggested imprisoning him in the back room and, by this ruse, was able to let him out quietly at the rear. The editor was back at his office hardly long enough to barricade it before a siege began. After considerable delay, one Criterion man launched an attack singlehanded; a group of honest people arrived just in time to break up the siege by killing the gunslinger.

Another problem which faced Byers and other Colorado publishers before 1871 was an occasional shortage of newsprint, which was shipped in from the East. However, there was a mill at Golden which produced wrapping paper and in emergencies every editor had to use it.

Religion came to Denver on November 21, 1858, when the first sermon was preached to a congregation of about a dozen at one end of a cabin while a gambling game continued without interruption at the other.[14] Indeed, the pioneer preachers spoke wherever they could find a place—in private homes, dance halls, saloons, gambling rooms, store buildings, or even in the open air. The first ministers officially assigned to the area were the Reverend William H. Goode and the Reverend Jacob Adriance of the Methodist Episcopal church. By the close of 1860, there were six organized churches in Denver.

When O. J. Goldrick first entered Denver, he created a sensation; he was wearing a silk hat, broadcloth suit, and kid gloves, yet was driving an ox team and using a regular bullwhacker's whip.[15] His much-discussed debut marked the arrival of formal education, for

[13] Hafen, *Colorado and Its People*, I, 223–36, II, 250–56.

[14] *Ibid.*, I, 193, 255–56, II, 199–202.

[15] Baker and Hafen, *History*, 1154–55; Hafen, *Colorado and Its People*, I, 193, 257–58.

Goldrick was a schoolteacher, among other things, and more practical than his first appearance suggested. In October, 1859, he began
instruction in a flat-roofed cabin at Auraria, the town that soon
merged with Denver; his students, thirteen the first day, paid him
tuition. By 1860, there were two rival institutions, and in 1862,
Denver started its first public free school.

Quite early some who had come west to prospect decided that
their best gold mine was to raise provisions.[16] In 1858, they sold such
produce as peas, lettuce, onions, watermelons, muskmelons, cabbages,
and squashes; they could not grow enough for several years to meet
the local demand. The first Colorado farmer to irrigate was David K.
Wall of Golden, who in 1859 netted two thousand dollars by diverting water from Clear Creek over a couple of acres in his garden. Also
in 1859, local cows, chickens, and their produce first became available.
Supplementary to these supplies were others brought in by ox team
from the Missouri River at a freight rate of four to six dollars per
one hundred pounds. Considering this charge, the selling prices for
produce in Denver were reasonable. Meat prices were kept low by
the abundance of wild game, easily killed and offered for sale fairly
cheap. Fresh fruit was almost unobtainable; apples were shipped in
to sell as high as a quarter each.

Denver soon had a considerable number of housewives. They were
very proud of their fair complexions and tried hard to preserve them
by wearing sunbonnets. Most women used ordinary calico as their
dress material; some could afford the better, higher-priced French
calico and Scotch gingham.

Twenty physicians settled in Colorado by 1860, mostly in Denver,
although a few went to the mountains, where they "sustained the
body by the practice of medicine and the spirit of hope by hunting
gold." Not until 1867 did the first dentist, Dr. B. Wesley Rogers,
establish himself in Denver.

Public attendance at the theater began in Denver on October 3,
1859, when Colonel Thorne's Star Company appeared in *The Cross
of Gold* at Apollo Hall, equipped with twelve candles as footlights
and seats for 350, those at the front being reserved for ladies.[17]

16 Baker and Hafen, *History*, 646–84; Hafen, *Colorado and Its People*, I, 182–84,
242–45, II, 122, 137, 380–81, 408.

17 Willison, *Dug Gold*, 82–83; Hafen, *Colorado and Its People*, I, 193, 258–68,
II, 441–53.

Thorne's group did not stay long and the real pioneer of the drama was the Haydee Star Company. It presented, among other things, Colorado's first locally written play, a tragedy by A. B. Steinberger called *Skatara, or the Mountain Chieftain;* this was not popular until remodeled into a burlesque called *Skatterer, the Mountain Thief.* By 1860, one Denver theater was regularly open each night and another usually ran three nights a week. That season, John S. Langrishe came to Denver and organized a stock company. For almost twenty years he was to dominate the city's stage, despite occasional rivals. He also established a theatrical circuit which included most of the mining gulches and mountain towns. To appear with his stock companies he brought in stars of national reputation. The golden era of Denver drama did not begin until the opening of Tabor's Grand Opera House in 1881. For twenty years everything that was great in the theater of the period appeared there. During its first ten years there were 345 weeks of plays, 54 of operas, 21 of minstrels, and over 40 of such other types of performers as magicians.

On a much less exalted level, but more important commercially, were the variety houses. These glorified saloons and gambling halls had fifteen to twenty numbers a night of dancing, singing, magic, and farce. Another attraction was the bevy of pretty, flashily dressed girls who allowed male patrons to buy them beer at a dollar a bottle and wine or champagne at from two to five dollars. For each sale the girl received a check from the waiter and immediately thrust it into her stockings; these slips showed the management whether she was to be retained at her job. Some of these women sold men keys to their hotel rooms for three or five dollars and few of the dupes later had the courage to complain that there was no such room number. A step below these variety houses was the famous Elephant Corral, a combined stable, hotel, cafe, and gambling house. Its owner simply rented tables and equipment to gamblers by the day, week, month or year; he calmly disclaimed responsibility for any scandalous cheating.

One problem common to gambling and reputable businesses was a shortage of coins.[18] Gold dust was generally used for payments, but some scoundrels were unprincipled enough to adulterate theirs in ways hard to detect quickly. It was scarcely accurate to make change

18 Hall, *History,* I, 255, II, 109–10; LeRoy R. Hafen, "Currency, Coinage and Banking in Pioneer Colorado," *Colorado Magazine,* Vol. X (1933), 81–90.

by calling a "pinch," the amount that could be held between the thumb and one finger, a quarter's worth. To help correct the situation, Clark Gruber and Company issued at Denver several thousand of their own $20, $10, $5, and $2.50 gold pieces; those of 1860 were so pure they were too soft, but those of 1861 fortunately contained a little more alloy. Also minting some money were J. J. Conway and Company of Georgia Gulch, with $10, $5, and $2.50 coins, and John Parson of Tarryall, milling $5 and $2.50 pieces. For subsidiary money, Clark Gruber and Company printed $1, $2, $3, and $5 bills, backed by the concern's gold coins, in 1861. The next year, C. A. Cook and Company of Denver issued 10¢, 20¢, 25¢, 50¢, and $1.00 denominations of paper money, which it would redeem when presented in $5 batches. The need for these makeshift devices began to vanish in 1863 when the federal government established an assay office and mint at Denver. For borrowing money during the sixties the interest rate on large amounts might be as low as 5 per cent a month and on small sums as high as 25 per cent. Even with the substantial collateral required, conditions were so unstable that those who made loans in Colorado were taking a considerable risk.

Denver, like many a mining town, had some difficulty preserving law and order.[19] The people there first took matters into their own hands in April, 1859, and hanged a convicted murderer. Not until the next spring did an organized vigilance committee arise. Its membership of one hundred was not sufficiently selective to exclude some allies of criminals, and news of its plans always reached intended victims before the committee did. Those who thought this deplorable reorganized the leadership of the vigilantes into less than a dozen, known as "The Stranglers" to those who opposed arbitrary violence and "The Bummers" to the disreputable element. The committee made a reciprocal agreement with its counterpart in Montana. The representatives from the north had hardly arrived before they pointed out two men, whom the Colorado group promptly hanged without any investigation; whether this met the ends of true justice is not clear. Certainly the committee did quash for a time the lawless element in Denver; then gradually conditions grew worse

19 Hall, *History*, I, 469–78; Willison, *Dug Gold*, 112–15; Francis S. Williams, "Trials and Judgments of the People's Courts of Denver," *Colorado Magazine*, Vol. XXVII (1950), 294–302.

again. A temporary vigilance committee arose on the night of December 1, 1868, removed a captured thief from the custody of the law, and hanged him. The following night, it cast its noose over a notorious desperado and stock thief, meekly surrendered on demand by his jailers. These warnings caused many of the lawless to depart abruptly.

To operate stagecoaches to Denver, William H. Russell and John S. Jones organized, in February, 1859, the Leavenworth and Pike's Peak Express Company.[20] First it laid out a 689-mile route from Leavenworth and Fort Riley, mostly along the Republican River. Then the company sent out an expedition of twenty wagons to establish, every twenty-five miles, stations for changing horses and feeding passengers. It started westbound service on April 18. Its operating expenses were about one thousand dollars a day; its equipment included fifty-two Concord coaches and one thousand mules. On May 11, the company purchased the contract of J. M. Hockaday and Company to carry the mail from the Missouri River along the Platte River route through Fort Kearny and Julesburg to Salt Lake City. The Leavenworth and Pike's Peak Express soon decided to transfer all its service, both Salt Lake City and Denver, to the Platte River route; it thus abandoned, after only a little use, its original road. The company's chief revenue from its Colorado service was, naturally enough, from the passengers who paid an advertised flat rate of one hundred dollars for food and transportation from Denver to Leavenworth. For letters carried as express, the fee was twenty-five cents each and for newspapers ten cents. The rate on express packages was twenty to forty cents a pound, according to size.

In 1860, a rival line started operations from Omaha to Denver. About a year later the original company fell into the hands of Ben Holladay, the celebrated western stagecoach operator, who soon merged it with the rival concern. Gradually local service began in Colorado. By the middle of 1869, there were two triweekly lines from Denver to Central City and a triweekly line each to the South Park area and to Boulder. When the famous Pony Express began its short-lived mail service to California in 1860, it dropped off Colorado

[20] Raymond W. and Mary L. Settle, *Empire on Wheels*, 27–85; Hafen, *Colorado and Its People*, I, 185–91, 295–97, 325–26; Baker and Hafen, *History*, 646–48, 797–99; Hafen, *Overland Routes*, 235–40; Taylor, *Colorado*, 27; Hall, *History*, I, 303.

letters at Julesburg, to be carried the rest of the way by stage. The first telegraph line to Colorado, a Denver branch from the new transcontinental wire at Julesburg, opened in 1863.

Transporting freight westward was a major business enterprise. The most famous of the wagon firms was Russell Majors and Waddell. The companies generally used oxen, rather than horses or mules, because they were cheaper to buy, were not so attractive to thieving Indians, and got along better on the grass available. The animals pulled wagons made by Studebaker, Schuttler, or Bain and Murphy. Illustrating the magnitude of the business, in the spring of 1860, one major Denver merchant had 4,800,000 pounds of freight moving west; from September, 1859, through May 1860, a total of 160 complete stamp mills were shipped from Missouri River points to Colorado. With the construction of the transcontinental Union Pacific through Wyoming, Denver citizens organized the Denver Pacific to connect their city with the main line at Cheyenne; it was completed in 1870. That same year, the Kansas Pacific finished laying its rails from Kansas City to Denver.

In the placer camps of the mountain regions, life was often primitive because the miners thought their stay in one place was probably quite temporary.[21] Their cabins seldom had a plank floor; instead they used sawdust sprinkled six inches thick and covered with a gunny-sack carpet. Their dishes were tin, their cook pots iron, their chairs woven from rope or rawhide, and their mattress filled with hay. If there were any wives in the camp, as many miners as possible boarded with them. These women also nursed those who were ill and perhaps worked harder than most men. The miners often wore their clothing until it rotted off. Not surprising were the frequent outbursts of skin disease and internal disturbances. The latter were not alleviated by the general custom of piling all refuse out of doors or by the large numbers of horses and mules.

More substantial than these temporary placer camps were the towns whose lode mines gave promise of endurance. Such were Black Hawk, Central City, and Nevadaville, once separate towns but soon continuous without visible division along the main gulch.[22] Each

21 Lavender, *Big Divide*, 69–70.
22 Caroline Bancroft, *Gulch of Gold: A History of Central City, Colorado*, *passim*; Ellis, *Teller*, 36; Taylor, *Colorado*, 55–68; Wolle, *Stampede*, 10–32; Muriel S. Wolle, "Adventure Into the Past, A Search for Colorado's Mining Camps," *Colo-*

had a single street, except in Central City, where some cross thorough-fares were possible. On the hillside above the main street was a row of houses, with pole foundations on the gulch side, which overlooked the roofs of the structures below. The homes, some of brick and stone but most of wood, were rich in gabled windows and that elaborately carved bargeboard, commonly known as gingerbread, which was the mark of good architecture in the 1860's. The business buildings, many of them wooden, very often contained saloons or "hotels, with pom-pous names and limited accommodations." When world traveler Bayard Taylor visited the area in 1866, he observed of Black Hawk that "the sole pleasant object is the Presbyterian Church, white, tasteful and charmingly placed on the last step of Bates Hill." He thought prices at Central City outrageous but found the mining activity in the area impressive. It attracted many, but he was hardly prepared to meet a Norwegian merchant he had last seen several years previously in Lapland.

Religious services began in Central City as early as 1859 and that year also saw the first private school opened. Black Hawk is said to have laid out the first cemetery in the state. In 1863, the two towns established public schools and in 1870 erected the first two permanent school buildings in the state. At first the instruction left much to be desired; by 1870, however, it compared favorably with that in the older cities of the East. Although there was some lawlessness in the area, always a considerable number of men strove quickly to make their town as quiet as a New England village. Certainly Black Hawk and Central City were more law abiding than other major Colorado mining centers. About the only compromise was to allow gambling and prostitution in certain areas, provided they did not flout con-ventions too much. By 1870, these cities had all the comforts of contemporary civilization. Central City may have been second in size to Denver that year, but it ranked first as a center of wealth and

rado Magazine, Vol. XXVII (1950), 11–23; Lynn I. Perrigo, "The First Decade of Public Schools at Central City," Colorado Magazine, Vol. XII (1935), 81–91; Lynn I. Perrigo, "Law and Order in Early Colorado Mining Camps," Mississippi Valley Historical Review, Vol. XXVIII (1941–42), 41–62; Lynn I. Perrigo, "The First Two Decades of Central City Theatricals," Colorado Magazine, Vol. XI (1934), 141–52; Lynn I. Perrigo, The Little Kingdom: A Record Chiefly of Central City in the Early Days, passim; Hal Sayre, "Early Central City Theatricals and Other Reminis-cences," Colorado Magazine, Vol. VI (1929), 47–53; Caroline Bancroft, Historic Central City, 8.

culture. In it Henry Moore Teller, the political leader, opened the four-story Teller House in 1872; at the time it was the largest and finest hotel in the state, well justifying its cost of sixty thousand dollars. When President U. S. Grant walked up to its entrance in 1873, he could hardly believe the information that he had just crossed about fourteen thousand dollars' worth of silver bricks, laid especially for the occasion. Central City, Black Hawk, and Nevadaville were all in Gilpin County, the smallest in Colorado but so powerful that it dominated the territory politically in the early days and came commonly to be called "The Little Kingdom of Gilpin."

Drama came to Central City in the form of the three Wakely sisters; for male support they would hire whatever man happened to pass by on the street. Early players ad-libbed considerable profanity, suiting the taste of the miners. When the completion of the railroad to Black Hawk made it convenient for traveling companies to reach the city, during the seventies and eighties Central City saw the finest dramatic talent available in America. The town's major catastrophe came in 1874 when a fire, starting in a Chinese home, burned all the buildings in the city except Senator Teller's hotel. A special train rushing aid up from Golden went so fast that it shook one man off and had to back up a considerable distance to retrieve him. The city was quickly rebuilt better than ever, for much more brick was used and the streets were widened.

Georgetown, the center of a silver craze in 1867, became a permanent mining town.[23] In the earliest days, Methodist Deacon Smith, riding circuit, held occasional church services there and summoned his congregation by blowing lustily on a four-foot horn that could be heard for miles. Gradually the first excitement gave way to more restrained and orderly progress. The first pretentious hotel, the Barton House, opened in 1867, and in that same year the first newspaper, the *Georgetown Miner*, began publication. Two years later, the first theater, McCellan Hall, seating nearly four hundred people, opened its doors. Its productions and the public dances held at various places met the approval of the town's Catholics and Episco-

23 John W. Horner, *Silver Town*, 77–280; Wolle, *Stampede*, 116–21; WPA, *Colorado*, 203–204; Hafen, *Colorado and Its People*, I, 336; Gene M. Gressley, "Hotel de Paris and Its Creator," *Colorado Magazine*, Vol. XXXII (1955), 28–42; James E. Russell, "Louis Dupuy and the Hotel de Paris of Georgetown," *Colorado Magazine*, Vol. XIII (1936), 210–15.

palians, but not that of the Presbyterians, Baptists, or Methodists. Nobody officially sanctioned the red-light district. The townspeople must have read with interest in the local paper about one of the new girls there, who promptly acquired the nickname "Tid-bit." Two weeks after Tid-bit's arrival, a young woman from Kansas City came inquiring for a sister who in a fit of rage had deserted her husband and fled west. The description fitted Tid-bit, by now more than willing to cast aside her scarlet role. In 1870, a public bathhouse opened, advertising its hot or cold water at seventy-five cents "per ablution" as preferable to a washtub in front of the kitchen stove.

In appearance, Georgetown became New England transplanted, especially with its carved wooden posts and picket fences. A pleasant local custom was for the men to pay a complimentary call on their lady friends on New Year's Day and receive refreshments. A less agreeable aspect was the general lack of sanitation, illustrated by the complaint of a housewife to the local newspaper editor that grocers set vegetables on the walks outside their stores without adequate covering from passing dogs; she suggested placing the edibles "above high water mark." In the 1870's, a child had only a fifty-fifty chance to live until its third birthday.

Among accident victims was the French miner Louis Dupuy. With the generous collection taken up for him he established the Hotel de Paris, which had the air of a small provincial establishment in France. Its ten bedrooms and four overflow rooms were more than satisfactory, but its fame rested especially upon Dupuy's excellent cookery and the fine wine cellar from which he would serve only with meals. He was reserved, gruff to people he didn't like, but hospitable to other guests. He enjoyed inviting a select few of his patrons to talk philosophy, science, and mechanics with him until the small hours of the morning. At one such interview he discussed the importance of diet and cookery with James E. Russell, who later as dean of Teachers College, Columbia University, was stimulated by the memory of the discussion to help greatly in developing domestic science as a field for university instruction. Dupuy's library contained three thousand volumes, many of them concerned with social and radical theories of the day or else upholding materialistic philosophy. His hotel, with its fine etchings, engravings and photographs, was a place of much refinement.

On a far lower level was the illiterate Georgetown barkeeper who did not realize that an angry sign painter had placed over his saloon the words "We sell the Worst Whiskey, Wine and Cigars." This attracted so much attention that he let it stay.

Another Georgetown man much discussed was Willam C. O'Boyle. He became expert at falsifying assays by having a little vessel filled with filings concealed up his coat sleeve in such a way that simply by passing his hand through ore samples, ostensibly to see that the crushing or stamping was properly done, he could sift in more silver. His downfall came from boasting.

The history of such mining cities as Georgetown is clear enough, but the various attempts to have Colorado created a separate territory or state are confusing.[24] At first the Denver area lay within Kansas Territory, but other parts of the present state lay within the territories of Utah, New Mexico, or Nebraska. In 1855, Kansas created Arapahoe County in the Denver region, then waited until 1858 to appoint local officials. Prospectors rushing to the mines paid almost no heed to political divisions. In February, 1859, Kansas abolished the county of Arapahoe, which had never functioned, and created instead five new ones. These never came to life because the people's reply was to elect officials for Arapahoe, although it was now legally dead, and some of them actually served their terms.

In April and June, 1859, conventions met to discuss the problem of regional government. They called an election for the people to decide whether to try to become a state or a territory; the latter won. A third convention drew up a constitution for self-styled Jefferson Territory and nominated its officials; all this the voters then approved. Some Coloradans acknowledged the authority of the new territory; few proposed to pay its one-dollar poll tax. Although Jefferson Territory did manage to perform a few functions, by the summer of 1860 it was almost wholly impotent.

Never effective were the pretensions of a much lesser organization calling itself, despite its location, Idaho Territory. Law and order were generally on an improvised local basis. That fall, the citizens of Denver, tired of having various groups try to assert authority, organized "The People's Government of Denver" and for a time suc-

24 Ellis, *Teller*, 65–75; Hafen, *Colorado and Its People*, I, 199–221, 280–300, 355, II, 374–76.

cessfully retained complete independence. Finally, in December, 1860, Congress created Colorado Territory. President Lincoln appointed William Gilpin as governor. The new executive, taking office in May, 1861, thought the Civil War situation so serious that he promptly raised local troops and paid their expenses with drafts on the national treasury amounting to $400,000. When these were not honored because they were unauthorized by Washington officials, consternation prevailed. Federal authorities finally agreed to pay the bill. The troops Gilpin raised helped turn back, at Glorieta Pass, a Confederate invasion of New Mexico which, if unchecked, might well have pressed into Colorado itself.

During territorial days each justice of the supreme court also rode circuit, acting as a local trial judge. In his trip he had, as retinue, court officials, lawyers, litigants, Spanish interpreters, and prisoners for trial. The group traveled in a caravan of mules, horses, wagons, and buggies through dusty sage mesas and over snowy mountain ranges, at night gathering around the roaring campfire to sing and to tell tall tales. By the middle 1870's, the territory's leading lawyers lived in Central City, Black Hawk, and Georgetown, where many a complicated suit tested the powers of the best attorneys available.

No sooner was Colorado a territory than some politicians began looking forward to statehood. The Republicans, in their national strategy of 1864, decided to create Colorado, Nevada, and Nebraska as states. They thought this would help the party keep its hold on the electoral college and force through postwar amendments to the federal constitution. In Colorado a state constitution was drafted but not passed. In 1865, another proposed constitution was drawn up, and it carried, perhaps by fraud, but President Johnson vetoed the federal act authorizing admission. The issue became even more involved in partisan politics than ever. Finally, in 1876, Colorado became a state, a move by then well justified by its increasing population and the prosperous outlook for its economy.

In the late 1860's and early 1870's, between one-half and two-thirds of Colorado's mineral wealth came from the Little Kingdom of Gilpin, especially Central City and Black Hawk. By 1872, Clear Creek County, particularly Georgetown, began producing enough to rival Gilpin. During the seventies there were considerable mining developments elsewhere in the territory; each had its own rush.

Much of the excitement was in southwestern Colorado.[25] The treasures of the area, hidden in 1860 from the Charles Baker group, were first revealed in 1870 and 1871 by discoveries which were themselves minor, though enough to cause a rush. Riches in the Alamosa Creek area led to the foundation of Summitville, whose elevation was 11,300 feet. To serve as gateway and supply point for it and other developing mineral areas the valley town of Del Norte was founded in 1871. When the railroad reached there from Alamosa in 1881, the Summitville mines shipped out more than three hundred thousand dollars in gold ores the first three months.

John Moss and his party made such valuable discoveries along the La Plata River in 1873 that, before the area was officially open to whites, they made a private treaty with Chief Ignacio and his Utes for rights in the region. The next year, these miners founded Parrott City.

Other prospectors explored the headwaters of the Animas River. By 1873, most of the big mines of the area had been uncovered. One of them was the North Star on King Solomon Mountain, whose entrance at 13,300 feet is said to have been the highest in Colorado. The region was a vast treasure chest, between 1882 and 1918 yielding sixty-five million dollars in minerals. In 1874, its chief town, Silverton, was founded. Soon a wagon road from there over Stony Pass to Del Norte was thronged with wagons and pack trains, charging a freight rate of thirty dollars or more a ton. These became outmoded when a railroad from Durango to the south reached Silverton in 1882. The town's population reached a maximum of three thousand people. Silverton's social life in the eighties and nineties centered in the many fraternal organizations. Most of the mines at first concentrated on silver production; in the 1890's, there was virtually a revolution which shifted more than half the area's output to gold. The reason for this was the declining price of silver, a matter discussed in the preceding chapter.

Not until 1874 did prospectors in the Lake City region find much rewarding; then Enos Hotchkiss uncovered the mine known as the Golden Fleece and caused a rush to the area, a boom to the town.

25 Bancroft, *Colorado*, 497–501; Wolle, *Stampede*, 421–33; Baker and Hafen, *History*, 455–60; Hafen, *Colorado and Its People*, I, 334–40; Fred Espinosa, "Del Norte—Its Past and Present," *Colorado Magazine*, Vol. V. (1928), 95–102; L. C. Kinkin, "Early Days in Telluride," *Colorado Magazine*, Vol. XXVI (1949), 14–26.

The rest of the seventies were good years, followed by a decline in production because of transportation problems; when the railroad came in 1889, it ushered in a decade of prosperity. There were other rushes elsewhere, giving rise to Rosita in 1872 and to Telluride and Rico in 1878.

In 1875, A. J. Staley and Logan Whitlock, while on a hunting and fishing expedition, discovered the Trout and the Fisherman lodes. Shortly, A. W. Begole and Jack Eckles located a series of extremely rich parallel veins in an area of forty acres they called the Mineral Farm. These discoveries, at first developed for their silver, led to a stampede and the founding of Ouray.[26] Ore of the area varied in worth from one hundred to two thousand dollars a ton, but before the railroad came, none valued at less than a thousand dollars could profitably be shipped out to the smelters.

Ouray had three newspapers; certainly the notable one was David F. Day's *Solid Muldoon*. From 1879 to 1892, this able editor filled his paper with vigorous remarks, often too forceful for others to reprint, caustic wit, and biting sarcasm. He once had forty-two libel suits pending against him at the same time, but did not moderate his language. He crusaded especially against dishonest mining promoters and the Republicans. Typical of the twist he could give even routine news were the following items:

A tenderfoot over in the Animas Valley ascended the Golden Clothes Pole last week; the ascension being caused by getting outside the wrong brand of mushrooms.

No people, young people ever before enjoyed such a season of undisturbed courtship as the belles and beaux of Ouray are now experiencing. Not a drop of coal oil or candle in the village.

Backward, turn backward
Oh, Time in your flight,
and make us a boy again
Just for two nights.

Nine miles south of Ouray, in the Mt. Sneffels district, rich mines were discovered in 1875 and 1876 above the timber line.

[26] Hafen, *Colorado and Its People,* I, 339–40; Wolle, *Stampede,* 371–77; Stone, *History,* I, 296; Fritz, *Colorado,* 429–32; Chauncey Thomas, "Ouray, The Opal of America," *Colorado Magazine,* Vol. XI (1934), 17–22.

Also near Ouray was the famous Camp Bird mine, discovered in 1870 and worked with fair success until 1881, its operation then being suspended because it was so terribly isolated. It lay idle until 1895, when smelter owner Thomas Walsh hired Andy Richardson to prospect for certain types of ore. Among the samples taken were some from the Camp Bird. They showed gold running as high as $3,000 a ton. Walsh hastened to buy the old mine and the adjacent properties for $20,000. He also saw that Richardson got an adjoining claim. From his purchase Walsh extracted $2,500,000 in gold; then, in 1902, he sold out for $5,100,000 and by 1918 the new owners had removed $18,000,000 more. Walsh's wife at one time owned the famous Hope diamond.

8

LEADVILLE, CREEDE, AND CRIPPLE CREEK

THE year 1877 was the year of the stampede to Silver Cliff.[1] The excitement began when R. J. Edwards and others found almost pure silver scarcely deeper than the grass roots. There was much jumping of claims and mines, giving considerable employment to armed guards. When Louis Salvich opened the second saloon in town, he cleared two thousand dollars in ten weeks. With such money to be made and with water so scarce, he simply washed his glasses in the morning and left them on the counter all day so that his customers could drink from the handiest. By 1882 the boom was over and the miners began to drift away.

The most important Colorado mining boom of the 1870's was at California Gulch.[2] In 1873, miner William S. Stevens and capitalist Alvinus B. Wood decided there was still considerable gold to be secured in the lower portion of the defile. They purchased a large tract of mineral land, built a ditch to facilitate sluicing, and on their fifty-thousand-dollar investment secured annually a 20 to 30 per cent return. The next year, they investigated the black rock which had annoyed miners in the area so long and learned from an assay that it was carbonate of lead containing silver. They kept this fact a secret for two years until certain placer claims expired so that they could secure these for themselves as quartz claims. Starting in 1876, others found additional deposits. One of the new claims was purchased by John L. Routt while he was still governor of the state. He discarded his dignity and responsibilities by personally working with a small crew of men to develop the property, grudgingly making a few trips

1 Wolle, *Stampede*, 287–93.
2 Griswold, *Leadville*, 23–272.

to Denver to perform the minimum functions of his office. When his term expired, he turned full time to the silver mine and in April, 1879, uncovered an immense body of valuable ore.

As early as 1877 many of the people in California Gulch moved up to a new town called Leadville. In that year the settlement got its first foundry, first grain store, first hardware store, first hotel, first physician, first lawyer, first regular church service, first threat of lynching, and even its first speech—by Susan B. Anthony. The next year, Leadville was incorporated, whereupon it elected city officials and began to prosper.

A storekeeper there was H. A. W. Tabor, who, with his wife, had unsuccessfully sought a treasure in Colorado since 1859. Two unpromising prospectors, former shoemaker August Rische and former steelworker George Hook, asked him to grubstake them for a one-third interest in what they might find.[3] Tabor, busy, told them to help themselves, and tradition has it that they included a jug of whiskey. The two climbed up Fryer Hill and started work at a point which they later admitted selecting only because it was in the shade of a big pine tree. Twice they returned to Tabor for additional supplies, bringing his total investment to about fifty dollars. On May 1, 1878, at thirty feet, they struck silver so rich that the first wagonload from the mine netted about $200. The two had indeed been fortunate, for they had selected the only point on the whole hill where minerals were so near the surface. If they had decided to dig elsewhere instead —a few rods in any direction—they likely would have found nothing before quitting in disgust. By July the Little Pittsburg, as the mine was christened, was yielding $8,000 a week. In September, Hook sold his share for $98,000, in November, Rische sold out for $273,500, and eleven months later, Tabor disposed of his portion for $1,000,000.

News of the Little Pittsburg inevitably precipitated a wild scramble of men to reach Leadville, now famous throughout the world.[4] That summer of 1878 probably saw a maximum of six thousand people in what came to be nicknamed "the Cloud City" because

3 Griswold, *Leadville*, 37–42; Lewis C. Gandy, *The Tabors: A Footnote of Western History*, 173–74, 188; Willison, *Dug Gold*, 102; Hafen, *Colorado and Its People*, I, 362.

4 Griswold, *Leadville*, 75–150; Willison, *Dug Gold*, 173–261; Hall, *History*, II, 456–95; Wolle, *Stampede*, 41–66; Hafen, *Colorado and Its People*, I, 361–67; Bancroft, *Colorado*, 5–10; Fritz, *Colorado*, 497.

its elevation was 10,208 feet. Freight generally came on the rails of the expanding Denver and South Park as far as Dean's, then lay stacked about in huge piles as teamsters struggled to carry it forward. Newcomers to Leadville had great difficulty finding a sleeping place, the fortunate paying a dollar a night for a blanket and some space in a boarding tent, while others simply lay down on the dirty, sawdust floor of a saloon with the hope that regular patrons would leave them alone. When the Reverend Thomas A. Uzzell came over from Fairplay, he called at all places of business, including gambling dens and dance halls, to announce his first service. Among his listeners were some of the girls and cardsharps who had teased him so much as he made his rounds. When his church building was completed, he kept the arrival of its bell secret; it rang out loudly one Sunday morning, allegedly causing a surprised miner far up one of the gulches to say to his companion: "I'll be damned if Jesus Christ hasn't come to Leadville too." Enough families arrived for the town to start a public school with Mrs. Louise H. Updegraff as instructor. One day Willie Morris and Inez Hill came back from lunch with real revolvers and told fellow students they were going to kill the teacher. A pupil slipped off to warn a member of the school board, who came and disarmed the two.

The boom of 1878, big as it was, seems small when compared to the rush of people in 1879. That summer, new arrivals, coming from all over the world, averaged 100 a day; the record was set on July 15 with 236. So many people thronged Chestnut Street and patronized its 226 business or professional establishments that pedestrians often deserted the sidewalks to make more speed by using the middle of the street. The post office handled a larger amount of mail than either Kansas City or San Francisco: it issued $351,911 in money orders and canceled $32,000 in stamps. Its general-delivery windows were at the rear to provide some shelter for the long waiting lines.

At first people had built wherever they wished, but by the fall of 1878, thoroughfares had been laid out and the following year the city gave those who still had shanties in the way of a street ten days to remove them. With the order published, Mayor William H. James discovered he had put his own stable where he shouldn't; he had no choice but to tear it down. The city expanded so rapidly that in May, 1879, there were thirty sawmills running night and day to turn out an estimated 3,600,000 feet of lumber weekly. At the peak demand it sold for sixty-five dollars per thousand feet, but later dropped to eighteen. For a time brick was cheaper than lumber and for business buildings it was preferred because it was more substantial. In 1879, the Clarendon Hotel, with 151 bedrooms, opened; it is said to have paid for itself in the first thirty days of operation. That same year, the Leadville Illuminating Gas Company began service.

There was much demand for town lots, causing prices to advance so sharply that one man who had seen both declared that the rise in Leadville was more rapid than in gold-rush San Francisco. The situation attracted so-called lot jumpers, who simply seized possession of a lot they wanted and sometimes boldly tore down a building thereon, depositing the debris and the interior furnishings on the street. In such affairs there were often threats of armed violence, and there occurred at least one fatal shooting. Needless to say, these operations also caused much confusion in legal titles.

It is no exaggeration to say that Leadville was very lawless in 1879. Daily there were quarrels and general turbulence, with whiskey often inciting the participants to drastic actions. Holdups were routine, thefts from moving wagons ordinary, burglary of homes day or night commonplace, and even raids on the cloakroom of the schoolhouse not unknown. A wise man did not go out after dark if he could help it; two pedestrians meeting in the early evening tried to give each other a wide berth, and those who had to walk late at night kept their pistols habitually drawn and often cocked.

The police force of 1879 was certainly too small to cope with the situation, and many a Leadviller would have added, too dishonest. That fall, the merchants established their own private force, which worked from sunset to daylight. In July, two rival groups hired armed forces to seize control of the Highland Chief mine, but finally decided to let the courts adjudicate. Less restrained in September were those who fought for possession of the Buckeye Bell; the hundreds of shots they exchanged killed only an innocent, if foolish, bystander and one band eventually forced the other to surrender by creeping up on them Indian fashion. Finally the town had enough and vigilantes arose. They took Edwin Frodsham, whose gang of lot jumpers was infamous, and bandit-murderer Patrick Stewart from the jail on November 20 and hanged them. The vigilance committee warned that it might take further drastic action and claimed that it was seven hundred strong. It aroused enough concern among honest working miners, who distrusted a leadership of the economic elite, that they organized among themselves a second committee, which never took any action. The first one brought down on Leadville citizens a horde of threatening letters from the roughnecks, to anybody they didn't like, warning that they controlled the city. This was idle boasting; within twenty-four hours after the hanging, an estimated four hundred undesirables left town.

The boom above ground was matched by increasing riches from Leadville's mines. When Tabor sold his share of the Little Pittsburg, he went on a claim-buying spree. Whether he knew that the Matchless, one of his purchases, was salted and thought valueless by the seller is a question on which no evidence remains. At any rate, his men dug deeper and found a rich deposit; at the maximum, Tabor's clear profits from it ran $100,000 a month. Another major mine, owned by others, was the Robert E. Lee, which in 1880 made a net income of nearly $1,000,000.

Such mines raised many problems in operating procedures, in ore refining, and in financing. The usual plan was to work slowly enough to secure everything worth extracting in a given area and then abandon it permanently.

To refine the ore from these mines required the development of considerable facilities. When Stevens and Wood announced their discovery in 1876, California Gulch was one of the most isolated spots in the nation. The next year, August R. Meyer of Alma established a sampling works, for determining the value of ore, and soon persuaded Edwin Harrison, president of the St. Louis Smelting and Refining Company, to build in the gulch the Harrison Reduction Works. In the early days Meyer did everything possible to foster the area's growth, such as persuading large wagon-freight companies to move in from other parts of the country and thus keep rates down. By the fall of 1879 there were seventeen smelter concerns operating in Leadville. To determine the value of the ore they bought from the mining companies, they usually took a sample from every tenth wheelbarrow load; to be certain there was no cheating, the sellers took one, too, and had a different assayer test it.

Inevitably the major Leadville mines were incorporated and their stock traded on the New York market. A favorite with the speculators was the Little Pittsburg, about which the best mining experts of the time expressed unbounded confidence. In February, 1880, its leading owners began selling stock in such a flood that the price fell from thirty-five dollars a share to six. They kept secret as long as they could the news that the Little Pittsburg simply had no ore left that was worth mining. This catastrophe caused a sharp decline in other Leadville stocks. To make matters worse, at this time the Chrysolite Company announced it had so overproduced that its mine was temporarily exhausted. Before too long, further exploration fortunately revealed additonal minerals and in the first year of resumed production the mine yielded four million dollars. These two episodes brought an end to speculative plunging. Thereafter companies were generally more economical in their methods, more careful and diligent in their exploration and development work, and more accurate in fixing the boundaries of their mines.

A cause of much dispute was the apex right. The federal law of 1872 authorized quartz claims not over 1,500 feet long and 600 feet wide. It gave the owner the right to all the veins throughout their entire length whose apexes were located within the area of the claim, even if the veins ran laterally in any direction and even if they undercut adjoining claims. The definition of apex, as eventually fixed by the courts, was the end or edge or terminal point of a vein nearest the surface of the earth, even if not at or close to the surface. At Leadville the veins often ran nearly horizontal and also crossed each other at many angles. The result was many expensive lawsuits.

The first serious labor dispute in Leadville started on May 26, 1880, when the Chrysolite mine imposed irritating regulations about talking and smoking during working hours.[5] The strike quickly spread to other companies, not on the original complaint, but with four new demands: every man to get a dollar-a-day wage increase; no man to work for less than four dollars a day; no man to work more than an eight-hour day; and the men to select their own shift boss. The strikers closed down almost every mine but did not carry out their proposal to shut off the pumps and flood some of them. The Miners Union denied responsibility for threats of murdering the mine owners and of laying the town in ashes. Neutral citizens staged a parade of fifteen hundred armed volunteers to overawe the strikers; the miners started such a countermarch that it was the citizens who were overawed. On June 13, the governor declared martial law. Troops promptly arrived, "requested" various "unde-

5 Griswold, *Leadville,* 181–98; Hafen, *Colorado and Its People,* II, 314.

sirable" people to leave, and announced that they would arrest as vagrants all men who could not show visible means of support. The intimidated strikers agreed to go back to work at the old rates of pay. The chief mines promised an eight-hour day and said they would try to persuade the smaller ones to grant it, too. The financial effects of the three weeks' conflict bankrupted many of the town's smaller businesses.

Business in normal times was good. It was said that in 1880 a million dollars' worth of goods was usually en route to Leadville.[6] Trade was helped by the establishment of banks, although four of these had failed by 1884 because of mismanagement.

Leadville's businessmen and clerks normally appeared in suits, although often working without their coats. Others generally wore wide-brimmed soft hats or loose-fitting caps; shirts of wool, cashmere, flannel, or cotton; work trousers or blue jeans; and mining boots or heavy, high-topped shoes. Many liked brown cotton or wool shirts; however, the younger ones preferred those of blue wool and also wore flowing blue ties.

In winter everybody had to use flannel underwear, taking particular care to protect the throat and feet. The air of the Cloud City lacked oxygen and "a man had to breathe fast to keep going." With stoves indoors kept red hot and the temperature outside often thirty degrees below zero, a person stepping outdoors inevitably took in a gasp of freezing air. It is not surprising that pneumonia was a noteworthy scourge in Leadville. Dozens of its victims, beyond dispute, were buried secretly in the middle of the night to prevent the news of so many deaths from slowing down the influx of newcomers. The wintry snow glare was serious enough for most men to wear dark glasses. Those who worked outdoors did not wash often; open pores invited the cold air and the scorching reflection of the sun to peel off the outer layers of the skin in great flakes.

Another winter problem for Leadville was its streets. Built simply out of the natural rock soil, they degenerated into soft mud by ten o'clock in the morning, and not until seven in the evening were they again hard enough to support an empty wagon and mules.

By April, 1879, sanitation demanded attention. In three weeks city crews removed five thousand wagonloads of accumulated filth from

6 Griswold, *Leadville*, 199–216; Lavender, *Big Divide*, 120–21; Gandy, *Tabors*, 255; Anne Ellis, *The Life of an Ordinary Woman*, 72.

the streets and alleys. Lack of sewers, bad housing, bad food, and excessive liquor all took their toll in health and lives. There were epidemics of smallpox and typhoid fever. The reckless riding of horses and the wild driving of teams were a hazard that caused much complaint; however, few serious accidents resulted. Leadville's altitude was high enough for newcomers to be well advised to take time to adjust to it. In the mines, accidents occurred from exploitation too rapid or too greedy to timber properly and provide other safeguards.

Horse racing began at a track three miles west of Leadville in 1879.[7] It attracted entries from various parts of the state and there was considerable betting. Always active were the "silver exchanges," the saloons, gambling houses, and dance halls, sometimes separate, sometimes combined into a single establishment. They were most active on Saturday night, Sunday afternoon, and Sunday evening; many never closed their doors all week. Their games were continuous, usually amidst much confusion; the dealers and bartenders worked eight-hour shifts. Most famous of these establishments was Pap Wyman's. One of its unusual fixtures was a large Bible, placed on a stand near the entrance of the building, which was reportedly in constant use and read by thousands. Another was a large clock which had printed across its face the legend "DON'T SWEAR." In the early morning children sat in the gutters in front of such places as Pap's, sifting their fingers through the sawdust sweepings to find overlooked gold dust and coins.

Leadville had an infamous red-light district. Some of the girls there were thought by eastern relatives to be schoolteachers, clerks, or holders of other respectable positions. The most notable house of ill fame was Winnie Purdy's, financed by a Leadville bank. To the rear of the district lay Tiger Alley, Still Born Alley, and Coon Row; these spots were notorious, among other things, as the places where drunken miners, after being plied with whiskey mixed with snuff until they became very ill, were robbed.

Very popular in the summer of 1879 were beer gardens, where so-

7 Griswold, *Leadville*, 219–45; Lavender, *Big Divide*, 130–31; Wolle, *Stampede*, 42, 48; WPA, *Colorado*, 92, 174; Hafen, *Colorado and Its People*, I, 486–87; Dorothy M. Degitz, "History of the Tabor Opera House at Leadville," *Colorado Magazine*, Vol. XIII (1936), 81–89.

called schooner skippers did the serving. Many a man found recreation and companionship by joining one of the military companies organized and financed by wealthy mine owners, who supplied splendid uniforms. Supposedly these groups were to protect the city if the Utes ever attacked, which was very unlikely; actually they satisfied chiefly a craving for splendor. Other men found social outlet in the volunteer fire companies; still others loafed around cigar stores and billiard halls.

Leadville miners, like others in the state, participated in rock-drill contests. Often they trained for two weeks in order to "get their wind in proper shape." During the fifteen minutes of the contest they frequently rained down sixty-seven or sixty-eight blows a minute and some could average as high as seventy-five. Much of their success depended upon their partners, the drill-turners, who had to keep the hole round. To sharpen the drills for such a contest was a fine art which few mastered. Prizes, especially at a state-wide competition, ran as high as five thousand dollars and there was much betting on the outcome.

At Leadville's variety or wine theaters the patrons sat at tables on the floor or in boxes flanking the stage. They were seldom charged admission, but were expected to patronize the bar, and the lapses between acts were long enough to satisfy the thirstiest. The show began about nine in the evening and the curtain was not finally rung down until four or five in the morning. At the "amphitheaters" there were variety acts, running or walking races, wrestling matches, and prize fights.

Of the legitimate playhouses, the most famous was the Tabor Opera House. This eight-hundred-seat theater, built by the wealthy mine owner at a cost of forty thousand dollars, was opened in November, 1879. At first most presentations were by the resident stock company; later the completion of a railroad to Leadville brought all of the era's notable performers on tour, especially since this offered an opportunity for some quick profits on the way from the Middle West to California. One memorable appearance was that of Fanny Buckingham in *Mazeppa,* in which the climax was for her to be carried off tied to a horse. Her specially trained charger balked at traveling in a narrow-gauge-railroad boxcar, so she had to come without him and accept as substitute a docile milk horse. Just as she began the ascent of the scenery's mountain on his back, the sound of a fish horn rang through the theater. Hearing the familiar signal for a delivery, he stopped; she kicked; he went on; he heard another blast and stopped again. The audience rejoiced. Miss Buckingham spoke words not written by the play's author, and the curtain in haste descended.

The best known of the Tabors' performers who lived in Leadville was perhaps Charles Vivian, a variety actor and ballad singer. Previously he had founded a club called the Jolly Corks and had been its national president when it evolved into the fraternal organization called the Elks. One of the notable sights in the Leadville of 1880 was his long funeral procession as it returned after the services were completed; the band struck up "Ten Thousand Miles Away," his favorite song, which he had sung countless times before the town's footlights, and the group joined in until the mountains themselves seemed to ring with it as a farewell tribute.

While it is easy to paint the seamy side of Leadville, there were also substantial and admirable aspects.[8] Many of its men were kindly, honest people of good will, fine character, and high standards who contributed to the community's cultural, social, and spiritual advancement. It had business and professional men of high caliber.

The most famous Leadville fortune was that of H. A. W. Tabor.[9] His grubstake for the prospectors who found the Little Pittsburg was the start of his good luck. Probably not even he knew how much money he cleared from his various mines; the best estimate is between eight and nine million dollars. He was a man of kindness, generosity (although too often misplaced), great courage, and real intelligence. He likely kept no record of what must have been the large amount he gave to old friends as "loans." He was always seeking new and profitable ways to use his surplus funds. Living in a gambling atmosphere, he made many speculative investments. Many of them failed, "but Tabor was too good a poker player to expect to win every bet." He bought much Denver real estate. He built and operated there the Tabor Grand Opera House, of whose physical structure Edwin Booth, probably the finest actor of his generation, said that it was the most beautiful and best equipped theater he had ever seen.

8 Griswold, *Leadville*, 238–70; Hafen, *Colorado and Its People*, I, 367–68.
9 Gandy, *Tabors*, 198–269.

One of the prices Tabor paid for his wealth was the breakup of his marriage to his first wife, Augusta, who had helped him so loyally and wisely in his years of adversity. She did not take kindly to the more flamboyant aspects of his life as a rich man and struck back with her sharp tongue, a usually effective weapon which now only drove them farther apart. She finally secured a divorce and a cash settlement, but was never willingly parted from her husband. He promptly married a beautiful and much younger woman whose companionship he had already often sought, Elizabeth McCourt Doe, generally known as Baby Doe. She at once became the object of gossip, much of it vicious; Tabor himself was an anathema to the women of Colorado.

Tabor's political ambitions prompted him to make large contributions to the state's Republican party in 1883. He hoped to be elected by the legislature to the vacant six-year term in the United States Senate; instead, it named him to the thirty days remaining in that of Henry M. Teller, just elevated to President Arthur's cabinet. In 1884, the magnate sought the governorship and the next year a federal senatorship, both without success.

In 1887, Tabor began to encounter financial troubles. Assuming that the Matchless mine would be a constant source of funds, he had put his money into investments which would yield a high return if all went well and had made no effort to keep some assets easily convertible into cash. Faced with increasing difficulties, he struggled along until the general financial panic of 1893 bankrupted him. Well past sixty, with a wife and two small children to support, he set to work as best he could. To the surprise of many, Baby Doe stuck by him with great loyalty. In 1898, he was appointed postmaster at Denver. In his days of wealth he had done much to upbuild Denver; it was a post well deserved. About a year later, he died.

Another well-known person was Carlyle Channing Davis, commonly called Cad, who made the *Chronicle* Leadville's leading daily newspaper.[10] He paid high salaries and had an excellent staff.

Mary Hallock Foote was the only writer of any significance to take part in one of the Colorado mining booms.[11] Her novels had conventional, trivial plots but gave an accurate picture of western mining

10 Hafen, *Colorado and Its People,* II, 265.
11 Mary Lou Benn, "Mary Hallock Foote, Early Leadville Writer," *Colorado Magazine,* Vol. XXXIII (1956), 93–108.

life. Of her books about Colorado, *The Led-Horse Claim* and *John Bodewin's Testimony* were chiefly concerned with mining itself. *The Last Assembly Ball* analyzed the difference between eastern and western social patterns.

The peak of Leadville's mine production came in 1882, although the camp remained quite active until after the turn of the century.[12] With the sharp decline in the demand for silver in 1893, the mining corporations placed much more emphasis upon gold. Some continued to exploit the spots they had always used, but most shifted, broadly speaking, a little to the east where larger quantities of gold were intermixed with the silver and lead. In the hard times of 1893 the companies cut the pay of miners to $2.50 a day. By 1896 some had raised wages to $3.00 and others had left them at $2.50; the labor union called a strike to enforce a uniform scale of $3.00. It pointed out that 65 per cent of the miners were married; that on the average their grocery, rent, fuel, water, and clothing bills amounted to at least $63.00 a month; and that this left almost no reserve above ordinary, unavoidable expenses. The strike was long, bitter, and at times violent; it resulted in at least three deaths, and a number of mines were so badly flooded when the pumps were forcibly shut off that they never reopened. The sheriff was friendly to the union; the troops sent in by the state governor certainly were not. Finally the strike was broken and the miners returned to work on the owners' terms.

A more pleasant, earlier event in the Leadville of 1893 was the opening of the Ice Palace on New Year's Day. Built in the form of a Norman castle, it was 320 feet wide and about one-half mile long and had ice-block walls, eight feet thick, into which articles on exhibition were frozen. Stonecutters were employed to trim the blocks, but they proved too slow and were replaced by specially imported Canadian wood choppers, whose work with a broadax was faster and neater. The palace included a skating rink, a grand ballroom, lesser ballrooms, and several banquet rooms; admission was fifty cents. No intoxicants were sold in the building, although somehow the tea had a peculiar flavor not found at tea parties.

At various times there was mining excitement in the Gunnison

12 Mrs. James R. Harvey, "The Leadville Ice Palace of 1896," *Colorado Magazine,* Vol. XVII (1940), 94–101; Willison, *Dug Gold,* 261; Griswold, *Leadville,* 55, 199; Lavender, *Big Divide,* 186–87; Wolle, *Stampede,* 58–61.

area, southwest of Leadville across mountain barriers.[13] The town itself was founded in 1874; no mines were ever found adjacent to the city limits, but it prospered as a commercial center. In the region around Tin Cup, placer operations on a modest scale began as early as 1861; then in 1878 came the discovery of the Gold Cup mine and men rushed into the area, thinking it was going to be a second Leadville. The ore proved to be a mixture of gold, silver, lead, iron, copper, and sometimes other metallic substances, so that smelting was expensive and the net profit small. Once when a freighter with his six-mule team brought in thirty-five hundred pounds of flour, he found himself selling the hundred-pound sacks, at fourteen dollars each, almost before he had stopped his wagons. Gradually the mining excitement waned. Tin Cup became almost a ghost town, then, from 1904 to 1910, revived as a gold-mining center.

Adjacent to Tin Cup was Pitkin, founded in 1879 as the result of a fortunate accident. Two prospectors who had searched the region for two unfruitful years were saying at lunch that they might as well leave the area. One, in his disgust, picked up a rock and hit another one a couple of times. This knocked off a chunk, but it did not fall to the ground; instead, it hung suspended. It was so-called wire silver and a subsequent assay of the discovery showed it to be 80 per cent pure.

All of these developments helped to make Gunnison prosperous. In 1881, a railroad line of the Denver and Rio Grande reached town; in 1883, a branch of the Denver and South Park came. Between 1893 and 1895 there was more mining excitement in the Gunnison area, this time over gold, and thousands of men hurried into the area. Typical of the outlying mining towns was Spencer, established in 1894. By fall it had a newspaper and three operating mines. Its mineral formation was so similar to Cripple Creek's that men of that city and Colorado Springs invested much money in Spencer. Unfortunately, however, the veins of mineral pinched out as they went deeper and by 1898 gold operations had almost ceased. Of the mining towns which surrounded Gunnison, the most enduring was Crested Butte, founded in 1880 because of its precious metals but long lived because

13 S. E. Poet, "The Story of Tin Cup, Colorado," *Colorado Magazine*, Vol. IX (1932), 30–38; C. E. Hagie, "Gunnison in Early Days," *Colorado Magazine*, Vol. VIII (1931), 121–29; George A. Root, "Gunnison in the Early Eighties," *Colorado Magazine*, Vol. IX (1932), 201–13; Wolle, *Stampede*, 178, 182–84; Hafen, *Colorado and Its People*, I, 445; Stone, *History*, I, 287–88.

of its extensive coal deposits. The town was notable for a winter snowfall so deep that to provide proper entrance at all seasons its householders had to build two-story privies.

North of Gunnison and west of Leadville lay Aspen.[14] To its area the original prospectors were attracted by the immense amount of float debris. They started looking for silver lodes, made the initial discovery on July 3, 1879, and soon had claims strung out for forty-five miles. That fall, men from the area talked at Denver with B. Clark Wheeler and Charles A. Hallam, agents and partners of Cincinnati capitalist D. M. Hyman; the two Coloradans made conditional purchases of several mines. The following January, Wheeler led a group of five snowshoers into the region for a seventeen-day trip over drifts averaging five to seven feet on the level. What he saw convinced him that the area had a great future and he speedily gave enthusiastic reports to the newspapers. In May he returned, surveyed the streets of the newly established town of Aspen, and undertook to develop it as a real estate venture. Much more important were his lectures far and wide on its potential wealth and his influence in attracting conservative men of capital to invest their funds in the area's mines.

In March and April, 1880, there was a major rush to the Aspen region. It was a very exhausting trip to hike over the rugged mountain range from Leadville, so rugged that many turned back short of their objective. Those who pushed on knew little, but expected much, of what they would find; instead of securing immediate wealth they at first faced a struggle for existence in a largely unexplored region. For several years the mines around Ashcroft seemed the most promising because the lodes at Aspen were buried beneath glacial gravels and the ore-bearing rocks were less distinguishable from the ordinary ones than was usual. By 1884, however, Aspen had clearly shown its superiority and most of the houses at Ashcroft were dragged the twelve miles to it. In the Emma mine, a single chamber the size of an ordinary bedroom netted the owners a half-million dollars. Unusually large nuggets were occasionally found; the largest on record

14 Len Shoemaker, *Roaring Fork Valley, passim;* Frank L. Wentworth, *Aspen on the Roaring Fork,* 22–23, 115–316; Wolle, *Stampede,* 232–41; Henderson, *Mining in Colorado,* 45–46; Hafen, *Colorado and Its People,* I, 446–47; C. S. Thomas, "An Argonaut of the Roaring Fork," *Colorado Magazine,* Vol. VII (1930), 205–16.

came from the Smuggler mine in 1894, a solid chunk of 2,060 pounds, 93 per cent pure silver. Many of the mines, above the timber line, used gravity-powered or electric tramways to carry their ore to the mills at the base of the mountains. There were innumerable lawsuits about title to valuable ore bodies, and development was delayed thereby. By 1889 the town had thirty-three lawyers.

Health conditions in early Aspen were poor. The serious outbreak of malarial fever in 1883 was attributed to many causes: the fruit, tainted by decay; the cabbage, so high in price it was not trimmed down to the solid head; the home-delivered water, left standing in its barrel for as much as a week; the outhouses, almost none with a cesspool as much as five feet deep; and the back yards, partly filled with decaying matter. In 1888, there was a bad epidemic of scarlet fever.

At first Aspen's nearest source of supplies and its ore market was Leadville. Burro transport originally cost one hundred dollars per ton; competition eventually drove the rate down to twenty-five. In 1887, both the Denver and Rio Grande and the Colorado Midland railroads arrived. The top year of production, ten million dollars in ore, was 1889. Aspen was the greatest silver camp on earth in 1891 and 1892, with eleven thousand residents, a streetcar system, ten churches, three banks, and six newspapers. B. Clark Wheeler built there an excellent opera house and a substantial hotel, each costing about eighty thousand dollars. A unique recreation was the Bathing Train, which left Aspen at six in the evening for the forty-one-mile trip to the widely known Glenwood Springs and returned at ten; round-trip fare, including a swim, was two dollars.

Aspen was hard hit by the financial panic of 1893; almost all the mines closed down without notice on July 1. Workers whom they had for years provided with almost limitless employment at good wages were now cast adrift. Most employees had only small savings, and these were soon swept away when the local banks failed; moreover, the good years had not taught thrift. Many families remained in Aspen, despite much suffering and distress. Finally some companies agreed to reopen, with wages cut to $2.50 a day, and by 1897 there were two thousand miners regularly at work. The boom was clearly over, however, and gradually Aspen declined.

From the early days through the turn of the century, the separating of Colorado's gold and silver from the rock in which it was imbedded proved to be a difficult problem for refiners.[15] The ore would not yield much under methods normally practiced in California and Nevada. At the first stamp mills in the state, water, carried through wooden flumes, moved the overshot water wheels of large diameter; coupled directly, these turned the camshaft, which lifted the stamps and let them fall by gravity. Later, steam was substituted for water power. The mills came to be built with a deep mortar and their stamps used a long, slow drop of thirty or forty times per minute. In the 1860's, the mills recovered about half of the gold at an average rate of $25.00 per ton; gradually they revised their methods until by 1925 they secured all the gold, about $6.82 a ton.

The first great advance in Colorado methods came with the establishment of a smelter at Black Hawk by the Boston and Colorado Smelting Company. Thanks largely to the work of N. P. Hill, its methods were a decided improvement over those previously used. Difficulties arose because many a claim had been sold, at one time or another, with the aid of a fictitious assay which exaggerated its value. When the smelter processed its ore, the yield was so much less than the owners expected that they were sure the company was cheating them; only gradually could it convince Coloradans of its honesty. The company charged high prices, at first $60 a ton to handle ore assaying $120 a ton. It produced a gold, silver, and copper matte (or mixture) which it originally shipped to Vivian and Sons, Swansea, Wales, who completed the refining process. In 1873, the Black Hawk firm enlarged its works into a complete refinery. By 1877, however, the company faced another problem: fuel. It had been using wood, which was growing increasingly scarce in the area; then, too, the federal government was becoming unpleasant about the unauthorized removal of large quantities of timber from its land. A further difficulty was the condition of the roads, what with some teams hauling wood and others ore in all kinds of weather. The company decided to shift from charcoal to the coking coals of Trinidad. To facilitate rail transportation, it moved its works from Black Hawk to Argo, just outside Denver. In its new plant the greatest improvement was the fuel economy gained by delivering red-hot ore from the roaster directly to the smelting furnaces.

The Boston and Colorado had major rivals at Golden and Lead-

15 Baker and Hafen, *History*, 701–16; Hall, *History*, I, 442–45; Bancroft, *Colorado*, 784–86; Hafen, *Colorado and Its People*, I, 448–49, II, 498–503.

ville. In 1899, almost all the state's plants fell into the hands of the American Smelting and Refining Company.

The Colorado smelters employed four different methods in ore extraction, depending upon the nature of the rock. Amalgamation was to have mercury, sometimes called quicksilver, combine with the gold or silver in ore crushed by a stamp mill; to remove the waste rock; and then to heat the fused material until the mercury escaped, leaving a pure mineral residue. Roasting was a heating process valuable for the many ores containing sulphur, which burned readily and could thus be eliminated. Chlorination added chlorine to ore after it had been crushed and roasted; this formed soluble gold chloride, from which the gold could then be easily precipitated. The cyanide process mixed crushed ore with potassium cyanide to form a soluble compound from which the gold was secured by electrolysis.

An early supplement to such methods was the so-called Gilpin County Bumping Table, which by a series of sharp bumps so agitated the water carrying crushed ore over it from the stamp mill that the minerals would settle to the bottom while the waste rock, which was lighter, would float away. An improvement on this was the Wilfley Table, across which the water carried, simultaneously, various metals of different specific gravities; each flowed in distinct streaks and so could be collected separately.

Most of the very early machinery for Colorado mines was made by Hendrie and Bolterhoff at Burlington, Iowa, often from plans drawn up in San Francisco. In 1869, Peter McFarlane established at Central City a machine shop and foundry which equipped many a mine, mill, and smelter. He contributed much to the perfection of the Gilpin County Bumping Table. At Silver Plume, also in 1869, Charles Burleigh invented a power-driven rock drill which came to be used widely throughout the West.

Transportation into mining areas was a constant problem to Coloradans.[16] The first method used to carry freight into a new camp was the burro; thus in 1881 regular pack trains ran from Grant to Aspen. A large one contained between sixty and one hundred burros driven

[16] Baker and Hafen, *History*, 803–804, 834–40; Lavender, *Big Divide*, 127, 137–49; William M. Dinkel, "A Pioneer of the Roaring Fork," *Colorado Magazine*, Vol. XXI (1944), 133–40; Elmer R. Burkey, "The Georgetown-Leadville Stage," *Colorado Magazine*, Vol. XIV (1937), 177–87; D. H. Cummins, "Toll Roads in Southwestern Colorado," *Colorado Magazine*, Vol. XXIX (1952), 98–104.

by two mounted men and two shepherd dogs which bit the heels of any animal that strayed. Soon, demand would arise in the new camp for a road to replace the burro trail. In the 1860's and 1870's, this was generally met by organizing a toll-road company as a business venture. It is clear, despite lack of detailed records, that a network of such roads developed, especially in the area immediately west of Denver. Typical fees varied from fifty cents to a dollar for each vehicle drawn by a single span of animals, with extra charges for a larger team. The road companies had to allow free passage to or from funerals or other religious services, which inspired many an impecunious miner to travel on Sunday. They tried to locate their collection stations in narrow canyons or similar points where evading the toll by detouring through the woods would be impossible. The most important builder and owner of Colorado toll roads was Otto Mears, who from a shoestring start constructed 450 miles of them over fifteen mountain passes, some more than eleven thousand feet high. His greatest achievement was the road from Ouray to Silverton, which used a shelf gouged out of solid rock a thousand feet above the canyon floor and then crossed Red Mountain. (It now forms the base for the present-day Million Dollar Highway, generally held to be the most beautiful and spectacular in the state.) In the 1880's, many toll roads were built primarily as a service to the community rather than from much hope of profit; funds were subscribed by many people of the area.

The wagon-freight services over Colorado roads were often operations of considerable magnitude. Thus in 1879 between five and seven thousand men were employed in those from Denver, Canon City, and Colorado Springs to Leadville; on the last-named route alone twelve thousand animals were kept busy. In wagon freighting generally there was much competition, with rates usually not being as important as expeditious service. The criterion for the best driver was whether he could deliver the biggest cargo in the shortest possible time and return for another. He was expected to do his own loading and unloading. If his trip was long, he used the stations established to give him and his animals a night's rest. On the steep upgrades the driver might use a team as large as twenty animals, hitched five abreast. He then rode the left wheel mule, telling his team which way to go by means of jerks or a steady pull on the line. Often he hauled two wagons hooked together, with just enough space between to allow him to negotiate sharp curves. His vehicle had large wooden blocks for brake shoes, which he applied from his saddle by means of a rope reaching to the large wooden poles used as lever arms. The driver reckoned the average life of his wagon and team to be three years. He had to be especially skilled on the many narrow roads with turns so sharp that the only way to go around was to get up speed, bunch the animals, and allow momentum to carry the wagons safely through. Under such conditions upgrade, he used an assistant to direct mules placed behind the vehicles and harnessed to a long push pole. In winter the teamster replaced his wheels with runners and shod his animals with calks or, in rare instances, bolted to their hoofs flat board snowshoes equipped with calks. While small freighting outfits were numerous, the great bulk of the traffic fell to a few large concerns. Expenses were high, but so were the profits.

For passengers there was stagecoach service. Of coaches operating through difficult terrain, typical perhaps was the Georgetown-Leadville line. From the railway at Georgetown the stage company built in 1879 a road called the High Line and by the next year was running in each direction two daily coaches regularly, a third occasionally. Its chief difficulties came in the winter, when it used sleighs equipped with a unique snowshoe-like brake, to run over the top of the mountains to connect with stages on either side. It employed three to six men on this portion of the route to help the homemade plow keep the road clear and, when needed, to pull the horses back onto the hard-beaten trail quickly enough to prevent their becoming buried in the snow. The drivers wrapped their feet in burlap, warmer than overshoes and less likely to slip. In spring the company's chief concern was with washouts and unsafe bridges; its stages carried long bridge planks to use in getting across dangerous places.

In certain mining communities a strictly local institution was the so-called self-returning horse. A man would rent the animal in town, ride him high up the mountainside to a mine, tie the reins to the saddle horn, and let him go. The horse knew he was free, unless mounted at the mine, and would bolt on the way down whenever anybody tried to snatch him for an unpaid ride.

Eventually railroads were built to the more important mining camps.[17] At first these were narrow-gauge lines, with their rails three

[17] L. L. Waters, *Steel Trails to Santa Fe*, 100–27; Baker and Hafen, *History*, 816–50.

feet apart instead of the usual four feet, eight inches; many were never widened later. Cheaper to construct, with sharp curves made possible by shorter cars, and often with steep grades, the narrow gauge seemed to many an excellent means to escape the heavy expense of building a standard line into mining areas whose duration was speculative. The baby roads, as they were sometimes called, operated at comparatively slow speeds, even on straight, level track, but their diminutive equipment was fully the equal of that of their larger contemporaries. On through passenger trains, for example, they carried sleeping and parlor cars as well as day coaches.

The foremost of these narrow-gauge lines was the Denver and Rio Grande. When Leadville showed signs of becoming a major mining camp, both it and the standard-gauge Atchison, Topeka and Santa Fe decided, in 1877, to build from Pueblo or Canon City through the Royal Gorge to Leadville. Unfortunately, in the narrowest part of Royal Gorge there was room for only one railroad. With the enmity the two lines had developed in their conflict over Raton Pass between Colorado and New Mexico that year, the idea of a compromise occurred to neither side. When the Rio Grande began taking steps to occupy the coveted spot, the Santa Fe moved faster, recruited a force of men at Canon City in the middle of the night, and occupied the gorge first. To protect its new possession, the AT&SF imported about a hundred toughs from Dodge City; for its own offensive, the D&RG hired combat troops from various mining camps. These forces placed some reliance upon trenches but much more on stone forts. Although a few shots were exchanged, most of the fighting was left to the exceedingly complex maneuvers of opposing lawyers in local and federal courts. Finally, in 1880, the Denver and Rio Grande secured exclusive rights to the Royal Gorge and the Santa Fe abandoned its attempts. Released from warfare with its standard-gauge rival, the narrow gauge's various lines reached Leadville in 1880; Silver Cliff, Durango, and Gunnison in 1881; Silverton in 1882; Ogden, Utah, in 1883; Aspen and Ouray in 1887; Lake City in 1889; and Creede in 1891.

Considerably earlier, another narrow gauge, the Colorado Central Railroad, built from Denver to Black Hawk in 1872, to Georgetown in 1877, and to Central City in 1878. The slim-sized Denver and South Park started west in 1872, secured running rights for the last miles into Leadville in 1880, and two years later built its own line there.

In 1883, the South Park line completed to Gunnison a branch distinguished by the lofty situation of its Alpine Tunnel. In 1899, toll-road builder Otto Mears turned to railways, completing a short line from Silverton to Red Mountain and Ironton. His lines are now remembered especially for the fancy annual passes given to certain of Mears's favorites; they were solid silver, silver filigree, or buckskin. In 1891, Mears finished his narrow-gauge Rio Grande Southern from Ridgway, near Ouray, to Durango.

Into the empire of diminutive trains the standard-gauge Colorado Midland began to intrude from Colorado Springs, reaching Leadville in 1886 and Aspen the next year. Its advantage of a shorter distance than the Rio Grande had from Denver to these mining camps was more than offset by severe grades. In 1890, to meet the Midland's competition, the Rio Grande standard-gauged a main line from Denver through the Royal Gorge to Leadville and Ogden.

The Colorado mining rushes attracted people of various races.[18] To Central City and Black Hawk large numbers of Cornish miners came early. Generally known by the nickname of "Cousin Jacks," they aided sound development of the mines, especially by their skill in sinking shafts and in tracing gold-bearing veins through the rock. They devised the so-called Cornish pump for removing water from underground recesses and popularized the plan of renting a certain portion of a largely undeveloped property for 10 or 15 per cent royalty. When first Irish and then Tyrolese miners from Austria came into Gilpin County, the Cornishmen initially clashed with them; before long the dislike was dispelled. The first Chinese arrived in Colorado shortly after the completion of the transcontinental Central Pacific Railroad. Apparently the first attempt to hire them as miners was near Central City in 1873 and the first organized resistance was at Caribou the following year. Into a fair number of the camps, especially Leadville, Chinese were not allowed to enter. Whatever the pretense, the real reason for exclusion was that they would work for less pay than a white man.

The Colorado frontiersmen had the usual difficulties with Indians. Originally the whole area was in theory set aside for the red men. To

18 Lynn I. Perrigo, "The Cornish Miners of Early Gilpin County," *Colorado Magazine*, Vol. XIV (1937), 92–101; Patricia K. Ourada, "The Chinese in Colorado," *Colorado Magazine*, Vol. XXIX (1952), 273–84; Fritz, *Colorado*, 203–209, 285–89; Ellis, *Teller*, 43.

solve this problem of trespassing, in 1861 the federal government negotiated a new treaty in which the Indians relinquished what the white man thought desirable and retained a reservation in eastern Colorado. When the tribes came to realize fully what they had done, they grew resentful and seized the opportunity produced by the Civil War to go on the warpath. In the 1864 debacle at Sand Creek, the Colorado militia, commanded by Colonel John M. Chivington, attacked a group of Arapahoes, under Chief Left Hand, and Cheyennes, led by Chief Black Kettle and others, who thought they had completed surrendering to a federal Indian agent. The militia slaughtered as many men, women, and children as possible in what became the most controversial episode in Colorado history. It roused resentment in few of the territory's inhabitants at the time; they only turned against Chivington when he later did something they considered unworthy: when his son died, he married the widow. Not until 1867 were the Cheyennes and Arapahoes finally quelled.

To the west of these Indians were the Utes, a very nomadic tribe. They were given a very large reserve in southwestern Colorado in 1863; its eastern boundary was just west of the future town of Gunnison. In 1873, they surrendered from it the area of the San Juan Mountains, soon swarming with gold seekers. The Utes grew restive as they saw how slow the federal government was in removing white intruders from another part of their preserve, Uncompahgre Park, and how dilatory it was in its payments of promised annuities. An attempt in 1876 to civilize the tribe in one generation caused a massacre and revolt which only the U. S. Army could put down. Finally the Utes were removed almost entirely to New Mexico and Utah in 1880, eliminating the last limitation on roaming Colorado prospectors.

Developments in various parts of the state continued. Nicholas C. Creede and George L. Smith were searching the headwaters of the Rio Grande in the spring of 1890 when they discovered the Holy Moses mine.[19] Its silver ore, assaying eighty dollars to the ton, aroused David H. Moffat and other substantial capitalists to buy various adjacent claims. Their investment convinced lesser businessmen, miners, and speculators that the region had a bright future. The real rush

19 Nolie Mumey, *Creede: History of A Colorado Silver Mining Town, passim;* Mrs. A. H. Major, "Pioneer Days in Crestone and Creede," *Colorado Magazine,* Vol. XXI (1944), 212–17; Wolle, *Stampede,* 320–26; Hafen, *Colorado and Its People,* I, 457–60; Lavender, *Big Divide,* 132–33.

did not come until 1891, however, and it was stimulated by additional rich discoveries. The town of Creede sprang up almost overnight in a canyon so narrow that there could be but one main street. The jumping of lots was frequent and the only certain way to retain possession of one was quickly to complete a building on it. In 1891, the Denver and Rio Grande Railroad extended a branch to Creede. At first there was such demand for freight service that the clamor of people eager to receive their goods created conditions of near riot at the station. The branch earned its cost of construction in the first four months of operation. Early in 1892, between 150 and 300 people a day were arriving in Creede by various means; in April, the total population was at least 8,000. The railroad parked sleeping cars to help provide newcomers with temporary quarters. At its height the town had at least seventy-five saloons, three dance halls, one variety theater, and nearly a hundred "hotels." Such conditions prompted Cy Warman, founder of the *Creede Chronicle,* to write a poem whose memorable lines were:

> It's day all day in the daytime
> And there is no night in Creede.

When "Soapy" Smith, already a notorious confidence man and later to make an unenviable reputation in the Alaska-Yukon gold rush, arrived in Creede, he found it without much local government. After a slow start to become sure of the situation, he informed the sporting element of the community that he was in charge and all but one accepted his declaration without even protesting. Almost at once he became the town's dictator; his decision on all municipal matters was final. He successfully kept both the honest merchants and the dishonest elements satisfied. His policy was to make few arrests; instead, he would not admit known troublemakers into the town, and those who became difficult after their arrival, he immediately chased away. He collected tribute from every gambler in Creede and probably received money from various other shady undertakings. Smith was full of civic pride, encouraging all kinds of enterprises, proper and improper, and spending his money freely in many ways. He picked for city office men he knew would do his bidding and they were elected. When Parson Uzzell of Leadville and Denver first came to Creede, he preached from a table in a new pool hall. That evening as he slept, some of Smith's men cut a hole in his tent and stole the trousers containing the proceeds of his collection. When Soapy learned of this, he forced his subordinates to return the pants with more money in the pocket than had been purloined.

Early on June 5, 1892, there broke out in Creede a fire which destroyed almost the entire town. The highly inflammable dried pine, used in most buildings, and the pitch made a fierce inferno. There was no loss of lives, but somewhere between a half-million and a million dollars' worth of property was destroyed or stolen. The fire was followed by a wild debauch, but the respectable elements finally organized themselves to keep the lawlessness from going too far. The fire destroyed Creede's glamour. Many a prospector, broke and homeless, left; many a gambler and dance-hall girl, without customers, soon followed. The town's "wide open" days were over. Developments continued, however, until the financial panic of 1893 and the repeal of the Sherman Silver Purchase Act destroyed the demand for silver. As the decline became clear, businessmen had time enough to start thinking about their municipal government. Soapy Smith, analyzing the situation, left Creede permanently before he lost power and control.

Colorado's last mining rush, and one of the biggest, was to Cripple Creek. The first stampede was to an area west of Cripple Creek, the Mt. McIntyre region. At the time this was mistakenly called the Mt. Pisgah rush: in fact, Mt. Pisgah was at the site of the future Cripple Creek.[20] The excitement began when a prospector named Chicken Bill widely announced a rich find; about five thousand men poured into the area. Louis Liverman drove over from Alma with a wagonload of beer, sold it all the first day, decided he had found a unique bonanza, returned to Alma for more, and arrived back at the new camp after an absence of four days. To his astonishment, no customers remained. The miners, quickly concluding that the alleged find was a fake, had departed. This rush was important, however, because it endowed the entire Cripple Creek region with an undeservedly bad reputation.

The yard-wide stream which eventually lent its name of Cripple Creek to the famous city was itself christened, according to an entertaining tradition, because so many cows lamed themselves or broke

20 Wolle, *Stampede*, 451–52; Marshall Sprague, *Money Mountain: The Story of Cripple Creek*, 22–29.

their legs while crossing over its rocks.[21] Robert Womack was a cowboy employed by the ranch which surrounded the rivulet and occupied the future townsite. In 1878, he discovered a stray bit of rock which assayed two hundred dollars a ton. While going about other tasks, he kept looking for its source. Grubstaked in December, 1889, Womack finally made his big discovery the following October and staked his claim on the El Paso Lode. There was no rush at first, for everybody remembered the previous Mt. Pisgah excitement and resolved not to be fooled again. In 1891, a fair number of tenderfeet came into the camp, so many of them farmers that it was commonly said they "mined with pitchforks." Certainly they knew little of mineral geology and had almost no practical experience as prospectors. Perhaps it was just as well, for the gold-bearing lodes of Cripple Creek ran so contrary to the ordinary rules that expert knowledge was almost a handicap; in the early days the amateur was as likely to find riches as the expert. The filing of claims did not make the finders suddenly wealthy, for much capital was needed to develop the lodes. By September, 1891, it is doubtful that as much as twenty-five thousand dollars in actual gold had been extracted from the area. Those who had money to invest were skeptical. Finally, Count James Pourtales, a German nobleman living at Colorado Springs, announced in November, 1891, that he was buying the Buena Vista claim for eighty thousand dollars; he shortly secured financial backing from J. J. Hagerman. Other capitalists, now aroused, purchased the holdings of many a pioneer. Womack parted with his share in the El Paso for three hundred dollars, several years later sold another claim he owned for five hundred, and eventually died in poverty.

The owners of the cattle ranch where Womack had worked, the Denver realty firm of Bennett and Myers, laid out the townsite of Cripple Creek and prospered from lot sales. In the spring of 1892 came a big rush of fortune seekers. The area was so close to Colorado Springs (about fifty miles) and Denver that primitive conditions prevailed a much shorter time than in most new mining regions. By 1893, Cripple Creek had a population of five thousand, a public water system, electric lights, and twenty restaurants. Much of the housing was one- or two-room shacks, built from green lumber, heated by

21 Sprague, *Money Mountain*, 18–83, 105; Wolle, *Stampede*, 452–53; Harry J. Newton, *Yellow Gold of Cripple Creek*, 13, 18–21.

wood or coal stoves, and illuminated by kerosene or sometimes electric lights. The ceilings were lined with canvas, the outside boards were vertical, with the cracks covered by wooden strips, and the interior boards were horizontal. The shacks cost about five hundred dollars to build and rented for fifteen dollars a month.

In 1893, two great mines, the Independence and the Portland, proved their exceptional richness.[22] The former belonged to Winfield Scott Stratton. He had long been a contracting carpenter in Colorado Springs, esteemed for his fine workmanship and his ability to make accurate estimates of what a job would cost. As early as 1874 he hunted for minerals during the summer and supported himself by the carpentry he did in the winter. He prepared himself methodically by working for a week on a dredge, spending many months in a mill using the amalgamation process, and taking courses in metallurgy at both the Colorado School of Mines and Colorado College. He continued prospecting, with no better results. By 1890, he estimated that he had spent twenty thousand dollars of his own money without finding a paying mine. Disgusted with gold and silver, he was unimpressed when he first heard of Womack's El Paso Lode.

Stratton got a grubstake in the spring of 1891 from a plasterer, Leslie Popejoy, to search for cryolite, a mineral useful in making aluminum. He went to the Cripple Creek area, turned instead to hunting gold, and staked the Independence and Washington claims. These failed to impress Popejoy, who finally sold Stratton all grubstake rights for $275. Stratton began cautiously developing the Independence. In 1893, he gave a thirty-day option on it to a prospective buyer. Before relinquishing the property, Stratton decided to have one last look around and on the fourth crosscut, disused for a year, he found a vein assaying $380 a ton. The next thirty days he must have been very nervous and uncomfortable as he waited to see whether the prospective purchaser would also find the vein. The buyer didn't; in fact, he uncovered nothing promising enough to warrant the $115,000 asked and handed the mine back to Stratton. The former carpenter developed it cautiously, hired old friends in supervisory capacities, and secretively forbade any employee to discuss its wealth. He limited its yield to a net of $2,000 a day. When his men located

22 Frank Waters, *Midas of the Rockies: The Story of Stratton and Cripple Creek*, 107–27, 207; Sprague, *Money Mountain*, 112–29; Newton, *Yellow Gold*, 23–30.

rich layers of gold, he generally left them intact until he might need the money.

On the same Battle Mountain as the Independence, whose richness was just being uncovered in 1893, was the claim of James Burns and James Doyle. These late-arriving amateurs had managed to find a vacant 0.069-acre plot and sink a shaft, the Portland, but were discouraged. They told John Harnan they would give him a one-third interest if he could find a gold vein in it. He managed to uncover one without much difficulty, if tradition is to be believed, simply by moving the ladder and digging where it had been. The Portland proved to be a very rich mine. At first the three owners removed the ore under the cover of night and took it secretly to Pueblo for refining. They feared they would not be able to defend themselves from lawsuits sure to be brought by surrounding claim owners. The three entered into an unwritten mutual-assistance pact with Stratton to defeat these rivals and to secure all Battle Mountain. It was mid-November by the time the first suits reached the courts. Meanwhile, the three partners had built up their cash reserves to about $125,000; Stratton had a similar sum and also unlimited bank credit. Faced with twenty-seven suits against the Portland, the allies bought up the lesser claims first and then used them to threaten countersuits against the larger litigants. This defense worked so well that before long the four owned all the claims on the mountain. The Portland mine, with its holdings enlarged to 183 acres, was then incorporated; the resulting distribution of stock gave 731,000 shares to Stratton and 600,000 shares each to Burns, Doyle, and Harnan. By the end of 1910, the mine's gross yield was $30,000,000 in gold.

The year 1893, when the wealth of the Independence and the Portland seemed omens of the future Cripple Creek, was one of economic misfortune throughout the United States; especially hard hit were the silver mines of Colorado. Many of the destitute swarmed to Cripple Creek; almost inevitably, labor troubles erupted.[23] The standard wages were three dollars a day, but with such prices prevailing as firewood at fifty-five cents a cord and water at five cents a bucket, they hardly covered expenses for the average miner's family. The workday, varying from mine to mine, was eight, nine, or ten hours long. There were more men available than there were jobs to fill. The first hint of trouble came in August, when the Isabelle mine ordered its men to work ten hours, rather than eight, for the same pay, then rescinded the directive. The workers in the whole district speedily formed a union and affiliated it with the Western Federation of Miners, an organization then two years old.

The mine owners took the offensive in January, 1894, by ordering generally the ten-hour day. They pointed to the country's labor surplus, to the hours prevailing in other mines of the state, and to how much nicer it was to work in the dry, well-ventilated shafts of Cripple Creek than in those of most other areas. The union, unimpressed, called a strike against all mines demanding more than eight hours; these centered in the Bull Hill and Battle Mountain areas. The labor leader, John Calderwood, managed well, tightly controlling his men and establishing a central kitchen at Altman to feed them. By March they were still holding out so effectively that the owners became impatient and secured a court injunction restraining the union from interference with the operation of the mines. When six deputy sheriffs tried to serve this order on the strikers in Altman, municipal officials ran them out of town. Calderwood then organized his men in military fashion, established a picket line, and announced that nobody would be allowed to cross it without a pass. The alarmed sheriff asked the state's Populist governor, David H. Waite, to send the militia. He did, the miners passively accepted eighteen warrants for arrest, the troops withdrew, the eighteen were acquitted at their trials, and the strikers again required passes of those who wanted to enter the Bull Hill area.

When Calderwood shortly departed for a tour of the state's other mining camps, he left in charge Junius J. Johnson, miner and former West Pointer. Johnson improved the defenses of Bull Hill, but could not control the minority rough element which wrecked saloons, robbed stores, and beat up non-union men. To retaliate, the mine owners hired as deputy sheriffs some former Denver policemen and firemen, recently removed in a shake-up of those departments. As these invaders neared Bull Hill the miners gave them a general warning by blowing up the surface workings of the Strong mine. The offensive train began backing in retreat, whereupon the defenders sent a flatcar of explosives coasting down toward it. The car gained such speed that before reaching the train it left the tracks, obliterating one cow and three goats in an adjacent pasture. Calderwood returned the next morning, too late to prevent the strike's degenerating into class warfare. He took every restraining action possible, such as persuading local saloonkeepers to close their doors. He had about seven hundred men in his group on Bull Hill, and to oppose them, the mine owners next hired an army of twelve hundred fighters, swearing them in as deputies. The forces made a formal exchange of prisoners of war—five strikers for three company men. Governor Waite intervened and tried to arbitrate between the two disputants at a Colorado Springs meeting which an angry mob of townspeople broke up. The mine owners' deputies launched several unsuccessful attacks against Bull Hill before the state militia again arrived to intervene.

Shortly the strike was settled on the following terms: wages of three dollars a day for an eight-hour day in all mines; the deputies to disband; the miners to hand in their arms; the militia to stay until the mines were operating normally; and Calderwood and three hundred miners to stand trial for alleged criminal acts. Under the last proviso, only two men actually served time in the penitentiary, supposedly for blowing up the surface of the Strong mine. The strike lasted 130 days, cost about three million dollars in lost production, unpaid wages, and upkeep of the various armed forces, and left much bitterness in both Cripple Creek and Colorado Springs.

After the strike was settled, Cripple Creek experienced its biggest boom.[24] In June the narrow-gauge Florence and Cripple Creek Railroad reached the city, and the Midland Terminal, a spur from the standard-gauge Colorado Midland's Colorado Springs–Leadville line, built into adjacent Victor that fall and into Cripple Creek itself early the next year. Not until 1901 was the Colorado Springs and Cripple Creek District Railroad complete.

In earlier times, smelters were built at Cripple Creek, Pueblo, Florence, Denver, and Colorado City to serve the mines of the area. Various towns grew, such as Victor, where the chief gold vein was uncovered accidentally during excavation for the foundations of a proposed hotel building. Cripple Creek was always the region's largest settlement. Trading in the stock of mining corporations began as early as 1892 on the city's curbstones, where the shares of the Buena

24 Sprague, *Money Mountain*, 162–298; Newton, *Yellow Gold*, 49–70; Wolle, *Stampede*, 456–72; Hafen, *Colorado and Its People*, I, 470–72.

Vista advanced in one day from $1.75 to $5.00. In 1896, the Cripple Creek Stock Exchange opened its doors; in 1900, about $6,250,000 worth of securities were sold through its facilities. There were also two stock exchanges at Colorado Springs. In Cripple Creek, most of the ground-floor locations on the main street were occupied by stockbrokers or by saloons.

The gambling and red-light district was easily available. No account of sin there would be complete without a mention of what happened to writer Julian Street in 1914. He published an article about Cripple Creek in *Collier's,* supposedly a well-rounded account of all aspects of the town's activities but actually devoted almost entirely to the houses of ill-fame on Myers Avenue. Enraged at the distortion, the city council took the only means of retaliation open to it by officially renaming the avenue Julian Street.

Fire twice hit Cripple Creek in 1896. The first one started on Saturday, April 25, when a lighted gasoline stove tipped over. The resulting blaze destroyed the structures on thirty of the town's three hundred acres. The next Wednesday, a maid overturned a pot of grease on the stove in the kitchen of the Portland Hotel. With a very stiff wind blowing, the fire raged out of control until it destroyed virtually every building remaining in the city. To aid the stricken townspeople the citizens of Colorado Springs dispatched two relief trains of supplies and shortly supplemented them with goods secured by a house-to-house canvass. This prompt, generous action did much to allay in both cities the bitterness remaining from the 1894 strike. The mining town was promptly rebuilt, with its business district of brick.

A constant problem was theft from the mines. If a miner took away only a few pieces of valuable ore, so-called high grade, from where he worked, he doubled or trebled his day's wages. He carried it out in his dinner bucket, in his shoe, or in a secret pocket. He sold the ore to a dishonest assayer, who quickly crushed it so that it could not be identified as coming from any particular place. The miner, if he did not like to deal directly, delivered the ore to a saloon, cigar store, haberdasher, or even a laundryman. Although he generally stole while at his regular job, he might secretly enter the mine while off duty and go to an especially rich spot. Those implicated in these thefts permeated every level of Cripple Creek society from top to bottom. Stolen high grade was even dropped into church collection plates. To protect themselves, the mine owners took such precautions as hiring guards, shaking the dinner buckets of those coming off shift, or even requiring the outgoing miners to undress almost completely, but they never managed to prevent all thievery. What eventually stopped it was that the mines ran out of high grade. Although many men regarded taking a little ore as being nearly legitimate, personal property was almost always inviolate. This was well and good, for often the keys given lodgers in rooming houses would fit a series of doors.

From 1890 through 1953, the 475 mines of the Cripple Creek district produced officially $412,974,848 in minerals, 99.5 per cent gold, and as stolen high grade an estimated $20,000,000 more. The gulch where Womack made his original discovery contributed, up to 1928, a total of $7,500,000.

By 1899, the area created at least twenty-eight millionaires. The leader of them, the dominating force of the camp in his time even though he lived elsewhere, was Winfield Scott Stratton. In his prosperous years he purchased an ample but unpretentious house which he had built earlier as a carpenter in Colorado Springs. Although generally husbanding his fortune, he allowed himself some luxuries, such as having clean sheets on his bed each night, and gave some money away, once buying a bicycle for each laundry girl in town. In 1899, after Stratton had removed $3,837,360 in ore from the Independence for a net profit of $2,402,164, he sold his mine to an English group. He received $10,000,000 for it, and the man who arranged the transaction got a commission of $1,000,000 in addition.

It was not as good an investment as the Englishmen had hoped. By 1914, they had taken out $19,583,060 in ore for a net profit of $5,237,-739; they then sold the property for $325,000. They felt they had been cheated, so with Stratton now dead, they sued his estate, charging misrepresentation. They failed in court because of a vital technical point. Legally speaking, they had not purchased the mine from Stratton; rather, they had helped him to form his own corporation, Stratton's Independence, Limited, and it had issued him stock for his mine. The Englishmen had then formed an entirely separate company, the Venture Corporation of London, and made a contract to sell Stratton's stock for him. Outside the courtroom, observers were particularly impressed by testimony that the Englishmen had not taken Stratton's word for what was in the property but had hired an independent expert, the renowned mining engineer John Hays Hammond, to make an examination and had then followed his recommendation to acquire it. Hammond may have made a mistake in judgment, but not even the disgruntled purchasers dared to hint that he was dishonest.

The money in Stratton's estate, a huge amount since he had spent comparatively very little during his lifetime, went in large part to the establishment of a home for unfortunates near Colorado Springs; still in operation, half of its occupants are orphans and half elderly people. An interesting item in the official inventory of Stratton's estate at the time of his death carried a bookkeeping value of zero—the team he had originally used around Cripple Creek, long since pensioned to a nice pasture.

The mining excitement in Colorado lasted intermittently from 1857 until the turn of the century. Its three major peaks were the early rush, which revealed especially the wealth of the Little Kingdom of Gilpin, the Leadville stampede, and the Cripple Creek bonanza. Aspen, Creede, Ouray, Silver Cliff, Silverton, Georgetown, and the area surrounding Gunnison also attracted prospecting hordes. In the early and last years, the quest was for gold, but during the middle period, silver was almost equally attractive. All major discoveries were made by the turn of the century; some mines had been exhausted long before, and others have continued in production down to the present time. From 1858 through 1922, the state yielded gold valued at $666,470,261 and silver worth $497,359,655, or a total of $1,163,-829,916.[25] Colorado's mining rushes, early lawlessness, development of miners' codes, attempts at early government, and social conditions were typical of the mining frontier. Its transportation problems through an area so mountainous were exceptionally difficult.

[25] Henderson, *Mining in Colorado,* 103.

9

MONTANA GOLD AND SILVER

BY 1950, Montana had produced $2,957,779,814 in minerals. To be more precise, between 1862 and 1950, the state yielded 17,319,824 fine ounces of gold worth $390,647,052, a total of 775,324,501 fine ounces of silver valued at $570,765,138, and 13,611,188,000 pounds of copper priced at $1,996,367,624.[1]

The great era of placer mining was from 1862 through 1876, yielding about $150,000,000 in gold from roughly five hundred gulches which varied in length from a half-mile to twenty miles.[2] The pay streak, usually ten to fifty feet wide, was covered with five to a hundred feet of dirt and gravel. Devices used to extract gold from the surrounding waste material were the pan, the rocker, the long tom, the sluice, and the hydraulic hose.

The earliest discovery of gold was probably made by François Finlay, a half blood better known as Benetsee, in the Deer Lodge Valley of Montana in 1852.[3] Although he took some to the Hudson's Bay Company post near Flathead Lake, the traders did not encourage him. John Silverthorn likely got some gold from his old friend Finlay in 1856 rather than discovering any himself. At any rate, he brought it to the agent of the American Fur Company at Fort Benton and

[1] Merrill G. Burlingame and K. Ross Toole, (eds.), *A History of Montana,* I, 334.

[2] W. A. Clark, "The Origin, Growth and Resources of Montana," *Contributions to the Historical Society of Montana,* Vol. II (1896), 49–50; T. A. Rickard, *A History of American Mining,* 344.

[3] Hiram M. Chittenden, *The Yellowstone National Park: Historical and Descriptive,* 54; Clark, "The Origin, Growth and Resources of Montana," *Contributions to the Historical Society of Montana,* Vol. II (1896), 49–50; Paul C. Phillips and H. A. Trexler, "Notes on the Discovery of Gold in the Northwest," *Mississippi Valley Historical Review,* Vol. IV (1917–18), 89–97; William J. Trimble, "A Recon-

traded it for $1,000 worth of goods; its value proved ultimately to be $1,525. Neither Finlay's nor Silverthorn's gold touched off excitement enough to make anybody go out looking for more.

James Stuart, his brother Granville, and Reece Anderson were returning in 1857 from the California gold area when Granville became so ill at Malad Creek, Utah, that clearly he could not travel farther without a rest. While he was recuperating, the three met Jake Meek, a horse trader, and before long they decided to winter with him in Montana. The next spring, the three wandered into Deer Lodge Valley. On May 2, 1858, the Stuarts did some prospecting at what is now known as Gold Creek, sinking a hole about five feet deep and taking out ten cents' worth of gold. This is the first authenticated discovery of precious metal in Montana. The men were so exposed to hostile Blackfeet that shortly they sought safety at Fort Bridger. Not until the fall of 1860 did the Stuarts return. Earlier in the summer, Henry Thomas came and sank a shaft; his work never brought him more than $1.50 a day, often less. James and Granville continued prospecting in the area, for in 1862 they had made a find which seemed promising. As the Stuarts worked, other men passed by on their way to the mines of Idaho.

One of the groups going through from Colorado to Idaho was led by John White;[4] it wintered in the Deer Lodge Valley. On July 28, 1862, the major discovery was made on Grasshopper Creek by White himself. When news of this reached those still on Gold Creek, they nearly all rushed over to the new area and helped to found the settlement named Bannack; five hundred people spent the winter of 1862–63 there. The placer deposits were mostly ten or twelve feet above the stream. On its banks a man could occasionally pull up a sagebrush, shake off the sand and gravel from its roots into a pan,

sideration of Gold Discoveries in the Northwest," *Mississippi Valley Historical Review*, Vol. V (1918–19), 70–77; Rickard, *American Mining*, 344; Helen F. Sanders, *A History of Montana*, I, 170; Tom Stout, *Montana: Its Story and Biography*, I, 184–86, 189; Granville Stuart, *Forty Years on the Frontier*, I, 118–39, 155–65, 185–212, II, 30; Granville Stuart, "A Memoir of the Life of James Stuart," *Contributions to the Historical Society of Montana*, Vol. I (1876), 47–48.

4 Hubert H. Bancroft, *History of Washington, Idaho and Montana, 1845–1889*, 723–27; Clark, "The Origin, Growth and Resources of Montana," *Contributions to the Historical Society of Montana*, Vol. II (1896), 51; Stuart, *Forty Years*, I, 225, 231–32; James M. Hamilton, *From Wilderness to Statehood*, 133, 219; James A. MacKnight, *Mines of Montana*, 6; Rickard, *American Mining*, 344–45; Merrill G. Burlingame, *The Montana Frontier*, 84.

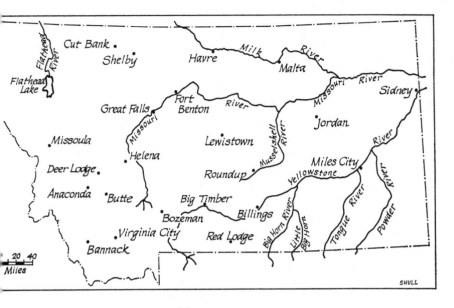

SHULL

MONTANA

and collect about a dollar's worth of gold, so prospectors delighted to say that they could "pan gold out of sagebrush." Lode mining began with the discovery of the Decotah Lode on November 12, 1862. Its owners fashioned a water-powered mill of traditional design, with its stamps made out of wagon tires, to process their ore. Apparently Montana's hydraulic mining began in this area when N. G. McComb started operations on Zoller's Bar in September, 1866. By that same year, enough silver had been discovered to warrant the establishment of a smelter for it in Bannack.

When production in Bannack began to decline, James Stuart and others set out on the prospecting trip now commonly referred to as the Yellowstone Expedition of 1863.[5] The group left Bannack on

5 Bancroft, Montana, 630, 725; Henry N. Blake, "Historical Sketch of Madison County, Montana Territory," Contributions to the Historical Society of Montana, Vol. II (1896), 82–85; C. B. Glasscock, The War of the Copper Kings, 21–22; Hamilton, From Wilderness, 241; Nathaniel P. Langford, Vigilante Days and Ways, 172–78; MacKnight, Mines, 6; Rickard, American Mining, 342; Peter Ronan, "Discovery of Alder Gulch," Contributions to the Historical Society of Montana, Vol. III (1900), 143–51; Stuart, Forty Years, I, 66, 225, 247, 263–67; James Stuart, "The Yellowstone Expedition of 1863," Contributions to the Historical Society of Montana, Vol. I (1876), 151–52; Robert Vaughn, Then and Now, 40.

April 9, drove off two attacks by Crow Indians, and arrived back safely on June 24. Six men who had expected to join the group but missed a meeting with it were Barney Hughes, Tom Cover, Henry Rodgers, Bill Fairweather, Henry Edgar, and Bill Sweeney. They pressed on. The Crows captured them and threatened them with death if they continued their search. They fled. As they neared civilization, roughly seventy-five miles away at Bannack, they prospected on Alder Gulch and got as high as $5.10 from one pan.

With such obvious riches at hand, Hughes was sent on to town for more supplies. He refused tempting offers to slip back secretly. When he did leave, quite openly, somewhere between three and four hundred men followed him. After traveling awhile he stopped and held a meeting. He said the total panned out so far was $189, told what the prospects appeared to be, and then warned that he would go no farther unless the stampeders promised to give each of the six discoverers two hundred feet of ground, rim to rim, as claims which could never be jumped or taken away from them. To this the prospectors agreed and then proceeded to draw up a general mining code for the new district. That night, when almost everybody was asleep, Hughes and some of his particular friends stole away at eleven o'clock so that they could stake as close as possible to the discovery. The rest of the stampeders, angry now, arrived on June 6, 1863, in time to get good claims for themselves. Later in the month a fire accidentally set in dry grass was fanned by a high wind so that it swept rapidly down the gulch and consumed the belongings of many prospectors. Those whose goods escaped the flames shared their supplies with those who had lost everything until the settlement's first shipment of merchandise arrived.

The townsite, 320 acres laid out on June 6, was soon called Virginia City, causing some confusion in mail service with the famous Nevada city of the same name. That summer, men lived in dugouts, wagons, tents, caves, and wickiups of alder and pine boughs or else simply slept outdoors in their blankets. Lumber from the nearest saw mill, at Bannack, cost $250 per thousand feet in Virginia City at first; six-by-eight windows cost a dollar a pane. Near by was plenty of good timber for logs. The first building erected was for the Mechanical Bakery; certainly this was one of the very few times in the history of mining towns that the first structure housed something

other than a saloon. Later, the larger buildings were made of por-
phyritic stone.

The mining area grew until it was strung for seventeen miles
along Alder Gulch, in appearance one long shoestring of settlement
along the crooked creek. By 1864, there were at least ten thousand
people in the area and possibly fifteen. Men at first worked the
bars on the sides of the creek, then turned both to the stream bed and
to the hillsides. They found the best deposits at bedrock, which was
never more than fifty feet from the surface. They prospected the
side gulches extensively, sometimes finding nothing and never making a spectacular discovery. They found about one thousand claims
profitable enough to work when wages were $10.00 to $14.00 per day.
The miners initially exploited placer deposits; in January, 1864,
they found the first lode; in October, 1864, they started the first water-
powered stamp mill; and in December, 1865, they began using the
first steam mill. Perhaps by 1865, certainly by 1868, they had extracted
$30,000,000 in gold from Alder Gulch, and by 1900, the total yield
was over $85,000,000. Gold dust was bought by dealers in Virginia
City and Bannack at $19.00 or $19.50 per ounce; they usually resold
it for $22.00.

In the first two or three years after the discovery at Alder Gulch,
various groups looked for new riches in adjacent areas with little
success. A forty-two-man party went in 1863 through Lower Geyser
Basin in what is now Yellowstone National Park but failed to see
any significance in the hot springs they viewed. A dozen mining
groups in all had some contact with the Yellowstone area in the
1860's, and none publicized the scenic wonders there.[6]

Various stampedes, based on little more than rumors, proved an
exciting waste of time for those who took part.[7] Thus in January,
1864, there were rushes to the Gallatin River, to Wisconsin Creek,
and to Boulder Creek. One of the most unusual was triggered in the
fall of 1865 by an old mountaineer named McClellan whose Blackfoot squaw had so many relatives dropping in frequently that he
had to come to town for more supplies. Thinking of all the domestic
comforts with his Indian housekeeper, he told a friend, "I have got

[6] Merrill D. Beal, *The Story of Man in Yellowstone*, 103–105; Chittenden, *Yellowstone*, 55–59.
[7] Stuart, *Forty Years*, I, 270–72; Vaughn, *Then and Now*, 109–12.

as good a thing as I want." This remark was misinterpreted. About twelve hundred men followed him out of town, although the temperature was thirty-five degrees below zero and a foot of snow was on the ground; of course they found nothing.

David B. Weaver, Frank Garrett, and David R. Shorthill discovered the real riches of Emigrant Gulch.[8] In the lower portion they saw that the miners were not making expenses and moved upstream. Five miles above the third waterfall, on August 30, 1864, the three got a dollar's worth of gold in their first pan. The mines were organized into the so-called Shorthill District on September 12. By the close of 1867, the Shorthill District had yielded $180,000 in gold.

Another discovery in 1864 was made by John Thompson at Confederate Gulch, in the Big Belt Mountains about thirty-five miles southeast of another area settled the same year, Helena.[9] This ravine probably produced more gold per square yard in less time than any other placer in Montana. Its total yield was somewhere between ten and twelve million dollars. Its town, Diamond City, had at the maximum a population of ten thousand. In the 1870's, the area was so badly flooded that almost all of the white men left, leaving the Chinese to clean up what gold remained; by 1878, they, too, had departed.

A third placer development of 1864 was Last Chance Gulch.[10] John Cowan, Robert Stanley, and Cabe Johnson made the original discovery in July; not satisfied, they looked elsewhere without finding anything better and returned there in September. On the thirtieth of that month a public meeting named the settlement Helena; sponsors of the name intended the accent to be on the second syllable, but the miners' great familiarity with the word "hell" soon shifted

[8] Stout, *Montana*, I, 213; David B. Weaver, "Early Days in Emigrant Gulch," *Contributions to the Historical Society of Montana*, Vol. VII (1910), 73–96.

[9] Glenn C. Quiett, *Pay Dirt: A Panorama of American Gold Rushes*, 233; Muriel S. Wolle, *The Bonanza Trail: Ghost Towns and Mining Camps of the West*, 191–92; Vaughn, *Then and Now*, 63.

[10] Bancroft, *Montana*, 721–26; Cornelius Hedges, "Centennial Address on Lewis and Clarke County," *Contributions to the Historical Society of Montana*, Vol. II (1896), 109–18; MacKnight, *Mines*, 57–60; M. Murray Schreiner, "Last Chance Gulch Becomes the Mountain City of Helena," *Montana Magazine of History*, Vol. II (October, 1952), 33–42; Stout, *Montana*, I, 210–12; Daniel S. Tuttle, "Early History of the Episcopal Church in Montana," *Contributions to the Historical Society of Montana*, Vol. V (1904), 304–305; Vaughn, *Then and Now*, 58.

the emphasis to the first syllable. The meeting also decreed that the size of lots be thirty feet by sixty, ruled that putting up a foundation would establish a right to one for ten days and that claim to ownership entered with the recorder would hold it for ten days more before construction of a building had to begin, and established a commission of three to decide disputed lot titles until regular civil law was established. Not until June, 1872, did the United States Land Office issue title to the townsite of Helena. For years town government was carried out simply by justices of the peace and constables. Finally, civic needs overcame the fear of higher taxes and a complete governmental structure for the city was organized in 1876.

Gradually the early settlement expanded. By March, 1865, there were perhaps a thousand inhabitants; by 1867, four thousand people and a hundred business establishments, of which only three closed on Sunday. The original cabins, poorly chinked and with roofs covered by a thin layer of loose dirt, were so uncomfortable and unhealthy that they were gradually replaced. The first permanent stone building was put up in 1866. That summer, a large portion of Main Street was mined, causing such continued complaints that bridges were built to allow easy passage along the street. Early Helena, like most mining towns, was prey to fire. The nine suffered before 1876 inflicted a total of slightly less than two million dollars in damage.

The total yield of Last Chance Gulch was over thirty million dollars in gold, at first only from placers and later also from lode mines starting with the location of one by James W. Whitlatch in 1864. Gold was also found in the country surrounding Helena. New York Gulch, discovered about fifteen miles away in 1866, proved quite productive. First Chance Gulch for a time yielded nearly a thousand dollars a day, and Montana Bar was very rich.

The area around Butte, now so famous for copper, developed first as a gold-mining region.[11] The initial discovery, made in 1864 at Silver Bow in the valley below Butte by Budd Parker, P. Allison,

11 Forrest L. Foor, "The Senatorial Aspiration of William A. Clark, 1898–1901: A Study in Montana Politics" (unpublished Ph.D. thesis, University of California), 3, 5; Glasscock, War, 56–62, 85, 158–60; MacKnight, Mines, 31–32; William D. Mangam, The Clarks: An American Phenomenon, 30–32, 46; Rickard, American Mining, 345–49; Stout, Montana, I, 213, 326–33, 371–73; K. Ross Toole, Montana: An Uncommon Land, 175–77; Charles S. Warren, "The Territory of Montana," Contributions to the Historical Society of Montana, Vol. II (1896), 64–75; Montana Writers' Program, Copper Camp, 17, 259.

Joseph Esler, and James Esler, caused a stampede. Among the prospectors were George O. Humphrey and William Allison, who sold their holdings, moved up to what became Butte in May, and began placer mining. Others came in and made rich discoveries that fall. The deposits were quite shallow, yielding about one and one-half million dollars; by the fall of 1867, they were exhausted and only a few dozen men remained in town.

As a silver rather than a gold camp Butte began to revive in 1875. Silver had been found earlier, but first attempts to separate it locally from the intermixed gold were failures. The possibilities, however, still intrigued William L. Farlin, who noticed that the owners of the Travona Lode failed to do the amount of work required by law to hold their property. A few minutes before midnight on New Year's Eve, 1874, he posted notice that he was now claiming the Travona as his own. Development work proved so promising that he borrowed $30,000 from William A. Clark's bank to build a smelter. Before long, he could not meet his installment payments and turned his entire property over to Clark to operate until the debt was paid. Somehow, Clark could not seem to find profitable ore in the mine, so he apparently had no choice but to foreclose; as soon as he obtained ownership for himself, astounding as it may appear, the lode began to yield a rich supply of silver and continued to do so for many years.

Other mines developed; Butte boomed. The climax of silver production came in 1887, when five mills with a total of 290 stamps were treating about four hundred tons of ore daily to extract an average of twenty-five dollars in silver and a little gold from each ton. Most mines were actively operated until 1893, when the steady decline in the price of silver became sharper. By 1896, the only silver being secured was an incidental by-product of the rapidly expanding copper mines, whose development will be treated in the next chapter.

Butte's age of silver saw the arrival of two men destined to play major roles in the area's development—Marcus Daly and William A. Clark. Daly came as an expert for Walker Brothers, mine financiers, to examine the Alice silver mine; they bought two-thirds of it and he one-third. He shortly secured the Anaconda mine, with co-operation from James B. Haggin, George Hearst, and Lloyd Tevis, and eventually developed it, not for its silver, but for its copper. Daly, an uneducated man of great wit and charm, was spontaneously generous but never forgot an affront.

Clark began his mining career in Colorado in 1862 and moved to Bannack the next year. Realizing that merchandising would yield good profits, he turned to it. When a shortage of tobacco developed at Blackfoot City in the winter of 1866–67, Clark made a round trip of five hundred miles to haul in as much tobacco as his wagon would hold; the temperature was about twenty below zero and the profits were more than 300 per cent. In 1872, he began investing in Butte mines, making loans, buying several undeveloped properties, leasing others with rental dependent upon earning and with an option to buy. He did not start to develop his Moulton mine until Daly's Alice proved rich. He was always careful to work at a slightly higher level than his neighbor and to allow the water in his property to seep into the Alice so that Daly could pay the cost of pumping it out. At his Mayflower mine Clark in two instances ordered his superintendent to suspend work and was twice disobeyed; the first time a $2,000,000 ore body was found, and the second saw a $2,500,000 deposit uncovered. When Clark died, his fortune was somewhere between $150,000,000 and $250,000,000. Once when a hack driver complained at receiving only a dime tip, when the magnate's two sons always gave him a dollar, Clark replied, "Yes, I know; Willie and Charlie have a rich father—I haven't."

The pioneer silver camp of Montana was not Butte but Phillipsburg, where Hector Horton made the initial discovery in February, 1865.[12] The first silver processing mill in the state was erected there. When the pans for it were shipped in from San Francisco, both wagon and pans sank from sight in quicksand at a river crossing, lay buried for several weeks, and finally were extracted by means of derricks.

To reach Montana, the gold and silver seekers used various routes.[13] The most obvious way was the Oregon Trail to Fort Hall,

---

12 Bancroft, *Montana*, 765–67; Burlingame and Toole, *Montana*, I, 341–42; MacKnight, *Mines*, 6.

13 Burlingame and Toole, *Montana*, I, 142–46, 153, II, 58–63; Bancroft, *Montana*, 729; Martin Barrett, "Holding Up a Territorial Legislature," *Contributions to the Historical Society of Montana*, Vol. VIII (1917), 93–98; Harold E. Briggs, *Frontiers of the Northwest*, 58–59; Burlingame, *Montana Frontier*, 136–37, 145–46; Mer-

thence northward to Montana. As a cutoff to this roundabout approach, John M. Bozeman and John M. Jacobs set out from Bannack in May, 1863, to go directly to Fort Laramie. Over the so-called Bozeman Trail which they had pioneered, a moderate number of wagon trains rolled until the Sioux Indians forced the federal government to abandon it. Another cutoff was Bridger Road, which branched off from the Oregon Trail west of the present town of Casper, Wyoming.

In 1862, because no established way led west from Minnesota, James L. Fisk secured federal money to organize a Montana-bound wagon train which would follow the route of the 1853 Stevens railroad survey. His first group—117 men, 13 women, 168 oxen, 8 mules, 14 teams of horses, and numerous dogs—traveled an average of seventeen miles a day until it reached Fort Benton, where the military escort turned to other duties while the party continued on to Helena and Bannack. In 1863, 1864, and 1866, Fisk again led emigrants westward, the last group as a private venture.

Within Montana, many prospectors used the Mullan Road, opened by the federal government in 1860 for the 624 miles from Fort Benton to Fort Walla Walla, Washington. With regard to local toll roads and bridges, the public resented the heavy charge of one to three dollars on each, especially where actually little or no improvements had been made. Eventually the state revoked the charters of the racketeers and purchased the rights of the others.

An important route for freight and passengers to Montana was the Missouri River, meandering roughly 2,500 miles from St. Louis to Fort Benton. Its side-wheel steamers carried about 500 tons of freight each. The upriver rate of twelve cents a pound for freight and $150 per passenger made possible profits of $16,000 to $65,000 per ship in 1866; captains earned $200 monthly and first-rate pilots $1,000. The climax of Missouri River trade came in 1879, when 47

rill G. Burlingame, "John M. Bozeman, Montana Trailmaker," *Mississippi Valley Historical Review,* Vol. XXVII (1940–41), 542–53; Hamilton, *From Wilderness,* 146–70; Hedges, "Centennial Address on Lewis and Clarke County," *Contributions to the Historical Society of Montana,* Vol. II (1896), 114; Langford, *Vigilante,* xx; Stout, *Montana,* I, 375; Stuart, *Forty Years,* II, 15, 22, 35, 37–38; William J. Trimble, *The Mining Advance into the Inland Empire,* 128, 225, 258; Tuttle, "Early History of the Episcopal Church in Montana," *Contributions to the Historical Society of Montana,* Vol. V (1904), 301; Vaughn, *Then and Now,* 113–14.

arrivals landed 9,444 tons of goods; by 1889, all the business had shifted to the new railroads. Some eastbound passengers went downstream in mackinaw boats, flatbottomed, broad, with square sterns, and generally propelled by the current, with only occasional assistance from oars or sails. As many as 200 of them, filled with 10 to 30 men each, left in a year. At St. Louis they were either sold or broken up.

For freight beyond the head of navigation, eight mules or nine to twelve oxen pulled three or four wagons filled with sixteen to twenty tons of goods. This service in 1866 required an estimated twenty-five hundred men, six hundred wagons, and three thousand teams. The charge for the 140 miles from Fort Benton to Helena was at first ten cents a pound, but competition soon forced the rate downward. Another heavily traveled route was from the Central Pacific Railroad at Corinne to Virginia City.

The pioneer stage line was A. J. Oliver and Company, opened in 1863 from Virginia City to Bannack and Salt Lake City; the initial fare for the four-day trip was $225. The next year, Ben Holladay obtained the new federal mail contract between Fort Hall and Virginia City. An intense rivalry with sharp rate cutting marked the competition between the two services until Holladay banished Oliver. In 1866, C. C. Huntley began service from Helena to Fort Benton. A telegraph line opened from Corinne to Virginia City in November, 1866, and went on to Helena in October, 1867. The charge in 1868 for a ten-word telegram from Virginia City to the eastern states was ten dollars.

The first railroad to reach Montana was the Utah and Northern, launched in 1873 to build from Salt Lake City; work progressed slowly. It sought subsidies from Montana counties without success and then asked the legislature for tax exemption for fifteen years. Its lobbyists dispensed liquor so freely that sometimes their parties ran all night and, at the next morning's session, the sergeant-at-arms had to be sent through the legislature to rouse drowsy members whenever a vote was to be taken. The lobbyists found themselves blocked by five solons who deliberately left Helena to prevent a quorum; when these travelers finally returned, the railroad company offered one of them five hundred dollars and a lifetime pass if he would vote for tax exemption, but to no avail. Despite this failure, the Utah and Northern, by then a subsidiary of the Union Pacfiic, reached Butte in 1881. The transcontinental line of the Northern Pacific, passing through Butte, was completed in 1883. A subsidiary of the Great Northern entered Butte in 1887 from Great Falls, and in 1894, the Anaconda Copper Mining Company opened a line from its mines in Butte to its smelter at Anaconda.

Law and order were as much a problem in Montana as on other mining frontiers.[14] The first regular court trial in the territory, a trespass case heard in March of 1862 at Hell Gate, was almost broken up when the defendant, a man named O'Keefe, suddenly addressed the justice of the peace as follows: "Say Old Brooks, who in hell made you judge? You are an old fraud. You are no judge; you are a squaw man, you have two squaws now. Your business is to populate the country with half breeds. You — — —."

More serious difficulties began when Henry Plummer arrived in Bannack from Idaho in the fall of 1862. Soon he secretly organized a gang of robbers, operating both there and in Virginia City, whose villainy eventually included the known deaths of 102 people. At first nobody suspected the existence of the group. When Plummer shot Jack Cleveland, a former associate, no one did anything about it. In January, one of the gang took an Indian squaw for a wife and so mistreated her that she returned to her tribe; in revenge, three of the ruffians killed a chief. They were given a trial by a twelve-man jury. Friends of the murderers surrounded the court during the hearing, making such threats that eleven of the jurors voted for acquittal and one for conviction with the death penalty; the compromise verdict was banishment and not even this was enforced. So powerful had the criminal element become that five months after the trial, eight or nine of the men who had served at it in some capacity

14 J. A. Burkhart, "The Frontier Merchant and Social History," *Montana Magazine of History*, Vol. II (October, 1952), 13; Thomas J. Dimsdale, *The Vigilantes of Montana*, 22–23, 25, 149, 229–38, 251–53; Hamilton, *From Wilderness*, 217–62, 321–26, 398–99; Joseph K. Howard, *Montana: High, Wide and Handsome*, 45–47; MacKnight, *Mines*, 58; Langford, *Vigilante*, xv, 110, 371–75, 388; Edward L. Munson, "Lyman Ezra Munson," *Contributions to the Historical Society of Montana*, Vol. VII (1910), 199–200; W. Y. Pemberton, "Montana's Pioneer Courts," *Contributions to the Historical Society of Montana*, Vol. VIII (1917), 99–100; Helen F. Sanders (ed.), *X. Beidler: Vigilante*, 28–29, 46–47, 106–107; J. W. Smurr, "Afterthoughts on the Vigilantes," *Montana: The Magazine of Western History*, Vol. VIII (Spring, 1958), 8–20; Stout, *Montana*, I, 288–90; Stuart, *Forty Years*, I, 199–200, 234–35.

had been killed, eleven or twelve had fled from the territory, and only seven of the original twenty-seven remained in the area.

Plummer ran for sheriff at Bannack in the spring of 1863 and won at an honest election. That summer, his gang continued to be very active. When Buck Stinson, Charley Forbes, and Haze Lyons tried to induce honest deputy sheriff D. R. Dillingham to join them in robbing three men going from Bannack to Virginia City, he refused and warned the travelers. Shortly, Dillingham himself went to Virginia City on official business; there the three outlaws shot him dead in the presence of a hundred men at a miners' court. The miners promptly tried Stinson and Lyons, found them guilty by unanimous vote, and ordered them hanged. The assembly then considered Forbes, who managed to talk so convincingly that he was acquitted. The other two then made a loud appeal for mercy, a second vote was finally agreed upon (although much of the crowd had dispersed), and those tallying the voters favoring acquittal deliberately allowed some men to walk past them twice. Stinson and Lyons were freed.

More successful was the trial of Plummer's subordinate George Ives, from December 19 to 22, 1863, for the murder of Nicholas Thiebalt, who had incautiously exhibited the gold he received from the sale of a span of mules. Accused as accessories were gangsters "Long John" Franck and George Hilderman. When a hunter discovered the frozen corpse, the three were taken to Nevada City for trial. To defend them, Plummer hired several lawyers; for the prosecution appeared attorney Wilbur F. Sanders, ably assisted by miner Charles S. Baggs. When a large number of men assembled on December 19, they voted to leave the decision to a jury of twenty-four, drawn equally from Nevada City and Junction.

The hearing was held on a platform made of two wagons, surrounded by the twenty-four jurymen's chairs hastily borrowed from a hurdy-gurdy hall, then encircled by a cordon of guards, and finally encompassed by about one thousand armed but good-natured citizens. When disputed points arose, what should be admitted as evidence was put to the vote of the people; these decisions would bring some of them rushing from the saloons and stores where they had retreated to warm themselves. When the trial adjourned for the night, threats were made against the lives of the prosecutors. The next day, Long John, who had witnessed Thiebalt's murder, frankly told what he had seen. The third day, the lawyers argued at length.

The jury took thirty minutes to return a written verdict, signed by twenty-three of them, that Ives was guilty. Sanders moved that he be hanged, the crowd voted approval, and an hour later it was done. The assemblage ordered Hilderman banished, Long John discharged.

The Ives trial, taking four days' time of about a thousand men, led directly to the formation in Virginia City and Nevada City of a joint vigilante committee. During the last week in December it began a roundup of criminals by arresting George M. Brown and Erastus "Red" Yager. Yager confessed his membership in the gang and gave the names of the entire group. This information enabled the vigilantes to capture the rest of the lawbreakers, twenty in all, including Plummer. Some of the gang who planned a last-minute dash to safety were apprehended, which shows that the vigilantes either sought revenge for past misdeeds or else feared the robbers might return later. Between January 4 and February 3, 1864, some of the criminals were hanged without trial; others were given a hearing, without any defense attorney, before the vigilantes' executive committee and then hanged. Since the vigilantes went unmasked, the secrecy of their trials apparently came from the critical attitude of some citizens who resented the group's lack of faith in the jury system. The Plummer gang was a great evil; its elimination was made more difficult by its secret password of "I am innocent." The committee's methods, however, are open to the same criticisms, discussed earlier, of a similar organization in California. When H. L. Hosmer, appointed chief justice of Montana Territory by President Lincoln, arrived at Virginia City, he told the grand jury (in December, 1864) that while vigilantes had previously been necessary, they should now give way to the courts, but in a few cases in 1865, the group still took its own action. In the 1865 diary of Virginia City merchant Isaac Rogers, however, the only disorder mentioned is a mild free-for-all at the first municipal election.

Other separate vigilante groups arose in Confederate Gulch and Helena. The latter committee executed a total of thirteen men on "hangman's tree." The group there was not as careful in gathering evidence or as conscientious as the men who wiped out the Plummer gang. The accounts written by contemporaries—which so glowingly and completely justify the initial group—say little about the Helena committee although apparently an equal amount of information was then available and some historians have suspected that there might be ample justification for an apologist to make the omission. When Lyman Ezra Munson, newly appointed justice on the Montana Territory Supreme Court, arrived at Helena in March, 1865, he was greeted by the swinging body of a man the vigilantes had hanged the night before. Their first duty, he told the other justices, was to insist that accused people have a jury trial, not such an execution, and he vigorously and repeatedly stated his conviction to the public. It was he, more than anyone else, who convinced Montanans they should depend upon the regularly established courts.

The miners' court, an institution already discussed in preceding chapters, proved ineffective in suppressing early Montana criminals but served well in regulating mining and all other civil matters.

The first formal attempt to establish effective government over the mining area came when Congress established Idaho Territory in March, 1863; it included all of the present state of Montana.[15] Its chief justice, Sidney Edgerton, was assigned to the judicial district which included Montana, and in the fall of 1863 he came to Bannack. Some citizens realized that they could expect no aid from the Idaho government in Lewiston, shut off by about eight hundred miles of snow-blocked road, so they raised $2,500 in gold nuggets to send him east pleading for a separate Montana Territory. His arguments were so effective that by May, 1864, President Lincoln signed an act authorizing its establishment and soon appointed Edgerton as its first governor. The capital was first at Bannack; in 1865, it was moved to Virginia City and in 1867 shifted to Helena. The first territorial election was in October, 1864; the first legislature sat from December 12 of that year until February 9 of the following one, doing its job well. Even after it adjourned, however, in many instances the laws of Idaho were observed rather than the new ones just passed simply because there were no copies of the new regulations available for some time and the brief summaries in newspapers were inadequate to meet attorneys' needs. In mineral procedure, the legislature, recognizing the customs and principles already adopted by the miners' courts, officially enacted them into law. One of the most

[15] Bancroft, Montana, 643; Hamilton, From Wilderness, 274–91, 327–28, 331, 338–42; Hedges, "Centennial Address on Lewis and Clarke County," Contributions to the Historical Society of Montana, Vol. II (1896), 109–11; Robert L. Housman, "The First Territorial Legislature in Montana," Pacific Historical Review, Vol. IV (1935), 376–85; Howard, Montana, 40–44; Stout, Montana, I, 281–83, 288–91.

important of these was the doctrine of prior appropriation—first in time, first in rights.

The first session of the district court, which had both territorial and federal jurisdiction, was opened at Virginia City in December, 1864, by Chief Justice H. L. Hosmer in the Planters House dining room, which had just been cleared of breakfast dishes. The meeting place was changed several times; for a while it was the Union League Room, entered by outside stairs from the back of the building. The first judges did not realize that the reasons why they made their rulings should be written down and published, since their decisions were foundation stones of judicial interpretation which generations of subsequent lawyers would want to examine; not until 1868 did the court begin publishing its opinions.

Religious activities started in the mining areas with the arrival, early in 1864, of a Baptist minister, A. M. Torbett, at Virginia City; a Methodist, a Catholic, and a Presbyterian also came that year.[16] When the Reverend G. G. Smith, a Presbyterian, was preaching his first sermon there in 1864, a dance band next door suddenly struck up a lively tune and the congregation began to beat time on the floor with hobnailed boots. He stopped, folded his arms, and then a ringleader promised him he would not again be interrupted if he would continue. Smith found out later that for the first six months he was followed by detectives; had he proved not to be a genuine minister, the vigilantes wanted to know what his real activities were. Daniel S. Tuttle, Episcopal bishop for Montana, Utah, and Idaho, came to Virginia City in July, 1867. In his first months there he spent "many dreadfully lonely hours." At his cabin his "white cat Dick was a constant, comforting and much loved companion. . . . I am not ashamed to say that my memories of him are of the tenderest and most grateful kind." During the thirteen years Tuttle was in Montana, he baptized 301 people, confirmed 240, buried 23, and married 21 couples.

16 Blake, "Historical Sketch of Madison County, Montana Territory," *Contributions to the Historical Society of Montana*, Vol. II (1896), 84–86; George Edwards, "Presbyterian Church History," *Contributions to the Historical Society of Montana*, Vol. VI (1907), 290–94; Hamilton, *From Wilderness*, 506–11; Hedges, "Centennial Address on Lewis and Clarke County," *Contributions to the Historical Society of Montana*, Vol. II (1896), 113; Tuttle, "Early History of the Episcopal Church in Montana," *Contributions to the Historical Society of Montana*, Vol. V (1904), 289–98; Stuart, *Forty Years*, I, 268.

The recreations available in Montana were typical of the mining frontier everywhere in the West.[17] At Virginia City and Nevada City every third business place was a saloon. When supplies of regular whiskey ran low, the taverns made their own "tanglefoot" by mixing a quantity of boiled mountain sage, two plugs of tobacco, and one box of cayenne pepper with one gallon of water; such a drink ordinarily cost twenty-five cents. The professional hurdy-gurdies, women who charged a dollar, were excellent dancers but far from good looking. Occasionally there were balls for families in Virginia City. A room and some beds were set aside for the small children, and parents took turns looking after them; a fine supper was usually served at midnight and the festivities continued for several hours more. Gambling and speculation were so much a part of life that few could resist. The first theater, the Montana, opened at Virginia City in December, 1864, and a rival, the Melodian, appeared the next year. In 1867, John S. Langrishe, a leader in Colorado's drama circles for twenty years, and his stock company started coming to Virginia City for several weeks twice annually. One time at Helena the United States marshal and all his deputies wanted to go to the theater, so they took along with them their only prisoner, an Indian being held as the witness of an illegal liquor sale to red men. All went well until the actors started killing each other "in great shape." The Indian, thinking it all in earnest, became frightened, jumped through a window onto the porch, ran to his horse, and dashed away. Occasional prize fights were held in the mining towns. In 1865, one in Virginia City lasted for three hours and five minutes.

Fraternal activities began in Montana when a Mason died in Bannack in November, 1862, after requesting a Masonic funeral; notices were posted throughout camp, and, to everybody's surprise, seventy-six members assembled. The territory's first Masonic lodge was organized at Helena in 1864; in 1867, the Odd Fellows established one there; the Independent Order of Good Templars opened

17 Sanders, X. Beidler, 136; Briggs, Frontiers, 83, 92, 109; Burkhart, "The Frontier Merchant and Social History," Montana Magazine of History, Vol. II (October, 1952), 7, 12–13; Dimsdale, Vigilantes, 11–12; Hamilton, From Wilderness, 511–13; Hedges, "Centennial Address on Lewis and Clarke County," Contributions to the Historical Society of Montana, Vol. II (1896), 114–15; Langford, Vigilante, 144, 173; Stuart, Forty Years, I, 265–68, II, 23–25; Trimble, Mining Advance, 162; Tuttle, "Early History of the Episcopal Church in Montana," Contributions to the Historical Society of Montana, Vol. V (1904), 294.

one at Virginia City in 1868. For a time the Fenians were important. With organizations at Helena and Virginia City, this brotherhood intended to join a simultaneous uprising of Irishmen in Canada, England, and Ireland. The Montana and Idaho contingent thought they might seize British Columbia.

Helena had a library association, organized in 1868 with four thousand dollars initially subscribed and the annual membership rate fixed at twenty-five dollars. By January, 1874, it owned two thousand volumes. In several camps the men organized lyceums, in which the members gave plays, musical numbers, essays, lectures, and debates. Thus one society had "a terrific debate" on the question "Resolved, that the Love of Woman has had more influence upon the Mind of Man that the Love of Gold." Certainly a fair number of men took little part in the less respectable forms of recreation.

The various business houses in the important mining towns were usually open on Sundays and, in Helena of 1868, also every evening until ten.[18] Merchants of the sixties generally made one trip a year to the East, taking with them their gold dust, paying their debts, and purchasing new supplies. The first center of trade to emerge in Montana was Virginia City. Firms used cellar warehouses because they were comparatively fireproof. One problem was a shortage of change; for example, in 1865, merchant Isaac Rogers had to pay a $10 premium to get $150 in small coins. Another difficulty was greenbacks, which miners refused to accept at face value until the legislature passed a law requiring it. An inadequate supply of money—gold or paper—available as a circulating medium in the territory sometimes curtailed business activities and cut down on everybody's profits. The first bank was the partnership of Allen and Millard, opening its doors at Virginia City in 1864. The firm charged interest of 2 per cent a month. Other early banks were operated by individuals or partnerships; the first one chartered under federal regulations as a national bank was established at Helena in 1866, and the second

18 Briggs, *Frontiers*, 61; Burkhart, "The Frontier Merchant and Social History," *Montana Magazine of History*, Vol. II (October, 1952), 6–10; Hamilton, *From Wilderness*, 376–84; A. M. Holter, "Pioneer Lumbering in Montana," *Contributions to the Historical Society of Montana*, Vol. VIII (1917), 253–70; Stuart, *Forty Years*, II, 28; Trimble, *Mining Advance*, 147; C. James Wall, "Gold Dust and Greenbacks," *Montana: The Magazine of Western History*, Vol. VII (Spring, 1957), 24–31.

one opened its doors in 1872. Montana banks of the territory period seldom failed and in fact enjoyed a large amount of success.

Finished lumber was scarce in the early days. The first mill near Virginia City sold its product for $750 per thousand feet; when a second one was opened in 1863, it cut the price on sluice planks to $140 per thousand and on ordinary boards to $125. Demand so exceeded supply that sometimes an anxious customer would simply load up his wagon and drive off without consulting the mill's office, then appear later to pay for what he had taken. Gradually, supply increased and prices came down; by 1867, sluice lumber was selling at $50 and ordinary planks at $40 in Helena.

The territory's pioneer newspaper was the weekly *Montana Post,* begun on August 27, 1864, at Virginia City.[19] Its first editor was Thomas J. Dimsdale, later best remembered for his book *The Vigilantes of Montana,* a detailed justification; the next one was Henry N. Blake, and Blake's successor was James H. Mills. Blake subscribed to Salt Lake City newspapers and about five days after they were issued there he published a condensation of the telegraph news. If the snows lay deep enough to cut Virginia City off from the outside, he occasionally ran so short of local items that he had to invent some to fill his vacant spaces. He saw to it that all brides were beautiful, all speakers eloquent, and all gold discoveries quite promising. The *Montana Post* prospered and became a triweekly. When the placers of Virginia City clearly began to decline, it was moved to Helena (in August, 1868) and became a daily; eleven months later, it suspended publication when its business manager defaulted. Other pioneer Montana newspapers were the *Montana Democrat* of Virginia City, 1865–67; the *Rocky Mountain Gazette* of Helena, 1866–74; the *Radiator* of Helena, 1865–66; and the *Herald* of Helena, which was started in 1866.

The earliest schools in Montana were private ones.[20] In October,

[19] Henry N. Blake, "The First Newspaper of Montana," *Contributions to the Historical Society of Montana,* Vol. V (1904), 253–64; Hamilton, *From Wilderness,* 480–85; Hedges, "Centennial Address on Lewis and Clarke County," *Contributions to the Historical Society of Montana,* Vol. II (1896), 113; James H. Mills, "Reminiscences of an Editor," *Contributions to the Historical Society of Montana,* Vol. V (1904), 273–88; Stuart, *Forty Years,* I, 267.

[20] Briggs, *Frontiers,* 100; Hedges, "Centennial Address on Lewis and Clarke County," *Contributions to the Historical Society of Montana,* Vol. II (1896), 114;

1863, Lucia Darling began teaching at Bannack, mornings only, in a schoolhouse that was mud covered and mud lined, with wooden benches and improvised desks. Since there were no textbooks available to buy, each student used whatever he could secure, and considerable variety resulted. Later that fall, Thomas J. Dimsdale started teaching at Virginia City, charging pupils two dollars a week. By October, 1867, Helena had four private schools with a total enrollment of 142. The first free public school opened at Virginia City on March 5, 1878, with 81 students and 2 teachers.

Food supplies in the mining camps were generally adequate.[21] Typical prices in November, 1862, at Virginia City were: raisins, one dollar per pound; potatoes, forty cents a pound; turnips, twenty-five cents a pound; butter, one and one-half dollars a pound; table salt, fifty cents a pound; bacon, forty cents a pound; and fresh beef, fifteen, twenty, or twenty-five cents a pound, depending upon the cut. For board and room, the California Hotel at Nevada City was charging fifteen dollars a week in 1864—lodging was a cot in a large bunkroom. For similar services in May, 1867, the Crystal Hotel at Helena asked eight dollars per week.

Food difficulties struck Virginia City in 1864–65. With snow fifteen feet deep in the passes, a shortage of flour seemed to develop, although it was well known there was an ample supply in town and the hoarding was obvious. The price for a one hundred-pound sack advanced steadily from twenty-seven dollars to one hundred dollars. One public meeting about the dangerous situation resulted in no action. At the second, men organized themselves in military fashion, searched the town, unearthed about 125 sacks, paid for it at twenty-seven dollars a hundred pounds, and under armed guard distributed it at cost to those who affirmed they were without—twelve pounds

---

Sarah R. Herndon, "The Pioneer Public School of Montana," *Contributions to the Historical Society of Montana*, Vol. V (1904), 198–99; S. W. Park, "The First School in Montana," *Contributions to the Historical Society of Montana*, Vol. V (1904), 191–95; Stuart, *Forty Years*, I, 267.

21 Briggs, *Frontiers*, 65, 70–71; Clark, "The Origin, Growth and Resources of Montana," *Contributions to the Historical Society of Montana*, Vol. II (1896), 54–56; Langford, *Vigilante*, xxix; Hamilton, *From Wilderness*, 345–52, 385–88; Sanders, *History*, I, 185; Stout, *Montana*, 335; Stuart, *Forty Years*, I, 262, II, 28–30, 34; Dorothy Winner, "Rationing During the Montana Gold Rush," *Pacific Northwest Quarterly*, Vol. XXXVI (1945), 115–20.

to each single person, twenty-four pounds to a couple and more if there were children. When three enterprising men thought this would be a good time for them to confiscate suits from a clothier, a leader of the vigilantes warned them that the first thief would be shot or hanged.

The various gold discoveries quickly prompted producers of beef, wheat, and potatoes to settle in the fertile valleys near by. Thus the rush to Bannack stimulated agriculture in the Bitterroot and Beaverhead valleys; those to Helena and to Confederate Gulch encouraged cultivation of the Prickly Pear Valley. Food commanded a high enough price that the most successful farmers had better incomes than the majority of miners. At first implements were scarce and crude; gradually, however, machines, adequate in number and variety, were imported. Although the territory's first flour mill had been established by the Jesuits at St. Mary's Mission in 1845, production of flour in Montana did not equal consumption until 1869. At that time the selling price was ten dollars for one hundred pounds; by 1876, this was down to five dollars. Some of the early cattle ranches were begun from the oxen and cows the immigrants used to pull their wagons west. In 1866, the first herd was driven into Montana from Texas. By the late 1860's, more than enough beef was raised to meet the local demand and Montana began her long economic role as an exporter of meat.

The Montana mines attracted a variety of races, but discrimination was shown against only two of them.[22] There were perhaps eight hundred Chinese in the territory by 1869, operating restaurants and laundries freely but allowed to take gold only from claims no white man wanted. They played an important role in the area's economy, but no careful study of their contribution has ever been made. A good example of the discrimination practiced against them was the law that all male persons engaged in the laundry business had to pay a tax of fifteen dollars per quarter; the only men in such enterprises were Chinese. Negroes were not allowed to vote; at Helena in September, 1867, however, they were permitted to take part in an election for the first time. Some of the whites objected to

[22] Burlingame and Toole, Montana, I, 132; Sanders, X. Beidler, 147–49; Briggs, Frontiers, 73; Glasscock, War, 72; Hamilton, From Wilderness, 180–89, 206–208, 423; Langford, Vigilante, 378–81; Warren, "The Territory of Montana," Contributions to the Historical Society of Montana, Vol. II (1896), 69.

this, and a man named Leech shot a Negro who said he didn't know whether or not he was going to vote; Leech was arrested but broke out of jail.

Another minority race, the Indians, were of course already in Montana and took no part in mining activities. The various tribes, as stipulated in an 1855 treaty, lived in different parts of the territory. In 1865, the government negotiated an agreement securing from the Blackfeet some land south of the Missouri and Teton rivers, but it was never ratified by Congress. Two actual Indian wars affected Montanans. The Sioux conflict of 1875–76 will be discussed at length later. The Nez Percé War of 1877 belongs essentially to Idaho's history, although the retreating red men fought with federal troops on Montana soil. In 1880, the United States drew up a treaty with the Crows excluding from their reservation grazing lands along the Yellowstone River and certain mineral tracts; the agreement was ratified in 1882.

The gradual increase in population, the expanding economy, and the arrival of railroads prompted Montanans to seek statehood.[23] Not until 1889 did the interplay of Democratic and Republican national politics allow Montana, Washington, and the two Dakotas simultaneously to become states.

On July 4, 1889, Montanans elected delegates to a second constitutional convention. Among the provisos it enacted concerning mineral development was one allowing aliens the same rights as citizens with regard to the ownership of mining property; this was a reversal of the earlier federal law prohibiting such ownership in the territories. Another section, aimed at the use of strikebreaking Pinkerton detectives, said that no armed persons could be imported into the state for preventing violence without the approval of the legislature or, if it could not be convened, the governor. A third specification exempted from taxation all mines, claims, and ore bodies—in other words, what would be the most valuable part of a rich property— but allowed taxes on what was potentially a considerably less important source of revenue: the annual net proceeds of mines that were operating, machinery, and surface improvements.

23 Hamilton, *From Wilderness,* 526–63; Howard, *Montana,* 62–64; Louis Levine, *The Taxation of Mines in Montana,* 16–77; J. W. Smurr, "The Montana 'Tax Conspiracy' of 1889," *Montana: The Magazine of Western History,* Vol. V (Summer, 1955), 55–56.

This was put into the constitution by the mining interests over the opposition of the cattlemen. It was not an issue in the election to ratify the constitution, which was approved 26,950 to 2,274, nor did the public at the time expect the proviso to be changed. The result, in the opinion of most observers, was that the mines did not pay their fair share of the state's taxes. Just after World War I, a vigorous controversy concerning the matter arose, and eventually it was at least partially corrected.

10

WITH the national collapse of silver's price in 1893 came a sharp decline in such operations at Butte.[1] Silver became simply an incidental by-product in copper mining. In 1902, for example, Butte's operations to secure 288,903,820 pounds of copper also yielded 10,106,884 ounces of silver and 46,051 ounces of gold. The area began to emerge as a copper producer just as the demand for that metal was beginning to increase. In 1876, wire made of copper was used to transmit speech and in 1882, at New York City, the nation's first electric-light generating plant opened. The world's annual consumption of copper in 1882 equaled what was used in an ordinary two weeks of 1957.

William J. Parks kept insisting that part of the Parrot silver lode would make an excellent copper mine. Unaided, with meager equipment, he set to work himself, filling a bucket, then climbing to the top of the shaft and hoisting it out. Finally, in 1876, at a depth of 150 feet, he struck copper ore, so pure it could be "shipped to hell and back for smelting and still make a profit." Within a short time he sold his property for $10,000; it eventually yielded $1,000,000

1 Burlingame and Toole, *Montana*, I, 201, 345; MWP, *Copper Camp*, 27–29, 45; Foor, "The Senatorial Aspiration of William A. Clark," 197–98, 286; Glasscock, *War*, 69–71, 85–86, 106, 203–20; Howard, *Montana*, 56; MacKnight, *Mines*, 17; Isaac F. Marcosson, *Anaconda*, 31–33, 45–57, 92–96, 105; F. E. Richter, "The Amalgamated Copper Company: A Closed Chapter in Corporate Finance," *Quarterly Journal of Economics*, Vol. XXX (1915–16), 397, 405; Rickard, *American Mining*, 350–54; Stout, *Montana*, I, 375; Toole, *Montana*, 195; K. Ross Toole, "When Big Money Came to Butte," *Pacific Northwest Quarterly*, Vol. XXXXIV (1953), 25–27; K. Ross Toole, "The Anaconda Mining Company: A Price War and a Copper Corner," *Pacific Northwest Quarterly*, Vol. XXXXI (1950), 317–29.

worth of the mineral. William A. Clark began developing copper mines in 1873. In 1878, he, Nathaniel P. Hill, and Richard Pearce joined to form the Colorado and Montana Smelting Company, the building of whose plant at Butte was crucial because it provided a local market for copper.

The Anaconda, which was to become the richest copper mine the world has ever known, was originally claimed in October, 1875, by Michael Hickey, who later took in Charles Larabie as a partner. In 1881, Marcus Daly examined the property and took an option on it; whether he then realized it was a copper mine as well as a silver location is not known. He turned to James B. Haggin, Lloyd Tevis, and George Hearst, already owners of the Homestake mine in the Black Hills. The purchase price is given as $30,000 by all except the latest researcher, Isaac F. Marcosson, who puts it at $70,000; the three financiers apparently gave Daly a free one-fourth interest. Development work continued and copper was found; by May, 1883, the workers were down to six hundred feet, where the vein varied from fifty to one hundred feet wide, 55 per cent copper. Initially the ore was shipped for processing to Swansea, Wales, where the amazed Welshmen wrote to ask if this was the product of a new refining process or if it was from some wonderfully rich mine.

As copper was increasingly produced at Butte, one of the problems was how to refine it locally. The cheapest, most common method was heap roasting, simply burning alternate layers of logs and ore. It gave off a suffocating smoke, filled with sulphur and arsenic fumes, which killed grass, flowers, and trees. Cats, when they licked the grime from their whiskers, risked being poisoned to death by the arsenic. Cattle, eating grass on the adjacent hillsides, literally plated their teeth with copper. On a windless day in the late 1870's or the 1880's, the smoke lay so heavy at midday that lamps were burned and thieves were as fearless at noon as at midnight. The practice continued—despite protests organized by Butte's women as early as 1885—until the middle of December, 1891. The Boston and Montana Company began roasting a new heap; within forty-eight hours, fifteen people had died and many others were confined to their beds; certainly some of this was caused by the fumes. The mayor had one hundred men pour sand on the heap until it was buried two feet deep and then got an injunction prohibiting further roasting until adequate precautions were taken.

The four partners in the Anaconda enlarged their ownership to include other valuable Butte mines. They also decided to erect a smelter, twenty-six miles to the west at Anaconda, to refine their ore. The plant, with an initial daily capacity of five hundred tons, opened in 1884. Its operations led adjacent ranchers to claim that fumes damaged their crops and livestock, and at first they secured considerable sums of money. In 1902, the miners hired a commission of experts who concluded that damage had really been done and $340,000 was paid to those injured. A system of flues and stacks was installed in 1903 to remove poisonous material before the smoke was released. Another of the miners' enterprises at Anadonda was the Montana Hotel, built in lavish fashion, fitted with a magnificent barroom that is still a show place, equipped with a dining room for five hundred people, and kept fully staffed, even though Daly was sometimes the hostelry's only occupant.

The Anaconda partners encountered price difficulties. Copper had been selling for seventeen or eighteen cents a pound in 1882, but the following year the producers in the Lake Superior region started cutting prices and Anaconda had to sell for as little as seven and one-half cents. In 1885, with the Lake Superior mines producing 77,000,000 pounds and all those at Butte 67,798,000 pounds, the general selling price was eleven and one-half cents. The lake companies cut the price to ten cents the next spring. After keeping its properties closed the following winter, Anaconda announced that it could thrive on ten-cent copper. At this point a syndicate of French speculators tried to purchase a world monopoly. Their plans went awry because scrap copper came on the market and buyers went on strike against higher prices. The French creditors of the speculators and the American producers agreed in 1889, after extensive negotiations, to peg the price at twelve cents.

Daly, Hearst, Haggin, and Tevis decided in 1894 that they could no longer act simply as a partnership, so they incorporated the Anaconda Mining Company. The next year, a foreign syndicate dominated by the Rothchilds purchased Hearst's portion and the whole enterprise was reorganized as the Anaconda Copper Mining Company. Before long it attracted the attention of Henry H. Rogers, who thought he saw the possibility of forming a copper trust; in 1899, he and his associates in the Standard Oil trust purchased it. At the time, about three-fourths of the state's wage earners were on the rolls of its varied enterprises. In addition to being the world's largest producer of copper, it was in the railroad, water, hotel, coal, lumber, newspaper, and electric-light fields. Daly remained the nominal head, but now the real power was in the hands of Rogers rather than J. B. Haggin.

As a holding company for Anaconda and such other copper properties as they might acquire, the Standard Oil interests formed the Amalgamated Copper Company in 1899. They issued $75,000,000 worth of common stock, floating it on the market at $100 a share; after the initial campaign, the insiders manipulated the price down to $75 and, squeezing out many of the original purchasers, bought much stock cheaply. In 1901, Amalgamated obtained two additional mining groups: the Boston and Montana Company and the Butte and Boston Consolidated Mining Company. The insiders raised Amalgamated's capitalization to $155,000,000 and pushed the price on the open market up to $130, when they unloaded much of their own stock. By cutting the dividend rate and plunging to $33, they then repurchased the shares at a good price. In 1910, Amalgamated obtained the three copper mines and the smelter—but not the lead or silver properties—belonging to William A. Clark. He accepted the the word of a trusted engineer that the three were nearly exhausted and disposed of them for five million dollars, a fraction of their true value. He did not realize he had been betrayed until his employee was in South America, reportedly with much money. It is a fact that within a year Amalgamated took out twice the total purchase price from just one of the three mines. Despite these successes, Amalgamated never obtained anything like a monopoly of copper; it came the nearest in 1899, when its subsidiaries mined 300,000,000 pounds and the total American production was 570,000,000 pounds.

The most serious threat to Anaconda and Amalgamated was F. Augustus Heinze.[2] As a twenty-year-old engineer graduated from Columbia University's School of Mines, he first arrived in Butte in 1889. Soon Heinze leased a small mine, unsuccessfully tried to raise

[2] MWP, *Copper Camp*, 43–44; Christopher P. Connolly, *The Devil Learns to Vote: The Story of Montana*, 185; Foor, "The Senatorial Aspiration of William A. Clark," 189–91; Glasscock, *War*, 107–10, 141–58, 223–311; Howard, *Montana*, 73–83; Sarah McNelis, "F. Augustus Heinze: An Early Chapter in the Life of a Copper King," *Montana Magazine of History*, Vol. II (October, 1952), 25–32; Marcosson, *Anaconda*, 107–108; Jerre C. Murphy, *The Comical History of Montana*, 55–59.

money for an independent copper smelter, and then went east for a year when his grandmother died. When he returned to Butte, he leased the Estella mine from James Murray, agreeing to pay a 50 per cent royalty on all ore containing at least 15 per cent copper but none on less. He promptly ordered his men to mix rock with the ore so that the yield would never reach the specified minimum; Murray, despite a lawsuit, never got any payment for his valuable property. Heinze rented the Glengarry, supposedly exhausted, and soon uncovered a rich deposit. He secured enough money to build his own smelter, then turned his attention to Trail, British Columbia, where his smelter and railroad activities became so successful that the Canadian Pacific Railway finally purchased all of his holdings there for $1,200,000.

Heinze next concentrated on Butte and started trying to wrest control of rich copper deposits from their owners. He battled for properties worth, at conservative estimates, $200,000,000. Always selfish, usually unethical, he used methods whose legality was hotly debated. At one time he faced 133 lawsuits with Anaconda; at the maximum he employed thirty-seven lawyers, and at the high point of legal proceedings the fees for attorneys fighting for or against him must have amounted to a million dollars annually. In fact, legal action became so complicated that Anaconda had to establish a special set of records to keep everything straight.

Many of the decisions favoring Heinze were made by William Clancy, a saloon lounger and curbstone lawyer, cunning, shrewd, coarse, vulgar, of little education, indifferent to his opponents but stubbornly loyal to his friends, who was unexpectedly elected district-court judge. In court he chewed tobacco, put his feet on a chair or a desk, looked out the window, dismissed a witness when he had heard enough, and appeared to focus his attention on the proceedings only to sustain the objection of a Heinze attorney or overrule one by an opponent. Elsewhere his undignified, slipshod personal habits seemed to endear him to the lower levels of society, whose votes kept him in office. Popular opinion insisted that he was "owned" by Heinze, yet nobody ever tried to prove it and several of his important decisions favoring the capitalist were sustained by the state supreme court. In 1900, Heinze supported strongly the re-election of Clancy and the initial election of Edward W. Harney. Both were victorious and both subsequently pronounced verdicts favoring the financier.

Heinze's superior knowledge of Butte's geology and his uncanny sense of mineral locations enabled him to uncover several immense bodies of ore whose existence rival engineers never even suspected. He posed as the champion of the common man and the independent mine owner, especially against the wicked ogre of Anaconda-Amalgamated, although it is now clear his only interest was the welfare of F. Augustus Heinze. Thus in 1900, as an electioneering device to help secure judgeships for Clancy and Harney, he announced that he and William A. Clark would adopt the eight-hour day in their mines. His struggles enabled a fair number of Butte miners to increase their pay without his knowledge by working one shift in one of his mines and another, on the same date, in an Amalgamated property; at the latter they did most of their resting. So intense did his feud grow that when President Theodore Roosevelt visited Butte in 1903, an equal number of Heinze and Anaconda men were invited to dinner. When everybody was seated, a large tray was laid before the President; the napkin covering it was lifted off, and there lay a dozen pistols which the police had found when they frisked each guest.

To recount all the maneuvers and all the properties in which Heinze was involved, to keep strict chronology accurate and the narrative clear, would require more space than this entire chapter; the following typical examples should make his methods clear.

Not long after his return from Trail, Heinze completed buying the Rarus mine. He thought his investment of $400,000 well justified because he believed that the apex of the Boston and Montana's Michael Davitt mine was actually in the Rarus; at law, whoever controlled the apex owned the entire deposit. He pushed his workings through increasingly rich ore into the Michael Davitt. Branded a thief by the Boston and Montana, he calmly offered it $250,000 for a property it thought worth $20,000,000. In the federal courts the Boston and Montana sued for uncontestable ownership of its Michael Davitt, for relief from trespass, and, insisting that the apex was in its property, for all the ore in the Rarus. The judge directed a verdict in its favor but the jury, defying him, gave it to Heinze. By the time a second trial began, the Boston and Montana had been taken over by Anaconda-Amalgamated. The hearing lasted forty-five days and again the jury favored Heinze. Amalgamated requested an appeal on the grounds that Heinze's public attacks against it had created prejudice; the right of appeal was granted and injunctions were issued to prevent either side from mining in the disputed property pending a final judgment.

To thwart these orders, Heinze evolved the brash theory that they applied only to his original corporation, so he established a new organization called the Johnstown Company. It promptly sealed the Michael Davitt off from the Amalgamated's Pennsylvania with concrete bulkheads, ran crosscuts into it from the Rarus, started mining, and hoisted the ore out of the Rarus. When an Amalgamated spy learned what was being done, Heinze doubled his working force. He thwarted a federal court order authorizing Amalgamated's engineers to examine the Michael Davitt. He slowed down the digging of crosscuts from the Pennsylvania by pouring slaked lime through air pipes to smother out the invaders; he tried to ward off counterattacks of steam and high-pressure water. Heinze had his men work faster than ever, snatching the ore away through secret passages. In the mass combats and private fights, officially only two men were killed and no record was kept of the scores doubtlessly injured. After days of struggle underground and legal manuevering, the United States Supreme Court finally ruled that Heinze had no legitimate title to the Michael Davitt. How much ore he removed by his device of the Johnstown Company was never revealed, but general opinion in Butte at the time was one million dollars' worth. He certainly never made any restoration to its owners.

Another phase of Heinze's activities was the discovery of an interesting triangular fraction on Butte Hill, about 375 square feet or one-twentieth of an average city building lot, to which nobody had ever sought patent as mineral land. Since it was between the shafts of the Anaconda, St. Lawrence, and Neversweat mines, all Amalgamated properties, he secured title, named it the Copper Trust, and announced that all three of those valuable ore producers apexed in his fraction. He got an injunction from Judge Clancy preventing the three from operating until a lawsuit could be decided. Amalgamated immediately closed the three mines down tight, threw three thousand men out of work, and announced that the cause was Clancy's support of an attempt to steal $100,000,000 in ore. Provocative agents unleashed by persons unknown stirred up a mob which clearly intended to hang the judge. He vanished from his usual haunts, sent word that he would revoke the injunction as soon as the Amalgamated lawyers drew up the necessary papers, and by midnight had done so. The next morning, the three thousand men were back at work and Heinze made no further serious attempts to exploit the Copper Trust.

Amalgamated persuaded Montana's legislature to pass a bill authorizing any company incorporated in the state, with the approval of two-thirds of its shareholders, to sell, lease, mortgage, or exchange its mining property for the stock of any other corporation, foreign or domestic. The measure was vetoed by Governor Robert B. Smith, who denounced it as a step in the formation of an American copper trust, but it was promptly passed over his protest veto and became law. Amalgamated acted under this authority and secured all but 2 per cent of the Boston and Montana Company's stock. It failed to get the one-fifteenth of 1 per cent belonging to John MacGinnis, one of Heinze's associates. He secured a temporary injunction from Judge Clancy preventing the Boston and Montana from paying any dividends to Amalgamated, and after two years, in October, 1903, the Judge made his order permanent. In answer, Amalgamated shut down all of its mineral and lumbering operations throughout the state, throwing out of work twenty thousand men, perhaps four-fifths of all Montana wage earners. Finally, Governor Joseph K. Toole agreed to call a special session of the legislature if Amalgamated would resume work at once. The solons promptly passed what the company wanted, what most states already had on their statute books, what was clearly reasonable and proper—a "fair trial" law providing that when either party to a suit suspected before the hearing began that the trial judge was prejudiced, it could shift to another jurist by the process known technically as "change of venue." To obtain this statute, Amalgamated had done a dangerous thing: it had coerced an entire state. To get precisely what it wanted took only three weeks. Shortly thereafter, the Montana Superior Court reversed Clancy's permanent injunction.

Twice Amalgamated tried unsuccessfully to purchase all of Heinze's Montana interests. Heinze left the state and settled in New York City. He began to speculate in the stock of the United Copper Company, a security with little intrinsic value, and forced the price up to sixty dollars per share; his enemy, Amalgamated, took such powerful action in 1907 that it slumped the price to ten. This cost Heinze almost all of his fortune. Apparently, Amalgamated's motives were revenge and to prevent Heinze's ever again having the ability to threaten it. He died in 1914 at the age of forty-one. His spectacular activities had kept Butte in an uproar for more than decade. He was an expert geologist, a superior mine operator, a scoundrel, and a thief. He sought his objectives with no regard for ethical standards; there is nothing that can be said to justify his actions. To resist him, Anaconda-Amalgamated found that it had to use his own methods; the alternative was a disastrous loss of extensive, very valuable property. No doubt this experience is one reason why the company maintained a dominating influence over Montana's political and economic development until well after World War II.

As spectacular as the great battles between Heinze and Amalgamated was the long-lived political feud which raged between William A. Clark and Marcus Daly.[3] Traditions give various debatable accounts of its origin; certainly at first, if there was any personal animosity between the two, which cannot be proved, it was not bitter. Then came the election of 1888. Clark, politically ambitious, won the Democratic nomination for territorial delegate to Congress. At this period in Montana, it would normally have meant automatic election in the fall, but when November came, Clark lost to a Republican, Thomas H. Carter, because he failed to carry Butte, Anaconda, and the lumber counties to the west.

Clark, quite bitter, correctly blamed his defeat on Daly. Probably Daly would never have opposed Clark except for one thing: Daly had been securing the timber needed for his deep mining operations from the Montana Improvement Company, owned by A. B. Hammond, E .L. Bonner, the Northern Pacific Railroad, and possibly other stockholders. The concern faced both civil and criminal suits for ruthlessly denuding the public domain of its trees. Thefts of this kind were all too common throughout the West. Had the Montana Improvement Company been found guilty, certainly the price Daly paid for lumber would have increased. Hammond and Bonner convinced him that with the Republicans in power nationally, the election of any Democrat, such as Clark, would not aid their selfish cause. The three of them and the railroad joined forces; in those

3 MWP, *Copper Camp*, 36; Connolly, *Devil Learns*, 97–98, 202–203; Foor, "The Senatorial Aspiration of William A. Clark," 9–15, 42–65, 80, 83, 126, 131, 178–279; Glasscock, *War*, 65, 117, 198; Hamilton *From Wilderness*, 581–600; Howard, *Montana*, 67; Mangam, *The Clarks*, 50, 70, 79–80; Toole, *Montana*, 27–32, 177–89.

districts where they controlled large blocks of votes, Clark lost. His-torians believe Carter promised to have the charges quashed; it is a fact that they were laid to rest in 1890. Subsequently, an Anaconda subsidiary, the Bitter Root Development Company, cut logs from a forest reserve and other government land. The value of the stolen trees, according to federal investigators, was certainly one million dollars and quite likely two. To Daly's defense came Carter, by this time a United States senator, but suits over the theft still threatened. Finally, Henry H. Rogers of Standard Oil went to Mark Hanna and warned him the Republican party need expect no more Standard Oil money anywhere unless the suits were abandoned. They were—through the intervention of President McKinley. At least all of this is what Montana newspapers friendly to Clark were publishing in 1900, corroborated by authenticated copies of correspondence, and the Daly papers made no attempt at all to deny the charge.

Earlier, in 1888, when Clark was defeated, the newspaper he had already owned for ten years, the *Butte Miner,* led the Democratic press in a strong attack on Daly. He retaliated by founding the *Anaconda Standard,* by spending perhaps five million dollars to launch it as "the best paper that can be made," by securing a large Montana-wide circulation, and by devoting its editorials to lam-basting Clark at every opportunity.

In 1892, Clark tried to win appointment as United States senator from the state legislature. He could have been elected by the regular Democrats and the Populists, with their majority of the joint house-senate assembly, except for the opposition of the Daly Democrats. In voting on the last day of the legislative session, the Clark forces came within three votes of victory. Afraid to risk another ballot, a Daly Democrat successfully moved that the session adjourn. Gov-ernor J. E. Rickards then attempted to appoint a Republican to the post, but the United States Senate refused to seat him.

The Clark-Daly feud flamed anew in 1894. Clark still hoped to be a senator; Daly wanted his home city of Anaconda to win perma-nent possession of the state capital rather than Clark-backed Helena. Had the two men been willing to co-operate, each might easily have secured the prize he sought; instead, each met defeat. The Republi-can majority in the legislature elected two of their own party to be United States senators. Helena won over Anaconda, 27,028 to 25,118, probably because of the Clark group's repeated warning that the Anaconda Company threatened political and economic tyranny in the state, a charge emphasized by the distribution of thousands of little copper collars. To celebrate Helena's victory, Clark paid the bill at each of the city's bars and "old-timers today declare it was the drunkenest night Montana ever had, which was going some." The battle of the state capital in the preliminary election of 1892 and the runoff of 1894 cost Daly and Clark one million dollars, according to a subsequent estimate by the United States Senate.

In the early summer of 1898, Clark and his friends again laid plans to make him senator, organizing a committee to elect favorable state legislators. The committee subsequently admitted spending $139,000. After the election, Clark or his agents had unusual business transactions with some of the legislators, such as buying the timber and sawmill of one and then installing him as manager.

When the legislature elected in 1898 met early the next year, one of its members was an independent Democrat named Fred Whiteside. Convinced there was much corruption in the elections and in the legislature itself, he deliberately laid a trap for bribers. Before long a Clark attorney, John B. Wellcome, was handing him $30,000; upon a vote for Clark being cast, this money was to be divided among the following legislators: $10,000 to Henry L. Meyers, $10,000 to W. A. Clark (of Madison County and no relation to the mining magnate), $5,000 to H. H. Garr, and $5,000 to Whiteside. When Whiteside arose on the house floor to make this public, he created such pressure that on January 9, the day before the proposed first ballot for United States senator, the two branches of the Montana legislature created a joint committee to investigate the charges of bribery. As the first witness, Whiteside produced the $30,000, mostly in $1,000 bills, and testified that the general idea had been made perfectly clear in his conference with Wellcome and financier Clark. Meyers and legislator Clark then confirmed this. The investigators voted to turn the matter over to a grand jury. At its hearings Clark's friends claimed the accusers had perjured themselves and that the $30,000 really came from Daly to be used as a smear. The jury reported on January 27 that there was insufficient evidence to convict anybody in a court of law. It was commonly said at the time around Helena that the foreman had received $15,000 and the rest of the jurors each $10,000, but nobody tried to prove it. On January 28, the day after the jury's report, the legislature cast its eighteenth ballot for the senatorship. Eleven Republicans favored Clark, amidst charges of corruption and the naming of specific sums of money as each man cast his vote. Clark was elected, fifty-four to thirty-nine. That night in Helena, rockets illuminated the heavens, red fire danced on the street corners, firecrackers popped, bands played, and so much free champagne flowed for cattle barons and mine muckrakers alike that the total of Clark's bills for liquor was commonly stated as $30,000.

Whiteside petitioned for the disbarment of John B. Wellcome. The Supreme Court of Montana, reluctantly taking jurisdiction and holding a trial, expelled him from the bar. Wellcome did not take the witness stand in his own defense. While the trial was going on, the Clark forces probably offered, in the opinion of a subsequent investigating committee of the United States Senate, bribes of $100,000 to both William H. Hunt and Attorney General C. B. Nolan; these were indignantly rejected.

When Clark went east, he was tentatively admitted to office but faced an investigation by the Senate Committee on Privileges and Elections. The committee concluded, among other things, that the election had cost Clark $330,000. It thought that some of those Republican legislators who voted for him on the eighteenth ballot had been bribed; it believed one of them had received $50,000, another $10,000, and a third $5,000; it asked unanimously that the Senate refuse to allow Clark his seat permanently because he was "not duly and legally elected." The report brought from Daly's *Anaconda Standard* the complaint that the election had cost Clark, not $330,000, but at least $750,000 and perhaps as much as $1,000,000.

Clark, who had occupied his seat from December 4, 1899, to April 11, 1900, promptly handed his resignation to the governor of Montana. Who should fill the vacant position? When unfriendly Governor Robert B. Smith was lured into investigating some California mining property at the request of Tom Hinds, an associate of Clark's, the president of the state senate, Edwin Norris, became acting chief executive. To displace him, Lieutenant Governor A. E. Springs rushed back from Iowa, officially accepted Clark's resignation, and then named him to the vacancy just created. Back hustled angry Governor Smith to revoke the appointment and select instead Martin Maginnis. What no doubt seemed a clever scheme to some Montana politicians aroused disapproval among United States senators and the large eastern newspapers. When Clark and Maginnis both presented their credentials, the Committee on Privileges and Elections allowed the question to rest for about two weeks until that session of Congress adjourned permanently.

In the spring of 1900, Clark again started making plans to gain the office. One of his first was to secure control of the delegates for the Democratic state convention, which would select those to represent it at the national nominations in Kansas City. He met with so little initial success that he allied with financier F. Augustus Heinze, who convinced him that they had to win labor's support. The two announced that in their properties they were granting the union's demand to cut the workday to eight hours but keeping the standard wage of $3.50. When the state convention met, the argument over seating of disputed delegates erupted into hand-to-hand combat so fierce that the sheriff and his few deputies stationed there were thrown out of the hall. The result was that two separate groups went to the national meeting as delegates and the one which favored Clark was admitted; this gave him control of the Montana Democratic machine. The state campaign continued. When the ballots were counted, Heinze had secured the election of Judges Clancy and Harney. Clark was elected senator for the long term starting March 4, 1901. His enemies charged that it had cost him $1,230,000. Clark soon reached some kind of co-operative understanding with Anaconda-Amalgamated; he and Heinze, no longer needing each other, gradually drifted apart. No service Clark rendered to the state or nation as senator could repair the great damage he inflicted on Montana's political structure by the twelve years of huge campaign expenditures, some of them illegal and corrupt, with which he sought to win office.

To protect themselves from Clark, Daly, and other owners, miners belonged to a union.[4] It was founded in the summer of 1878 by about one hundred men who successfully struck against a proposed wage cut in certain properties. In 1881, it was reorganized as the Butte Miners' Union, which was transformed in June, 1893, into the first local of the newly established Western Federation of Miners. By 1900, membership at Butte had grown to over eight thousand. The union enforced there a daily wage scale of $3.50 for all underground

4 Works Progress Administration, *Montana: A State Guide Book,* 68–69; Mac-Knight, *Mines,* 25.

mine workers. It built up a large financial reserve to provide its members with hospital care, sick benefits, and burial expenses.

Cats, horses, and mules also worked in the mines.[5] The cats attacked the numerous mice in the areas where feed was stored. The most famous was Kelly the Ghost, a big white cat living on the eight-hundred-foot level of the St. Lawrence mine. Kelly became a traveler, visiting the connecting Anaconda and Neversweat mines. Once he appeared on the six-hundred-foot level of the St. Lawrence; nobody knew how he got there, but the miners always insisted that he had climbed a two-hundred-foot ladder from his usual haunt.

Horses and mules were used to transport ore in the mines. They had very clean underground stables, the finest of fodder, and fresh water twice daily. They numbered, in 1910, at least one thousand. The animals were lowered blindfolded down the mine shaft in a special rope harness. Safely landed at his level, each was allowed two days of leisure before going to work. Soon his hide turned a greenish hue. He generally stayed below until bad illness, old age, or suspension of operations brought him to the surface, although occasionally he might be allowed a vacation above ground to gallop, kick up heels, and roll over and over. At work a horse or mule pulled a train of six cars, each filled with a ton of ore, from where it was dug out to where it was lifted to the surface. His train was handled by a driver and by an assistant who loaded the cars from chutes and threw the switches. Most animals could never be persuaded to pull more than six cars, or made to work more than the normal length of a shift, or induced to cut short the customary sixty minutes for lunch. Many of them became pets, stealing pie or chewing tobacco; at least one enjoyed inhaling the cloud of smoke from a group of miners having their noontime pipes. A deep affection developed generally between the animal and his driver, on rare occasions so strong that neither would work without the other. As an old miner's ballad lightheartedly had it:

> My sweetheart's a mule in the mine.
> I drive her with only one line.
> On the dashboard I sit
> And tobacco I spit,
> All over my sweetheart's behind.

5 MWP, *Copper Camp*, 46–47, 90, 92, 124–26, 141–42, 198–201, 231; Connolly, *Devil Learns*, 88; Glasscock, *War*, 162–65.

Above ground about the turn of the century in Butte were approximately ten thousand horses. Teams of six or eight pulled ore wagons, while smaller ones hauled the delivery wagons. They trod on streets so unevenly paved that the average horse could stand to work only four days a week and had to rest for three. At the city's score of livery stables one of the big annual events occurred in early spring when the horses were shorn of their winter hair with air-driven hand clippers. To assist at this, boys eagerly worked the bellows and happily accepted their customary reward of a shearing themselves. The most famous animal on Butte's streets was Jim the Firehorse, sole animal survivor of a great explosion in 1895, who lived in a special stall with no bars on it. Wandering about at will, he poked his head into all the cafes and candy stores, begging for sugar or apples, and followed young ladies to nudge their pockets for sugar or hard candy.

The talk about horses centered in summer on the races at the near-by Montana Jockey Club. Much of the discussion was about the high-quality stable of 90 to 120 horses which Marcus Daly maintained as a hobby. Some of his animals were national bywords in their day. Daly gave his miners the day off, with pay, to attend Jockey Club events; most of the rest of Butte went, too, for these were important occasions. Race days, St. Patrick's Day, St. George's Day, Miners' Union Day, and election day supplemented the regular American holidays in Butte and the miners guarded these as a traditional right.

Three miles east of the city's center William A. Clark built a typical trolley park of the era; it was named Columbia Gardens and was served by his street car line.[6] There were picnic tables, a dance pavilion, playgrounds for children, various concessions, band concerts—in fact almost everything the miners wanted in a summer resort if they could not afford to leave Butte. The one thing they missed was beer, which the law said could not be sold within a mile of the park. Exactly at the limit was Skibereen's One Mile Limit Ranch. "Skib" Mullins allowed large and hilarious parties, yet with an iron hand forbade fighting at the bar; if insistence grew too strong, he allowed it under supervision in the corral. There the normal occu-

[6] MWP, *Copper Camp*, 77–80, 173–86, 222, 224, 250; Archie L. Clark, "John Maguire: Butte's 'Belasco,' " *Montana Magazine of History*, Vol. II (January, 1952), 33–37; Glasscock, *War*, 92–97, 146, 161, 166–67.

pant was a solitary Holstein cow, normally placid but by "the extra-ordinary carrying-on" turned into a surly and suspicious animal.

Rock-drill contests were an interesting recreation as common to Butte as most mining towns, except that in Butte it was the biggest attraction and so could offer the largest prizes. The spectators almost all made some kind of a bet on the outcome. More unique to Butte was coursing, a race between two dogs to determine which was faster, which could better turn the rabbit they were chasing, and which could more adeptly avoid the holes in the hedged side of the track. The town's first theater was opened in 1885 by John Maguire. He brought to his seven Montana theaters all the top-ranking stars of the 1880's and 1890's with the single exception of Edwin Booth. Definitely below his establishment was the Comique, catering to the lowest and most depraved tastes in town. The stage show was a combination of vaudeville and burlesque; some of the acts supplied by the leading booking agents of New York City were really excellent vaudeville. On the main floor sat gamblers, pimps, and others who had no reputations to lose. For the rest of the audience there were rows of screened boxes from which patrons could look out without being seen. The conduct of the gentry in hiding was no different from that of the men exposed to public view. To them girls sold drinks, working under the incentive of commission payments.

The upper crust of Butte society never admitted attendance at the Comique. It sent its sons and daughters to the most expensive finishing schools of New York, Boston, and Paris or else to the best colleges. It condoned the institution of the mistress; it knew who the women were well enough to point them out, but it never accepted them socially. To prevent any mistakes, the chaperon was a very important institution. Certainly whenever a bachelor entertained at a dinner party there was a chaperon. If he had a mistress, she disappeared completely for the evening and even her photographs were removed. For a while a mistress of Heinze's amused herself by tacking her pictures so high on the wall that the inspecting chaperon would have to get a stepladder to take them down.

For those who wished to patronize it, Butte had a red-light district which came to rank with those of New Orleans and San Francisco as the most wide open in the United States. At the Casino, a combined saloon, dance hall, theater, and whorehouse, more than one hundred girls worked, often under a "nom de crib." In many of the brothels girls earned sixty dollars an evening. For the elite there were deluxe "parlor houses," ornately furnished, complete with Chinese servants and well-groomed girls; one of the madams, Lou Harpell, openly advertised on theater and race-track programs. Such establishments were the playground of millionaire copper kings and their friends, who thought nothing of spending several thousand dollars in an evening.

There were, of course, many places to gamble in Butte. All the usual games were available and also the petty one called *panguingui,* which some old-timers insisted was introduced "just to keep the pimps off the streets." In a faro game one time "Fat Jack" Jones, the city's best known hackman, staked his false teeth, lost them, went for a week on a very soft diet before he could raise the necessary money, and when he redeemed them, promptly ate three T-bone steaks at one sitting. In the saloons a Butte special was a "Shawn O'Farrell," served only to miners coming off shift. The "Shawn O," selling for a dime, was a full ounce of whiskey—supposedly to cut the copper dust out of a man's lungs—followed by a pint of beer to slake his accumulated thirst. It was commonly said that two of these made the miner a new man and so called for a third for the new man just created. Miners who were drug addicts had no difficulty in getting the supplies they wanted.

Of the food commonly eaten in Butte, three dishes deserve special mention.[7] Cousin Jack pastry, a combination of pie crust, beef, and vegetables, was excellent if made by an experienced cook but generally soggy if prepared by an amateur. When his wife put it in a miner's lunch bucket, this Cornish dish was called "a letter from home." Oaten cake was oatmeal, milk, and water pressed into a cake, then baked to an iron hardness. It was popular with the Scotch, Irish, and Nova Scotians. Stirabout was oatmeal mush, thinned with milk until it was a medium-heavy gruel. Many a miner ate two or three bowls of it for breakfast.

No Chinese ever worked in a Butte mine.[8] By the late 1890's, discrimination had driven them out of the restaurant, gardening, and vegetable-peddling businesses. They continued to run laundries, chop-suey houses, gambling rooms, lottery offices, and opium dens.

[7] MWP, *Copper Camp,* 243–46.
[8] *Ibid.,* 109–16, 139–49.

A brisk trade in slave girls was known to exist, but Butte officials never took steps to curb it. Neither did they concern themselves much when a ring of blackmailers in Chinatown used imported "hatchet men" to collect tribute for their countrymen. The Chinese were violently disliked by the city's early-day children, who bombarded laundrymen and vegetable peddlers in winter with frozen snowballs, in summer with rocks or cobblestones. Their attacks were so vicious that many Chinese finally secured a police permit to carry a gun; several children were killed.

Boys found a great variety of opportunities to earn money during the Clark-Daly political fights and the Heinze-Amalgamated battles. Most boys joined a gang, and much of a club's time was spent in recreation of a relatively wholesome kind, but there was also an obnoxious warfare between the various groups based upon race or geographical location. All in good fun was the swimming along Bell Creek. Somebody once dumped a large number of ancient eggs into the pond at its west end and they floated; the boys staged a memorable naval battle.

Butte had its share of disasters and fatalities.[9] In an ordinary year, deaths from accidents averaged somewhere between fifty and one hundred. In 1889, a major fire struck the Anaconda mine; six were killed. A conflagration at the Silver Bow mine in 1893 exterminated nine. On a freezing night in January, 1895, a small fire spread to the Kenyon-Connell and Butte Hardware Company warehouses. An hour after the first alarm a burst of flame abruptly shot upward several hundred feet and was followed by a concussion so terrific that men underground rushed to the shafts in fear their mine had suffered a disaster. Shortly there was a second explosion as strong as the first. Devastation was spread through the whole lower part of the city from tons of iron plate which had been stored next to blasting powder. This disaster killed about fifty-five people, including all but three of the city's firemen, and injured hundreds. In the autumn of 1899, a fire in the St. Lawrence and Anaconda mines killed four men.

Butte's major riot came in 1894 over the American Protective Association, an anti-Catholic organization. When the Columbia and Sazerac saloons included the letters A.P.A. in their decorations for July 4, somebody threw a stick of dynamite, destroying the former's

9 *Ibid.,* 147, 163, 171; Glasscock, *War,* 100–103, 134–38.

plate-glass window. This launched a battle royal between Cornish-men and Irishmen which lasted for three hours, despite the frantic efforts of Butte police to stop it. When shooting started, a call brought the fire department, which turned its hoses, not on the mob, but on the two saloons until everything inside was broken. Finally a platoon of militia drove everybody away.

The early development of Montana was typical of mining rushes. Bannack, Virginia City, Helena, and early Butte might equally well have been located geographically and in time on the California, Idaho, Colorado, or Black Hills mining frontiers. What sets Montana apart from the others is the evolution of Butte into a huge copper center, the Heinze-Amalgamated struggles, and the Clark-Daly political feud.

11

IDAHO MINES OF THE SIXTIES AND SEVENTIES

IDAHO'S golden age was the 1860's. The discoveries in the north near the Clearwater River and in the south at the Boise Basin precipitated rushes quite typical of the western mining frontier. In the middle 1880's, new finds developed the Coeur d'Alene area. Labor violence flared and was suppressed by federal troops; Idaho's former governor was blown up and the conspiracy trial for the murder attracted nationwide attention.

The first important gold seeker was Elias Davidson Pierce, who had served as a trader to the Nez Percé Indians at Lapwai.[1] In February or March, 1860, he accompanied them on a hunt and found just enough gold to convince him there was more. This discovery, not that false tradition about his belief in a tremendous diamond, prompted him to tell the council of the Nez Percés that he would return with a regular prospecting party. Their federal agent, A. J. Cain, opposed the plan and urged the red men to exclude such a group from their reservation. At Walla Walla, where Pierce tried

---

1 Merrill D. Beal and Merle W. Wells, *History of Idaho*, I, 281–88, 298; Ralph Burcham, Jr., "Elias Davidson Pierce, Discoverer of Gold in Idaho: A Biographical Sketch" (unpublished M.A. thesis, University of Idaho), 45–59; Ralph Burcham, Jr., "Reminiscences of E. D. Pierce, Discoverer of Gold in Idaho," (unpublished Ph.D. thesis, Washington State University), 44–45, 257–71; Byron Defenbach, *Idaho: The Place and Its People*, I, 259–69, 299; Hiram T. French, *History of Idaho*, I, 27; W. A. Goulder, *Reminiscences: Incidents in the Life of a Pioneer in Oregon and Idaho*, 204, 210; James H. Hawley (ed.), *History of Idaho, the Gem of the Mountains*, I, 103–105; John F. MacLane, *A Sagebrush Lawyer*, 78–79; Harry B. Averill, John M. Henderson, and William S. Shiach, *An Illustrated History of North Idaho*, 19, 22; Muriel S. Wolle, *The Bonanza Trail: Ghost Towns and Mining Camps of the West*, 216–22.

to recruit an expedition, the whites feared that gold hunting might stir up Indian trouble and perhaps war. Pierce secured only a handful of men, probably eleven, and set out August 10 or 12. They had an Indian guide, much more likely a man than a girl. Maneuvers dodging Nez Percés eager to turn them back so delayed them that it took about six weeks to reach the tributaries of the north fork of the Clearwater River. Here the initial discovery was made about October 1 by Wilbur Fisk Bassett, who shortly before sundown took a few pans from Canal Gulch just above its confluence with Orofino Creek. After testing enough to convince themselves of real prospects in the area, the group returned to Walla Walla with one or two hundred dollars in gold dust.

The news aroused considerable interest in Walla Walla, and a new group was organized under John Calhoun Smith. These thirty-three men, eluding the troops sent to intercept them, reached Orofino Creek on December 2, 1860, and erected eight cabins so promptly they were well housed when the snow really began to fall. They named the settlement Pierce and, in the tradition of the mineral frontier, organized the Orofino District on January 5, 1861, to regulate mining temporarily until regular government was established; they staked seventy-one claims that winter. Their success became public knowledge in early March when Smith and J. Davis snow-shoed out to Walla Walla with eight hundred dollars in gold dust. A fever seized the town and almost all available supplies were promptly used to outfit more prospectors. Letters carried the news to such areas as California and were published in the newspapers there.

To serve the rush, a Nez Percé Indian chief, Reuben, built a warehouse at what became Lewiston at the junction of the Snake and Clearwater rivers. William Craig installed ferry services there across the streams and one of them was soon collecting four thousand dollars a week in tolls. In May, the first steamship, the *Colonel Wright,* began operations on the two rivers, soon selecting Lewistown as its terminal. Pack trains carried freight from Lewiston to the mines.

The Nez Percés agreed on April 11, 1861, that the whites could work in the area north of the Clearwater River, but not south of it. Within a month prospectors had clearly violated this understanding. By August there were apparently 2,500 practical miners in the Pierce area and 5,000 additional men who made their living in other ways. They founded Orofino, located two miles from Pierce and about forty miles from the present Idaho city of the same name. Building lots sold for $100 or $200 and a good log house for around $1,000. Common laborers earned $3.50 to $6.00 a day, carpenters got $9.00 to $10.00, and the better claims were yielding $10.00 a day for each person working on them.

By 1863, pay streaks began to decline; Pierce left the area. By the end of 1866, the region had produced about $3,400,000 in gold. In the early 1870's, the annual yield was usually less than $70,000. Many of the claims were now worked by Chinese because the whites found the profits too small. One of the Orientals put gunpowder in a stick of wood, placed it in the pile where a miners' meeting was to be held, and when it was put into the fire, several miners were wounded. At his trial he was sentenced to twenty-five lashes with a black-snake whip. Then he had his choice of leaving camp forever or receiving seventy-five more; he preferred to leave.

In May, 1861, fifty-two prospectors set out from Orofino to explore the upper south fork of the Clearwater River.[2] When the Nez Percés warned that under the April terms of the agreement the area was closed, more than half the party turned back. Those who continued found gold the next month about 125 miles from Pierce, at what they named Elk City. The shallow but very rich concentrations of placer gold were scattered at a depth of two to three feet over a large area. Claims requiring hydraulic operation were also developed. The longest of the necessary water conduits was nine miles, had somewhere between 200,000 and 300,000 board feet of lumber in its flumes, and cost between $30,000 and $40,000 for the pick-and-shovel work on its ditches. Up to the end of 1866, the Elk City area had produced perhaps $3,600,000 in gold. By the 1870's, most of the whites had left, but a large number of Chinese continued at work. The Orientals had their opium supply mailed to them under the disguise of tobacco tins.

The Salmon River mines were discovered by a prospecting party of twenty-three who left Orofino in July, 1861, and found gold about

[2] Defenbach, *Idaho*, I, 270–71; Hawley, *History*, I, 105; Averill, Henderson, and Shiach, *North Idaho*, 22–23; Wolle, *Bonanza Trail*, 223–24.

110 miles southeast of Lewiston.[3] Settlement came to concentrate at the town of Florence. The gold, worth twelve dollars an ounce, was in narrow but very rich gulch deposits. The mines were well within the Nez Percé reservation, and the Indians unsuccessfully took the strongest measures short of war to prevent a rush, then in December agreed to the illegal intrusion. The winter was unusually severe, but men continued to force their way into Florence as late as February. They walked single file along a narrow path beaten down firm. If their customary precaution against snowblindness (a compound of pulverized charcoal and bacon grease) failed, they assigned a man whose vision was still good to the lead, then each placed the blade of a shovel under his arm and extended the long handle back for the person behind to hold onto as a guide. To travelers in serious difficulties the Nez Percés gave food and shelter. At Florence a severe food shortage developed; the cheapest thing available was flour at two dollars a pound, and only a wealthy man could afford bacon, sugar, or dried beans. The suffering would have been more severe had not the Indians sold the miners what surplus food they had.

Reports of the richness of the Salmon River country spread rapidly and exaggeratedly to Oregon and California. These temporary placers acted, in the summer of 1862, as a magnet, drawing in a considerable population. The mines at Florence were insufficient to hold permanently some of the prospectors, who then turned elsewhere for greater opportunities. Partisan feeling at Florence between Northerners and Southerners was so strong that some people feared trouble; none developed. A committee for the Fourth of July celebration brought down a considerable quantity of snow, drenched it repeatedly with water, and the chill of the high altitude froze it into a solid block of ice. On it Charles Ostner went to work, hidden from sight by tarpaulins, until on the great holiday several thousand watched the unveiling of what proved to be an ice statue of George Washington on his horse. Florence's placers produced abundantly until 1863, moderately until 1869, and then the Chinese worked over

3 Beal and Wells, *History*, I, 281–85, 298; Defenbach, *Idaho*, I, 272–74; M. Alfreda Elsensohn, *Pioneer Days in Idaho County*, I, 55, 67–68; Goulder, *Reminiscences*, 219–21, 240–42; Hawley, *History*, I, 105–107; Averill, Henderson, and Shiach, *North Idaho*, 24–27; Wolle, *Bonanza Trail*, 224–25.

what remained for another decade. The value of the gold taken out before 1867 was about $9,600,000.

Adjacent to the Florence area, gold was discovered by James Warren's party.[4] He was a college man of loose morals who drifted into such bad company that at least one of the men with him was an outright desperado, yet the settlement called Warrens, which arose in 1862, never had much trouble with ruffians. Some of the miners there amused themselves with an association called the Hocum Felta, devoted to dead-pan humor. The member performing and those watching deliberately refrained from smiling. The entertainer's words and deeds were intended to provoke mirth, and sometimes he succeeded with consummate skill. By the end of 1866, Warrens had yielded approximately six million dollars' worth of gold.

The supply point for Pierce, Orofino, Elk City, Florence, and Warrens was Lewiston. Many of the buildings erected there had simply a pole frame and rafters, with brown muslin or sheeting for the sides or roof. They had no windows because the sunshine came in well enough during the day; at night the reverse happened as the lamps and candles shone out to light up the street. Idaho's first newspaper, the *Golden Age,* was published at Lewiston from August 2, 1862, until 1865. The first time the American flag was raised over its office, Confederate sympathizers reportedly fired twenty shots through it.

Lawlessness developed around Lewiston.[5] In the spring of 1861, Henry Plummer, a professional gambler, and his wife came to town. Before long it developed that she was not his wife and that he no longer wished her company. Otherwise, Plummer appeared quite respectable and nobody realized that he was the leader of a robber gang. The group operated two roadhouses, one between Lewiston and Walla Walla and the other between Lewiston and Orofino. Both were surrounded by high hills. The gang at Lewiston sized up whether a man had anything worth stealing and if he did they sent

4 Beal and Wells, *Idaho,* I, 298, 312–14; Defenbach, *Idaho,* I, 286–87; Elsensohn, *Idaho County,* I, 81, 100–101; Hawley, *History,* I, 107; Averill, Henderson, and Shiach, *North Idaho,* 27–28.

5 Beal and Wells, *History,* II, 55; Defenbach, *Idaho,* I, 267; French, *History,* I, 27; Goulder, *Reminiscences,* 191–92, 231–32, 279; Hawley, *History,* I, 364; W. J. McConnell, *Early History of Idaho,* 59–77, 106–10, 143–52.

an agent ahead to the roadhouse with a forged bill of sale for his pack animals. Those who were wise surrendered their possessions promptly; otherwise they were killed. When the group murdered a jovial saloon owner named Hildebrandt, there was a meeting at Lewiston to discuss possible action but the plausible Plummer talked so strongly on the horrors of anarchy that nothing was done. The one man there outspokenly demanding action was Patrick Ford. Shortly the gang demolished his saloon in Orofino, killed him, and then defied the rest of the townspeople. Plummer changed his headquarters to Florence and before long left for Montana, where his exploits led to his death at the hands of vigilantes. The men of Lewiston finally took action against the outlaws in October, 1863, when they arrested David English, William Peebles, and Nelson Scott for the robberies of Neal McClinchey, Joseph Berry, and John Berry. They hanged them without a trial; by daybreak the next morning, other undesirables had all fled. The following January, the ordinary process of a regular court trial was held for the murder of Lloyd Magruder and the theft of his thirty thousand dollars; three men were hanged and one was freed.

Another important area of Idaho mining was far to the south of the towns just discussed.[6] It was the Boise Basin, 30 miles northeast of the present city of Boise, an area of 250 square miles separated from the rest of the country by mountains. By the end of 1866, it had yielded approximately $24,000,000 in gold.

The pioneer of the area was Moses Splawn. In North Idaho he met by chance the same Indian thrice in the summer of 1861—at Elk City, at Florence, and then on the Salmon River—and the third time the red man, who had watched the miners intently, told him of a basin surrounded by mountains where he believed there was gold. The next spring, Splawn joined a group of about fifty men under Captain Tom Turner in a search for the Blue Bucket Diggings, an unknown spot where emigrants in an 1845 wagon train had supposedly filled a blue bucket full of yellow metal without realizing it was gold. Before long Splawn and seven others split off to look for

6 Annie L. Bird, *Boise, the Peace Valley*, 97–108, 114, 127–28, 131; Sherlock Bristol, *The Pioneer Preacher*, 274–75; Defenbach, *Idaho*, I, 278; John Hailey, *The History of Idaho*, 36–37; Hawley, *History*, I, 108–11, 128; MacLane, *Sagebrush Lawyer*, 65–69 73; McConnell, *Early History*, 79–83, 126, 188, 290, 357–58; Wolle, *Bonanza Trail*, 228–35.

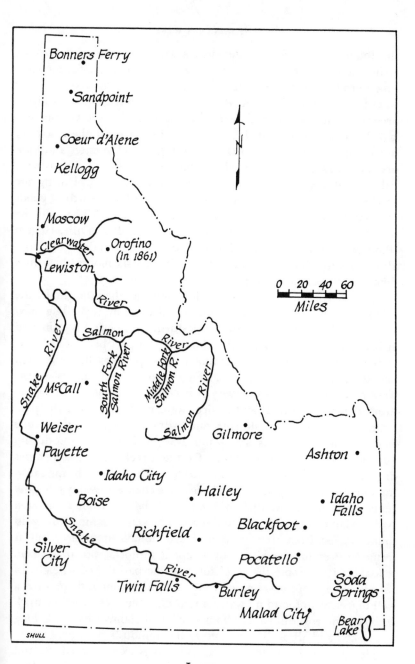

Bonners Ferry

Sandpoint

Coeur d'Alene

Kellogg

Moscow

Clearwater   Orofino
             (in 1861)
Lewiston

River

Salmon   River

Snake River   South Fork Salmon River   Middle Fork Salmon R.   Salmon River

McCall

Weiser   Salmon   Gilmore

Payette   Ashton

            Idaho City

       Boise   Hailey   Idaho
                                          Falls

Snake   Richfield   Blackfoot

Silver
City   River   Pocatello

        Twin Falls   Burley   Soda
                                           Springs

                     Malad City
                                      Bear
                                      Lake

SHULL

IDAHO

the Indian's basin. Shortly they met a party of eight led by George Grimes and the two groups joined forces. In August, 1862, the combined group began prospecting in the basin and the first discovery was made by Dave Fogus. As their search continued, hostile Indians fired at them upon several occasions and after George Grimes was killed, the group retreated from the basin. News of the discovery quickly spread. The basin was comparatively easy to enter and hundreds of prospectors came in that fall. Early important groups were led by Relf Bledsoe, Jeff Standifier, and Marion More. During the first ten days of November, twenty thousand dollars' worth of goods was purchased at Walla Walla by those going there. That fall the towns of Idaho City (at first known as Bannock), Placerville, Hogem (Pioneer), Centerville, and Buena Vista were founded. Virtually all those who came to the basin within the first six months had little difficulty in locating rich placer claims.

The rush began in 1863; operations were at their height in the middle sixties, but there was an obvious decline by 1870. The maximum number of people in the basin during the period is estimated at between twenty-five and forty thousand. In part because it had a warmer climate than most mining camps, perhaps half the men had their families with them. Mining districts and miners' courts were organized here as on every American gold frontier. The traditional placer methods and devices were used: crevicing, the pan, the rocker, the long tom, sluicing, and hydraulicking. Quartz deposits were developed. The first stamp mill was put into operation during July, 1864, by W. W. Raymond on Granite Creek. Private companies dug ditches, one and one-half to thirteen miles in length, for carrying water to placer operations. The average charge was sixty to eighty cents an inch for twenty-four hours and daily consumption at a typical claim cost one hundred dollars. The actual value of the gold found varied from sixteen to nineteen dollars an ounce, but it seemed easier for everybody to accept a uniform rate of sixteen.

Idaho City became the chief town of the basin. At its height in 1865 it had 250 business houses. In the early days a man there hired a well digger, who found no water but at eighteen feet struck bedrock with gold in it. Within a half-hour a string of claims a half-mile long was staked and all of them proved to be fabulously wealthy. It is no wonder that as the miners kept working they excavated streets and undermined homes. In June, 1864, the little son of Dr. J. B. Atkins

264

fell from the back door of his house four or five feet into a cut being run under the structure and fractured his left knee.

Until 1869, the commonest way for people to enter the area—and almost the only way for freight—was from Columbia River steamships landing at Umatilla.[7] Along the route roadhouses kept by bachelors served bread, bacon, and coffee for a dollar. Stretches of the way were very alkaline, so that a rider was enveloped in dusty clouds and became excessively thirsty; the best cure was thought to be alcohol at a roadhouse, where it cost twenty-five cents "per prescription." These roads occasionally crossed streams at privately owned ferries. A typical set of fees was as follows: one team with wagon, three dollars; each extra team, one dollar; pack animals, seventy-five cents if loaded and fifty if empty; horse and rider, seventy-five cents; a footman or each loose animal, twenty-five cents.

At first all freight was carried in by pack trains. In 1863, an average mule cost $250, the packers were paid $100 to $125 a month plus board, and the charge from Umatilla to the Boise Basin was twenty-five cents a pound or $500 a ton. Jesus Urquides was the most famous of the packers. With the completion of a wagon road the next year, pack rates had to be cut in half. Overstocked older merchants found themselves losing money as they had to reduce their prices to match those of newly established competitors. With the completion of the first transcontinental railroad in 1869, almost all freight hauling shifted to Kelton, Utah, which was about forty miles nearer the basin than Umatilla.

For passengers the cheapest way to get to the Boise Basin in 1863 was by so-called saddle train from Umatilla or adjacent Wallula for a fee of fifty dollars in advance. The trainmaster furnished a horse, a saddle, food, the necessary cooking utensils, and hauled a small amount of baggage for each person. On the trip he looked after the animals and the patrons cooked the food. By 1863, stage service began. Ben Holladay, whose experiment of a private pony-express mail service into the basin was so unsuccessful he had to discontinue it, in 1864 got a contract to carry United States mail triweekly the 675 miles from Salt Lake City to The Dalles. He himself ran the stage line from Utah to Emmett, Idaho, where he turned the mail over to the coaches of a subcontractor, Thomas and Greathouse. The

[7] Beal and Wells, *History*, I, 393–408; Bird, *Boise*, 103–106; Hailey, *History*, 61–63, 95–97, 126; McConnell, *Early History*, 121, 137, 181–89, 298–99.

latter's chief business, however, was on the portion of its route between Wallula and Placerville, in rivalry to the stages of Ish and
Hailey between Umatilla and Placerville. The Umatilla partnership
got almost all the patronage because it was a day faster, handled the
Portland newspapers to Placerville for half its rival's charge, carried
private mail for a fifth of it, hauled fast freight for less, and carted
large quantities of gold at freight rates if the owner assumed all the
risks.

There was a ready market in the basin for food.[8] Before 1867, not
enough was grown to supply the demand and farmers charged the
monopoly price of not less than twenty-five cents a pound for their
produce, often more. The first watermelons arrived in Buena Vista
at exactly the same time as the first respectable (and lovely) girls; a
young man bought one melon for them at a cost of eight dollars.
Essential supplies of another sort, lumber, first became available
when B. L. Warriner opened a sawmill on Grimes Creek in the
winter of 1862-63. Charging one hundred to two hundred dollars
per thousand feet, he found that everything he cut in a day was sold
by the next sunrise.

At the pinnacle of the business, social, and recreational structure
of the mining camps were the saloon owners.[9] By adding water, burnt
sugar, and a chemical, they could make either bourbon or cognac
from their kegs of alcohol in about five minutes. They were the community's bankers, safekeepers of valuables, leaders in every charitable enterprise, arbitrators in disputes, trusted advisors, and friends
of the needy. They generally kept their establishments open twenty-
four hours a day. At one of them the notable attraction was that
superb fiddler, the highly paid John Kelly. He performed on a
swinging platform over the heads of his audience; whenever any
shooting took place, he faced the disturbance, placed his violin
behind him and gave the instrument maximum protection from any
stray bullets. Kelly adopted an Indian boy of six who became a con-
tortionist to provide variety at the concerts and eventually developed

8 Bird, *Boise*, 106, 115–16; Bristol, *Pioneer Preacher*, 276–82; McConnell, *Early
History*, 121–23.

9 Beal and Wells, *History*, I, 312, II, 49, 64; Bird, *Boise*, 120–60; Goulder, *Reminiscences*, 240–41; Hawley, *History*, 119–21, 129, 367; MacLane, *Sagebrush Lawyer*,
70; McConnell, *Early History*, 138–40, 181, 189–91.

into as wonderful a fiddler as the master himself. There was a strong bond of affection between the two. When they were visiting Ireland and the boy was eighteen, he died from a congestive chill. The hurdy-gurdies, poor but pure girls who entertained by dancing for hire because they had to do so, often married the men who patronized them and made fine mothers. The greatest of outdoor sports was sledding. Every town had at least one club devoted to it, which held contests with those in adjacent villages. Billiards, cockfighting, dancing, checkers, gambling, fraternal lodges, and the theater were also available. There was at least one circulating library in the basin. The first newspaper in South Idaho, the *Boise News,* was established in the fall of 1863.

The early emigrant wagon trains coming west to the basin in the summer of 1863 were full of people escaping guerrilla warfare in Missouri and Arkansas. They brought with them almost the first nice girls. The result was a number of speedy courtships, and Governor W. J. McConnell insisted that none of these marriages ended in a divorce. At a ball in 1865, the favorite fabrics for the women's gowns were silk, lace, merino, and tarleton. The first school was the private one operated by Mrs. Smith at East Hill; it began in 1863 with twenty-one pupils enrolled at a dollar a week each; the first public schools opened in 1865. The earliest Catholic priests in the area, Fathers T. Mespile and A. Z. Poulin, arrived in the summer of 1863. Protestants, too, became active, the first being a Methodist, the Reverend C. S. Kingsley. The chief way of raising funds for religious purposes was to give balls and parties. The county maintained a hospital for the indigent sick at Idaho City.

Fire was a serious danger because most of the buildings were wooden, small, and one story. The first major one hit Idaho City on May 18, 1865; one on May 16, 1867, destroyed 440 buildings, another on June 19, 1868, was quite serious, and the fourth, in August, 1871, destroyed one-third of the town. During the 1860's, there was remarkably little stealing in the basin; cabins were seldom locked. Valuable claims were as likely to be transferred by an oral understanding as by a simple bill of sale. There was no stigma to fighting and killing a man, provided both parties had willingly agreed in advance to the contest.

Perhaps 0.5 per cent of the men who came to South Idaho had

criminal inclinations.[10] Vigilantes arose, not first in the mines, as was usually the case on the frontier, but in the agricultural area. When W. J. McConnell, then a farmer and years later to be Idaho's governor, lost some horses, pursued the thieves for 250 miles to recover his property, and learned from one of the dying robbers that a regular gang of horse thieves existed, he organized a vigilance committee at Payette. Certainly many of its leaders were Masons, and in later years McConnell always insisted that there was a close connection between the two organizations. It first took effective action against horse thieves. The committee captured the Washoe Ferry gang of highwaymen but could not prove at a vigilante trial that any of them were murderers; it acquitted one, banished one, and sentenced two to be hanged for thievery. This verdict McConnell considered too severe, so he arranged for the two to escape. Not long afterward, one of them, Alex Stewart, returned and brought a suit for twenty thousand dollars against the man who had saved his life. McConnell warned him to withdraw his action within twenty-four hours or he would not live forty-eight; he canceled it and left. The Payette group rid the area of a "bogus gold dust" syndicate. When the outlaws of Ada County succeeded in electing David Updyke sheriff, they had about forty of these vigilantes arrested and taken to Boise for trial; all the attorneys there served on the defense and won acquittal. Soon the first United States grand jury found three bills against Updyke and forced him out of office rather than punishing him. He was later executed by employees of Ben Holladay for burning the stage line's hay.

The outlaws disliked Sumner Pinkham, appointed to serve as sheriff of Boise County until an election could be held. When Fred Patterson arrived from Portland with a murder to his credit and fame for literally having scalped his mistress there, the roughs had him murder Pinkham. This, plus the fact that only ten of two hundred men had died natural deaths in Idaho City within eighteen months, led to the formation of a vigilance committee there in the spring of 1865. At first the vigilantes planned to storm the prison to remove Patterson and several other notorious murderers, but

10 Defenbach, *Idaho*, 340; MacLane, *Sagebrush Lawyer*, 80; McConnell, *Early History*, 20, 133, 192–93, 208–10, 242–50, 268–73; W. J. McConnell, "The Idaho Inferno" (MS in Bancroft Library, University of California), 2–72.

they reconsidered when the sheriff, a man named Crutcher, called the roughs of the area to man the walls in defense. After considerable discussion the vigilantes agreed not to attack the jail and to allow Patterson a regular court trial, even though they knew the evidence had already been rigged to acquit him. Crutcher withdrew his men and ended the crisis. He probably never knew that the vigilantes of Payette, arriving secretly as reinforcements, had placed themselves to join the fray when the shooting started. Patterson was acquitted and went to Walla Walla, where "arrangements were made to have him killed." The criminals in Idaho City were terrified and there was no further need for vigilantes.

There was some trouble with Indians who did not look kindly upon the white men's intrusion and stole whatever they could; if it was a horse, often they ate it.[11] In March, 1863, a group of Boise Basin unpaid volunteers led by Jeff Standifer conducted a two-month campaign against the Paiutes. The red men's activities, the rich deposits, and the presence of many Confederate sympathizers were all factors in the government's decision to erect a fort for the region. Construction of Boise Barracks on a military reservation containing 638 acres started in late June, 1863. This promptly stimulated the founding of a town named Boise, which in the following year became the territorial capital.

Another racial group the miners disliked was the Chinese. For a while the whites excluded them from the basin. In 1864, the territorial legislature passed a discriminatory tax of four dollars a month to prevent or discourage their participation in placer mining. By 1867, the yield in the basin had begun so obviously to decline that many whites sold their claims to Chinese. In addition to mining, the Orientals engaged in various enterprises. Recalling the era, Thomas Donaldson commented that he never knew one of them in a reputable business to refuse payment on a debt, but he knew of hundreds of cases where whites cheated them. Often they traded with white merchants because they wanted protection. The Chinese feared to resist a wrong and certainly did not care to go to law, for Donaldson pointed out that not one judge or jury in a hundred

11 Beal and Wells, *History,* I, 314; Bird, *Boise,* 119, 168–71; Bristol, *Pioneer Preacher,* 281; Thomas Donaldson, *Idaho of Yesterday,* 48–49; Hailey, *History,* 49–50; McConnell, *Early History,* 120–21, 180, 302, 332–41.

would give a decision in favor of an Oriental when he obviously was entitled to it. When a Chinese had to testify involuntarily before a court, he often protected himself by pretended failure to understand the questions asked and by such an incomprehensible sequence of words in his replies that at length the baffled lawyers simply abandoned their examination in complete frustration.

Adjacent to the Boise Basin the so-called South Boise mines developed along the middle fork of the Boise River about sixty miles from Idaho City.[12] Early in 1863, placer discoveries were made at Rocky Bar and Atlanta. By the end of 1866, the district had produced about $800,000 in gold. The mineral was easily available at the high edges of the bars, leading to a serious overestimate of the richness of the placers, a rush of far more people than could possibly find paying claims, and a quick decline in activity.

More enduring were the quartz deposits, the first one of which was found on Bear Creek in May, 1863. Surface indications of the narrow veins and the productive capacity of the small arastras first used to extract the gold from its surrounding ore both seemed to give promise of greater profits by far than was actually to be the case. Thus misled, enthusiasts organizing a company to promote a claim were willing to pay extravagant prices for contiguous properties in order to have a good-sized mine. All too often they then failed to do any development work on their holdings until they had erected a refinery. When operation on a good-sized scale finally began, the yield often proved insufficient to justify the investment. Besides such poor management there were some companies which were simply fraudulent creations designed to fleece innocent investors.

The years 1867–69 were a period of conservation readjustment in the South Boise mines, in the era 1869–76 the most obvious of riches were removed from mines with little thought for their future development, and after 1886 modern mining methods were introduced. The original Goodrich Trail into the region was difficult for pack animals to negotiate. It was replaced in September, 1864, by the Newberg Road, a toll route constructed at a cost of sixteen thousand dollars by the South Boise Wagon Road Company.

12 Hawley, *History*, I, 111; Robert L. Romig, "The South Boise Quartz Mines, 1863–1892: A Study in Western Mining Industry and Finance" (unpublished M.A. thesis, University of California), 7–87.

Another South Idaho mineral development was in the Owyhee Basin, named by a Hudson's Bay Company trader who was trying to spell Hawaii in honor of an employee from the Islands.[13] Along Jordan Creek, Michael Jordan's group found gold in paying quantities on May 18, 1863. They stayed there about ten days, drew up rules for a mining district, and each man staked three claims: one for discovery, one as an ordinary prospector, and one for a friend. Their news precipitated a rush of about two thousand men from the Boise Basin within forty-eight hours after the group's return. The newcomers found that practically all of the good placer claims had already been taken and soon left. The deposits, not extensive, were exhausted within two years.

In the fall of 1863, silver-bearing quartz ledges were discovered. Apparently the first one was located by R. H. Wade in Whiskey Gulch on October 14, 1863. The chief mines developed on War Eagle and Florida mountains, served by the permanent town of Silver City and an early temporary settlement a mile away, Ruby. The richest property was the Poorman, found in 1865. The claim for it and the Hays and Ray property overlapped. Who owned what was a matter of intense dispute because the wealth involved was so obvious. Each side put up miniature forts near the disputed ground and employed professional gun fighters while taking the question to court. Neither would accept defeat, rumors had it; a number of United States marshals and a company of infantry from Boise Barracks were sent to Silver City. In the midst of the 1866 trial came an Indian alarm and the judge adjourned court for ten days so that all who wished to do so might fight the red men. When the lawyers and fighting men returned from their inconclusive jaunt, they found that the litigants had used the time "to reason among themselves" and had decided to work all the property jointly. Eventually it was sold to a New York syndicate and by then had produced about two million dollars in silver and gold.

A dispute over boundaries between the Ida Elmore and Golden Chariot mines arose in 1867, and by the following March both had hired fighters and erected strong fortifications. The Golden Chariot's warriors stormed the works of their opponents on the twenty-fifth,

[13] French, *History*, I, 142–45; Hailey, *History*, 65; Hawley, *History*, I, 110–11, 371; McConnell, *Early History*, 335–42; Wolle, *Bonanza Trail*, 237–45.

killing two men and losing one of their own. The governor sent in the federal cavalry and a compromise was arranged on the twenty-ninth, but bad feeling continued.

Ore from Silver City's mines was hauled by ox team to Umatilla on the Columbia River, then carried by ship to Portland and San Francisco. Eventually corporations, many of them overcapitalized, took over most mines. By 1875, the area is alleged to have produced thirty million dollars in mineral wealth. That year the Bank of California failed, causing a money crisis in the Owyhee Basin which precipitated a serious slump. In the late 1880's and the 1890's, the region revived and large-scale operations were resumed. The area's leading paper was the *Owyhee Avalanche*, established at Silver City in September, 1865.

On Napias Creek, a tributary of the Salmon River, five Southerners discovered gold on July 16, 1866.[14] Veterans of the Civil War almost came to blows over what to name the settlement they founded but finally compromised by calling one end of it Grantsville and the other Leesburg. By 1874, the placers had declined sharply in production. In the fall of 1869, there was a stampede to the middle fork of the Salmon River, where Nathan Smith and "Doc" Wilson found gold at Yellow Jacket, later renamed Oro Grande. In 1870, gold was discovered on Caribou Mountain; the area eventually produced perhaps fifty million dollars in gold. The major settlements were Keenan City, Caribou City, and Eagle Rock.

The Wood River mining district, located in the central part of southern Idaho, did not begin to develop until 1879 and there was much activity there in the 1880's. The most important silver and lead producer was the Minnie Moore, sold in 1884 for $450,000. Considerable quantities of California and British capital were invested in the area. The mines centered at Bellevue and at Bullion, both tributary to the commercial center of Hailey. There the usual prejudice against Chinese showed itself at a meeting held on February 1, 1886, which resolved that the Orientals had until May 1 to get out of town. The Chinese hired lawyers, placed an advertisement in the newspaper saying they would not leave, and they actually stayed without interference as long as their business success warranted.

14 Beal and Wells, *History*, I, 572–74; Barzilla W. Clark, *Bonneville County in the Making*, 56–64, 90–94; George A. McLeod, *History of Alturas and Blaine Counties, Idaho*, 5–88; Wolle, *Bonanza Trail*, 226.

Originally, Idaho was a part of Washington Territory, established in 1853.[15] The creation of a separate government for the area became merged with the fight between Olympia, Vancouver, and Walla Walla for Washington's capital; Olympia and Lewiston united to help secure the separation. In 1863, Idaho Territory was established, some think as a wartime measure because of its wealth, to include present-day Idaho, Montana, and Wyoming. The next year, Montana became independent and Wyoming joined Dakota Territory.

As the first governor of Idaho, Lincoln appointed W. H. Wallace. Nothing was said about where the capital should be and Wallace selected Lewiston, at least in part because of the good mail service. The first legislature did not place the structure of territorial and county government in operation until February 4, 1864. This meant, ruled the courts subsequently, that no law existed in the area between its separation from Washington and that date; no crime committed during that period could be punished because no existing statutes had been violated.

Wallace's successor, Caleb Lyon, felt that the capital should be moved to Boise; Lewiston resisted. Lyon escaped southward from an alleged duck-hunting trip on December 29, 1864, and exactly three months later the U. S. Army helped to transport the official records to Boise. In the spring of 1866, Lyon learned that then Territorial Secretary Horace C. Gilson had obsconded with $41,062 in official funds; Lyon himself then hurried eastward with all the money not yet distributed to the Indian tribes, some $46,418.40. In territorial days, most of the law cases were petty, involving no great principles or much money. The majority of lawyers did not understand the elementary rules of practice and had almost no books to guide them.

---

[15] Beal and Wells, *History*, I, 325–81; Bird, *Boise*, 168; MacLane, *Sagebrush Lawyer*, 20–23; McConnell, *Early History*, 111–18.

12

THE COEUR D'ALENE LABOR TROUBLES

AT a later period than events discussed so far and north of the Clearwater mines came the development in the 1880's of the Coeur d'Alene region, approximately ninety miles east of Spokane, Washington.[1] The initial excitement came from the discoveries by A. J. Prichard, of placer deposits on Eagle and Prichard creeks about four miles east of the present town of Kellogg in April, 1882. As an ardent supporter of the Liberal League, he hoped he could save perhaps all, and certainly the best locations, for fellow members so that they could have a city of their own and so that the mining claims would support all of them. He wrote enthusiastic letters to various Leaguers, even though he knew some of them only slightly, urging them to meet him and emphasizing that everything should be kept secret. His plan met with fair success and his discovery did not become general knowledge until the fall of 1883.

In February, 1884, the Northern Pacific Railway issued a booklet about the Coeur d'Alene area by H. C. Davis, who claimed that every man could expect to make twenty-five to one hundred dollars a day. While few people took such an account at its face value, they did expect to find profitable opportunities. Settlements quickly sprang up, especially at Murray. There the queen of the underworld, "Molly b' Dam," had made an appearance which gave no hint of her occupation; she carried herself with an air of culture, quoted from Shakespeare, Milton, and Dante, gave liberally to charity, and helped nurse the sick; she also robbed the unwary and could swear

1 Beal and Wells, *History*, I, 572–75; W. Earl Greenough, *First 100 Years of the Coeur d'Alene Mining Region*, 9–17; Averill, Henderson, and Shiach, *North Idaho*, 984–93; William T. Stoll, *Silver Strike*, 6–52.

as well as the most expert man. When it became clear that more prospectors had rushed in than could secure mines, there was a vigorous move to reduce the size of claims from twenty acres to ten, but the federal courts upheld twenty. By the middle of 1885, the rush had definitely subsided and primitive methods of extraction were giving way to hydraulic operations.

When the building boom subsided at Murray in 1885, one of those caught in the slump was Noah S. Kellogg, an unemployed carpenter already in his sixties.[2] He set out looking for the obvious, gold, but fate made him the finder of a different kind of mine, the kind upon which the great fame of the Coeur d'Alene district rests, a producer of silver intermixed with lead and zinc. In the first sixty years after his discovery the district yielded more than a billion dollars' worth of the three metals. None of this Kellogg foresaw when, as a last resort, he turned to prospecting. He obtained as grubstake a jackass and a seventeen-dollar outfit from O. O. Peck, a small contractor, and J. T. Cooper, once a surgeon in the British navy. He tramped around in the mountains for two difficult days and on the late afternoon of the third discovered a large-sized vein of silver and lead. More than likely, he had been seeking his runaway jackass and, finally catching him, had sat down to rest when his eye caught the first sign of the great discovery; however, a few people insist that the animal was not even with him and many more romanticize the episode by alleging that the beast gazed in such astonishment at the ledge that Kellogg noticed it for the first time.

Kellogg promptly made two claims, giving a half-interest in each to himself, a quarter to Cooper, and a quarter to Peck. He knew the value of what he had discovered. His resentment against Cooper and Peck for their penury in the niggardly equipment of his grub-stake was deep and long abiding. It prompted him, upon his return, which was at night, to disregard his Murray backers and go instead to talk with Jacob "Dutch Jake" Goetz, a noted gambler. Before day-break the next day, Kellogg, Phil O'Rourke, Con Sullivan, and Alec Monk were on their way. They tore down the original notice of

2 Beal and Wells, *History*, I, 574–75; Greenough, *First 100 Years*, 17–23; Averill, Henderson, and Shiach, *North Idaho*, 995–1000; 13 *Pacific Reporter* 350; Robert W. Smith, *The Coeur d'Alene Mining War of 1892; A Case Study of an Industrial Dispute*, 2–11, 23–24; Stoll, *Silver Strike*, 51–151; Jim Wardner, *Jim Wardner of Wardner, Idaho*, 58–59, 67–68.

claim, obliterated all marks on the stakes, and made two "new" locations in the names of Kellogg, O'Rourke, Sullivan, and Goetz. They called one the Bunker Hill and the other the Sullivan, filing official papers on them at Murray and proclaiming the great discovery.

With the news out and a rush immediately underway, Peck and Cooper were very perturbed. They retained lawyers William T. Stoll and W. W. Woods to represent them on a basis at least initially thrifty—no money down and one-fifth of any property recovered. At Milo Gulch, Stoll picked up a torn, dirty scrap of paper which proved to be the original location notice of the Bunker Hill in Kellogg's own handwriting. No such evidence was available about the Sullivan. Stoll and Woods, with W. B. Hayburn as an associate, took the Bunker Hill case to trial before Judge Norman Buck in the territorial district court at Murray. Kellogg insisted that he had exhausted his grubstake of thirty-five pounds of bacon, ten pounds of beans, and fifteen pounds of flour before his discovery; he testified that he then formed the new partnership, found the Bunker Hill within twenty-four hours after again leaving Murray, went directly to it, and was at least a hundred feet ahead of the younger men when he made his discovery. Although it was supposedly an equal partnership, he received a half-interest in the Bunker Hill and Sullivan. The jury returned a verdict favoring the defendants; this Judge Buck overruled as contrary to the evidence. He said the jury was in some measure influenced by the strong climate of opinion in Murray against the plaintiffs. The crucial point, he declared, was that the contract did not expire until the grubstake was exhausted and he did not believe Kellogg's testimony about having used it all up with such miraculous speed. On appeal, his decision was upheld on the ground that deliberate fraud was clearly involved.

Late in 1886, Simeon G. Reed of Portland purchased both the Bunker Hill and the Sullivan properties, probably for $650,000. In 1890, he sold them to a group of California and eastern capitalists headed by the famous mining engineer John Hays Hammond. Practically every silver-lead mine of any importance in the Coeur d'Alene district was discovered in 1884 or 1885; they were gradually bought up and developed by corporations.

Within sixty days after Kellogg's discovery the new town of Wardner had a population of almost four thousand; originally, each lot sold for $2.50. Kellogg, Osburn, Gem, Burke, and Mullan arose to serve adjacent mines; Wallace had no big ones in the immediate vicinity but was a trading center. Wardner, Gem, and Burke were distinctly canyon camps, jammed into the bottom of a gulch; Wallace, Mullan and Osburn were mountain-meadow towns.

Electric lighting was just reaching the area in early 1891. Many of the men found recreation at saloons and gambling clubs; there were twenty-eight of them in Wallace. Dancing was always popular; the big balls on Christmas and New Year's started at nine in the evening and lasted until almost dawn. Baseball, local racing of horses, and boxing matches were important. The big holiday of the year, the Fourth of July, included a parade, speeches, dancing and a hard-rock drilling contest. Several of the towns had disastrous fires.

The first railroad into the area, a Northern Pacific subsidiary named the Coeur d'Alene Railway and Navigation Company, was completed as a narrow-gauge line from the head of Lake Coeur d'Alene to Wardner in April, 1886; it reached Wallace in the fall of 1887. The Union Pacific completed a roundabout route from Spokane to Wallace in December, 1890. Twelve months later, the Northern Pacific finished a connection from Wallace east to its main line near Missoula. In the early nineties, the two reached some kind of an agreement not to overlap their lines.

All of the Coeur d'Alene mines lay within the boundaries of Shoshone County. The census of 1890 showed that 3,993 people lived in the mining region and extracted that year about ten million dollars in ore.

Local miners' unions had been formed by the fall of 1890 in Wallace, Burke, Gem, and Mullan,[3] and the four merged on January 1, 1891. From this simple beginning came eventual consequences nobody could have dreamed of at the time: the intervention of federal troops, the murder of a former governor, and a nationally famous trial. Not all of the complete records on these events, in files belonging to a considerable variety of organizations, have been made freely available to scholars, nor are they likely to be. Many facts are not clear and probably a considerable number are as yet unknown. It seems unlikely that an absolutely accurate and complete account will ever be written.

The unions were formed because at times ambitious mine mana-

3 Smith, *Mining War*, 18–120.

gers, anxious to show a profit, wanted to lower wages or to skimp on essential safeguards or to extract an unreasonable profit from the monopoly of a company-owned store or a company-owned rooming and boarding house for unmarried employees. The members' objectives were to maintain high wages, to curb mining companies' commercial monopolies, to secure better safety precautions, to care for the sick or injured, and to bury decently the dead. From these purposes developed incidentally the dances, parties, and parades, the social and fraternal aspects of a union which often made its hall the center of community life.

In the winter of 1890–91, the union went on strike for the Butte standard of $3.50 a day to all men working underground, a scale which had prevailed in the Coeur d'Alene area before 1887, and by the middle of 1891 it had again secured the rate from all mines except those around Wardner. It also campaigned for a miners' hospital at Wallace. Everybody co-operated except the Bunker Hill and Sullivan mine; it changed its mind in August after a seven-day strike.

Union activities led the large mines, shipping regularly to smelters outside the district, to form the Mine Owners' Protective Association, certainly active by April, 1891. This organization hired a Pinkerton detective named Charles A. Siringo to work in the Gem mine under the name of C. Leon Allison and to join the union. In December, he started a seven-month term as the union's recording secretary, with access to all its records; he made regular reports to his employers.

Sometime in the fall of 1891 (the precise date was never made public), the railroads of the area increased by two dollars their rates on ore shipped out of the district. The Mine Owners' Protective Association, protesting, closed down their operations on January 15, 1892. By early March, the railroads had restored the old rate. The association said it would reopen the mines with actual miners getting their usual $3.50 for a ten-hour day, but carmen and shovelers would be cut fifty cents to $3.00; the union insisted upon the previous scale of $3.50 for everybody. The owners refused, issuing an eight-thousand-word statement: "It is unpleasant reading even today, and must have been much more so in 1892." The mines were not opened, locking out the men. The union secured the aid of about $30,000 monthly from various Montana miners' organizations. It was hindered by a court injunction which restrained it from trespassing on mine property, interfering with operations, or intimidating any workers. The owners recruited armed guards and began importing nonunion employees. A crisis arose on July 9 at the town of Gem when the miners, after many discouragements in their attempt to follow a peaceful and legal policy, learned that Siringo was a spy. At five o'clock in the morning, fighting broke out at the "old" Frisco mill; who fired the first shot could not be determined in three long court trials. After the mill was dynamited, the struggle spread to the Gem mine and mill. When the battle had killed five men, the Gem employees surrendered; they were escorted to Wallace and given twenty-four hours to leave the area. Siringo escaped by crawling underneath a board sidewalk. At Wardner, the union men captured three concentrators and vowed to destroy them unless all nonunion men were dismissed; the owners complied. As 132 of the exiles awaited the arrival of a Lake Coeur d'Alene steamboat, down swooped eight or twelve men, scattering and robbing them.

When the fighting started at Gem, Governor Norman B. Willey of Idaho called out six companies of the Idaho National guard and also secured federal troops; by November 15, the last of the soldiers had left the troubled area. The mines began working on a large scale, paying the rate they had proposed in March; the owners ended the company boarding house monopoly and the hold of company stores was weakened. A total of about 600 men were arrested for strike activities; the maximum held in confinement at any one time was about 350. The first case tried was for contempt of court, shown by violating an injunction, and thirteen miners were sentenced for terms varying from four to eight months. The next was for criminal conspiracy to violate an injunction. At it defense attorney Patrick Reddy declared: "Concert of action alone does not constitute conspiracy. The birds sing in concert, but they have no agreement to do so." The jury found ten of the men innocent and four guilty; later, the United States Supreme Court released those convicted because the crime was against Idaho rather than the federal government. The last trial was of a union man alleged to have killed a "scab" at the Gem mine. His defense was that at the time of the shooting he was lying in a saloon, "dead drunk," a condition in which he had been observed scores of times, and it won him acquittal. By March, 1893, indictments against all the remaining men were dropped.

From these Coeur d'Alene strikes the miners at Butte and elsewhere learned that a more effective union was necessary to protect themselves. They formed the Western Federation of Miners, which by 1903 had about fifty thousand members and two hundred sub-unions. Its constitution, showing the lesson learned from the Coeur d'Alene excitement, included the following among its objectives: pay compatible with the job; pay in money, not by other means; employment of its members rather than nonunion men; no hiring of armed forces for any illegal use; and repeal of conspiracy laws directed against the rights of labor.

A major conflict again hit the Coeur d'Alene region in April, 1899, when the Western Federation determined to unionize the Bunker Hill and Sullivan Company property.[4] The corporation finally yielded enough to raise its wages to the union scale but refused to recognize the organization or to discharge nonunion men. Hundreds of its employees quit before a formal strike was called; the company raised a small private army and started hiring what scabs it could. On April 29, miners captured the nine cars of the regular Northern Pacific freight train at Burke, boarded it, went to Wallace (partly over Union Pacific tracks, to the great perturbation of the crew), picked up there about 1,200 Wallace and Kellogg men, and went on to the Bunker Hill and Sullivan concentrator at Wardner. Part of the group, according to subsequent testimony of some mine owners, thought the expedition was simply a demonstration of strength. Each wore a strip of white handkerchief in the buttonhole of his coat or else had a strip of white cloth on his arm, which suggests that the trip had been well planned. Some of the miners scattered the sixty scabs, put in the concentrator three thousand pounds of dynamite taken from the Frisco mine at Gem, and touched off an explosion which demolished the $250,000 plant.

The company promptly appealed to Governor Frank Steunenberg for troops. He belonged to a union himself but felt that in the mining area anarchists had taken over the movement. Since the Idaho National Guard was in the Philippines, regular federal troops arrived in the Coeur d'Alene area on May 2 under the command of Brigadier General H. C. Merriam. The General's civilian ally, the Governor's appointed representative with dictatorial powers not authorized by any Idaho law, was state auditor Bartlett Sinclair. Martial law was

4 Beal and Wells, *History*, II, 106–18; Hawley, *History*, I, 251–55 (Hawley was a prosecution lawyer in the Cocoran case); Vernon H. Jensen, *Heritage of Conflict*, 74–87.

declared by Steunenberg on May 3. Most of the men who had taken part in the dynamiting had already left for British Columbia or hiked over the hills, through deep snow, to Montana. Those who remained, mostly spectators, were arrested and placed in an improvised "bull pen," a two-story hay barn and warehouse without any sanitary facilities, later supplemented by two box cars used to hold one hundred men each. The state failed to secure extradition of suspects from Montana, perhaps because an army expedition had earlier attempted to capture miners there before getting Montana warrants for their arrest. Sinclair ruled that nobody would work in a Coeur d'Alene mine unless he had a state permit, secured either by swearing he did not belong to the union or else declaring he took no part in the dynamiting and promising to quit the Western Federation. The practice was in fact stricter, for permits were issued only to those who could prove they were actually at work in a mine when the dynamiting occurred; this was obviously a state-imposed blacklist to break up the union. The suppression of the Western Federation of Miners aroused workingmen's protests throughout the nation. Even conservatives criticized the permit system. Adverse comment about the army's role forced the Committee on Military Affairs of the House of Representatives to make a thorough investigation. The majority found that the charges of misconduct were not sustained; the minority thought they were.

The state of Idaho based its court action against the union members on one of the grounds used in the 1892 troubles—conspiracy. At the explosion of the Wardner concentrator, James Cheyne and two other scabs were captured by union pickets; they were soon released with orders to run and were followed by a fusillade of bullets which killed Cheyne and wounded one of the others. This, according to the criminal-law codes, was more serious than blowing up the plant and so was made the basis of the prosecution. The state felt that a large number of men in the bull pen could be charged with being part of a conspiracy and therefore guilty of any action by anybody who was also part of the conspiracy. It took the position that a murder society was operating in the guise of a legitimate labor organization. Its attorneys laid plans to try nine union officials.

Picked for the first suit was Paul Cocoran, secretary of the Burke local. He was certainly not at Wardner at the time of the dynamiting, but the state's prosecutors believed that his conviction would be an excellent example to union members of what the law could do. He was found guilty on July 28, 1899, of creating a conspiracy and sentenced to seventeen years in prison. (He was pardoned on August 14, 1901, apparently because the purpose of his trial, a warning to others, had been accomplished.) The state was unable to take legal action against the eight other union officials because they escaped from the bull pen and disappeared. It did have federal suit brought against thirty-two miners for tampering with the United States mail on that commandeered freight train, and ten were sent to a federal penitentiary for two years. Martial law in the Coeur d'Alene area was ended on April 11, 1901; the Western Federation was completely broken in the region. The mines were at work, but a bitter legacy of hatred remained.

Governor Steunenberg's dreams of becoming a United States senator were dashed by the Coeur d'Alene troubles, so he resumed his private business enterprises.[5] Some six years later, returning late on the evening of December 30, 1905, to his home at Caldwell in the southern part of the state, he opened his front gate and was blasted by dynamite; he died an hour later. Within two days officials arrested Harry Orchard for the crime. The eight possible theories on why Steunenberg was killed are as follows: (1) the whole Western Federation of Miners was involved; (2) only an "inner circle" of the orgaanization knew of it; (3) some mine owners conspired to have it done for foul anti-union purposes; (4) one member of the Western Federation directed the murder without any other person's knowing of it; (5) not Orchard, but some disgruntled Coeur d'Alene miner actually did it and was never suspected; (6) Orchard's motive was revenge for losing his one-sixteenth interest in the Hercules mine as a result of the 1899 Coeur d'Alene troubles; (7) rivals of lumberman Steunenberg had him murdered; and (8) cattlemen wanted sheepman Steunenberg removed.

It is puzzling that Orchard made no attempt to leave town or to

[5] Beal and Wells, *History*, II, 209–19; Hawley, *History*, I, 267–71; Stewart H. Holbrook, *The Rocky Mountain Revolution*, 185–273 (Holbrook accepts everything Orchard said as true); Claudius O. Johnson, *Borah of Idaho*, 78–84; Leedice Kissane, "Steve Adams, the Speechless Witness," *Idaho Yesterdays*, Vol. IV (1960), 18–21; Marian C. McKenna, *Borah*, 48–63; Stephen Scheinberg, "Theodore Roosevelt's 'Undesirable Citizens,' " *Idaho Yesterdays*, Vol. IV (1960), 10–15; Irving Stone, *Clarence Darrow for the Defense*, 191–245; Arthur Weinberg, *Attorney for the Damned*, 410–88.

destroy incriminating evidence at his hotel room; it was almost as if he wanted to be caught. He was a self-confessed perjurer, kidnaper, thief, firebug, and murderer; he was also a member of the Western Federation of Miners who had worked in Colorado as a spy employed by the Mine Owners' Association. It was the responsibility of the state to prosecute him for his Caldwell crime. The Pinkerton Detective Agency was hired to help gather evidence, and among the people assigned to the case was detective James A. McParland, widely known for his work thirty years earlier in breaking up the Mollie Maguires labor organization at the Pennsylvania anthracite mines. For the past twenty years he had been a leader in the Colorado mine owners' anti-union activities.

McParland ordered Orchard placed in solitary confinement for ten days and then, partly through converting him to religion, induced him to write a confession. This extraordinary document left hardly any destruction in a western mine unaccounted for. It stated that Orchard had already dynamited more than twenty enemies of the Western Federation of Miners, including Steunenberg, on orders of union officials and had been financed by the organization's funds. The key question about the confession, never solved, is how much of it is true. Certainly Judge Luther M. Goddard of the Colorado Supreme Court must have had considerable confidence in it after he read it, went home, and dug up unsuspected traces of a misfired bomb in his yard, but that every word of it could be correct is almost incredible. Probably only part of the confession is accurate and what the size of that portion is or where it may be found in the document or how truth and falsehood may lie intermixed in the same sentence, nobody can possibly know. In giving testimony or undergoing cross-examination during the various trials, Orchard stuck to exactly what he had written. The confession was so complex, some say, that no man could possibly have fabricated it and then on the witness stand have remembered it without deviations and inconsistencies. Others reply that there was ample time between his arrest and the first trial for an unprincipled man, assisted by cynical detectives, to have learned a pack of lies.

The state acted as if every word were true. It resolved to try top officials of the Western Federation of Miners for conspiracy to murder Steunenberg; conspiracy was, of course, a charge previously used in the 1892 and 1899 Coeur d'Alene cases. The state directed its action against Charles H. Moyer, president of the Western Federation, William D. Haywood, secretary-treasurer, and George Pettibone, formerly active in the union but now a Denver storekeeper and the alleged contact man for Orchard. The first problem was that none of them had been in Idaho at the time the crime was committed, a requirement if the law of extradition was to be used to get them out of Colorado. McParland worked secretly with various Colorado state officials, including the governor, and received their approval of the only feasible plan. He had the three accused men arrested without a warrant by a county sheriff at Denver, shortly placed on a special train to Boise, and put into the death house in the state penitentiary. In other words, he had the men kidnapped. Their supporters promptly took action to try to get them released. The manner of their arrest caused more and larger contributions to their defense fund than would have been given otherwise. The majority of the United States Supreme Court, hearing on appeal a suit for their release, said that once the men were in Idaho, the issue was not how they got there but whether the state had the authority to try them; it did. The minority of the court objected that any kidnapping "is a crime, pure and simple." This preliminary exchange at law delayed the hearings on conspiracy cases a little more than a year.

The state intended to try Haywood first, then Pettibone and Moyer. For conviction, Idaho law required that the testimony or the confession of an accomplice had to be corroborated by independent evidence. To support Orchard's statements, the Pinkerton detectives secured a confession from a man he named as an accomplice, Steve Adams. Whether improper pressure was used in obtaining it is a matter of debate which can probably never be settled; certainly he later repudiated what he had written and refused to testify at any court hearing. Other witnesses which McParland promised to have on hand simply disappeared or else would not testify.

The trial lasted from May 9 to July 28, 1907, with national attention focused on it. For the prosecution William E. Borah and for the defense Clarence Darrow did such outstanding work that both won widespread reputations as lawyers of superior ability. If the state had been able to secure independent testimony in support of what Orchard said, its case would have been impregnable. Since it could not, Judge Fremont Wood instructed the jury clearly that conviction was impossible under the provisions of the state's laws and the twelve men acquitted Haywood. The six weeks' hearing on Pettibone produced the same result, so the state made no attempt to try Moyer. Judge Wood sentenced Orchard to life imprisonment, making it clear that he believed the confession completely and that he thought both Haywood and Pettibone were guilty in fact although conviction under Idaho law was impossible. Orchard was never pardoned, despite vigorous efforts on his behalf, and after serving forty-six years died on April 13, 1954, a repentant sinner.

13

THE BLACK HILLS: INDIANS AND GOLD

THE Sioux Indians considered the Black Hills to be one of their choicest possessions and therefore tried to keep the gold there a secret, fearful that white men would come, seize the treasure, and dispossess them of the area. The histories of the Black Hills gold rush and of the Sioux tribes are so closely connected that the story of the one cannot be told without discussion of the other.

The Black Hills, lying in southwestern South Dakota, are about 125 miles in length from north to south and average approximately sixty miles wide.[1] There the Sioux liked to wander, to secure medical herbs, to gather wild fruit, to harvest berries, to bathe in the curative waters of the hot springs, to cut poles for their tipis, and to dig out flint for their arrows. The area was a sacred region in their religion. Despite its many attractions and pleasures, they did not care to live there permanently. The red men found the area frightening because of a great noise, perhaps rolls of thunder echoing or perhaps gases escaping from burning coal seams.

Surrounding the Black Hills were the plains, which the Sioux loved more deeply than almost any white man of the era could understand. When across them came the wagon trains of westbound emigrants, bringing strange diseases and prodding the buffalo to desert their accustomed ranges, the red men were seriously concerned. The Sioux held a council of their entire nation in 1854 and determined to resist every form of white encroachment, following that policy consistently until they met their final defeat. They did not take the initiative, for what they wanted most was simply to be left alone.

[1] Roderick Peattie (ed.), *The Black Hills*, 38–39, 244; Agnes W. Spring, *The Cheyenne and Black Hills Stage and Express Routes*, 39–40; Jesse Brown and A. M. Willard, *The Black Hills Trails*, 18; Edgar I. Stewart, *Custer's Luck*, 8–19.

The Sioux in the Great Plains area caused little trouble during the Civil War period until in 1865 the government started building the Bozeman Trail, intended to shorten the route from the East to the booming mines in Montana.[2] It cut northwestward from the Oregon Trail and ran through the headwaters of the Powder and Yellowstone rivers, an area rich in game which the Indians had long regarded as their prime hunting area. War broke out at once. The army proved ineffectual in its fighting and Washington authorities, who could not decide whether to reinforce the soldiers in the field or to sue for peace, took no effective action. Under such conditions the Sioux more than held their own. Just as a serious shortage of ammunition finally made them vulnerable, the government decided it had to have peace and bribed the Indian chiefs with goods. In the resulting treaty of 1868, the United States established as a reservation all the present state of South Dakota lying west of the Missouri River, including the Black Hills. It recognized the area farther west, especially the Powder River and Big Horn Mountains country, as "unceded Indian territory" through which no white man could go without permission; this meant that federal authorities were abandoning the Bozeman Trail. The treaty also stipulated that the Indians had to keep away from the line of the Union Pacific Railroad, including their traditional trading post at Fort Laramie, and that they had to learn to become farmers; these provisions, the important chief Red Cloud was later angrily to insist, were never read to the Sioux.

Years before (nobody knows when), the Sioux had discovered gold in the Black Hills.[3] During the first half of the 1800's, they turned in a little at trading posts at Fort Laramie and along the Missouri River. They told the famous Catholic missionary Father DeSmet about the gold; he cautioned them to keep it strictly a secret for fear they would bring down upon themselves an invasion of white treasure seekers. Some whites who had taken Sioux wives and lived with the tribe came to share the secret, as did certain traders, who did not want a gold rush upsetting their well-established enterprises.

2 George E. Hyde, *Red Cloud's Folk: A History of the Oglala Sioux Indians*, 102–77; Stewart, *Custer's Luck*, 33–51; Peattie, *Black Hills*, 69–70; Howard R. Lamar, *Dakota Territory 1861–1889: A Study of Frontier Politics*, 102–107, 122.

3 George W. Kingsbury, *History of Dakota Territory*, 861–75; Spring, *Routes*, 20–25; Brown and Willard, *Trails*, 30; Harold E. Briggs, "The Black Hills Gold Rush," *North Dakota Historical Quarterly*, Vol. V (1930–31), 76; Annie D. Tallent, *The Black Hills*, 58.

At what time the first whites entered the Black Hills seeking gold can never be established, but enough physical survivals were unearthed in the later 1870's to indicate that men had prospected there earlier. It is a known fact that in 1853, Lieutenant John Mullan led a small group of soldiers through the area. Experienced in the California mines, he found such good prospects in the Black Hills that he was afraid to tell his men about them. Tales of the area's wealth were spun by Jim Bridger, but nobody took his declarations seriously. F. V. Hayden, an eminent scientist connected with the Smithsonian Institution, made a trip into the Black Hills in 1866; he shortly was telling an audience of Dakotans at Yankton that although he was mostly interested in other matters, he had found many evidences of mineral wealth and concluded there was "every indication of rich gold deposits."

About this time groups of men became interested in prospecting the area. The impetus for one was provided by two Swedes who appeared at Fort Laramie in the fall of 1865. They reported finding seven thousand dollars' worth of gold, either in the Black Hills or the Big Horn Mountains, shortly returned to their claim, and were never heard of again. The next spring, a body of 150 men organized at Fort Laramie to seek gold, but the military forbade them to enter the Indian reservation. A year later, in the spring of 1867, another group, 100 strong, met at Yankton, Dakota Territory, only to have Generals W. T. Sherman and Alfred H. Terry virtually forbid the expedition. A third group, under Captain P. B. Davy, began organizing at Yankton in the fall of 1867; its 300 well-equipped members were almost ready to set out when the military announced it would use force to bar the expedition from the Black Hills. In 1872, Charles Collins, editor of the *Sioux City Times,* tried to organize a colony for Black Hills settlement; General W. S. Hancock warned that he would use troops to keep it out.

Curiosity about the Black Hills continued to be lively. In 1874, the army sent an exploring party, headed by General George A. Custer, into the area.[4] His expedition had ten companies of cavalry, two

[4] Stewart, *Custer's Luck,* 62; Spring, *Routes,* 18–19; Brown and Willard, *Trails,* 37–40; Tallent, *Black Hills,* 15–16; Peattie, *Black Hills,* 85–86; Kingsbury, *History,* 882–90; William Ludlow, *Report of a Reconnaissance of the Black Hills Made in the Summer of 1874, passim.*

of infantry, a battery of three Gatling guns, some army engineers, sixty Indian scouts, and a few civilian specialists. It entered the Black Hills from the west side, explored the major portion of the interior, and passed out through the easternmost range, marching in all about six hundred miles. Custer concluded from his trip that no region in the United States had better or richer pasture land. More important was the discovery of gold. When he was encamped on French Creek one day in late July, Horatio Nelson Ross and William McKay, two experienced miners, brought back to camp with them some yellow dust wrapped in a page from an old account book. The substance was promptly cut, chewed, tasted, mixed with mercury, washed with acid, and examined with a microscope until everybody was convinced that it was gold. Only one person stood aloof, Professor N. H. Winchell, the official geologist for the expedition, who most of the day had been away climbing a mountain and upon his return was highly irritated that nobody officially consulted him about the discovery. He was so angry that he later made no mention of gold in the final report of his summer's work. The expedition, after moving on for a distance, stopped where the town of Custer now stands. Here, from the first through the fifth of August, almost all of its members dug numerous prospect holes which clearly indicated gold in paying quantities.

News of the discovery was first printed in the *Chicago Inter-Ocean* on August 24, 1874. It was soon spread from coast to coast, especially by a page-length article in the widely circulated *Harper's Weekly* for September 12, 1874. When Custer finally made his report, he declared that virtually every panful of gravel on some water courses yielded gold in paying quantities, which an amateur could find at the expense of only a little time and labor.

The return of Custer's force prompted Charles Collins again to try forming an expedition.[5] When General Phil Sheridan ordered that the plans be dropped, Collins issued a newspaper statement saying that he was obeying but at the same time sent out confidential letters declaring that actually he was not. Secretly a force of twenty-six men, one woman, and one boy set out from Sioux City with John Gordon as leader, while Collins, the organizer, remained at his task of editing

[5] Tallent, *Black Hills*, 18–97; Peattie, *Black Hills*, 92; Spring, *Routes*, 53–67; Kingsbury, *History*, 895–96.

a newspaper. For guidance the band depended as much on a pocket compass as on Gordon's memory of military routes, which it must carefully avoid using. Delayed by its caution to avoid both the army and the Indians, the Gordon party took seventy-eight days to reach its destination; on December 23, 1874, it settled about two and one-half miles below the present-day Custer.

Satisfied with what gold could be found, the interlopers devoted the next two weeks to erecting adequate shelter. With pine trunks thirteen feet high they threw up a stockade around an area eighty feet square, added bastions at the four corners, installed double gates, and within the enclosure erected seven log cabins. Meanwhile, the army learned of the group's departure from Sioux City and sent troops to exclude it from the Black Hills. These failed to find the party, abandoned the search, encountered temperatures of forty degrees below zero, and finally, in desperation, put their horses to a wild gallop, fearing that otherwise both animals and riders would soon freeze; by chance they stumbled onto the safety of a squaw man's ranch. Thwarted for the moment, the army sent out another force the following April and removed the Gordon party.

News from the group, sent out before the military arrived, caused excitement. Despite a declaration from Secretary of War W. W. Belknap that no one else would be allowed to enter the region, many men thought exploitation by whites would soon be possible. They organized groups, some of considerable size, in Boston, Brooklyn, Chicago, Harrisburg, Kansas City, Lancaster (Pennsylvania), Memphis, Milwaukee, New Orleans, New York City, St. Louis, and San Francisco. From most of these cities contingents came west to Wyoming, hoping to press northward prospecting together; government disapproval continued. Some members returned home, but others attempted clandestinely to cross the Platte River and reach the Black Hills. The hard way was to swim it. An easier way was to bribe the man who ran the ferry. A third way was to pay well for being hidden in wagons, filled with Indian trade goods, which had a legitimate right to use the ferry. To turn back such trespassers starting from Wyoming, the army assigned a patrol under Captain Edwin Pollock. He followed his orders to the letter and handed over those captured to civilian authorities, who promptly released them without bail. One interloper later admitted that within a period of three months he was escorted out

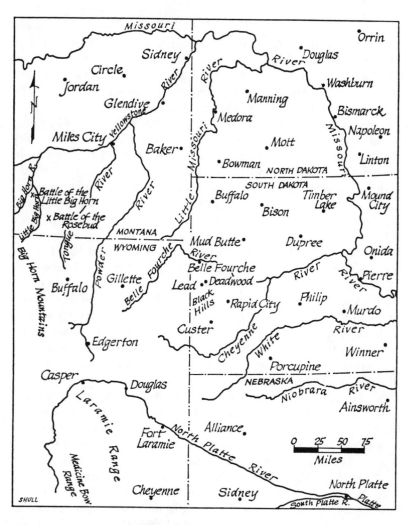

BLACK HILLS REGION

of the Black Hills four times, only to return again. Men sneaked into the area from Dakota Territory as well as Wyoming. A conservative estimate would place the number illegally prospecting the Black Hills in July at six to eight hundred.

The government, pressured because General Custer said there was gold in the area while the geologist of his expedition ignored the possibility, decided to have a more careful survey made. It hired Walter P. Jenney of the Columbia School of Mines, Washington, who set out from Fort Laramie on May 20, 1875, with a military escort of four hundred men.[6] He made a thorough examination of the southern portion of the region where Custer's men originally discovered gold on French Creek, but could not be as painstaking in the north, where Deadwood shortly arose, because the thick forest made access very difficult. Jenney was unimpressed with the French Creek area, concluding that work there with pan or rocker would not pay but that if a sluice could be devised, it would be profitable. He thought that any definitive conclusions about Black Hills placer deposits should await further prospecting, commenting that they were not remarkably rich when compared with those in California or Australia. He found no quartz ledges, a difficult task which required time and facilities not available to him. Jenney commented that there was gold enough in the Black Hills to bring about thorough economic development there. When the placer deposits were exhausted, he prophesied, the inhabitants would turn to stock raising. Jenney's preliminary report was published by the government in 1876; the final and complete one was not issued until 1880. Before anything came out, it was widely gossiped that in one creek he had found enough placer gold to liquidate the national debt.

In the year of Jenney's investigations, 1875, the government made two attempts to secure the Black Hills from the Sioux Indians.[7] In April, it escorted a number of Sioux chiefs to Washington, then told them that the purpose of their visit was to give up part of their reservation. When the federal negotiators mentioned the Powder River and Big Horn Mountains areas, it caused such an outburst of anger that they were careful not to raise the subject again. They discussed a surrender of the Black Hills. Finally the chiefs flatly refused to take any action until they had consulted their tribesmen. Their decision left the federal government obligated, under the treaty of 1868, to exclude all interlopers.

Meanwhile, whites continued to enter the Black Hills, despite the

6 Walter P. Jenney, *The Mineral Wealth, Climate and Rain-fall and Natural Resources of the Black Hills of Dakota*, 11–56; J. D. Irving, *Economic Resources of the Northern Black Hills*, 56; Kingsbury, *History*, 905, 909; Tallent, *Black Hills*, 124–28; John S. McClintock, *Pioneer Days in the Black Hills*, 4.

7 Stewart, *Custer's Luck*, 68–69; Spring, *Routes*, 63–64; Hyde, *Red Cloud's Folk*, 231–38; Kingsbury, *History*, 897–900.

efforts of the military to keep them out.[8] Sometimes the army intercepted a considerable group. It captured a party of 176 interlopers in May, 1875. The soldiers burned all the wagons and supplies of these trespassers except the load of merchandise that a certain Mrs. Brocket sat upon; they were too gallant to remove her by force and thus she saved much of her husband's goods. Despite such episodes, many people escaped the military. When the federal government decided to hold a general council with the Sioux Nation, hoping to arrange the sale that had failed in the East, it thought to put the red men in a more cooperative mood by removing as many trespassing miners as possible. It sent out a force under General George Crook. He mingled with some of the prospectors, even panned a little gold, and urged them to meet together, at what later was the town of Custer, to arrange an orderly withdrawal. At the gathering, held August 10, they voted that all claims which they held should be valid and not subject to trespass by anybody else for a period of forty days after the Black Hills were legally declared open to white occupancy. The rule gave more protection to men working where there was a considerable body of miners than to those in an isolated party because it could be enforced only by pressure or action from those in the area. Some prospectors formed societies to protect each other's holdings and not to reveal their discoveries to nonmembers. The miners, with definite plans to return as soon as possible, and Crook's force then left together, theoretically removing all whites from the Black Hills. Actually this was not the case, for some prospectors were working in such remote areas that they never heard of the big meeting, others with no intention of departing took pains to hide from the military, and still others were just secretly entering the forbidden area for the first time. Apparently, however, the great proportion of the miners voluntarily withdrew from the region for a time. That they did was a diplomatic triumph for General Crook, unmatched in any other western gold rush.

The grand council of the Sioux tribes and the negotiators of the United States government met in September, 1875.[9] There were

8 Tallent, *Black Hills*, 120–23; Spring, *Routes*, 67–69; Brown and Willard, *Trails*, 44–45; Kingsbury, *History*, 907–908; McClintock, *Pioneer Days*, 29–30.

9 Peattie, *Black Hills*, 96–100; Robert J. Casey, *The Black Hills and Their Incredible Characters*, 133–34; Hyde, *Red Cloud's Folk*, 241–49; Kingsbury, *History*, 915–16.

about twenty thousand Sioux, some of them very warlike in their attitude toward the whites and even against the more tractable of their own tribesmen. In attempting to hold discussions with as many of the Sioux as cared to gather around, the white negotiators met with strong demands for much money. It became obvious that many of the wilder Sioux would never approve any sale. One day at the council, a naked young warrior, Winchester rifle in one hand and a fist full of cartridges in the other, abruptly burst in and shouted that he was going to kill the whites who were trying to take land away from the Sioux. Other Indians disarmed him amid intense excitement. Suddenly, Young-Man-Afraid-of-His-Horses dashed up with some warriors of his band. In the first confusion some government men thought the fight had begun; instead, the chief was coming to their support. He ordered the rest of the Sioux to their lodges and forbade holding a council until their tempers had cooled. He was obeyed.

The white negotiators did not choose to hold any more mass councils. Shortly they called twenty young chiefs to discuss matters. The red men made extreme demands, although it is not clear whether Red Cloud actually asked $600,000,000. The whites countered with a definite offer of $6,000,000 for a sale of the Black Hills or $500,000 annually for a lease of the mineral rights, which could be terminated if the whites gave two years' notice. Neither side would accept the proposals of the other and the negotiations were adjourned.

At these discussions of the Black Hills some of the Sioux were violently angry at the idea of a sale and others that their price was not met; certainly their open hostility shook the white negotiators. The Indians probably had no better idea than the whites of the mineral potential of the area.

With discussions ended, the federal government was still legally obligated by the 1868 treaty to keep the whites out. Authorities feared to take drastic steps because of the expense and, more important, a political situation so unstable that the Republicans did not wish to alienate any voters. (How justified was their concern was proved the next year, 1876, in the disputed Hayes-Tilden presidential election.) The officials were discouraged by the ruling of U. S. Attorney General Edward Pierrepont. He decided in May that the federal law (excluding white trespassers as "foreigners" from the Sioux reservation unless they had a pass from officials of the Departments of War or the Interior) applied, not to United States citizens, but only to those who owed their allegiance to other nations. His remarkable perversion of the plain intent of the statute was never tested in the courts; instead, the federal government ceased bringing the interlopers to trial. Those miners who wished to risk Indian attack were welcome to enter the Black Hills and take their own chances; the government would neither hinder nor aid them.[10]

The United States at the same time undertook to confine the Sioux more strictly to the boundaries of their reservation; this was the immediate cause of the Sioux War of 1876, highlighted by the Custer disaster.[11] It would be "worse than idiotic" to say that federal authorities precipitated the war simply to get the Black Hills. Actually both they and the red men recognized that the treaty of 1868 was only a truce, poorly observed by each side. The government now proposed to end the long conflict, to force the Indians to give up their old, free, wild life, to keep them permanently within the reservation, and, until they became self-supporting, to give them a dole. It did not think many of them would dare to oppose and those few the troops could round up with little difficulty.

The late fall of 1875 found the Sioux, as always in the winter months, widely scattered. Abruptly the government ordered all tribesmen to report back to their agencies by January 31, 1876, or be treated as disobedient, hostile Indians. This directive did not reach some of the agencies until December 22. It was relayed by messengers to the red men as promptly as possible, but some of the couriers themselves could not get back until after the deadline set. Virtually none of the wandering Sioux obeyed the order; later they gave the unlikely excuse that it was too difficult to move in winter. Actually none of the Indians took the order seriously; they had no idea that a major change of government policy was involved and probably would have cared little if they had known, and they took the attitude that when spring came, they would start thinking about obeying. The federal authorities themselves moved slowly. Later, in the spring, many of the less-than-friendly Indians followed their annual custom of trekking away

10 Stewart, *Custer's Luck*, 69; Kingsbury, *History*, 910–20.

11 Stewart, *Custer's Luck*, 71–490; Hyde, *Red Cloud's Folk*, 249–93; Peattie, *Black Hills*, 103–105; Kingsbury, *History*, 946–60; Lamar, *Dakota Territory*, 184–89; Richard B. Hughes, *Pioneer Years in the Black Hills*, 237–38; Works Progress Administration, *South Dakota: A Guide to the State*, 37.

from the agencies toward the Powder River country; the army made no effort to prevent their going.

A military campaign began. General Crook marched north from Fort Fetterman, Wyoming. On March 15, he approached an encampment headed by Crazy Horse. He resolved to surprise it, not a difficult task. Contrary to general belief, the Sioux were habitually so careless about sending out scouts or guarding their lodges that in many instances they knew nothing of white men's presence until suddenly confronted with pale faces. Thus it was in this case; the soldiers, under the immediate command of Colonel J. J. Reynolds, drove the startled red men from their camp. Instead of obeying his orders to hold it for Crook and to confiscate the large amount of food stored, Reynolds fired the lodges and withdrew. This forced Crook, his plan ruined, to retreat back to Wyoming; he complained bitterly of Reynolds as a bungler.

In April, Sitting Bull, beyond any possible doubt a great leader, called a council of all the roving camps to meet on the Tongue River. Here he told the assembled leaders that the whites wanted a war and he would wage it. He then sent out messengers urging those red men normally peaceful to join him now in a mighty effort. In response some Sioux came in, but others refused.

General Crook headed his forces north again on the offensive and on June 17 met the Sioux at the Battle of the Rosebud. He had learned that the Indians were in the vicinity of his command and planned to surprise them. He had just started his advance when some of the scouts came plunging down from a hill with the enemy in hot pursuit. This time the Indians had been on the alert and had made a night march toward the military. Whether or not the red men had a plan of battle is a matter of dispute. It would have been some kind of decoy-and-ambush trick, for this was the only maneuver the Sioux practiced; they employed it with such variety and ingenuity that veteran whites who thought they were quite familiar with it were frequently fooled. If there were such a plan, it went awry. The Sioux disdained their usual circling at a safe distance with little risk and instead put their horses to a dead run, charged, and fought hand to hand. The battle itself was like "an old-time frontier barroom brawl, with every man for himself." Eventually the Sioux retired from the field. Their attack forced Crook to abandon the offensive and to stop for six weeks to await reinforcements.

Even before the Battle of the Rosebud, another army force was heading into the general area and was to fight on June 26 the more famous Battle of the Little Big Horn. This expedition, the so-called Dakota Column, was led by General Alfred H. Terry and included the Seventh Cavalry. Its commander was George A. Custer, actually a lieutenant colonel (his rank in peacetime) but commonly called General Custer because he had held that grade during the Civil War. He had been the center of considerable dissension ever since his assignment to the Seventh. A supreme egotist, with boundless ambition and limitless faith in his own destiny, Custer was especially resented by two older men in the regiment who held lower rank, Captain Frederick W. Benteen and Major Marcus A. Reno. He had recently been placed in the unenviable position of having to obey the order of a Congressional investigating committee to testify about certain illegal dealings in military and Indian trading-post licences which involved Orvil Grant, brother of President Grant, and Secretary of War W. W. Belknap. What he had truthfully said made the President so resentful that only after humiliating petitions was Custer allowed to resume charge of the Seventh Cavalry.

What happened at the Little Big Horn and how some things should have been done differently has been a matter of much heated controversy for years; the outstanding study is the well-balanced, thorough, and objective appraisal by Edgar I. Stewart, published in 1955 under the title *Custer's Luck*.

As the Dakota Column, marching westward, neared the hostile Sioux, whose chief leader was Sitting Bull, General Terry did not work out a clear-cut plan of battle. He divided his force to approach the Indians from two directions, sending Custer's cavalry to follow the Rosebud River while he with General John Gibbon's infantry went along the Big Horn. He did not order the two commands to cooperate or to make a joint attack. Terry realized that the cavalry could move faster and should reach the enemy perhaps a day before the infantry did.

Custer pushed forward so eagerly that he approached the Little Big Horn River nearly a day earlier than he had anticipated. Since it was obvious that the Indians knew of his coming, he could either attack at once, in midmorning, or wait until the traditional time, the next dawn. The General attacked, which analyst Stewart thinks was the only possible decision to make. How many warriors faced Custer is unknown, the best estimate being around four thousand, a force large enough to outnumber the soldiers by about eight to one. He divided the regiment, three troops to Benteen, three to Reno, and five for himself. He sent Benteen scouting to the left, partly to find any escaping Indians; whether he suggested that the Captain attack the Sioux village from the left is not clear. The General ordered Reno, in the center, to advance toward the village. The Major went forward, stopped his troops short of contact with the enemy, was strongly attacked, and finally fell back across the river, a maneuver in which he completely lost control of his force. As the last of his men were struggling up the bluff from the stream, Benteen returned from his scout and united his force with Reno's.

Custer, who was so uncertain of just where the Sioux were that he had no clear plan of battle, apparently had at first considered holding his immediate command as a reserve for Reno's forward thrust. Changing his mind, he went to the right, crossed the river, and probably expected to catch the enemy between his own and Reno's forces, rolling up the red men between them. If what he thought had been true, that the main village was in flight and the Indians had left only a rear guard, his tactic might have worked well. Unfortunately for him, the Sioux had not retreated; they were in a belligerent mood and Reno's retreat released a number of badly needed warriors just as Custer was pushing forward to the attack. Precisely what happened to the General's immediate command has been the subject of a vast amount of speculation, but this much is clear: his men fought with extreme bravery; they had no shortage of ammunition; a large number of their overheated carbines jammed; and they died to the last man, completely surrounded by Indians. With every indication that Custer was heavily engaged, Reno and Benteen took no steps to make contact with him or to aid him; they withdrew their combined commands to a hill. Here they withstood attacks that night and the following day, until in the afternoon the Sioux abruptly departed as Terry approached with the infantry.

The Indians had no desire to fight further; they had glory enough and plunder enough from their victories over Crook, and now Custer, to last them for the rest of the year. Their defeat of Crook had been distorted by the army so that most Americans thought the victory belonged instead to the General, for the red men had left the field of battle. No such intentional misrepresentation could cover up Custer's massacre, and the news of it deeply shocked the nation. The army, previously so overconfident, now desperately looked for someone to blame and brazenly accused the Department of the Interior of supplying inaccurate figures on the number of hostile Sioux, as if the military had not been watching these same red men for many years. The Indians, with no idea of the sensation their victory had caused among the white men, went about their usual routine. Many of them held the incredible belief that, as usual, the government would feed them during the winter and allow them to go off the reservation to hunt the next spring. Eventually a portion of their dissolving forces was overtaken by General Crook's soldiers and the minor Battle of Slim Buttes was an inconclusive stalemate.

Slightly earlier, on August 15, Congress finally passed the customary appropriations bill for the Sioux Indians but added a very important proviso: it stipulated that the red men would not get any money unless they relinquished the Black Hills, Powder River, and Big Horn regions and agreed to settle either in a reservation along the Missouri River or else in Indian Territory (the present state of Oklahoma). In other words, the Sioux were to surrender unconditionally and to give up everything the white man thought was of any value. Federal authorities plainly told those tribesmen who had remained friendly, staying entirely out of the conflict, that if they didn't join the hostile red men in signing the treaty, government rations would be withheld while they starved and also that troops might be set against them. The Sioux knew they were being robbed of their land, but they could do nothing about it. Many of their chiefs signed the necessary agreement on September 26, but there was no attempt to abide by the requirement, in the treaty of 1866, that it could be modified only by securing the signatures of three-fourths of the adult male Sioux. (This failure to observe the proper amendment procedure actually made the agreement relinquishing the Black Hills illegal, a fact Congress admitted in 1883 when it rejected a third treaty, giving up still more land and signed by only a few chiefs, on the grounds that the required three-fourths had not consented.)

The Sioux War of 1876 hindered the gold seekers entering the Black Hills, but many hurried into the area in spite of the obstacles.[12] In-

[12] Kingsbury, *History*, 910–11, 922–29, 978; Tallent, *Black Hills*, 171–77, 237–39, 249, 252, 262, 325–34, 370–72, 419–21; Spring, *Routes*, 77–78, 140–41, 147; McClintock, *Pioneer Days*, 31–32, 41, 55; Hughes, *Pioneer Years*, 26–27, 51, 72, 77, 105,

deed, some of them had never left it, avoiding Crook's round-up of the previous August, and others were continually slipping in. The military made no effort to stop them.

Late in the previous summer (1875), the first discoveries were made in the Deadwood area, which was to become the center of the Black Hills gold region. Most authorities say the initial find was made in August by Frank Bryant. Either it was not satisfactory or he felt that he had to leave because of Crook's evacuation orders. Bryant and a member of his party, John Pearson, returned early in November and staked a claim. Other first arrivals in the area were the William Lardner, William Smith, and A. S. Blanchard parties. None of these men, quite naturally, made any attempt to stake a claim in the area flooded by a beaver dam; as luck would have it, this was the very spot which was richest of all.

During the winter months of 1875–76, little work could be done. Early in the spring the great rush to the Deadwood area began. Some men came from elsewhere in the Black Hills. The largest single contingent from afar was a group of more than two hundred men from Montana who set out from the Yellowstone River area on March 20; all were experienced frontiersmen. The various newcomers found that while the diggings at Deadwood were rich, they were not extensive. Hundreds could not find a satisfactory claim, for the good ones there were all staked by the end of January. Perhaps half of those miners who took gold out of Deadwood Gulch purchased their claims from others. Gradually the men extended their placer mining into the neighboring Whitewood, Gold Run, Black Tail, and Bob-Tail gulches. Some prospectors returned to other areas of the Black Hills, concluding that what they had abandoned was better than the less desirable locations around Deadwood. Others grew discouraged, denounced glowing reports as a snare, and, with their resources exhausted, departed in bitterness. Still others remained in the region only a few days and then left as quickly as they had entered; mostly these were men from settled states, such as Iowa and Nebraska, who were unaccustomed to roughing it. Those who came from farther west, especially from other mining districts, were willing to stay long

117, 150, 189–95; Casey, *Incredible Characters*, 220; Briggs, "The Black Hills Gold Rush," *North Dakota Historical Quarterly*, Vol. V (1930–31), 89, 97; Brown and Willard, *Trails*, 492–93; Muriel S. Wolle, *The Bonanza Trail: Ghost Towns and Mining Camps of the West*, 454, 460.

enough to make a fair try. One authority has estimated that of those who came, half had no idea of working with a pick and shovel but expected, by their wits and abilities, to find their own kind of bonanza. Many of those who took part in the rush were veterans of a dozen previous mining camps, many had never really settled down since their experiences as soldiers in the Civil War, and many had not recovered from their reverses in the financial panic of 1873.

The Indians in the war year of 1876 kept careful watch on the groups entering the Black Hills; probably no whites went north without the red men's being aware of it. Late in the summer, after the Battle of the Little Big Horn, there was a considerable increase in Indian aggression. The number of deaths, however, was much smaller than it would have been in a general uprising. Most of the attacks were made by turbulent young warriors in small parties who could not be restrained, and they seldom came near Deadwood. The raids were held in check by the fact that the Sioux were essentially horsemen and did not like to penetrate deeply into an area where they could not use their animals freely. Of the forays, Spotted Tail once remarked that the whites took the red men's gold from the area without permission and in return the Indians stole from the interlopers without thinking it very sinful.

In 1876, there were stampedes out of Deadwood to areas where supposedly better claims could be staked. One of these was False Bottom Gulch. Actually this was a practical joke, men salting the diggings of a friend with gold from elsewhere and intending only a few moments' amusement; they had no thought of starting a stampede. When the truth was admitted, those who had rushed to the area took their disappointment good naturedly. Information about the apparently rich prospects on Polo Creek was given in the strictest secrecy to a very few people, but these in turn passed on the tip confidentially to others until the number of miners hurrying there all at once was large; nobody found much. The stampede which became a disaster was the winter one to Wolfe Mountain. Nobody seemed to know exactly where the new claims were, but many were very anxious to go search them out. When they looked for horses, they found that they had to turn to "Red" Clark, who asked very high prices because everybody else had sent their animals away for winter pasture. The prospectors charged out into the wilderness with more enthusiasm than wisdom. They did not know in which direction to start, how far they should go, or what travel in winter would be like. They suffered much, indeed a few of them died, but they found no gold. There was no Wolfe Mountain, except in the fertile imagination of some wicked hoaxer, probably Red Clark.

Before the winter of 1876–77 cut Deadwood off from the outside world completely, many men left, some vowing to return the next spring while others abandoned their fortune seeking. To supply those who remained, the merchants had adequate stocks, and none of them charged unreasonable prices, with the one exception of "Coal Oil Johnny" Spencer, who bought up all of the kerosene available and then raised the price to $3.75 a gallon. When spring came, more gold seekers hurried in and the Deadwood gold rush reached its peak. By summer, most of the placer claims that showed any possibility of producing satisfactorily had been taken up throughout the region. This caused the influx of newcomers virtually to cease. In October, 1877, the population within a radius of ten miles of Deadwood was about twelve thousand people. Indian attacks continued.

The first discoveries of gold in the Black Hills were placer claims.[13] They were located from French Creek (near Custer) on the south to Whitewood Creek (near Deadwood) on the north, a distance of fifty miles with thirty-eight gulches and creek valleys in between, all of which contained some gold. The claims proved to be less extensive and less productive than those in many other parts of the United States. The total amount of gold obtained in some areas was considerable, but when divided among the large number of men working there, it often made their earning less than reasonable wages. From no claim anywhere in the Black Hills did a prospector make a large fortune.

Part of the gold in the various gulches was in the present stream beds. Part of it was in one or two dry, covered beds, older in geologic time, which lay higher on the side of the hills, the one perhaps fifteen to twenty feet above the floor of the gulch and the other usually from one to three hundred feet above. The lower of the two was usually mined by diverting to it water through a ditch from upstream. For the higher bed there were two methods: to haul water up to it

13 Peattie, *Black Hills*, 245–51; Hughes, *Pioneer Years*, 74–79; Briggs, "The Black Hills Gold Rush," *North Dakota Historical Quarterly*, Vol. V (1930–31), 97; WPA, *South Dakota*, 272; Wolle, *Bonanza Trail*, 442–43; Tallent, *Black Hills*, 141–42, 398, 445–69; McClintock, *Pioneer Days*, 98, 104.

by man or donkey or to cart the dirt down, in some kind of wheel-barrow, to the creek in the bottom of the gulch. From whatever source the vital water came, the device used to extract the gold from sur-rounding impurities was the rocker or the sluice. During the early spring and late fall, the mercury placed in the sluice boxes to help recover the gold would become sluggish and would not collect as much as in more temperate weather. At best the Black Hills sluices saved about 65 per cent of the gold run through them. Where the prospects seemed particularly promising and water was especially scarce, the miners might bring it from a considerable distance by flume. The most notable example was the seventeen-mile flume from Spring Creek to the nearly dry placers at Rockerville; the project was built in 1880 at a cost of $300,000 and in two years helped recover $500,000 in gold. By 1883, Rockerville was virtually exhausted. In some areas traditional hydraulic methods of extraction, explained earlier, were used.

The first mining district in the Black Hills, aside from that of Custer's soldiers, which never really operated, was organized along French Creek on May 29, 1875.[14] Sixteen men established the district, elected a recorder, and, in much the same fashion as pioneer miners out beyond the jurisdiction of the law ever since the rush to Cali-fornia, kept a record of who owned which claim. The district author-ized claim size to be 300 feet along the gulch from rim to rim. This example was followed by many other districts organized later. At Deadwood in April, 1876, a number of men, who had arrived late and found remaining little that was worth having, listened to three agitators named McNabb, Smith, and O'Leary. Under the leadership of these men the late comers proposed to reduce the size of claims from 300 feet along the stream to 150; if done, this would confis-cate thousands of dollars not yet extracted by the pioneers. The old-timers held a miners' meeting, with five hundred in attendance, voted unanimously to make no changes, and elected three men to lead them should they have to fight for their prior rights. Their opponents num-bered only one hundred; when they came down the gulch and saw the

14 Tallent, *Black Hills*, 163, 279, 380–84, 399–400, 449–68; Brown and Willard, *Trails*, 473–75, 494, 501; Hughes, *Pioneer Years*, 105, 112–13, 126, 287–98; Wolle, *Bonanza Trail*, 447–48, 469; Peattie, *Black Hills*, 260–69; Briggs, "The Black Hills Gold Rush," *North Dakota Historical Quarterly*, Vol. V (1930–31), 90; George M. Smith, *South Dakota: Its History and Its People*, III, 25–28, 32.

angry, grim, determined faces of the veterans, they abandoned their venture permanently. Later, the legislature of Dakota Territory passed a law authorizing a claim to be no more than 300 feet wide and 1,500 feet long, ten acres in all, upon which the owner had to perform at least one hundred dollars' worth of work each year in order to retain title; it placed no limit upon the number of claims a man could own.

As the placer deposits gradually became exhausted, prospectors turned increasingly to seeking quartz mines. The gold was intermixed with a variety of other natural products; at some spot or other in the Black Hills it was deposited with silver, copper, tin, antimony, iron, nickel, lead, uranium, mica, graphite, asbestos, salt, granite limestone, gypsum, porphyry, and clay suitable for brick or pottery. Sometimes it was encased in rocks so hard that it was called "cemented ore." Many such deposits were uncovered throughout the region; almost all of them proved so difficult to refine that they were unprofitable. In a typical one the developers would be exerting their maximum effort two years after the discovery and within five would have abandoned their efforts completely. Another type of ore was the Tertiary; if bluish in color, it was very hard to refine profitably, but if reddish, it could be handled inexpensively.

Typical of the many towns which arose in areas of quartz mining was Rochford, where gold was discovered on Montezuma Hill in 1876. By December, 1878, five hundred people were in the town and as many more in the area immediately adjacent. The village had a solid line of store buildings a block long, with connecting wooden canopies covering the sidewalk. Several stamp mills were installed. They proved unable to extract the gold effectively from the ore found in the area and there was not enough of it being mined to warrant buying much new and complicated machinery to refine it further. Obviously, additional expenditures were not justified, present methods were not profitable, operations ceased, and the town faded away.

The first arrastra in the Black Hills, a crude device for separating gold from quartz, was set up in August, 1876. That fall, a stamp mill, similar in principle to those used in California, was erected. Eventually in the Deadwood area the first crude stamp mills were improved, as was described in the discussion of Colorado, with amalgamation, chlorination, and cyanidation processes. To haul the raw ore from the outlying mines to the three major mills in the town, a network of narrow-gauge railroad lines was built.

Capital was at first slow to come into the Black Hills.[15] Financiers were suspicious, and rightly so, that men with money might be defrauded; they frequently were. Those who intended to cheat eastern investors often worked so quietly and skillfully that there was little opportunity for honest Dakotans to give the outsiders a warning; when they did manage to do so, the words often fell on deaf ears. The best of specialists were sometimes fooled. Thus one of them was especially careful to keep his bag of ore samples where he could watch it. In hopes of thwarting him, the sellers had an identical bag made and filled with rock much richer than any to be found in their mine. When he finished his final inspection on the last day and was just leaving the mine, they asked him to turn back and give his opinion about a formation that looked to them like black lead. For a moment he relaxed his vigilance, leaving his sack in the wagon as he briefly re-entered the mine; he inadvertently allowed them just enough time to switch the bags and make the deception. In another instance of fraud, where exceedingly elaborate precautions against it were taken, both at the mine and at the mill where the ore samples were to be processed, a man apparently drunk came up to the place where the rocks were being shoveled from a wagon into the mill's chute, stumbled, and dropped his bottle into the chute. It was not the liquor bottle it seemed to be; it was full of gold chloride and greatly enriched the resulting assay.

Many of the investment opportunities offered outsiders were quite legitimate. The original discoverers of a mine would work it until it was clearly profitable, then sell out to those with greater resources, who would develop it on an extensive scale. If the mine continued to show promise, it would likely fall, in turn, into the hands of the Homestake Mining Company, which came to possess all of the Black Hills mines really worth owning.

[15] Smith, *South Dakota*, III, 24; Hughes, *Pioneer Years*, 126, 287–98.

14

THE BLACK HILLS: DEADWOOD AND LEAD

THE Homestake, giant of the Black Hills mining companies, centered its activities at Lead (pronounced "Leed"), four miles southwest of Deadwood.[1] At what was to be the site of this city on Gold Run Gulch, Thomas E. Carey made the first discovery of placer gold in February, 1876, and built the first cabin, but the area was to become more notable for its lode mines, developed later, than for its original placers. The lode deposits differed from those in California, Colorado, and Montana, where the gold was found in "leads" (well-defined veins of quartz between two walls, generally of granite) and where the richest gold was encased in quartz that was hard, white, and flinty. Around Lead there were enough geologic structures called leads to give the town its name; however, they contained almost no gold. Gold had to be sought, instead, in so-called blowups, quartz deposits found initially on the surface as if thrown there by a volcano; these were intermixed with a slate formation or, more commonly, with a mass of soft, dark-colored matter.

The great discovery at Lead was made by prospector Moses Manuel. He and his brother Frederick arrived in the Black Hills in December, 1857; their partners were Henry Harney and Alex Eng. The four first engaged in placer mining, then, with the coming of spring, decided to try to find the lode from which the gold they were taking out must have been washed down centuries earlier. They

---

1 Smith, *South Dakota*, III, 25, 28, 32; Brown and Willard, *Trails*, 366–68, 373–76, 463–75, 496; Wolle, *Bonanza Trail*, 472–74; T. A. Rickard, *A History of American Mining*, 213–19; Peattie, *Black Hills*, 262–64, 283–87; Tallent, *Black Hills*, 510–14, 526; Irving, *Economic Resources*, 57–66; Hughes, *Pioneer Years*, 105, 125; Casey, *Incredible Characters*, 216–19.

met with so little success that three of the men finally abandoned the search, leaving Moses Manuel to continue it alone. In about a week more, on April 9, 1876, he located the lode and the partners claimed it, giving their mine the name "Homestake." They shortly extracted a two-hundred-pound lump of quartz, which proved to be the richest ever taken out of the property. They continued diligently at development work, securing ample working capital for the Homestake by selling another mine they had come to own in the same general area, the Golden Terra, for $35,000. During the winter of 1876–77, they took $5,000 in gold out of the Homestake. The next spring, engineers representing George Hearst, who had made a fortune from Nevada mines, J. B. Haggin, and Lloyd Tevis inspected it, recommended its purchase, and the sale was made at a price generally given as $70,000, although sometimes quoted at $105,000. The three capitalists promptly incorporated the Homestake Mining Company, issuing 100,000 shares of stock at the theoretical par value of $100 each; actually they paid in an assessment of $200,000 and apparently this was all the money necessary to put the original Homestake mine on a self-sustaining, profit-making basis for the corporation.

As the various mines developed around Lead it became clear that there was a valuable series of properties forming a belt one and one-half miles long and one-half mile wide and extending in a north-westerly direction from Gold Run on the south to Deadwood Creek on the north, from the Homestake mine on the south through the Highland, Golden Star, Old Abe, Caledonia, and Deadwood Terra to the Fr. DeSmet on the north. These the Homestake Mining Company set about acquiring rapidly. The group as a whole contained ore of such very low grade that no visual inspection would show whether it was worth mining and refining; to determine this, a sample of it was taken for analysis each day from each face in the mine being worked. To succeed financially, the Homestake Mining Company had to handle very large quantities of ore at very low cost. At first, since its deposits lay on steep slopes, it worked them as open cuts or quarries. Finally the company exhausted this mode and turned to vertical shafts and horizontal tunnels. Underground it copied the methods of Nevada's Comstock Lode mine operators, including their famous square-set system of mine timbering.

To separate the gold from the rock surrounding it, the company employed traditional methods. As the first step it used stamps; by the turn of the century it had one thousand of them in various mills. As the second step the company at first used the amalgamation method; by these devices it extracted between 75 and 80 per cent of the gold, considering that the expense of saving the rest would exceed the value of any additional amount recovered. In this belief the company let slip away deliberately perhaps as much as one-half million dollars gross. In 1890, the company changed its policy and gradually installed the cyanidation process, finishing the task about the turn of the century; when completed, the recovery of gold was 95 per cent. The Homestake continued to improve its techniques, and after the turn of the century, two important processes were perfected for it; these were eventually used in many other areas of the world. J. V. N. Door devised the Door classifier to separate particles into the finer and the coarser, which received somewhat different cyaniding treatments. Charles W. Merrill invented a better method of treating the finer particles after they had been classified.

Up to June 1, 1900, the Homestake Mining Company had extracted $59,246,340 in gold from its various mines and had paid out $15,445,468 in dividends; to April, 1931, it had taken out $233,564,312 and had paid dividends of $57,868,584. By 1924, its shafts had penetrated to a depth of 2,200 feet below the surface and from them ran 60 miles of tunnels. In the late 1890's, the Homestake had about 1,500 men in its employ and was paying the miners $3.50 a day, the mine laborers $3.00, and the surface laborers $2.50. Almost all of them were laid off for four months in 1897 when a big fire in the company's mines could be controlled only by flooding.

A constant problem was the procurement of adequate supplies of lumber; choppers soon surrounded Lead with a host of dead stumps. The company built a narrow-gauge railroad line to haul wood, gradually extending it until it ran from Lead to Piedmont. How much right the Homestake people had to take all of the timber they did is not clear, for in 1894, the federal government brought suit against them, asking for $700,000 as damages. for removing large quantities from the "natural forests."

In its earliest days the Homestake Mining Company collided violently with the Fr. DeSmet property, which was at that time independent. Each corporation was convinced that it held the richest gold prospect in the world and eagerly gave battle on every slight issue to secure every possible advantage for itself. A major conflict developed over water, so essential for stamp-mill operations. An important aspect of the struggle began when an independent organization built the Foster Ditch to supply several smaller lode mines with water and happened to pass the Fr. DeSmet along the way. Before too long, the Foster Ditch lost so many customers that it could not survive financially and looked for a purchaser. It found one in the Homestake, which secretly secured the property, although it had no immediate use for the water. Shortly the Fr. DeSmet, under similar circumstances, bought up the Boulder Ditch, which it thought its rival would sometime need. To help preserve the Boulder Ditch's rights, the Fr. DeSmet had to have the water put to some use. It offered to furnish the city of Deadwood with all the citizens needed, free of charge, for a year. This aroused the Homestake to try to supply the town, too. A race followed, with each hurrying to complete its ditch into Deadwood as quickly as possible. The Homestake made an alliance with the City Creek Water Company, which was already delivering water to the townspeople, and also secretly purchased a local newspaper to champion its cause. An election was called so that the voters could decide which organization should serve them. On the day set for it, somewhere between ten and fifteen thousand voters assembled to participate, to sample some of the gallons of champagne dispensed without charge from what the Homestake chose to call "Information Booths," and to form themselves into blocs of several hundred members each while their spokesmen negotiated with the highest bidder for the sale of their votes. By midafternoon the Fr. DeSmet interests decided that they surely had a majority of the votes in the ballot box. To prevent more votes' being cast and to save themselves expense, they ordered the polling places to be packed; this was done so effectively that hundreds of would-be voters could not get within fifty feet of them. When the tellers made the count, however, the victory went to the Homestake's City Creek Water Company; obviously, the Fr. DeSmet had made some kind of miscalculation. Not long after this, the Fr. DeSmet sold out to its generally more successful rival, the Homestake.

An interesting example of the Homestake Mining Company's tactics in the late 1870's came to general public attention when a young man of Lead who owned property where the corporation wished to erect a mill demanded an exorbitant price for his land. He refused to be intimidated by the company's negotiator and then turned a deaf ear when the company's gunmen threatened to shoot him; they did just that, killing him. The murderers were promptly arrested. While they were lodged in jail, a deputy sheriff reported that he was offered five thousand dollars to open the jail door for them. At their long and sensational trial, the jury brought in a verdict of not guilty. The astounded judge, Gideon C. Moody, immediately declared that the decision was not in accord with the evidence and plainly told the jury that he held no doubts about their having received Homestake money. Nobody made a reply and nothing could be proved, but it was a well-known fact that several of the jurors had plenty of cash after the trial.

The Homestake was certainly the giant of the Black Hills gold producers, in some years extracting as much as 90 per cent of the area's total output; the remainder was mined by many companies and individuals. To 1924, the total yield of gold taken out of the Black Hills was more than $230,000,000.

For any mining community the development of adequate transportation facilities was important. Stagecoach service to the Black Hills began on January 27, 1876, when the Cheyenne and Black Hills Stage, Mail and Express line started operating from Cheyenne to Custer via Red Cloud Agency.[2] On February 12, it was sold to Gilmer, Salisbury and Patrick, who made Luke Voorhees superintendent. They bought thirty Concord coaches and six hundred horses, mostly eastern or southern bred. A team was usually six horses, sometimes four, and rarely only two. The animals were shod at least once a month, had their own particular sets of harness, and were kept loosely hitched, with free play of the reins, to get the best pulling power from each horse with the least amount of strain. How often a coach's team was changed depended upon the character of the country; a driver used several teams and covered an assignment of forty to

2 Spring, *Routes*, 81–334, *passim;* Casey, *Incredible Characters*, 229; Brown and Willard, *Trails*, 47–50, 59, 270, 445–46; Estelline Bennett, *Old Deadwood Days*, 68–69; Hughes, *Pioneer Years*, 259–60; Peattie, *Black Hills*, 250; Tallent, *Black Hills*, 191–92; Briggs, "The Black Hills Gold Rush," *North Dakota Historical Quarterly*, Vol. V (1930–31), 87; Harold E. Briggs, "Early Freight and Stage Lines in Dakota," *North Dakota Historical Quarterly*, Vol. III (1928–29), 246.

sixty miles. In wintry weather the passengers were kept warm with buffalo robes and, occasionally, with hot rocks or bricks wrapped in gunny sacks as foot warmers.

On April 3, the new firm changed to a more direct route. For the trip of 178.5 miles from Cheyenne to Custer it charged twenty dollars to through travelers buying combined stagecoach–Union Pacific Railroad tickets; more economical were the fees for accompanying its wagon trains—fifteen dollars second class (four days' travel time) and ten dollars third class (six days). On September 25, Gilmer, Salisbury and Patrick extended their stage line to Deadwood. The through trip took forty-seven to fifty-two hours in dry weather, sixty to seventy when the roads were muddy. Gilmer, Salisbury and Patrick sold their stage line to Russell Thorp in May, 1883; he continued operations until 1887, when railroads had come to serve most of its area.

In 1876, stage service began from Sidney, a town on the Union Pacific Railroad some 102 miles east of Cheyenne, to Deadwood; to passengers from the eastern states it offered a shorter distance over a better road than that of the stage from Cheyenne. Two years earlier, service began from Fort Pierre, approximately due east of Deadwood, and from Bismarck, to the northeast, both in Dakota Territory. Each coach on the Fort Pierre route was accompanied by a through messenger who had charge of all mail and express, checked the time of drivers between stations, collected the money at meal stations, and made himself generally useful. Eventually stages also ran to Deadwood from Medora, Dakota Territory.

Even in such a lively mining camp the arrival of the stages, especially the daily one from Cheyenne, was an important event. A distinctive rumble unmistakably announced its approach when it was a mile away. It swept into town, a fine sight, with a beautiful team of six white horses and a skillful driver, all conscious they were the center of attention. True, this was a specially selected team and man, better than found on any other stretch of the road; it was intentionally a show and people enjoyed it.

An important assignment undertaken by Gilmer, Salisbury and Patrick was to handle gold dust in express shipments on their Cheyenne-Deadwood stages. At first it was carried on any scheduled run in a chilled-steel container known as a "salamander," which was protected with heavy locks and secured to the coach's floor in some manner. In 1878, the firm put into service two special coaches, called "The Iron Clad" or "The Monitor," with an interior lining of steel plates, five-sixteenths of an inch thick, which, tests showed, could easily turn aside rifle fire from a distance of fifty feet. When outbound, these treasure coaches would not carry passengers; instead, there were eight guards—four in the coach, two on horseback in advance, and two to the rear—armed with rifles, six-shooters, and sawed-off shotguns.

There was lawlessness, at first attributed only to the Indians, along the Cheyenne to Deadwood road the stages traveled. By early 1877, some of the crimes were quite peculiar for red men to commit. Thus two mail carriers were killed and scalped in traditional fashion; however, the only thing taken from their sacks was registered mail. It gradually became clear that along the road there were many bands of outlaws, not just one.

An obvious target for robbery was the stagecoach and the frequency of the holdups increased until they became almost routine hazards of the road. The brigands usually lined the passengers up in a row, had them empty their pockets, then examined their hats, inspected the women's hair (often long enough to serve as an effective hiding place), passed their hands over everybody's clothing for unnatural bumps or bulges, and finally searched the men's boots and the women's shoes.

Only once was the famous treasure coach robbed. On September 26, 1878, at the stage stop of Cold Springs, five bandits captured the station and gagged the employees. When the unsuspecting driver brought the southbound coach to a halt and threw down his lines, they sent a hail of bullets at it, killing one guard and a passenger for whom an exception to the rigidly enforced rule had been made. The company's armed men retreated to the adjacent timber, maintaining a heavy answering fire. The bandits captured the driver, used him as a shield, and threatened to kill him if the messengers did not stop all shooting. Their demand was met, the guards retreating farther; the thieves then extracted about $27,000, bound the driver to a wheel of the coach and made their escape. They were recognized and pursued; within six weeks, three-fifths of the money was recovered.

The development of freight transport matched that of passenger service.[3] The chief method was to haul the freight in by ox team from Sidney or Cheyenne on the Union Pacific Railroad, from Bismarck or Dickinson on the Northern Pacific Railroad, or from Pierre, where it arrived at first on Missouri River steamships and in later years on Chicago and North Western trains. The freighters used wagons, manufactured by Studebaker Brothers, with square boxes and canvas tops. To a large lead vehicle and two shorter trailing ones they hitched twelve yoke of oxen. If they were operating on a large scale, they dispatched twelve such teams together in what was called a "bull outfit," supervised by a wagon master who had complete command while on the road. He traveled about ten miles a day, mostly during the cool period; sometimes he rested his oxen from nine or ten o'clock in the morning until three or four in the afternoon, then drove long after dark. On steep, descending mountain grades he often used heavy chains, known as "rough locks," to hold the wheels immobile. At the night stop he habitually placed his wagons in a circle or corral. Where the ground proved soft or muddy, he turned his train aside to make a new road; those following later used it for a while, until it, too, became worn down, then either went back to the old road or else started a third one. There were almost no bridges; fording was necessary. Sometimes when a stream was at flood stage and the crossing had a bottom of quicksand, the feat was difficult; once, under unusual circumstances at the Platte River crossing of the Sidney Trail, twenty-one yoke of oxen were required to get a single wagon across.

The work of the drivers, or bullwhackers, was hard and they generally took their pleasures strenuously. Unique was Madame Canutson, the only lady bullwhacker in the business, who simultaneously drove ten yoke of oxen between Deadwood and Pierre and took care of her year-old baby while her husband worked on their homestead. She was widely admired for her skill in handling her animals, and when she addressed them, it was generally admitted that her vocabulary of profanities equaled that of the most proficient men.

Some of the freighting was done by individuals acting independ-

3 Brown and Willard, Trails, 68–70, 432, 448–49; Tallent, Black Hills, 189–92; Briggs, "Early Freight and Stage Lines in Dakota," North Dakota Historical Quarterly, Vol. III (1928–29), 244–52, 260; Kingsbury, History, 1140; Briggs, "The Black Hills Gold Rush," North Dakota Historical Quarterly, Vol. V (1930–31), 87–99; Bennett, Days, 97–98; Spring, Routes, 172–77; McClintock, Pioneer Days, 63–64.

ently; much of it was in the hands of a few major concerns. On March 26, 1876, the Merchants Transportation Company began operations from Fort Pierre, across the river from Pierre, to Deadwood. It charged $4.75 to haul one hundred pounds of freight. By the next spring, the line had enough business to dispatch west from Fort Pierre each Monday a wagon train with a carrying capacity of seven hundred tons. It soon had competition on the route from the Northwestern Express and Forwarding Company, the Witcher Company, and the F. T. Evans Freight Line. In 1876, the Northwestern Express Stage and Transportation Company started freight service from Bismarck, and Gilmer, Salisbury and Patrick operated wagon trains from Cheyenne.

On the Missouri River were the six large steamers of the S. B. Coulson Line, operating northwestward from Yankton to Fort Pierre and Bismarck. They had competitors. One indication of the size of these various river operations is the fact that at the end of the season of navigation in 1880, fifteen steamboats were placed in winter storage at Yankton.

Quick freight, so called, was a wagon hauled by four or six horses or mules. It carried items for which there was a heavy demand in the Black Hills, such as butter, eggs, dressed hogs, sausages, and lard; charged eight, ten, or even fifteen cents a pound for its service; and made a good profit. Another kind of service was the "shotgun freight outfit"; its owner bought supplies for which there was a demand in the mining area, hauled them in, and sold them. Most runs were prosaic, but not the one on which the dance-hall girls of Deadwood asked Phatty Thompson to bring them some cats for pets. He procured his supply by telling the children of Cheyenne that he would pay twenty-five cents for each cat, with no questions asked about who owned it, and quickly accumulated a wagonload. He encountered objections only from a German brewer, who accused him of having the family's pet stolen, and the two engaged in an animated conversation with voices that could have served as foghorns; Phatty finally surrendered the disputed animal. On the return trip he upset his wagon and distributed his load along a gulch. He put out some food and lured all of the cats back except one, which climbed a tree and did not respond favorably to his profanity; some passing miners helped him recapture it. When he got to Deadwood, he found a very brisk demand for cats from the girls and also from many men who wanted a pet. He sold no cat for less than ten dollars and for some he got as much as twenty-five.

An important transportation service was carrying the mail.[4] At first the United States government did not provide service to the Black Hills because the area still officially belonged to the Indians and was closed to whites. Mail was brought in by wagon trains. Upon arrival at the store to which the train's freight was consigned, the mail was alphabetized. A man then stood on a box in the street and read off names while a helper collected from the recipients fifty cents a letter and twenty-five cents a newspaper. Later a list of mail not yet claimed was posted. In August, 1876, Richard Seymour and Charles Utter started as a private enterprise a weekly pony-express service from Fort Laramie to Deadwood; before long they had competition from H. T. Clark's Centennial Express, operating from Sidney to the Black Hills. The partners charged twenty-five cents a letter in addition to the regular postage, Clark ten cents. Clark provided his customers with Centennial envelopes, so small they could be enclosed in ordinary envelopes outbound from the Black Hills and thus insure a prompt reply. Late in the year the Cheyenne stage line of Gilmer, Salisbury and Patrick started hauling the mail as a private venture. In March, 1877, it got a formal federal contract to provide the service and in April one was given to operator of the Sidney stage line.

A telegraph line from Cheyenne to Deadwood was built by Willard H. Hibbard. When he exhausted his own money, he raised five thousand dollars more from Black Hills businessmen by selling them scrip to be used later to pay message charges. Hibbard completed his line on December 1, 1876.

The area's first railroad was the Black Hills and Fort Pierre, a narrow-gauge line owned by the Homestake Mining Company. In 1881, it was opened from Lead to Woodville, twenty miles, chiefly to haul timber for mine operations. In 1885, the standard-gauge Fremont, Elkhorn and Missouri Valley Railway, a subsidiary of the Chicago and North Western which was subsequently incorporated

---

4 Brown and Willard, Trails, 86, 94, 276, 421–22; Casey, Incredible Characters, 235; Briggs, "Early Freight and Stage Lines in Dakota," North Dakota Historical Quarterly, Vol. III (1928–29), 253; Tallent, Black Hills, 193–97, 377–79; Irving, Economic Resources, 61; Kingsbury, History, 983, 1453; Peattie, Black Hills, 286; Spring, Routes, 151–69.

into the parent organization, reached Rapid City from Omaha, extended to Whitewood in 1887, and in 1890 entered Deadwood. The Burlington and Missouri River Railroad, eventually combined with its parent, the Chicago, Burlington and Quincy, built from Edgemont, at the extreme southwestern edge of South Dakota, to Deadwood and Lead. After 1891, the two major railroads competed sharply for mineral business and built spurs to every mine of importance. In 1901, the Homestake Company sold to the Burlington Route its narrow-gauge line, which it had gradually extended to a connection with the Chicago and North Western at Piedmont.

The city which first seemed destined to dominate the Black Hills was Custer.[5] In March, 1876, it organized the Custer Minute Men, a group of 125 men ready to chase off the Indians who occasionally appeared to do mischief on its outer fringes of settlement. It ambitiously established what it called the Provisional Black Hills Superior Court, which was to have jurisdiction in all matters over the whole area until regular courts were opened; this temporary tribunal proved to be of little importance. In the summer of 1876, Custer opened a public school, the first in the Black Hills, with Carrie Scott as teacher. The town's fortunes began to decline as the rich discoveries around Deadwood increasingly attracted prospectors to the northern part of the Black Hills, yet it endured permanently because it was a convenient stopping place on a main route into the region.

The site of Deadwood was laid out on April 26, 1876, by Craven Lee, Isaac Brown, J. J. Williams, and others at a point below the junction of Deadwood and Whitewood creeks.[6] The town received its name from the large number of dead trees in the area, a characteristic of several locations in the Black Hills, caused, as later scientific investigations revealed, by an invasion of pine beetles in prehistoric times. The town grew rapidly, by autumn having a population of about seven thousand. It was so crowded during its early boom days that for sleeping purposes both beds and chairs were at a premium; those who could afford neither simply curled up near some building. To buy a meal without dessert generally cost one dollar.

5 Tallent, *Black Hills*, 287–91, 408–409.
6 Brown and Willard, *Trails*, 463–72; Tallent, *Black Hills*, 346, 361, 375–76, 489; Bennett, *Days*, 5, 20–21; Hughes, *Pioneer Years*, 104, 109–12, 346; Spring, *Routes*, 308; McClintock, *Pioneer Days*, 63, 72, 75, 141.

The settlement expanded along the gulch, partly with substantial log houses, partly with cabins built of green lumber and so frail that a man feared to lean against a wall lest he push it down. Merchants were so uncertain how long the camp would remain prosperous that many of them preferred to pay a high rental fee rather than build. After supper in the early days somebody at one end of the gulch usually cried "Oh, Joe!" The shout was taken up by his neighbor and gradually spread with increasing volume until it finally died away at the other end of the gulch. How or why this unusual custom arose, nobody knew. For the first two or three years there was only one main street and virtually no cross streets. This was either aswirl with dry dust or knee deep in mud, with very few plank crossings. Another problem was the congestion of ox-drawn wagons, sometimes blocking the street for half a day at a time; over or through them, men, but not women, dared to climb.

As Deadwood grew, side streets developed at right angles to the chief thoroughfare and climbed up the sides of the gulch. At Mc-Govern Hill, the principal avenue split, with one arm, called Main Street, following Deadwood Creek, while the other, Sherman Street, went along Whitewood Creek.

The spreading settlement faced a problem of land title. The miners who had earlier staked claims insisted that they were entitled to the surface the width of the gulch. Those who wished to use the area for commercial or residential purposes alleged that the prospectors could only use as much of the ground as was necessary to extract minerals. Often the miners seized the initiative by proposing to sink a shaft from the middle of a building already optimistically erected by a squatter and then settled the matter for a good price by signing a release, sometimes called "bedrock title."

In September, 1876, the citizens of Deadwood had to organize a municipal government, termed "provisional" because Deadwood was still an illegal settlement within an Indian reservation. They had managed well enough at first without local authorities; then it became apparent that unless the respectable element took action, the town would fall under the domination of a lawless group.

As the town boomed, most businessmen, whatever their line, made more money than they had anticipated. In business the last of September, 1876, the town had one assayer, four auctioneers, a bath-house, three butchers, two blacksmiths, one banker, two breweries, four billiards establishments, three barbershops, six bakeries, eleven clothing stores, a dentist, five doctors, four druggists, one dry-goods shop, two dance halls, three fruit dealers, fourteen gambling houses, twenty-one grocers, two hardware merchants, five hotels, three jewelers, four drayage firms, eight laundries, seven lawyers, three livery stables, one milliner, one newspaper, three painters, a photographer, three shops selling earthenware, six restaurants, twenty-seven saloons, two sawmills, three shoemakers, and three tailors. For miners and skilled mechanics, the pay that fall was five to seven dollars a day.

In the early days the chief money circulating was gold dust or gold coin; only a few paper dollars floated around before the turn of the century.[7] Many men carried money in larger amounts than most people do nowadays. The weight—for example, one and one-half pounds for five hundred dollars in gold—was enough for them usually to hang their pants on a stout hook at night. In stores, merchants evaluated gold dust with scales and a "blower," a shallow receptacle, six inches wide at one end and three at the other, from which they gently shook the dust proffered by a customer while blowing on it to separate impurities from the pure gold deposited on the scale pan. The Miner's and Mechanic's Bank, Deadwood's first, opened in the summer of 1876 and initially had only an ordinary iron safe in which to keep money. The chief business was gold dust—buying it, selling it, and shipping it for its owners to the United States Assay Office, which tested it and then bought it, with a certified check as payment. To handle the gold, the banks charged two dollars an ounce, virtually a 10 per cent fee.

Deadwood's first newspaper was the *Black Hills Weekly Pioneer*, which began continuous publication on June 8, 1876.[8] Its copies sold at twenty-five cents each, a price insuring a substantial profit. Waiting at the printing plant on the days of publication was a line of customers until well along in the evening. The town's first daily, the *Times*, first appeared on April 7, 1877, and on May 15, the *Pioneer*, too, became a daily; eventually, five papers were publishing simultaneously. They were intense rivals, indulging among themselves in much bitter controversy and vituperative abuse. They em-

[7] Tallent, *Black Hills*, 274; Hughes, *Pioneer Years*, 110; Casey, *Incredible Characters*, 222–24.

[8] Hughes, *Pioneer Years*, 119–20; Brown and Willard, *Trails*, 487; Tallent, *Black Hills*, 269–71.

ployed excellent writers and also made considerable use of telegraphic news, for despite its excessive cost, none could do competitive battle without it.

A major recreation in Deadwood was attending the theater.[9] Its first stars were John S. Langrishe and his wife. They were talented and could have had a good career in the East, but they chose to spend their lives on the frontier. They began their acting in San Francisco in the early 1850's, later went to Colorado, and then in July, 1876, arrived in Deadwood. They charged an admission of $1.50 for sitting or standing room. Although Langrishe was an all-round actor, he was best at comedy; he was held in high esteem both for his dramatic abilities and his sterling qualities as a man. At one of his performances Mrs. Adams, wife of the postmaster, caused considerable discussion when from their box seats she and her guests used, with many a flourish, the first pair of opera glasses in town. A few nights later an old prospector got a seat up front; when the performance was well launched, he pulled out a board two feet long and six inches wide with two beer bottles stuck in it. As Langrishe appeared on stage, the old-timer raised the board to his eyes in an affected manner and peered through the bottles. The veteran actor forgot his lines, the whole group on stage joined in the laughter, and even Mrs. Adams, who was there, thought it funny. After some three years in the Black Hills, the Langrishes returned to Colorado.

Another theatrical enterprise in Deadwood, well known but considerably less reputable, was the Gem Theater, managed by Al Swearengen. It secured some of the best traveling companies available and was the first to persuade the Sioux Indians to stage their war, squaw, and scalp dances for the entertainment of the palefaces. Tarnishing the Gem's reputation considerably was the regular sequel to each performance: the girls who had been performing on stage now devoted themselves, for pay, to the pleasure of the male audience. Each dance—and there was informal dancing after performances— ended with the caller's saying, "All promenade to the bar and make room for the ladies." At the end of any drink the man might go away with the girl. The last dance was "The Hack-Driver's Quadrille." During the prosperous years, the Gem took in five thousand dollars on an ordinary night and sometimes as much as ten. For

9 Bennett, *Days*, 6, 21-24, 106-22; Hughes, *Pioneer Years*, 113; Peattie, *Black Hills*, 114; Tallent, *Black Hills*, 277-78; McClintock, *Pioneer Days*, 70-75.

scores of girls, many of whom were quite innocent upon arrival, this perhaps meant suicide, but much more likely it simply foreshadowed drifting into a bad life. Little attention was paid to this at the time, but many years later a county official inspecting the undertaker's records of the 1880's was appalled at the number of girls who had taken their own lives but had been listed in the local newspapers as victims of pneumonia or mountain fever. The only one of them to defy Al Swearengen was a singer named Inez Sexton; given the alternative of rustling the boxes or shooting herself, she walked penniless out of the theater, took a hotel room, and told the owner her story. He spread it, the church people arranged a musical to benefit her, and with the proceeds she left the Black Hills forever.

A step down from the Gem was the red light district, the so-called bad lands, where the police never interfered after six in the evening. The span of glory which the girls there had was so obviously brief that it left little illusion in the mind of the town's youngsters about the desirability of such a life.

In addition to the usual complement of saloons, there were quite a few gambling establishments spread throughout Deadwood. Some were notorious, others honest. A problem faced by even the best ones was the loser who loudly but falsely proclaimed that he had been cheated, when in reality fortune had simply been against him; the usual technique was to eject him so forcefully that he did not care to return. The gambling influence was widespread enough in the town for the four young children of Judge Granville G. Bennett to play poker for matches, the loser going to bed in the dark, until their father discovered and stopped the practice.

In the summer of 1876, three partnerships—Mark V. Broughton and Oliver Dotson, John and Rasse Deffenbach, and the Ward brothers—brought herds of beef cattle to the Black Hills.[10] Some were sold to miners as meat; the rest were stolen by the Indians. Later, other herds were brought in, for the Black Hills was an ideal stock-raising area, and by the turn of the century more than 300,000 cattle were grazing there. In 1878, John D. Hale drove in a large number of hogs, which he quickly sold to miners; in 1879 and in 1880, he imported more, on the hoof. Feed for horses was so expensive in Deadwood that those not needed for immediate use were sent to

[10] McClintock, *Pioneer Days*, 77–78, 226; Brown and Willard, *Trails*, 100–101, 482–84; Tallent, *Black Hills*, 353; Hughes, *Pioneer Years*, 92; Bennett, *Days*, 15, 93.

the fertile valleys of the foothills. Many of them were kept in the so-called Montana herd, whose owners charged two dollars a month, cash in advance, to care for an animal and maintained a daily service to deliver horses to town. Some pioneers quickly turned from mining to farming on the plains immediately adjacent to the Black Hills. They did not raise any fresh vegetables until the latter 1880's; consequently, these and fruit commanded enormous prices at Deadwood. Apples, which were imported during the winter, generally arrived frozen solid and the merchants made them into cider. For those who had time to gather them, there were wild chokecherries, Oregon grapes, serviceberries, and red raspberries.

The first school in Deadwood was a private one, opened in the autumn of 1876 by William Commode. The next fall, there was a public school, with Dolph Edwards and Eva Deffenbacher as teachers.[11]

As early as 1877, Deadwood had a Chinatown. Eventually it became quite large and had many laundries, numerous gambling games, and a Chinese temple.[12] There were shops filled with Oriental silks, china, sandalwood, teak, carved ivory, and embroideries. The Orientals held colorful funerals, marching along and scattering little pieces of paper, which were intended to divert the Devil's attention away from the dead. Most Chinese men wore long shirts and loose, dull-blue trousers. Some of them sold opium, but nobody thought much about it. All Chinese women lived in the red-light district—except one. She was the wife of the leading Chinese merchant, Wing Tsue, who brought her over from the old country to a house which was ordinary looking outside but which within was heavily draped, thickly carpeted, and filled with teak and enamel goods. She never spoke a word of English, although her children went to the public school and to Sunday School. The whole family eventually returned to China. Apparently, in Deadwood there was not much of the prejudice against Chinese so abundant elsewhere.

The first minister active in the Black Hills was the Reverend Henry Weston Smith of the Methodist Church.[13] He arrived in Custer, held his first service for miners on May 7, 1876, then walked on to Dead-

11 Tallent, *Black Hills*, 350, 484.
12 Brown and Willard, *Trails*, 357; Bennett, *Days*, 27–30.
13 Bennett, *Days*, 174–85; Brown and Willard, *Trails*, 396–98; Tallent, *Black Hills*, 275.

wood. There, generally mounted on a dry-goods box or other informal platform at the corner of Main and Gold streets, he held
outdoor meetings and was never without an audience. On August
20, he set out for neighboring Crook City, unarmed, despite warnings,
and met his death at the hands of Indians.

The first Deadwood church building, completed by the Congrega-
tionalists in July, 1877, was at the foot of McGovern Hill. At the
first tolling of its Missouri River steamboat bell, twenty or thirty
men at work in their placer claims on Deadwood Creek straightened
up from their tasks, removed their hats, and stood at reverent attention until the last echo died away down the gulch; they never mentioned the incident afterwards, but it was observed. The only Deadwood preacher ever to attack "King Faro, Prince Stud Poker, Bacchus
and Gambrinus," as well as female depravity, was the newly arrived
R. H. Dolliver. When the local newspapers commented mildly that
he might like the town better after living in it longer and perhaps
should suspend judgment meanwhile, he took the hint. The most
unusual experience of a Deadwood minister was likely that of an
Episcopalian named Molyneux, who was called to the bedside of a
dying miner named Sam Huston. While Molyneux was there, the
mortally ill man lay with one of his two partners sitting at one side
of the bed and the second at the other. Several times the two inquired
if Huston had on his mind anything he would like to say. Finally he
whispered: "I wanted to die like our Lord—between two thieves."

Deadwood, like most mining towns, had several disasters.[14] The
first was a three-day snowstorm in March, 1878, which deposited
seven feet of snow on the level of the adjoining prairie. A second
disaster struck at 2:20 A.M. on September 26, 1879, when a fire started
from an upset coal-oil lamp at the Empire Bakery. The flames spread
to the hardware store of Jensen and Bliss, touched off eight kegs of
blasting powder, showered sparks in all directions, and started many
new fires. Shortly it destroyed the building of the fire department,
with most of the equipment still inside; this, plus an inadequate
water system, made the city nearly helpless. Hundreds of people
climbed the side of the gulch with a few valuables and watched their
other property go up in flames. The conflagration consumed everything in an area one-half mile long and a quarter of a mile wide.

14 Brown and Willard, *Trails*, 437–39, 450–51; Tallent, *Black Hills*, 486–90.

In May, 1883, came the third disaster, a big flood, doing in all about a quarter of a million dollars' worth of damage.

Four people stand out in Deadwood's history as unique.[15] One was Robert Jones, a miner generally known as "Smokey," a man with straggly beard and hair worn down to his shoulders, famous for his excellent imitation of the howl of a timber wolf. Eventually he discovered a mine, sold it for a good price, and left the area. Later he returned, well dressed, smooth shaven, and with hair neatly cut. He went unrecognized until one evening at the theater he supplemented the applause by a wolf howl from his box.

Deadwood Dick was a notorious young desperado, a character existing only in fiction yet more widely known than all but two of the Black Hills area's inhabitants. He was an important hero of dime novels, those sensational, poorly written stories so dear to the hearts of the younger generation and so roundly denounced by Sunday School teachers. He appeared in the Beadle and Adams *Half-Dime Library*, each paper-backed issue of which contained a story of 35,000 to 40,000 words printed in sixteen pages of rather small type. His author, Edward L. Wheeler, wrote the first story in 1877 and produced thirty-two more before killing Dick off beyond revival. Perhaps Wheeler was not the murderer, since the story appeared about the time of his own death in 1885. Interest in the series was so strong, however, that Deadwood Dick, Jr., arose to ride through ninety-seven stories, author or authors unknown. In these yarns the geography was quite inaccurate, but would seem convincing to one who knew nothing of the Black Hills.

Wild Bill Hickok's last days were spent in Deadwood. James Butler Hickok was born in La Salle county, Illinois, in 1837, grew up on what was then the western frontier, helped his father spirit Negro slaves to freedom along the Underground Railroad, acted as a Kansas constable, served on the Santa Fe Trail, participated in the Civil War, and then for three years was scout and dispatch rider with

[15] Hughes, *Pioneer Years*, 68, 158–64; Edmund Pearson, *Dime Novels; or, Following An Old Trail in Popular Literature*, 202–205; Albert Johannsen, *The House of Beadle and Adams and Its Dime and Nickel Novels*, I, 5–6, 294–96; McClintock, *Pioneer Days*, 106, 118, 134; WPA, *South Dakota*, 109; Peattie, *Black Hills*, 155–58, 165–72; Casey, *Incredible Characters*, 157, 163, 175–77; Brown and Willard, *Trails*, 402–17; Duncan Aikman, *Calamity Jane and the Lady Wildcats*, 20–113.

General Custer. He next became the peace officer in Hays, Kansas, and then at Abilene, Kansas, where his salary was reported to be one thousand dollars a month. He then moved on to other ventures, including two unsuccessful attempts at the "Wild West" show business. He was, some writers have theorized, essentially a man of the frontier whose real problem was that the conditions he understood were too quickly swept aside by the advance of civilization. However that may be, certainly while he was alive he had with the public a greater reputation as a gunman than anybody else, except possibly Wyatt Earp. Hickok could probably draw faster and shoot more rapidly and more accurately than any other man then living. He killed many men, most likely twenty-seven, although nobody cared to ask him. He was always within the law and justified, usually being a trifle too quick for the other fellow. Hickok was neither wild, boisterous, nor quarrelsome; he was quite mannered, absolutely fearless, and always in control of himself, although quick tempered. He came to Deadwood in 1876 as a professional gambler. Although he was careful to observe the ethics of that fraternity, he apparently collected some winnings because his opponents did not care to discuss the fine points of the game with him. On the morning of August 2, 1876, he was gambling in a saloon called Number 10 with several men; Jack McCall threw his sack of gold dust into the pot and shortly Hickok won it all. Although Wild Bill was a bit irritated when examination revealed that the sack was about three dollars short of what it should have been, there was no altercation. That afternoon, he violated his usual rule of never sitting where he could not see everybody who entered the room; McCall came up behind him and shot him dead.

Closely linked with Wild Bill Hickok's name in the myths of the West is that of Martha Jane Canary, generally called Calamity Jane. Most of her history has been so embroidered that the statements which can be made about her with certainty are surprisingly few. She was born about 1851 and grew up in Missouri, whether of dissolute parents or not is debatable. How she came west and precisely what she was doing in the years from 1860 to 1875 is not known. Certainly she gained experience as a prostitute, became expert at tying a diamond hitch, learned how to handle teams, and often wore men's attire; she could swear like a trooper, drink like a sailor, and rough it with the roughest. Probably she served as a teamster with the troops attached to Jenney's geological survey of 1875. It is usually said that she was with General Crook's forces in 1876 and that officers did not learn of her presence until they spied her form among those of troops taking a swim.

Jane entered Deadwood for the first time in early August, 1876. That she knew Hickok more than slightly cannot be proved; that she was his mistress is false. It is not even certain that at the time she came to the Black Hills she was beautiful and had a fine figure, although more writers speak for her on both counts than speak against her. Jane is generally reported to have been openhanded in helping the unfortunate. During the smallpox epidemic of 1878, she willingly acted as a nurse to the afflicted when nobody else would do so, despite the warning of Dr. L. F. Babcock that she might (but did not) lose a most important asset to a woman of her character, her "good looks."

Calamity could play the role of a real lady when she wished. She was always very fond of children and watched her conduct when among them. After staying in the Black Hills for several years, she wandered away and returned again in 1895. That she was someone special is proved by the actions of the notables of the town, respectable citizens all, who welcomed her back when she got off the train. In telling of her, old-timers seem never to have remembered her faults; certainly they did not think they were of any importance. No doubt in another age and environment she might have been a famous horsewoman, a distinguished athlete, a resourceful spy, or a nurse at the battle front where the need was greatest.

How to maintain law and order was a problem which faced the pioneer miners in Deadwood.[16] They solved it in traditional ways, probably because many of the men had taken part in earlier mining rushes elsewhere. The first major test came when Jack Hinch was murdered. A participant in the deed, John R. Carty, was returned to Deadwood by Deputy United States Marshal I. C. Davis. When most men of the town assembled as a miners' court, many of Hinch's friends talked of summary punishment and many of Carty's of a fair trial. Both groups were heavily armed. Despite the excitement,

16 Tallent, *Black Hills,* 364–66; McClintock, *Pioneer Days,* 105, 141, 269; Hughes, *Pioneer Years,* 114–17. 153–56, 162–67, 196–200; Casey, *Incredible Characters,* 141, 156, 163; Brown and Willard, *Trails,* 287–340, 349, 407–10; Bennett, *Days,* 36, 41–42.

the crowd promptly elected a judge and a jury. The throng was by now so large that no building in Deadwood could have held a tenth of it. Adjacent to the outdoor spot where the trial was being conducted was a partially finished log cabin with light spruce poles as rafters. Over these spectators swarmed for seats, despite the fears of the owner that the weight would break them. His warnings and demands met with nothing but laughter until he reappeared with a shotgun trained on the men and shouted, "Now, damn you, will you climb down?" They did.

Meanwhile, tempers and tension mounted at the trial until the threat of lynching Carty was serious. Up rose courageous federal officer Davis, demanding a fair trial, promising that he would help hang the accused if found guilty, and warning that in the meantime those who would injure Carty would first have to walk over his own dead body. The proper procedures then continued without further interruption. The evidence revealed that Carty was simply an accessory to murder, since he did not inflict the fatal injuries, and his punishment was fixed at being escorted out of town on August 2, 1876.

That was the day, by coincidence, that Jack McCall shot Wild Bill Hickok; why he did it, nobody really knows. He was promptly captured. The next morning, the prosecuting attorney, the defense counsel, and a jury were chosen; the trial got under way. McCall claimed that Hickok had killed his brother in Kansas. The jury apparently believed him, for it ruled that he was not guilty of murder. Later he was so ill advised as to boast in a Cheyenne saloon that the story about his brother was not true. He was arrested by federal officials, taken before a federal court, and his protests against double jeopardy were brushed aside. He was tried, convicted, and hanged.

Another event causing much discussion occurred at a vaudeville show. Singer Dick Brown was on stage when Ed Shaughnessy walked down the aisle and threw an ax onto the platform with unfriendly intent; Brown drew a revolver and killed him. At the trial, he successfully pleaded self-defense, saying that female singer Fannie Garretson had come to the Black Hills with him, leaving Shaughnessy, who had then followed them, seeking revenge. To a newspaper whose account stated she was Shaughnessy's wife, Fannie wrote a letter complaining that their report injured her reputation—she had never been his wife, she said; she had simply lived with him.

When Deadwood established a temporary local government in

September, 1876, it also opened a provisonal court. Since the tribunal had no legal standing, it handled only minor matters, such as assault, petty thievery, and disturbing the peace, which could be settled by a fine or a short term in the local jail. For major crimes and cases, the miners' court served. In September, a vigilance committe was organized; it took no action and at last disbanded, but its mere existence restrained the lawless; there was never a lynching in Deadwood. Outside the city it was tacitly understood that those clearly guilty of horse stealing would be hanged when captured.

In Deadwood's early days, individuals who had altercations which in a more settled community would have caused them to hire lawyers often settled the matter out of court in a manner likely to call for the services of an undertaker. The majority of these fatalities came from a dispute over priority rights to mineral land, town lots, or a woman of ill repute. Deadwood's skilled gunmen, Wyatt Earp told his biographer Stuart Lake, were, as a group, as good as could be found in any town of the frontier West except perhaps Tombstone. Pioneer Deadwood had no pickpockets, burglars, or embezzlers, perhaps because a speedy getaway was impossible. This meant that a man's cash was safe in his pocket on the street day or night and also in a gambling or dance hall until he voluntarily pulled it out. If a man was not judicious, his money might fall into the hands of the gang of "sharpers" led by "Ten Die" Brown, whose chief associates were "Pancake Bill," an expert decoy or capper for games of chance which the victim had no chance of winning, "Kentuck," whose air of diffidence and deference made him the town's most successful capper, and "The Miner," who posed as a hard-working prospector soliciting capital to develop a mine.

The first legal court session was held in Deadwood on June 5, 1877, after the President had appointed Granville G. Bennett federal judge.[17] About ten o'clock that morning the lawyers could all be seen heading toward the improvised courtroom, chairs in hand, since none were available there; at the session about fifty attorneys were admitted to practice before the bar. Most of the cases coming before Bennett involved conflicts over mining property, and many of his decisions helped to create and interpret Dakota's mining laws. In one unusual case he ruled that miners on strike who had settled

17 Bennett, Days, 39, 41–42, 51–52; Tallent, Black Hills, 383; Kingsbury, History, 981; Lamar, Dakota Territory, 171.

down to live in the mine tunnel had to leave the property. Disobeyed, he had them removed, uninjured, by dropping enough asafetida down the shaft to make a stench.

Bennett had not held office long before the Homestake Mining Company offered him a chance to buy two thousand shares of its stock, his payments for it to be extended over as long a period as necessary; he refused. In 1878, Bennett became territorial delegate to Congress. His judicial post was taken by Gideon C. Moody, who had denounced the jury which freed the gunmen of the Homestake organization in a murder trial. Moody made various decisions on mineral and water rights which involved millions of dollars' worth of property. He then retired to become an attorney for the Homestake Mining Company, a leader in the Republican party, and, after South Dakota had become a state, a United States senator.

When the Black Hills were legally removed from the Sioux reservation, they became a part of Dakota Territory. In February, 1877, the territorial legislature organized there three new counties: Lawrence, Pennington, and Custer.[18] It also empowered Governor John L. Pennington to appoint the first sheriff, prosecuting attorney, district judge, and three county commissioners. As commissioners he named a man from each of the two leading towns and another from the territorial capital of Yankton. Their first major task was to select a county seat. When the decision was finally made, the outsider cast his vote for the home town of one of the local commissioners. Another question was how long these various officials whom Governor Pennington had appointed should hold office before there was an election. They all insisted there should be none until 1878, but the law courts ruled that one had to be held immediately.

These first local elections were of special interest to the professional politicians who had come in with the miners in the hope that they would find their bonanza in the new governmental structure. Perhaps the classic example of a man seeking political advantage in a new mining area was James Clagett. He began in Nevada by serving in the house of representatives, both territorial and state; transferred to Montana, becoming territorial delegate to Congress; went to Colorado, where he found no political success; shifted to the Black Hills, where a profitable law practice offset his political failure; re-

18 Lamar, *Dakota Territory*, 159–270; Brown and Willard, *Trails*, 241, 353, 364–65; Tallent, *Black Hills*, 380, 397; Kingsbury, *History*, 976.

turned to Montana, where he tried mining but made little money; and moved to Idaho, acting as president of the state constitutional convention and then twice failing to win election as a United States senator. Such men as Clagett took leading roles in the Black Hills county elections in the fall of 1877. One set of candidates ran on the Democratic ticket; the other, actually Republican, called itself the People's party. Issues in the campaign were unimportant and personalities everything. At the polls the voters returned almost no officials who had been appointed by Governor Pennington. One of the disappointed ones was Seth Bullock, sheriff of Lawrence County, who had hired a large number of soldiers from Fort Meade to dress in civilian clothing and cast illegal ballots for him in the town of Sturgis. His opponent, learning of the scheme, had offered more money and so switched the vote. Bullock lost the election because of the ballots against him in Sturgis.

In July, 1877, the people of the Black Hills petitioned Congress to separate them from Dakota and make them a new territory called Lincoln, but they were unsuccessful. In that same year there was, for the first time, serious talk of making Dakota a state. It had more than the required minimum population, but the estimated cost of the proposed new government was more than most people thought the residents of the area could afford. Discussion continued at various times, prompted by such things as the colonial status of any territorial government and the obvious corruption of Governor Nehemiah G. Ordway, in office from 1880 to 1884. Generally there was apathy toward statehood; neither the farmers nor the miners were much interested, although some townspeople were. Finally, in 1889, Congress created North Dakota, South Dakota, Montana, and Washington as states. In South Dakota the framework of the new government was created chiefly by Republican lawyers and businessmen; the Farmers' Alliance, so active in economic matters, and the miners had virtually no connection with it.

Another problem which concerned people in the Dakotas was the Sioux reservation, created when the red men gave up the Black Hills.[19] Its twenty-one million acres of land divided the Black Hills from the rest of the territory. The whites argued that this was more land than was needed for twenty-four thousand Indians. The gov-

[19] Tallent, *Black Hills*, 697–99; Kingsbury, *History*, 1233–90.

ernment proposed to sell about nine million acres and divide the remainder into five reservations. In 1883, it secured the signatures of the chiefs and headmen approving the plan, but Congress rejected the treaty because it had not been signed by three-fourths of the adult Sioux males. From studies of the matter published thus far, the question appears to have been not whether a sale should be arranged but what the price should be. Finally, in 1889, a new agreement was made and ratified. For their acreages white homesteaders were to pay the tribe $1.25 an acre for land claimed within the first three years the act was in effect, seventy-five cents an acre for the next two years, and, finally, fifty cents an acre for the next five. For all then remaining unsold, the federal government was to pay the Sioux fifty cents an acre; it also presented them at once with a three-million-dollar bonus for signing the treaty.

The Black Hills mining rush was unique in its occupancy of an area which was supposedly reserved forever to the red men. Their resistance to its onslaught was never effective enough to halt the prospectors. Custer's disaster doomed any possibility that the Sioux would be paid a fair price for the gold area they surrendered. The whites worked first at placer deposits and then on lodes, following methods typical of the history of mining rushes to other areas. Traditional, too, were their informal methods of recording claims, their temporary governments, their enforcement of the obvious regulations in any civilized society (except that they had little use for vigilantes), their development of transportation facilities, their business expansion, and their recreation. But for the Sioux and the gradual rise of a single dominating corporation, the Homestake Mining Company, the Black Hills gold development differed little from others in the West.

15

THE discovery of gold by George Washington Carmack in 1896 precipitated a wild stampede from Seattle to the Yukon, one of the most isolated portions of Canada—a rush similar to the earlier ones in many ways but unique in the difficulties imposed by northward travel and in the problems raised by the harsh climate.

The interior Yukon Valley was an area of little snow or rainfall; of temperatures high in summer and exceedingly low in winter; of spruce, white birch, and cottonwood trees growing normally in the valley and quite stunted on the hillsides; of moose, woodland caribou, bears, mountain sheep, white goats, timber wolves, and such smaller animals as the muskrat, wolverine, mink, otter, and rabbit; of birds so abundant that they were to be heard even in winter; of trout and salmon. Arthur Harper, LeRoy N. "Jack" McQuesten, and Al Mayo were pioneer traders in the area, all arriving in the valley about 1871. The first two were originally employees of the Alaska Commercial Company but drifted into a casual relationship of virtual independence. These men at first concentrated on exchanging furs with the Indians, a business which gradually declined in volume, and later encouraged exploration for minerals.

As early as 1881, gold in limited quantities was discovered repeatedly on the various tributaries of the upper Yukon River, generally in a deposit so small that only one man could profitably work it. In 1885, gold was discovered on the Fortymile River, and in 1887 Harper and McQuesten opened a trading post called Fortymile where that river joined the Yukon. In Alaska there was a discovery on Birch Creek in 1892; the Yukon River settlement which arose to serve this area was called Circle City. It was these two areas which occupied most miners until the Klondike discovery.[1]

These pioneer prospectors regarded the theft of food as serious as murder; when a miners' meeting found a person guilty of it, he had to leave the country at once, no matter how, but leave. The early residents established the law-abiding character of the country years before the Canadian Northwest Mounted Police came into the area. Most of them were in debt to the trader who sold them supplies and generally never made quite enough money to pay off all they owed. One thing they would not do was to speculate in food; in time of shortage, they sold any surplus they had to their neighbors at cost. In an interesting annual custom at Circle City, on a certain day the squaws sewed several moose skins together and, one at a time, tossed all the white men in them. When each victim's turn was over, he put some food into the skins for the celebration which the Indians held afterward. No white man would aid or hinder another in the scramble. The honor of the first toss always went to Jack McQuesten; after a few preliminaries, he was thrown high enough that he could turn over in the air, and he always managed somehow to land on his feet, no matter how hard the women tried to upset him. At the last ceremony ever held, when he was over fifty years old, he landed on his back for the first time; the squaws, shocked, crowded around and patted him to show their sympathy.

Farther south along the Yukon River, Joseph Ladue established an independent trading post at Sixtymile and encouraged prospectors to work in his area.[2] In the summer of 1894, a newcomer to the area, Robert Henderson, a Nova Scotia-born veteran of the mines at Aspen, Colorado, arranged to finance his search for gold by the traditional method of a grubstake, in this instance furnished by Ladue. In 1896, Henderson acquired three partners: Ed Munson, Frank Swanson, and

1 Tappen Adney, *The Klondike Stampede*, 226–41, 267–72; Pierre Berton, *The Klondike Fever*, 14–15; William Ogilvie, *Early Days on the Yukon and the Story of Its Gold Finds*, 67, 112–13; Arthur T. Walden, *A Dog-Puncher on the Yukon*, 25, 60; Kathryn Winslow, *Big Pan-Out*, 17–20.

2 Adney, *Stampede*, 275–306; Berton, *Fever*, 24, 428; Ogilvie, *Early Days*, 130–33; Richard O'Connor, *High Jinks on the Klondike*, 97–98; T. A. Rickard, *Through the Yukon and Alaska*, 196; Winslow, *Big Pan-Out*, 21–25, 159–60; Walden, *Dog-Puncher*, 69–77.

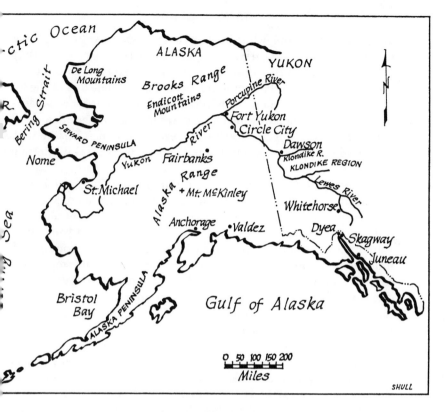

ALASKA–YUKON

Albert Dalton. The four undertook prospecting along an unsearched creek, shortly named Gold Bottom, a tributary of the then almost unknown Klondike River. By early that August they had taken from the creek $750 in gold and had run out of provisions, so Henderson went to Sixtymile for more supplies. He reported his find to Ladue, and some of the men at that trading post set out for Gold Bottom Creek. On his return trip Henderson sought to save time; instead of going in by Indian River, he used the short-cut route of the Klondike River. At the mouth of the latter he encountered four salmon fishermen—George Washington Carmack, a white man generally gnown as "Siwash George," who took it as a great compliment to be told that he was increasingly like the Siwash Indians; Kate, his Indian wife; her brother Skookum Jim, whose name Skookum, meaning "strong," was earned by such feats as carrying a 156-pound pack of bacon over Dyea Pass; and her brother Tagish Charlie, a principal chief in the tribe. Henderson followed the northern tradition of the time by sharing his good news. During the conversation, the miner somehow made a reference to the Indians which gave grave offense to the squaw man; authorities are in disagreement with regard to what it was he said. Henderson then went on and rejoined his partners on Gold Bottom Creek.

Carmack and the two Indians went unhurriedly there, too, looked around, did not stake any claims, and left, feeling that there was little to be excited about. On the way back they climbed to the headwaters of Gold Bottom Creek, hiked over the divide, and came back along Rabbit Creek, shortly to be renamed Bonanza Creek. About a half-mile below its junction with Eldorado Creek, the four stopped to rest; this was on August 16 or 17, 1896. Skookum Jim took a bit of dirt from the rimrock and panned it, with promising enough results that his two companions promptly stopped resting and started working. They staked four claims of five hundred feet each, one each for the Indians and two for the white man on the fiction that he was the "discoverer" of gold on the creek. They then went down the Yukon to Fort Cudahy, recorded their find with the police, and continued to the adjacent settlement of Fortymile. At first none of the loungers in Harry Ash's saloon took Carmack's claims seriously, since his reputation for honesty was not spotless, but none of them could identify the sample he showed as coming from any known source. About midnight men began slipping away to seek Bonanza Creek. Within two weeks of Carmack's discovery, Bonanza Creek was appropriated from end to end.

Old-timers were very skeptical of the new area. One of them, Louis Rhodes, staked a claim and then ashamedly said he would remove his name for twenty-five cents; nobody offered him the money and so he kept it, the next summer taking out about $44,000 gross from it. Veterans at Fortymile and Circle City kept repeating that the excitement was all "bunko." Not until January, 1897, did men at the latter place see a letter from Frank Densmore to Harry Spence saying that the Klondike mines were immensely rich. These two men were much trusted; that they were willing to abandon their extensive interests in the Circle City area was the final proof to the skeptics. Somewhere between three and four hundred miners left for the new discovery as fast as they could. The price of a cabin plummeted from $500 to $8. Those who were fortunate enough to own dogs used the team to haul their mining outfits and several months' supply of food. Combining several teams into one, they repeatedly sent their Huskies back; at Circle City these big groups were split up into smaller and smaller ones until finally, on the way to Bonanza Creek, there were outfits of one man and one dog. In this midwinter rush several miners froze their faces or toes.

While much of this was going on, Henderson and his partners continued working on Gold Bottom Creek; Carmack had never told them of his discovery, apparently breaking an explicit promise to do so because of his irritation over the slight to the Indians. Finally some miners walked over and found the four partners. They told them of the Bonanza Creek rush. At length Henderson asked them just where this creek was and they pointed over the hill to what had been Rabbit Creek. He threw down his shovel and sat on the bank, for some time speechless with discouragement. When he did go to the scene of the great excitement, he was able to stake only claims of little value. Eventually the Canadian government granted him a pension of two hundred dollars a month in recognition of his discovery.

Skookum Jim and Tagish Charlie were made honorary citizens of Canada. Jim had mining property which eventually brought him in ninety thousand dollars a year, but he followed the life of a prospector until, physically exhausted, he died in 1916. Charlie, proud of a citizenship which gave him the right to buy liquor when other Indians could not, became a hotel owner at Carcross and later drowned during a drunken spree. Carmack and his Indian wife, in their first burst of prosperity, toured the Pacific Coast. In both San Francisco and Seattle they enjoyed tossing money out of the hotel window and watching the mad scramble for it below. Kate had difficulty finding her way back to their room and blazed her trail through the various hostelries by nicking the wood in the halls with her fish-skinning knife. Eventually Carmack abandoned his Indian wife and their halfblood children and in financial ease lived with a second, white wife.

When in August, 1896, Joseph Ladue heard Henderson's original report, he set out to investigate and at the Klondike River learned of the strike on Bonanza Creek.[3] Perhaps too busy to notify Henderson, he promptly moved his store and sawmill to the confluence of the Klondike and Yukon rivers. Ladue laid out a townsite in September; the following spring, he and Harper enlarged it. Apparently, by summer, William Ogilvie had officially surveyed it, for certainly he gave the settlement its name, Dawson—after his superior in the Geographical Survey, George Mercer Dawson. The site lay on a flat some two thousand yards wide, extending northward for a mile and a half along the Yukon River from its junction with the Klondike. It was dry in winter but originally a swamp in summer. The streets were sixty-six feet wide; of these the most important was First, or Main, extending parallel to the river. Initially there were some attempts to jump property. The original selling price for lots was five hundred dollars each.

During the winter of 1896–97, the only claims worked were along Bonanza and Eldorado creeks, although discoveries were also made on Hunker and Bear creeks; in June, one was made on Dominion Creek. The sales of claims were few; prices paid were generally something like a sack of beans or a dog sled. When one claim was sold for $3,500, an old-timer left the room during the negotiations because he refused to be present when an honest man was "cheated."

Authentic information about the Klondike discovery reached the main portions of Canada and the United States only slowly.[4] The official report of it, dated June 5, 1897, was sent to the Canadian government by its civil servant surveying the Alaska-Canada boundary line, William Ogilvie. Unconfirmed tales had been spreading along the whole Pacific Coast the preceding winter; they were not taken seriously. Then letters describing the riches began arriving and local newspapers started publishing them. Finally, in the spring, came the traditional season for ships belonging to the Alaska Commercial Company and the North American Trading and Transportation Company to head north to St. Michael, Alaska, port of transshipment from ocean-going vessels to Yukon River steamers. The first to re-

3 Winslow, *Big Pan-Out*, 142–43, 168; Adney, *Stampede*, 176–80, 307–308; Russell A. Bankson, *The Klondike Nugget*, 86.

4 Adney, *Stampede*, 2–5; Winslow, *Big Pan-Out*, 26–35; Berton, *Fever*, 107, 122; Ogilvie, *Early Days*, 222–23.

turn, the *Excelsior*, landing at San Francisco on July 14, attracted no attention because everybody was thinking of the ship from India, with bubonic plague aboard, that had landed a few days earlier. On July 16, the *Portland* hove into sight off Cape Flattery in Puget Sound. Out hurried a tug bearing reporters and photographers of the *Seattle Post-Intelligencer;* then back it rushed them to Port Townsend to telephone the editor. The news had spread around the world by the next morning, when the *Portland* approached the dock in Seattle amidst hails of "Show us the gold," which finally induced more than one passenger to hold up a sack. The city's papers reported that the ship brought with it a ton of gold; actually, it was at least two tons. Interviews with each of the prospectors aboard reflected prosperity, optimism, and a determination to rejoin, as quickly as possible, a partner who was working their claim. Reports on later arrivals from the Yukon became exaggerated; thus when the *Excelsior* entered San Francisco a second time, with half a million dollars in gold dust, newspapers generously made it two and one-half million.

The Klondike discoveries produced a real gold fever in the United States and Canada.[5] The precipitous rush to the Yukon gained momentum in the summer of 1897, subsided when the winter months made northern travel impractical, reached its climax the following summer, and abruptly ended as a new enthusiasm, the Spanish-American War, gripped the United States. To stimulate the gold excitement there were numerous newspaper and magazine articles, special cars exhibiting Klondike material that traveled over the railroads, advertisements by those seeking to make a profit from the gold seekers, and the contagious enthusiasm of those convinced they could go north to make a fortune. Thus the Seattle Chamber of Commerce undertook such a vigorous campaign to secure the gold-rush trade that by the spring of 1898 it had obtained twenty-five million dollars' worth of the business; all the other Pacific ports combined had only five million.

In Pacific Coast cities hosts of advertisements appeared, offering businesses for sale so that the owners could go north. A local investor or syndicate might send out one or several fortune seekers. Another possibility was to buy stock in a company organized to do something in the Klondike area: a steamship line, a railroad, a toll road, a water

---

[5] Winslow, *Big Pan-Out*, 37–65; Berton, *Fever*, 124–25, 138; Adney, *Stampede*, 24, 37–48, 178; Ogilvie, *Early Days*, 217–19.

company, an electric plant, a carrier-pigeon mail service, a farm to raise gophers to claw holes in the frozen, gold-filled gravel—almost anything wise, stupid, or fraudulent which the mind of man could devise. By the end of the summer of 1897, investors in the United States had a choice of Klondike organizations whose total capital requirements were announced to be about $165,000,000. Some people talked of establishing colonies, such as a town near Circle City built from portable houses. There was even the project of sociologist Charlotte Smith to export four thousand New England spinsters as potential wives. Most of these various enterprises either failed or were never really begun; the amount of money the overspeculative, overenthusiastic, or unperceptive investors lost in them must have been tremendous. Equally unsuccessful were most of the inventions prompted by the Yukon excitement, such as an electric-powered, steam-heated sleigh, an X-ray machine for detecting gold deposits, and a complete thirty-day supply of chemical food tablets that could be carried in a pocketbook.

Some of the men who rushed to the Klondike were experienced miners. The great majority, however, had never even seen placer operations, and a considerable number were quite unaccustomed to outdoor life. Much of the hardship they met on the trip from the coast to the mine fields came from inexperience. Most of the men came from the United States and Canada, but Australians, New Zealanders, South Africans, South Americans, and even Samoans also took part in the rush.

The demand for space on northbound ships was tremendous. Thus when the *Portland* sailed on July 22, 1897, its owners had raised their price for a ticket from two hundred dollars to one thousand, and some speculators who bought at this price were able to resell for as much as fifteen hundred dollars. To supplement the established lines and steamers, new companies were established and additional boats secured. Freighters, tankers, whalers, pleasure yachts, coalers, and Atlantic liners were pressed into service on the Pacific Ocean. Ships which had operated on California's Sacramento and San Joaquin rivers were purchased at three times their original cost to increase the number of boats on the Yukon River. The problems of captains who had never sailed an ocean, often aided by an equally inexperienced crew, were numerous, especially if their vessels were ill adapted for passenger service.

The first men rushing up the coast from Puget Sound, over the mountain passes near Skagway, and downstream in the boats they had made came to a sign on the Yukon River reading "Danger Below. Keep to the Right." Naturally, they did; this course took them to what was officially named Klondike City but was always called Lousetown. It was a settlement of Indians and less-respectable whites. When word of the outsiders' arrival reached Dawson, Joe Ladue was especially annoyed, for he wanted them to be drinking liquor in his saloon rather than at his rivals' bars. To solve this problem, government surveyor William Ogilvie tied open the steam whistle on Joe's sawmill; when satisfactory explanations for the noise could not be given, the flotilla of boats left Lousetown, crossed the Klondike River, and came to Dawson. By October, 1897, there were three hundred cabins or other buildings there. The number of men who spent the winter in the town was perhaps six thousand.

The advent of so many gold seekers raised the problem of accumulating adequate food supplies.[6] The two veteran companies of the Yukon sought to cram as many supplies into the town's warehouses as possible. Five of their river boats made a total of fourteen trips that summer, landing by the middle of September about four hundred tons of food and four hundred of general merchandise. This would certainly have been enough had the population remained stable, but instead newcomers kept arriving. So concerned were the two companies to accumulate supplies at Dawson that they bypassed Circle City. The latter's miners grimly contemplated the shortages in the two local stores, calculated the total amount of supplies the settlement required, and took action when the next ship, which happened to be the North American Trading and Transportation Company's *Portus B. Weare,* docked. A miners' committee leveled their Winchester rifles at those on board and demanded no more and no less than the goods which the company's local branch required for its regular customers. These were unloaded, checked in by the committee, placed in the usual warehouse, and eventually purchased through the store in normal fashion. When the Alaska Commercial Company's *Bella* arrived a few days later, the holdup was repeated. On the *Weare,* a

6 Adney, *Stampede,* 183–92, 330–35, 365; Winslow, *Big Pan-Out,* 199–207; Edward B. Lung, *Black Sand and Gold,* 219; Walden, *Dog-Puncher,* 98–101, 104; S. B. Steele, *Forty Years in Canada,* 309; Frederick Palmer, *In the Klondyke,* 62, 184–85.

traveling artist was so impressed with the unique event that he sketched it; soon a miner came to his side and made detailed comments about his drawing of the men holding the rifles until he got the point, erased the faces, and substituted imaginary ones. Nothing was ever done to punish those who removed the supplies.

At Dawson, anxiety continued to mount. J. E. Hansen, assistant superintendent of the Alaska Commercial Company, went down river on the *Margaret*. When he learned that low water would prevent three of his company's ships from arriving at Dawson, he heroically pushed his way back upstream in a pole boat—one of the most difficult and unselfish trips ever made—to give warning. On September 30, after two additional lightly loaded boats had arrived, a public notice was posted that there was not sufficient food in Dawson to last the winter and that the only solution was for a contingent of miners to move down river to Fort Yukon, "where there is a large stock of provisions." The notice was signed by Inspector C. Constantine of the Northwest Mounted Police, by Collector of Customs D. W. Davis, and by Gold Commissioner Thomas Fawcett. John J. Healy of the North American Trading and Transportation Company, insisting that there was enough food in town to prevent starvation if the two companies pooled their resources, said there were few supplies at Fort Yukon and that any move should be to the coast, not down river. Most miners felt they could not leave because their claims might be declared forfeit and somebody might jump them.

Less than two hundred men took the situation seriously enough to accept the Canadian government's offer of free transportation down river on the *Bella* and the *Portus B. Weare*. The two got as far as Circle City, then stuck fast in the ice. Eighty of the *Weare*'s passengers forced their way by small boat and then on foot to Fort Yukon. Here they discovered not the mountain of supplies they had expected but only a limited stock. Had there been a mass migration, it would have been a major disaster. A group of miners brought such pressure upon two United States Army officers who happened to be at the settlement and upon the stores that supplies adequate to last seven months were issued to everyone. These were paid for upon delivery where possible and otherwise were on credit, with the United States government guaranteeing the merchants against loss. Some of the miners promptly hired themselves as woodcutters, piling up fuel for the rush of river boats anticipated the next summer; others went prospecting on the adjacent creeks and found nothing. A few men leaving Dawson went up river to the safety of Skagway.

When federal authorities in Washington heard of the threatened food shortage in Dawson, their solution was to buy 539 reindeer in Norway and rush them to the endangered miners. By March 7, 1898, these animals had come by ship as far as Seattle, where the supply of moss accompanying them ran out. They were pastured for nine days on the grass of a city park, which was bad enough, then shipped north to Dyea. Here the United States Army held them for a week, awaiting orders, and fed them dry alfalfa. This unaccustomed diet so weakened the reindeer that many of them died. By the time they could be driven over the mountain pass and north to the Yukon River, the need for them had passed; eventually, the 183 surviving were deposited at Circle City and there vanished from the pages of history.

The food shortage was never as severe as had been feared. The two companies and the Northwest Mounted Police co-operated to assure equitable distribution of what there was. Neither mercantile house attempted to profiteer; some small-scale operators did, with only mediocre success. Certainly most luxuries and some necessities were in short supply, some men cut their meals below the traditional daily three, but there was no starvation; indeed, when more food came, there was still available a month's supply of bacon, beans, and flour. When supplies finally did come from the Pacific Ocean, through Skagway and down the Yukon River, they arrived in rafts or small boats; thirty of these landed the first week and brought prices down fast. Thus the first eggs sold for $18.00 a dozen, but within five days the price was down to $4.00 and shortly fell to $3.00. An interesting speculator to arrive early was the man who brought in fifteen hundred pairs of boots; he paid $1.75 a pair for them at Montreal and sold them for $15.00.

The year 1898 was the year of the great rush to the Klondike.[7] The statistics themselves, even though not precise, are impressive. Perhaps one hundred thousand people set out for Dawson, thirty to forty thousand got there, fifteen to twenty thousand prospected, four thousand found some gold, fifteen thousand people out of the year's rush remained in the Klondike when winter closed in, and another five thousand departed before spring came. They spent somewhere between

[7] Berton, *Fever*, 127, 417; Mrs. George Black, *My Seventy Years*, 115, 125; Palmer, *In the Klondyke*, 165, 199; Steele, *Forty Years*, 321; Walden, *Dog-Puncher*, 69.

thirty and sixty million dollars for transportation and supplies, yet the yield of gold from the Klondike in 1898 was hardly more than ten million dollars.

In both 1897 and 1898, by far the most popular route of the gold seekers was from San Francisco or Puget Sound to Skagway or Dyea, over Chilkoot Pass or White Pass, and finally down a system of waterways to Dawson.[8] The steamship fare on the ocean segment of the trip was seventy-five dollars at the very minimum and as much more as the seller thought he could get. From Dyea or Skagway to Dawson stretched six hundred miles, where costs could be held to a minimum because the chief need was for muscle power and ingenuity of each individual prospector. Since many people took the route, they gave each other company and mutual protection. Because at least two men out of three lacked practical experience either in mining or travel in the wilds, often they formed a partnership. Sometimes this was an eduring alliance of great mutual benefit; sometimes it fell apart under the difficulties of the trail and the annoyance of continuous disputation. If the advice of a neutral outsider was sought, often a few good-humored observations mended the rupture. Perhaps the damage was irreparable and the partners split up their outfit fairly in a process popularly called "getting a divorce." In one extreme instance, two men were so irritated with each other that they literally sawed their boat in half, each patching up his end for further use, cut their tent in half, and pitched what couldn't be divided—an ax, a stove, and a gun—into the river.

At San Francisco or the Puget Sound ports the gold rushers purchased almost all the supplies they would need. Most were provisions, for the Northwest Mounted Police would not allow any ordinary person from Dyea or Skagway into the Yukon River system without his bringing 1,150 pounds of edibles for his own use and such essentials as a tent and tools. In addition, men needed equipment for building, for mining, for cooking, and for hauling their goods. Most men found that some of their purchases had been misguided, so they abandoned as useless a few items at Skagway or Dyea; they bought a few things there which, they had come to realize, would be essential for the task ahead.

The customs duty to be paid on these supplies was an expensive

8 Adney, *Stampede*, 14–28, 86–88, 360; Berton, *Fever*, 136; Walden, *Dog-Puncher*, 14–15; Winslow, *Big Pan-Out*, 42–44; Steele, *Forty Years*, 295, 302.

annoyance.[9] It was complicated by the long-simmering dispute between the United States and Canada over the precise location of the international boundary along the thin coastal arm of Alaska extending south to include such settlements as Dyea and Skagway. The argument arose in 1867 and was not finally settled until 1903. In February, 1898, Canadian officials had the Northwest Mounted Police plant customs posts, considerably nearer the Pacific Ocean than the United States wished, at the top of Chilkoot Pass and White Pass. This prompt action, Canadian Minister of the Interior Clifford Sifton declared later, saved twenty years of negotiation with the United States; certainly the boundary at those points was not changed later. Canadian customs-charged duty on goods bought in the United States averaged about 25 per cent of the purchase price. The police were lenient in collecting it, almost always taking a man's word for what he had rather than inspecting his belongings and accepting a day or two of labor as payment from a prospector short of cash. During the spring and summer of 1898, the Canadians took in more than $150,000 at the two passes.

Another customs question concerned goods bought in Canada which passed through the thin belt of Alaskan soil. They had to be landed at Dyea or Skagway and then accompanied to the international boundary by a federal customs official at a charge of six dollars a day. In March, 1898, after much negotiation, the United States decided to allow Canadian items to pass through without any kind of fee.

Dyea and Skagway were unique as mining-rush boom towns because they were so far distant from the gold fields.[10] Located three miles apart, Dyea was never more than a temporary town of tents but Skagway gradually acquired the physical attributes of a permanent settlement. Ships could approach the shore at neither place very closely. Unloading was a disorganized process of dumping cargo overboard into scows, then transshipping it into wagons nearer the shore; such items as barrels and lumber were simply floated in with the tide. When Skagway extended long, thin wharves out far enough for ships to come alongside easily, almost all vessels stopped there and few went on to Dyea, which gradually withered away.

9 Winslow, *Big Pan-Out*, 73–81; Adney, *Stampede*, 13, 33, 50, 135–36; Steele, *Forty Years*, 293, 314.

10 Adney, *Stampede*, 37–40, 65–68, 102, 385–86; William R. Collier and Edwin V. Westrate, *The Reign of Soapy Smith*, 213–53; Berton, *Fever*, 149, 346–64; Steele, *Forty Years*, 295–97; Walden, *Dog-Puncher*, 129–31; Winslow, *Big Pan-Out*, 95–113.

The half-mile of beach upon which Skagway arose was claimed by William Moore. At first he tried to drive intruders off his land, with no success. When the town was surveyed, he was offered a lot free and refused it; thereupon his tent was torn down and his goods destroyed. Later the courts awarded him damages equal to 25 per cent of the assessed value of all lots within the original townsite. More important, his venture of building a mile-long wharf out over the tidal flats was quite profitable and he died a wealthy man. By the end of the summer of 1897, Skagway was a town of twelve thousand tents and about one hundred frame buildings. Whiskey sold was of poor quality originally and adulterated with two-thirds water; cigars retailed at about ten times the Seattle price. The following summer, the town's population, including transients, was averaging between fifteen and twenty thousand people.

"The town of Skagway at this period of its existence was about the roughest place in the world." This expert appraisal by visitor S. B. Steele of the Northwest Mounted Police, a Canadian organization which of course had no jurisdiction over the town, was accurate. Robbery and murder were such a daily routine that they occasioned little, if any, comment. One Sunday morning, as Steele subsequently wrote, a pistol duel in the immediate vicinity of his cabin caused bullets to come through its thin boards; a fight was so common an event that neither he nor his companions bothered even to rise from their beds. The United States had almost no machinery for law enforcement in the area. A United States commissioner and a United States marshal were an inadequate force accomplishing little.

The leader of the lawless element was Jefferson Smith, commonly known as "Soapy." His activities in Creede, Colorado, and what he did in Alaska were much the same. When the Klondike excitement struck, he opened a saloon in Skagway. His real opportunity came that fall of 1897 when a crowd was about to lynch saloon owner John E. Fay for the murders of Andy McGarth and United States Deputy Marshal Rowan. Smith, who had been in town only twenty-four hours, got together a bunch of toughs, stopped the mob, and persuaded it to ship the guilty men off to Sitka for trial; he also collected $2,200 for the two widows. Smith promptly announced to the lawless element in Skagway that he was in command, that they would pay him a commission of 50 per cent on their various ventures, and that he would protect them when they got in trouble. His gang came to number between two and three hundred. In many ways Smith resembled a European dictator of later years, as Pierre Berton has pointed out, for he maintained such an effective spy system of "underground" operatives that it was dangerous for a man to speak his mind or disclose his finances; Soapy kept good relations with his neighbors, allowing no robbery of permanent citizens; he cultivated business, labor, the Church, and the press; he ostentatiously did charity work; and he even tried to volunteer for the Spanish-American War. However, his good deeds were far outweighed by his bad ones, for he was a ruthless dictator who fostered any type of disreputable enterprise that would separate a victim from his money and who did not shrink from the murders committed by his gang.

The cause of Smith's downfall was a most unlikely person—inoffensive, weak-willed J. D. Stewart, who was returning to his home at Nanaimo, British Columbia, with $2,800 in gold. Despite his friends' clear warnings, he fell victim to the blandishments of Smith's gang; shortly he found himself separated from his money. He wandered about the street telling people of his loss, the same sort of thing many a victim must have done before, but now suddenly Skagway had had enough of the reign of crime. A fire bell rang; a crowd gathered; a vigilante committee arose spontaneously; a demand served on Smith for the return of the money met a flat refusal. Then the United States district judge from Dyea gave Smith an ultimatum to restore Stewart's poke by 4 p.m. At the deadline the dictator stalked out of his saloon with his rifle in hand, demanding that the crowd forget the incident. His confederates, disloyal almost to the man, fled until the Northwest Mounted Police turned them back at the international boundary or else wandered off into the wilderness until the rugged conditions there forced them to return. The vigilantes met first at Sylvester Hall and then, fearing informers, at the far end of Juneau Wharf. Smith, impatient, finally headed to the wharf for a showdown. He disregarded guard Frank Reid's order to halt, the vigilante's gun misfired, Smith shot, Reid shot, and both fell. Smith, hit in the heart, died almost instantly; Reid lingered for twelve days before passing on. In a frenzy of excitement the vigilantes invaded dive after dive, slugging, shooting, and intimidating. They captured forty prisoners, talked seriously of lynching them all, but instead finally shipped the scoundrels off on the first boat returning to the United States, warning them never to return. Smith's worldly assets at the time of his death proved to be about five hundred dollars in cash; he had spent the rest of his funds as received, sometimes generously, sometimes flamboyantly, and sometimes in the worst illegal ways. His demise marked the end of Skagway's lawlessness.

In 1897 and 1898, the town of Dyea, entryway to Chilkoot Pass, attracted mostly those who did not own horses or dogs and lacked enough money to pay for somebody to carry their outfits over the mountains.[11] So obviously was it a "poor man's pass" that even the gamblers and criminals at Dyea were "second rate." The camp, a half-mile string of shacks, was located on the beach next to the Dyea River. Along the shore was usually a vast pile of goods, a chaos of mixed-up, burst-open, and water-soaked bundles at which travelers dived "like gulls over swill." Only the fortunate managed to rescue their outfits complete. The very few men who could afford to hire their goods carried over Chilkoot Pass employed a professional packer, a position at first monopolized by the local Chilkoot Indians until the demand became so brisk that they allowed other red and white men to enter the field. Most commonly, arrangements were made through Isaac, the chief of the Chilkoots.

The Indians used as pack straps two bands of cotton cloth, lined with a blanket, twenty inches long and two inches wide, which they fastened to the top and bottom of the load by means of a small rope; the loops of the straps were passed around the shoulders. There was also a head strap, which passed over the forehead, with ends fastened to the load behind. An Indian man carried a load of 100 to 150 pounds on his back, his wife 75, his children 25 to 60, and his dogs (who had to be lifted over the streams) carried 15 pounds each. Sometimes twenty or thirty people joined together to transport an entire outfit in a day. The red men at first charged five cents a pound, but increasing demand gradually drove the price up to forty cents. When carrying somebody's goods, if offered a higher price, they would immediately drop what they had.

Those whites who could not afford such rates but still had some money hired men owning strings of horses to move their freight

---

11 Adney, *Stampede*, 46, 90–119; Bankson, *Nugget*, 29–30; Berton, *Fever*, 245–57; Angelo Heilprin, *Alaska and the Klondike*, 20; Lung, *Gold*, 385; Palmer, *In the Klondyke*, 9; Steele, *Forty Years*, 306–307; Walden, *Dog-Puncher*, 4–7; Winslow, *Big Pan-Out*, 96–105, 115–26.

part of the way; the charge was about half that of the Indian packers. Often these horses were mistreated: many a load was improperly packed; many a saddle blanket was so wet that it rubbed a sore; many a saddle was incorrectly cinched or fitted. Inevitably, the horses were cut and bruised by the rocks on the pass. The price of hay was almost prohibitively high, so the animals were fed on packing straw or simply not fed. Starvation, injury, or the loss of a shoe (for which no replacements were available) soon made a horse useless for further service, so he would simply be turned loose to stray about camp until he collapsed, died, and his bloated, wormy corpse offered a precarious stepping stone to those crossing the filthy streets. Usually nobody would mercifully kill such a horse for fear some imposter would enter a damage claim.

Most gold seekers, unable to hire their loads carried over Chilkoot Pass, did it themselves. Ordinarily the minimum outfit for an individual prospector was two thousand pounds; if he had a partner with whom he could share some items, this weight could be cut a little. Their possessions were not moved over the pass, 3,500 feet high, a load at a time but, rather, were transported by relays from one convenient point of deposit to another about five miles away. In summer, most men carried a pack weighing between seventy-five and one hundred pounds; in winter, they often used sleds part way. Priced at ten dollars in Dyea, these were seven feet long and eighteen inches wide, with a bed of four long pine slats set upon four crosspieces of ash; the runners, also made of ash, had two-inch shoes made of brass (not iron, which split at low temperatures). The men pulled a load of four hundred pounds, using as harness a broad band around the body high under the armpits.

The route over Chilkoot Pass, until the summer of 1897 the only one used between the Skagway area and the headwaters of the Yukon River, began with the ascent of the Dyea River. It could be navigated by canoe for the first six miles, a very difficult task left mostly to Indians. Occasionally prospectors pushed flat-bottomed scows up the stream; more often they used the trail, which stuck close to the river for the first six miles, frequently crossing it, and then wandered somewhat away along the mountainsides. At several points enterprising men who had corduroyed difficult places collected a toll. Up river about thirteen miles was Sheep Camp, the last point on the trail where wood was available; during the rush there were seldom less than fifteen hundred people there. From it to the summit was a difficult four miles. The upward path was a succession of ice shelves in winter; for perhaps four months in summer it was instead a mass of slippery shale and granite boulders. From Sheep Camp, for the first two miles the trail followed a huge gorge until the valley narrowed to an end at the start of the pass. Up Chilkoot went a narrow footpath, from the bottom precipice (called "The Scales") ascending along a series of benches into and across Chilkoot Glacier. The general slope of the route was 30 per cent, but in a few places the men had to climb on hands and knees from rock to rock; over such spots a horse could go only if two or three men ahead pulled on a rope to prevent his tumbling over backwards. Across the glacier, a horse had to be blindfolded and a dog carried; neither could pack anything. The top of the pass was comparatively level. Beyond it was the head of another glacier, down which the prospectors slid goods on tarpaulins and at the bottom, on the shore of Crater Lake, cached their load. For the average man to carry his outfit from Sheep Camp to Crater Lake took at least three months.

The trail was safe in winter, when a falling man's worst fate would be to plunge into slush up to his armpits; in summer he would hit the rocks. In the cold season along the last steep stretch were hacked perhaps fifteen hundred steps in the ice; guy ropes were strung for added safety, and a toll was charged. To cross this portion usually took between three and six hours. Every fourth step had a resting place, many of which enterprising gamblers expanded, with seats carved out of the glacier for those who would try their luck at such swift sports as the shell game while relaxing. For one fee a man could make as many trips across the flight of steps as he wished; few wanted more than one. Over the trail to the summit, well defined and so narrow that once in place there was no getting out of it, men followed each other so closely that they were almost in lockstep; the pace was set by the slowest. When accident or illness struck, the whole line stopped and normally the ascent was hindered by a series of delays. When a storm struck, there was nothing to do but brave it out. Returning in winter, the prospectors used the short-cut of chutes worn deep in the snow; they got a swift descent and also a hot one unless they had a canvas pad.

Men crossing Chilkoot Pass complained that no matter how they bound themselves up, the winter wind seemed to reach them. Many made the mistake of not adopting parkas, of using instead clothing that was too heavy and made them perspire easily. Perspiration in such weather was dangerous; normal prudence dictated an immediate change into dry clothing, and experience taught the wisdom of the Indian practice to work so slowly that there was no overheating. When the day was done, few men took time enough to cook their flapjacks and beans adequately, especially when they knew their life depended upon collecting enough wood after supper to last the next day. At night they sought to keep warm but not hot, for perspiration could turn into ice and then there was no awakening. Most of the men became very weary and short tempered.

In 1897, although most material was carried from Sheep Camp on the backs of gold seekers, several cables were strung, powered by a small engine, which dragged packs up for eight to thirty cents a pound, depending upon the value of the goods handled. In 1898, a company erected a freight tramway from Sheep Camp to the summit.

On the ascent from Sheep Camp, avalanches constantly threatened. Of true Alpine type, they came from heavy beds of snow clinging with bare support to the steeply pitched mountain walls. The most serious struck on the evening of April 27, 1898, at The Scales, burying nearly seventy sleeping people. All except ten perished, despite prompt rescue work. These reported that the pressure imprisoned them in their blankets, that their breath melted a bit of snow from their mouths and nostrils, that they could hear their rescuers moving above, and that their own voices, howling for aid, did not carry to the surface.

Once the time-consuming haul over Chilkoot Pass was finished, the gold seekers paid a cent a pound to have their goods ferried across Crater Lake. They carried them over a four-mile trail to Long Lake and there paid another ferryman another cent a pound for a two-mile haul, portaged a few hundred yards to Deep Lake, hired a third ferryman for the one-mile trip across, and finally bore them overland to Lake Lindemann, usually to its junction with the trail leading over White Pass. From Dyea to Lake Lindemann was a total of twenty-seven miles.

The men who went from Skagway over White Pass were almost exclusively those who owned horses, oxen, or dogs to transport their goods or else could hire the service.[12] The original trail was cut in 1887 by William Moore, but it was little used. In 1897, it was greatly improved for the twenty miles to the summit by the company which planned to use it as an access path to the route of the railroad it was building from Skagway to Whitehorse; it allowed use without charge. The route led out of Skagway across a succession of hills, deceptively easy for three or four miles, then swung across the Skagway River and for three miles farther was broad enough to accommodate a wagon. The trail then narrowed and was seldom more than two feet wide, a route for horses. By June, 1897, the melting snows turned it into a seemingly endless series of mudholes, some so bad that horses sank in them down to their tails and could be extracted only with a violent struggle. At places there was corduroy over the quagmires, but the terrain was occasionally so steep that some of these had to be pitched at a forty-degree angle. Where there was little mud, there were many rocks. In places a single misstep would send the animal plunging five hundred to one thousand feet down to the canyon floor. Such a trail was very difficult for an experienced, careful horse which had been well packed. Often a poorly placed load so projected that a beast avoiding a rock on one side would find himself stepping over the path and onto nothing on the other; some horses were always clumsy, paying no heed to where they put their feet. The trail went over the summits of Devil's Hill, Porcupine Hill, and Summit Hill. At the last was the customs-collection station of the Northwest Mounted Police, a cabin so beset by snow in the spring of 1898 that a guard was placed at the door at night to shovel it away lest the occupants be smothered. From here the path went down a narrow funnel for about eight miles and then fanned out into various routes.

Such a route might have handled a small number of pack trains comfortably, but it was never suitable for the hordes of men and animals who sought to struggle over it. Late in 1897, the old-timers insisted on closing it to all travel for a few days while supposedly everybody pitched in to improve it by corduroying. When it was re-opened, heavy traffic soon made it as bad as ever. Cruelty to animals

12 Adney, *Stampede*, 35, 55–86, 123–25; A. A. Allan, *Gold, Men and Dogs*, 49–51; Berton, *Fever*, 153, 166; William B. Haskell, *Two Years in the Klondike and Alaskan Gold Fields*, 460–67; Rickard, *Through the Yukon*, 144; Steele, *Forty Years*, 289–90, 298; Walden, *Dog-Puncher*, 133–36; Winslow, *Big Pan-Out*, 124–25.

on this trail, according to all authorities, was widespread. It came from the so-called better classes. When horses sank into the mud so deeply that they seemingly could not be gotten out, frequently they were simply abandoned without the mercy of a bullet and often with their load still on them. These luckless animals quickly died as men and horses climbed across them. In one extreme instance the owner of an exhausted pair of oxen became so enraged that he built a fire under them; they were unable to move their load and so slowly roasted to death. Probably three thousand horses and mules were killed on the White Pass route. Undoubtedly, the trail also shattered the health and fortunes of hundreds of men. Scattered along the middle and far reaches of it were valuable goods abandoned by their owners; nobody would buy them or even take them as a gift.

The routes over White Pass and Chilkoot Pass usually met at Lake Lindemann, although some bypasses did not merge until they reached Lake Bennett.[13] At one of these two—Lindemann, nine miles long, or Bennett, thirty miles—the trip on the Yukon River system generally began. However, those who arrived in the winter or early spring often used dogs and sleds to carry their outfits across the frozen ice. Little frost balls could form under a dog's nails and between his pads, cutting like glass and quickly becoming so painful that he had to stop. A wise owner, at the first sign of a limp, thawed the frost by putting the foot in his mouth and then dried it with his shirt. It was common for a dog to stop, turn toward his master, and lift a paw pleadingly. When there was a wind on the lake, the owner hoisted a sail to ease the burden on his team.

As spring neared, men at the lakes turned to building boats in which to float downstream to Dawson. A typical boat was flat bottomed, flare sided, twenty-five feet long by six feet wide, square, and wide at the stern; it carried two or three tons of goods placed on slabs on the bottom cross ribs. It was usually driven by a sail made of a large canvas tarpaulin attached to a stout mast and supplemented when necessary by awkward, heavy, pine or spruce oars. These vessels were built of lumber so green that despite calking with oakum and pitch they leaked badly. The timber, mostly spruce and a little pine,

13 Adney, *Stampede*, 120–66, 385, 389–90; Berton, *Fever*, 276–77, 292; Heilprin, *Alaska and the Klondike*, 166–68; Ogilvie, *Early Days*, 81–82; Palmer, *In the Klondyke*, 14; Rickard, *Through the Yukon*, 171; Steele, *Forty Years*, 302, 310–12; Walden, *Dog-Puncher*, 19–21, 138–42; Winslow, *Big Pan-Out*, 126–39.

was secured two to five miles from the lake shore and cut into planks, nine inches wide and one inch thick, with planed edges. The sawing was done on a platform perhaps twelve feet high, with one man standing above and another on the ground; this process was irksome at best and caused a fair number of quarrels. Nails and pitch were in very short supply on the lake. The great majority of gold seekers cut their own timber and put together their own boats. When the time for launching came, everybody around lent a hand.

Life in these boatbuilding camps on the two lakes was more pleasant than in the passes. People became insensitive to illness and death, those afflicted usually cared for only by their partners. If for some reason a man lost his partner, often he turned back because the rest of the trip looked too difficult without assistance. Many gold seekers abandoned the trip after a careful appraisal of the boat they had just finished building.

As soon as the ice broke up at the end of May, the initial contingent set off downstream to Dawson and were followed as rapidly as possible by those who had reached the shore later. Many a boat carried a flag and a name. In 1898, under orders from the Northwest Mounted Police, they also bore an assigned number; in the official records the names of the occupants, their addresses, and their next of kin were recorded for each vessel. If the voyage started at Lake Lindemann, the first difficulty was the gorge leading down to Lake Bennett, rocky on the sides and clear in the center except for a submerged rock near the lower end. On Bennett itself, the wind was often stiff enough to capsize carelessly handled boats. Sometimes there was quite a flotilla on this lake; on one occasion Colonel Steele counted eight hundred boats under sail at the same time. At its foot, called Caribou Crossing, a sluggish stream with a current of four miles an hour carried the vessel into Lake Nares, three or four miles long. Next was Tagish Lake, seeming to the travelers more like a series of lakes than the single lake it actually was. Another slow river carried the gold seekers to Lake Marsh. Halfway down, the Northwest Mounted Police established what they called Tagish Post, where each boat had to register and show a customs receipt for its cargo. The police found that when roughly accosted, the best way to handle the malcontent was to be so especially polite that finally he became polite, too. Lake Marsh, almost twenty miles in length, was narrow, shallow, and long. Beyond lay Miles Canyon, one hundred feet wide and more than fifty deep, through which the Lewes River raced. The first danger was a bad whirlpool about halfway down, which was best avoided by keeping to the crest of the waves; then Squaw Rapids; then Whitehorse Rapids, boiling through a cut twenty to thirty feet high for a quarter of a mile.

Along this stretch nobody drowned in 1897, but by late May, 1898, ten had died. The Mounties then ordered all women and children to walk around it, forbade any boat to go through without first satisfying them that it could ride the waves safely, and insisted that unless there was a competent man among its owners, they should hire a pilot. These were at first Indians, but later whites also turned to the task. The charge varied from five to one hundred dollars but was usually about twenty. By returning on horseback, a pilot could make as many as ten trips downstream a day. One of them, later to become a famous novelist, was Jack London; he earned about three thousand dollars in fees before hurrying on toward Dawson. Around Whitehorse Rapids two tramways were built in 1898; they hauled goods around the obstacle for three cents a pound. The tramcars had cast-iron wheels, the rails were of wood, with occasional iron plates, and the ties were three to ten feet apart.

Beyond Whitehorse Rapids were no serious obstacles; the gold seekers drifted down the Lewes River. They complained more about the mosquitoes on the various lakes and rivers than about any aspect of their trip from the Pacific Ocean. They kept a sharp eye on the local Indians, pilfering thieves who were sometimes willing to exchange goods. At times they had difficulty finding the main course of the Lewes. The river widened into Lake Labarge, the most pictorial of all, thirty miles long and never less than two wide. Such a strong wind blew on it that often the voyagers waited at Windy Arm until the breeze died down a little. At the downstream outlet they steered around a reef exactly in the middle of the exit. Their next excitement was at Five-Finger Rapids, where five great blocks of reddish rock stuck out like the piers of a bridge to break the stream into two principal channels; a bit beyond, the river, very wide, was split into many channels by wooded islands. The gold seekers drifted on until they came to Dawson, where they anchored their boats as near as possible to the center of the city. By midsummer, 1898, the vessels were six deep for nearly two miles.

Starting in 1898, steamship service was available between Whitehorse and Dawson. The first steamer, the *Bellingham,* a forty-foot stern-wheeler with three decks and two funnels, arrived in Dawson on June 14 and within a week eight others had also come down. These boats were owned by various companies; one or another of them sailed from Dawson about every three days once normal operations had begun. On the stern-wheeler itself only passengers, mail, and express were carried. Freight was pushed ahead in one to three barges, 100 feet long, controlled by rope and tackle from the steamer; each barge carried 125 to 150 tons. The trip downstream from Whitehorse took forty hours; the fare of $75 included board. Upstream the time was four days, if the barges were empty, and the charge for passengers was $175.00, later cut to $95.00, with meals extra at $1.00 each.

The trail over White Pass was eventually replaced by the White Pass and Yukon Railroad, completed in 1900 to Whitehorse, which charged passengers twenty-five cents a mile.

The great majority of gold seekers used the route from Dyea or Skagway over the passes to Dawson. Next in popularity was the ocean voyage of almost three thousand miles from Seattle to St. Michael and then about fifteen hundred miles farther up the Yukon River to the Klondike.[14] This was the route of women, mine buyers, and government employees, seldom of ordinary prospectors. In 1898, only those passengers who could prove to United States Army officials at the military reservation established around St. Michael that they had the ability to care for themselves for a year were allowed to land and to go up river. The harbor at St. Michael, neither deep nor well protected, was on the shore of an island separated from the mainland by a narrow slough; no vessel could get nearer than half a mile to the beach. Goods were lightered ashore, except when a river vessel happened to be in port and could come directly alongside the ocean liner. Fare from St. Michael had traditionally been one hundred dollars, although in 1898 some fast boats got as much as one thousand. That summer there were thirty-five vessels in regular, scheduled service on the Yukon River, some run by the two old established companies and others by the six or seven new organizations. Earlier the steamers had used Eskimo and Indian pilots who knew only a portion of the river; twenty or more of them were needed to make a trip through to Dawson. As business expanded, the boats turned to employing white pi-

14 Adney, *Stampede,* 192, 388–89; Berton, *Fever,* 205; Haskell, *Two Years,* 231–33; Walden, *Dog-Puncher,* 91–92; Winslow, *Big Pan-Out,* 83–85.

lots, mostly from the Mississippi River, who quickly learned the new stream well enough to handle a vessel the entire distance. They were more successful than the mates, also imported from Dixie, who found that getting work out of Indians and Eskimos required techniques different from those used in handling Negroes.

When a steamer arrived in Dawson, its owners wanted it unloaded as quickly as possible, regardless of expense, so that it could begin another round trip. Its cargo was carried from ship to warehouse by a fast-stepping crew of men paid $1.50 an hour. When one of them became tired, wanted a meal, or was fired, he was given a tab showing the amount of money due him; if he resumed work, his record was started on another tab. When the work was nearly done and it was not practical to hire new men, the speed of the stevedores was stimulated with free liquor.

Five other routes from the Pacific Ocean to Dawson existed, but relatively only a handful of people attempted to use them.[15] The Jack Dalton Trail, with about 350 miles of hiking, began 7 miles south of Skagway, followed the Chilcat River for about 40 miles, crossed a couple of divides, and then ran along gently rolling valleys to the Lewes River. Here the traveler built a raft below Five-Finger Rapids and floated down the Yukon River system to the Klondike. Other gold seekers started from Wrangell up the Stikine River, following a trail or pushing their way up on a flat-bottomed boat, portaged across the mountains, then traveled by raft about 700 miles from the head of Lake Teslin to the Teslin (Hootalinqua) River, and floated down it to its confluence with the Lewes River. Perhaps 7,000 people used this route. Other prospectors went inland from Juneau for 70 miles along the Taku and Nahkeena rivers and trudged overland another 70 miles to reach the shores of Lake Teslin. About 3,500 men started out on the all-American route and perhaps as many as 20, near death, reached Dawson. They went from Valdez up the Copper River, crossed with great hardship the very difficult Valdez glacier, traveled through Kluteena River rapids bad enough to daunt the bravest, climbed over Mentas Pass, and then pushed through a great wilderness to the headwaters of the Fortymile River, which carried them to the Yukon River. A few hardy souls landed at the head of Yakutat Bay and began the truly dreadful undertaking

[15] Berton, *Fever*, 211–19; Winslow, *Big Pan-Out*, 86–88; Stratford Tollemache, *Reminiscences of the Yukon*, 27–31.

of crossing the tremendous Malaspina glacier, thence by various routes to the Klondike.

There were all-Canadian routes to the Klondike, all of them far less attractive than their backers admitted.[16] The Ashcroft Trail began at Ashcroft, 125 miles northeast of Vancouver, and ran north until it joined the route from Wrangell. In 1897, and 1898, at least 1,500 men undertook to use it in getting to the Klondike; only a handful actually reached Dawson. Another series of trails supposedly led northwest from Edmonton. According to that city's board of trade, a gold seeker could reach the Klondike in 90 days with horses, could buy needed canoes from the Indians cheaply (although in reality few red men were met), and might purchase any food needed from a Huson's Bay Company post (which in large part had been closed down) en route. It was almost murder to send an amateur out on a pathless trip of 2,500 miles along the Mackenzie River nearly to the Arctic Circle, then over a mountain divide to the Yukon River system, or on a journey of 1,700 miles using mostly the Peace River system. About 2,000 men started from Edmonton to the Klondike, at least 500 died, and by late 1899, only about 100 had reached Dawson, sometimes taking two years for the journey.

There was talk of building railroads, although none but the White Pass and Yukon ever laid a rail. A widely discussed project was that of two famous Canadian promoters, William Mackenzie and Dan Mann, to construct 150 miles of narrow-gauge track connecting the abandoned hamlet of Telegraph City, on the Stikine River up stream from Skagway, with Lake Teslin, where steamers would carry passengers and freight the rest of the way. The two demanded 3,750,000 acres of land adjacent to the proposed line as a gift; they didn't get it. Another proposal was to build a railroad from Hudson Bay.

[16] Berton, *Fever*, 224–43; Adney, *Stampede*, 384–87; Winslow, *Big Pan-Out*, 89–94; Rickard, *Through the Yukon*, 177.

16

KLONDIKE DEVELOPMENTS

THOSE prospectors who arrived in Dawson the summer of 1897 sometimes staked a claim of real value, sometimes were completely wrong, and occasionally found nothing they judged worth having. By about the middle of the next summer all the gold-bearing creeks were completely taken up and there was literally nothing left. The late arrivals, stunned and disappointed, milled aimlessly around Dawson until they reached a decision—to sell their outfit and return home at once, seek some kind of employment, or still look for gold somewhere. Many of those who determined to prospect had no real knowledge of how to find what they sought; they followed rumors or the advice of those allegedly more experienced than they were.

In such an atmosphere it did not take much to start a stampede to some spot; it usually lasted about twenty-four hours, included only men with little Klondike experience, and was seldom of any importance. In the winter of 1898–99, "Nigger Jim" made a famous bet. This white Kentuckian of the unusual nickname, an old-timer owning good mining property, wagered that he could tell just one friend in the strictest secrecy of his "rich new find" and then leave camp unaccompanied. When he had told his confidential news, he left Dawson in the middle of the night; at daylight he looked about and "thought he had drawn the whole town." He made a long trip and then camped in an effort to starve the men out. They promptly formed partnerships, sending one of their number back for supplies. Clearly beaten, Nigger Jim gave up, returned to Dawson, and paid his loss.

Most stampedes were the result of such ill-founded or misguided rumors; a few apparently were caused by those who had figured out

357

some cynical plan of selfish profit for themselves.[1] Up to July 1, 1898, more than nine thousand placer-mining claims had been recorded. Of all those who had a paying claim on the Klondike, former slave St. John Atherton made the trip north from the United States in hopes of finding enough riches that he could aid the aged and impoverished daughter of the man who had once owned him. He left the Yukon area with $30,000; what happened after that is unknown. Charles Anderson got drunk one night and was persuaded to spend the $600 dollars he had saved in buying a claim. When he sobered up, he begged for his money back but couldn't get it. His property ultimately yielded $1,250,000 in gold.

The Klondike area, eight hundred square miles, contained three hundred miles of gold-bearing creeks—the chief ones, their tributaries, and the "tributaries of tributaries," known locally as "pups." Eastward along the south bank of the Klondike River from Dawson, the first spur was Bonanza Creek (with Eldorado as its chief offshoot), then Quigley, next Hunker (with Gold Bottom as one of its branches), followed by five small streams, and then the last gold-bearing water course, Flat, with its tributary, All-Gold. These streams all had their headwaters on the north side of a chain of hills called "the ridge." On the south side of it, emptying into Indian River, Dominion, Sulphur, and Quartz were the chief gold creeks.[2]

The law governing the making of claims along these creeks varied from time to time.[3] Originally a claim could be five hundred feet long and the width of the valley, otherwise one hundred feet square. To measure and mark it properly took about half a day for a fair axman. At each of the four corners he placed a stake four feet high and on one face of it wrote "I claim . . . feet up [or down] stream for mining purposes" and signed his name. He then went to the gold commissioner, made an affidavit that he had discovered gold, paid a fee of fifteen dollars, and received a one-year lease, which could be renewed for one hundred dollars each year. Once it was officially recorded, the owner had to work on the claim for three months, daily except Sunday, doing whatever was most needed;

1 Adney, *Stampede*, 396–97; Bankson, *Nugget*, 70; Winslow, *Big Pan-Out*, 147–50, 177, 246; Walden, *Dog-Puncher*, 178–80; Rickard, *Through the Yukon*, 195–96.

2 Adney, *Stampede*, 384; Winslow, *Big Pan-Out*, 24, 157, 180.

3 Adney, *Stampede*, 263, 308–12, 323–24, 434–41; Haskell, *Two Years*, 423–25; Ogilvie, *Early Days*, 161–92; Steele, *Forty Years*, 327, 333; Winslow, *Big Pan-Out*, 24, 159, 185–88.

after three months, he was not required by law to work on it any more. All disputes were settled by the gold commissioner and there was no appeal from his decision to higher authority.

Not two weeks after Carmack made his discovery in 1896 came the first alteration in regulations, stating that instead of a man's staking a claim on each creek in the district, he could now have only one on one creek. When the news of the great Klondike find reached Ottawa, the Dominion cabinet passed an "Order in Council," making drastic limitations. These regulations caused a mass meeting in Dawson to send three Canadians to Ottawa with a vigorous protest. Before they arrived there was such an outcry in Canada generally that a new Order in Council was issued on January 18, 1898. It fixed a royalty at a flat 10 per cent of gross output, with an annual allowance of $2,500 to cover the cost of extraction, and established the size of creek claims at 250 feet, placing them in blocks of ten along the stream and reserving alternate blocks for the Crown. The order defined a bench claim, above the rimrock on either side of the stream, as 250 feet wide and 1,000 deep, and fixed all other claims at 250 feet square. The new regulation required each person who sought any mining work to take out a "Free Miners Certificate" at a cost of $15 each year. It insisted that each miner had to stake his claim in person if it was to be valid. It authorized the granting of dredging permits, in five-mile blocks along 1,500 miles of two streams too swift for other methods of exploitation, the Klondike and Yukon rivers. Subsequently the charge for renewing the annual lease on a claim was cut to $15. In March, 1899, the annual allowance for cost of production, used in calculating the royalty, was increased to $5,000.

When a gold discovery was made on a creek, the first claims were filed downstream, on the theory that the heavier deposits would likely be in the direction the current flowed, and only after a considerable number had been staked did prospectors start putting them upstream. Often enough a gold seeker broke the law by making a claim for a friend; the two were not likely to be found out if the other man promptly recorded it personally and falsely swore he had done all the work himself. Another common violation was to have a claim on several creeks, but not record any of them until developments gave some indication of which would be the more valuable. Somebody else might jump it if ten days had passed since the original person staked it. A famous instance of this sort was the claim numbered "40 above" on Bonanza Creek, unrecorded. It officially became vacant at 12:01 A.M. on a January morning, 1897, and such was the interest that a military policeman was on hand officially to declare the time. At the signal several men set out on foot to the recorder's office, then at Fortymile beyond Dawson; most of them soon dropped out, leaving only two rivals, Lereaux and Lowrie, each with a team of five or six dogs. They kept close together. The dogs did not like the idea of a race, preferring to follow the sled ahead; the lead team insisted on turning out of the trail toward each cabin passed, so there was constant alternation. The two racers arrived at the door of the office on a dead run, too exhausted for the moment to say why they had come. With such an obvious tie, the recorder insisted on dividing the claim between them; later it turned out to be worthless.

A number of claims were incorrectly or carelessly staked along Bonanza and Eldorado creeks in the winter of 1895–96. Part of the difficulty was that a good many of the men used the same rope for measuring, supposedly fifty feet long but actually forty. A mass meeting sent a petition with 130 signatures to the government surveyor at Fortymile, William Ogilvie, requesting him to come and correct matters. When he checked claims one to sixty below on Bonanza Creek, he found there was actually room for just fifty-two full-sized ones; the only equitable solution was to give each man a fractional area. He found other problems on the 110 additional properties. No one actively questioned his rulings, although considerable wealth was sometimes involved and the nearest policeman was sixty-five miles away; this is clear evidence of how law abiding the early Klondike miners were.

The most interesting situation which Ogilvie uncovered was at the claim of Clarence Berry and partner on Eldorado Creek. Obviously rich, it was too long by forty-one feet, six inches. Ogilvie was not a man to favor one prospector over another or to capitalize on any situation for himself. The mistake created a fractional claim, legally open to the first man getting possession; if this had become known generally, somebody would probably have gotten hurt. For once the surveyor violated his own strict code of conduct and, away from the other miners, told Berry of his findings. Pressed for advice, he finally recommended having some friend stake the claim and then later, as was legal, transfer it to Berry and his partner; the plan was executed. The gold taken from the fraction that season was worth $163,000.

A good many miners were unenthusiastic about paying royalty to the Canadian government. At first some of them threatened trouble if inspectors watched their operations closely, and they simply made an affidavit of what their output was; the receipt issued by the officials never showed the amount paid. In 1899, collection was made a duty of the Northwest Mounted Police, who took cubic measurements of the unprocessed extractions from a mine and then by a sampling method from different parts of it estimated the amount of gold in the dump. By this method the Mounties secured far more royalty than had been collected previously. At best it was very difficult to calculate exactly how much gold had been extracted and certainly there was much concealment of the facts; undoubtedly the Canadian government did not receive all to which it was legally entitled. One estimate places the loss in 1898 and 1899 at more than five million dollars. The royalty collected was insufficient to pay the expenses of the Yukon Territory government. The tax was heavy enough, however, to discourage prospecting in unproved areas and was a major factor in the exodus to Nome, Alaska, when discoveries there gave promise.

The selling of mining claims in the early days of the Klondike was quite informal.[4] As more people came into the area, the most common method continued to be direct negotiation between the owner and the buyer. Another frequent device was for the seller to offer his property at the well-conducted auctions of the Mining Exchange, a private enterprise; at times the bidding was spirited. The prospective purchaser made a 10 per cent down payment and then had a maximum of ten days to examine the claim more thoroughly and reach a final decision. Sometimes sellers used professional mine brokers. Occasionally they gave an option for six months to a promoter in one of the money capitals of the world.

The mining methods early used on the Yukon River were much changed by the turn of the century.[5] Initially the prospectors worked two summer months a year and seldom went down more than four

---

[4] Heilprin, *Alaska and the Klondike*, 60–61; Palmer, *In the Klondyke*, 103–106.

[5] Adney, *Stampede*, 242–52, 398–420; Berton, *Fever*, 192–93; Ogilvie, *Early Days*, 138, 231–34; Palmer, *In the Klondyke*, 97–101; Rickard, *Through the Yukon*, 215–18, 235–36; Tollemache, *Reminiscences*, 147–48; Winslow, *Big Pan-Out*, 162–86, 234–35, 246–47.

feet below the surface. In 1887, Fred Hutchinson adapted from the centuries-old practice of the Russians in Siberia the technique known as burning. He used fire to thaw the ground so that he could work twelve months a year rather than two; by the time of the Klondike rush, a precise method had evolved. It was best practiced by two men, who would start to work late in September and try to guess correctly where a former stream bed was, perhaps as much as fifty feet below the present one and following quite a different course, sink a hole to it, and extract the gold-bearing earth. They dug a hole four feet by six or seven down a distance from the surface, then started their burning. The two made a new fire each evening, sometimes with difficulty, and then left quickly to avoid the suffocating smoke. The next morning, with the fire burned out, they removed the ashes and then the dirt. As their hole got deeper, they installed as a windlass a spruce log six inches thick and four and one-half feet long. Gradually their dump of extracted earth rose higher; they put in cribwork and raised the hoist so that it was on top of the dump. When they got down a considerable distance, they perhaps struck the old stream bed; if not, they dug some tunnels twenty feet to the sides looking for it. If they did not find it, the pair simply started the process over again. Often they used thirty cords of wood, costing twenty-five or thirty dollars each, in their search and perhaps sank as many as six holes.

When the miners finally found the gold-bearing gravel, they were careful to pile it separately from the ordinary earth around the top of their shaft. After they had dug out all that was simply at the bottom of the hole, they would tunnel thirty or forty feet upstream and downstream; in the frozen ground they did not need the protection of timbering, nor did they have to worry about water. To be sure their gravel would repay the labor, they panned out a sample several times a day; ten cents a pan on the average meant the work would be profitable and twenty-five cents that it would be unusually remunerative. The two men continued to work until the surface water entered and put out the fire, sometimes as late as May.

As soon as they could no longer work below ground, the miners started preparing for the summer cleanup. They built a dam, costing perhaps one thousand dollars, to catch some water from the creek and send it into their flume, which fed it into a series of twenty to one hundred sluice boxes; the flume and boxes likely cost another one thousand dollars. When the sun had thawed their dump, they started sluicing. The miners generally ran the water for about twenty minutes, then let it settle and ran some more; at the end of the day, they took out the accumulated gold.

These techniques for working a creek claim, traditionally the only kind of any value in the Yukon area, were only slightly modified in developing bench claims. These were on the sides of hills because often the course of a prehistoric stream bed lay buried perhaps as much as eighty feet deep and yet was still above the valley floor. Bench claims were not developed until the winter of 1897–98, when such men as Albert Lancaster, Nels Peterson, Nathan Kresge, William Dietering, and Oliver B. Millett braved the derision of almost all miners to try them. At first such a claim had no standing in law; later it was recognized, its size defined, and a man prohibited from staking both a bench claim and a creek claim. To work the hillside prospect, the men sank shafts. For the cleanup, they either toted their gravel down to where a stream was available for sluicing or used a rocker.

Whatever kind of claim they had, miners in 1897 and 1898 worked with feverish haste to secure the maximum immediate yield because they feared that the Canadian government might reduce the size of their holdings and by such confiscation withhold some of the wealth they believed was theirs. This was never done, but fear of it made for extravagant methods of mining.

While many men worked their own property themselves or hired others to do it at a stipulated wage, another method was to grant a so-called lay. This was the lease of a segment, perhaps fifty feet wide across the stream in a creek claim, to a man who would sink at least one hole to bedrock in return for 50 or 75 per cent of the yield. The arrangement was not entirely satisfactory, for sometimes the so-called layman did not work steadily; sometimes the segment was so small that it did not pay the layman an adequate return.

Gradually the techniques of mining changed. In 1898, miner C. J. Berry observed that steam escaping from the exhaust of an engine had accidentally thawed a hole. This led him to experiments which proved that steam applied to frozen ground would thaw it along the entire length of a rubber hose in a few moments. He devised the "steam point." From a small boiler at the surface, steam was carried through a rubber hose to a piece of iron pipe, five or six feet long, pointed at the lower end and with an orifice there to apply the steam to the ground. It was inserted in the frozen gravel and then driven forward gently by taps from a hammer. Later there were some improvements on this rudimentary device; its use was widespread.

By the summer of 1899, the "poor man's rush" was over. Companies began paying good prices to buy up considerable blocks of claims along the creeks. They used steam for thawing, steam shovels to dig, steam-propelled water for the hydraulic washing down of hills, and otherwise mechanized tasks once performed by hand. In later years, dredging came to be used exclusively.

How much gold was secured by these various methods over the years? The question is easier to pose than to answer because the royalty which the Canadian government charged gave much incentive for concealment; the official tax returns are certainly not accurate. Probably a figure somewhere between $200,000,000 and $300,000,000 is correct.[6]

Certain of the governmental services provided the gold seekers of the Klondike area in 1897 were quite unsatisfactory; beginning in 1898, the deficiencies were remedied.[7] In the earliest days the Northwest Mounted Police informally handled a variety of matters. When the Canadian government received the official report of Carmack's discovery, it moved promptly to dispatch customs officers, land surveyors, more police, and three key officials—a judge, a gold commissioner, and an administrator (who was to perform much the same functions as a governor).

First of the chief officials to arrive was Thomas Fawcett, permanent gold commissioner and temporary head of the government in the area until Major J. M. Walsh should come. The kindest thing that can be said of him is that, thrust into Dawson from a government sinecure in British Columbia, he was incapable. When he arrived with two assistants in the summer of 1897, so great was the rush that there seemed no time during regular office hours to do anything but record claims. Perhaps there actually was not sufficient leisure to

6 Adney, *Stampede,* 415; Berton, *Fever,* 436; W. N. Robertson, *Yukon Memories,* 55–56; Adams Shortt and Arthur G. Doughty (eds.), *Canada and Its Provinces,* XXI, 633–34; Winslow, *Big Pan-Out,* 241.

7 Adney, *Stampede,* 437–41; Bankson, *Nugget,* 107–108, 127–29, 263–65; Berton, *Fever,* 329–31; Black, *My Seventy Years,* 123, 185–89; Rickard, *Through the Yukon,* 238; Winslow, *Big Pan-Out,* 146, 179–83.

allow any inquirer the right to see the registry books, but it was the custom everywhere else in Canada and its denial in Dawson caused much bitterness. Quickly the clerks started to capitalize on the situation by privately selling desired information to any person who would pay them cash or give them an interest in the claim. The clerks made some unintentional mistakes in the records. They were also bribed to make other changes, such as running a line through names and dates, erasing, scratching out, or even literally cutting out information and pasting in a substitute. Occasionally they rejected a claim and somehow another person, immediately informed, would appear to take it as his own. These unjust practices Fawcett, not a crook himself, apparently lacked the force of personality to change. It is difficult to understand why he arbitrarily dismissed complaints about specific mistakes which he clearly had the duty to correct. He began issuing passes to favored individuals, allowing them to go to the head of the line waiting to record claims; this was grossly unfair to ordinary men who sometimes had to retain their place in line for three days in weather forty degrees below zero. Commissioner Fawcett often refused to record fractional claims, yet he consistently allowed some favorites to make them. Another difficulty he faced was that the Canadian mining laws were not precisely adapted to conditions in the Klondike, a problem made worse by the vague and sometimes contradictory wording of the regulations; the different interpretations possible over a statute could cause honest differences of opinion and certainly those Fawcett adopted were criticized.

In February, 1898, additional Canadian officials arrived in Dawson. The judge performed his duties to the satisfaction of the entire camp. The crown prosecuting attorney, who was also lands agent, leased government-owned water-front property to private individuals—a proper procedure except that he was employed by them in an unofficial capacity to be their legal advisor before he arranged the rental. The two mine inspectors who came were not well qualified; one had previously been a dealer in horses and the other "an uncertified master" of a whaling vessel.

Finally, Major J. M. Walsh, who as administrator was head of the government in the Klondike area, arrived on May 21, 1898. Meanwhile, Fawcett had been letting many matters wait for his arrival. Walsh had agreed to serve only a year, so when he belatedly got to the Klondike he was already thinking about his successor and would not take a strong stand on anything; he left in July. He had had a distinguished career as a member of the Canadian Parliament; he managed during his brief stay in the Yukon to tarnish his reputation. When he hired Louis Carbeno as his cook, he required a promise that he, Walsh, would be given a three-quarters interest in any claim the cook might stake. Later, Fawcett closed a large portion of Dominion Creek to further entry because the staking there had been so haphazard that a new survey of the area had to be made; he said that the region would again be open for filing on July 11 to those who had obtained special permits. On the morning of July 9, Commissioner Fawcett posted a notice dated July 8 saying that Dominion Creek was at once open to further entry and no permits were needed. Carbeno and other favored stampeders had left Dawson on July 8.

On May 28, 1898, the Klondike region became the separate Yukon Territory. Its first governor was William Ogilvie, the Dominion surveyor, a sensible choice. He arrived, as promptly as possible, in September. One of his first duties was to conduct an investigation of misconduct reported in the gold commissioner's office. Many witnesses had already left the Klondike, while others cynically believed that nothing could be accomplished and lent no aid; the hearing was a fiasco. Ogilvie, despite this failure, proved an able governor, and conditions generally were much improved under his administration.

No hint of scandal marred the outstandingly good work of the Northwest Mounted Police in the Yukon area.[8] The first Mountie assigned there, Inspector Charles Constantine, came to Fortymile in 1894 and was joined the next year by 20 more men. By 1896, there were 30 on duty; they moved their headquarters to Dawson in the winter of 1896–97. In 1897, a reinforcement of 50 men arrived at the gold-rush city; in 1898, some 250 more came. The men of Dawson were the pick of the Mounted Police, which was itself a select group.

The officer in command at Dawson during the greatest excitement, Colonel S. B. Steele, had to stay awake nineteen hours a day to perform his duties. He did not assign his men to any specific beat because he wanted a lawbreaker to feel that anywhere in town one might suddenly appear. Steele used secret detectives to obtain the

8 Adney, *Stampede*, 432–33, 440; Berton, *Fever*, 320; Jeremiah Lynch, *Three Years in the Klondike*, 62; Steele, *Forty Years*, 288, 323–31; Walden, *Dog-Puncher*, 134; Winslow, *Big Pan-Out*, 145–46, 194–95.

names and histories of criminals so that his men could watch them carefully. His Mounties allowed the town to run "wide open," forbidding only obscenity, cheating, disorderly conduct, the sale of liquor to minors, and the employment of children in saloons. On Sunday they prohibited fishing, hunting, patronizing saloons, opening any place of business, or performing any labor, even sawing wood for one's own use. However, they allowed dancing, gambling, or patronizing a theater.

The police dealt effectively with the numerous minor thefts and misdemeanors. They were faced with almost no major crimes; that there were no such conditions as those at Skagway was a great tribute to their effectiveness. The Mounties used two chief punishments—the "blue ticket" and the woodpile. The ticket was an order to leave the Klondike. Sawing at the woodpile to supply fuel for the government buildings was hard work in summer and unpleasant indeed when the temperature was well below zero; fear of it proved a real deterrent to crime. Occasionally the police collected fines and the government used the money mostly to pay the hospital expenses of sick prospectors.

The population at Dawson in the fall of 1896 was four or five hundred people, five thousand in the summer of 1897, and the next summer thirty thousand. The summer of 1899 showed little change, and then a quick decline began. By 1908, there were only three thousand people left.

At first Dawson was a city of tents, some on lots on the river flat, others strung along the squirming trails up the hillsides.[9] Gradually there arose rough cabins costing $1,500 for labor and green lumber. By 1899, many of the houses were of brick and a few of them had bathtubs. Lots in the business district brought high prices, sometimes in 1898 as much as $20,000 for a choice corner suitable for a saloon, and speculation in them was lively. To keep up with the demand for building material that year, three sawmills ran constantly and men were waiting to cart away the boards as quickly as they were produced. The price of lumber was $150 to $200 a thousand feet. Most of the river-front sites were rented for $8 to $12 per foot per month.

[9] Adney, *Stampede*, 365–66; Haskell, *Two Years*, 357; Lynch, *Three Years*, 278; Tollemache, *Reminiscences*, 53; Walden, *Dog-Puncher*, 145; Winslow, *Big Pan-Out*, 143–44, 150.

In Dawson's winters the long darkness was from about December 1 to the middle of January.[10] Its location in a north-south valley made the sun visible longer than in the surrounding gold creeks, where often the darkness lasted from November until February. The long night cast a never ending gloom over the area. The temperature went down; in 1897–98, the lowest at Dawson was −54°F. and it was even colder on some of the surrounding hills. Old-timers judged the temperature by the fact that mercury froze at −40°, kerosene at −35° to −55°, according to grade, painkiller at −72°, St. Jacob's oil at −75°, and the best Hudson's Bay Company rum at −80°. Extreme cold usually hit the Klondike two or three times a year in snaps of a week or ten days. Many a northern veteran would say that −25° was invigorating, −40° decidedly chilly, and −50° extremely cold.

In such weather a person's face often felt numb from cold and it was hard to know when it had become frostbitten except that a small patch as white as a tablecloth would appear on it. Then prompt remedies were demanded and it was expected that anybody who saw such a spot would warn the person. Certainly it was common for frost to collect on eyelashes, eyebrows, mustaches, and beards. To prevent this harmless inconvenience, most men were clean shaven.

When the snow fell, it was nearly invisible. It usually accumulated to not over three feet deep, light as powder. Since there was no wind in the cold of midwinter, it clung to the trees and made whole mountainsides seem "chiselled from spotless marble." In February, as the temperatures started to rise, the breezes returned and blew the snow. To prevent snowblindness, most people wore dark glasses; its victims had to stay indoors for perhaps a week. An occasional winter sight was the aurora borealis, less spectacular on the Klondike than in some parts of the Far North; it would come for several nights in a row and would not appear again for weeks. In spring the great excitement came when the ice on the Yukon River melted enough to start moving downstream. Later the streams would fill high enough for part of Dawson to be flooded at times. In summer the sun shone twenty hours a day; from the mountains behind the city it could be seen for twenty-four. It was hard to go to bed under such con-

10 Adney, *Klondike*, 201–204, 352–54, 368–72; Lynch, *Three Years*, 178; Tollemache, *Reminiscences*, 14–15; Winslow, *Big Pan-Out*, 219–23.

ditions. When a man was asked the time of day, the next question would likely be: "Morning or evening?"

A variety of foods was available in Dawson by the summer of 1898.[11] C. A. Bartholam, who had brought in about fifty cents' worth of vegetable seeds, planted them. The dampness and the long hours of sunshine had much the same effect as a hothouse. His first crop took a month to raise; his net profit, $1,000.00, prompted competitors to enter the field. The first fresh milk in town, sold from a cow who arrived July 8, 1898, cost $30.00 a gallon. For those who did not wish to do their own cooking, the price of a good meal at a cafe averaged $1.50 to $2.50.

The early hotels, the second story of some eating or drinking establishment, were split into pens as high as a man's head or else left undivided. On the double-deck bunks the bedding was rough blankets and a very small pillow. Ventilation came through the cracks in the wall; in winter, torrid heat from the stove made it all too obvious that the hotel was filled with unwashed men who had taken off only their shoes and outer coats. In the summer of 1898, the Fairview Hotel, by far the best in town, opened. This three-story frame building was lighted by electricity, heated with hot air. For board and a room ten feet by twelve, the monthly charge varied from $125 to $250, depending on the room's location.

Dawson's water in winter came bubbling to the surface from holes dug five to six feet deep in the ice of the Yukon River.[12] Every night a few inches would freeze on top and were cut away the next morning until abruptly the entire hole turned to solid ice; then a new hole was dug. In summer the water came from surface springs back of the town and from the Klondike River. The water which the men of Dawson drank was contaminated by the garbage washing down the Klondike River, by inadequately safeguarded cesspools, by seepage from the decaying vegetable matter in the bog on which the town was built, and by mineral salts. It caused a severe epidemic of typhoid and dysentery in the summer of 1898, with deaths from it averaging

---

11 Adney, *Stampede,* 349, 374–80, 392–93; Heilprin, *Alaska and the Klondike,* 102; Winslow, *Big Pan-Out,* 150, 152.

12 Adney, *Stampede,* 350–51, 429–30; Haskell, *Two Years,* 155–56; Heilprin, *Alaska and the Klondike,* 174–75; Steele, *Forty Years,* 321–22, 331–32; Tollemache, *Reminiscences,* 77; Winslow, *Big Pan-Out,* 150, 154–55, 222, 225.

about two a day. Instituted reforms prevented another epidemic the next summer.

One persistent health problem was malaria, whose then unknown cause was the numerous mosquitoes active from about the first of June to the first of September. In the almost constant daytime they were perpetually on the attack; the only effective defenses were gloves and netting. People in Dawson were less likely to fall prey in winter to scurvy than those who lived out of town. The first symptom, feeling tired, was hard to detect when everybody was tired anyhow; additional evidence as the disease progressed was a hardening of the tendons, especially under the knee, and a darkening of the skin. The illness was rarely fatal to men in town; some prospectors in isolated areas became disabled before they realized what was happening and eventually died unless a providential visitor discovered them in time.

To care for the ill, Dawson had about seventy doctors in the summer of 1898. So few had lucrative practices that the Canadian doctors, far outnumbered, had several United States physicians fined and jailed for practicing without a Canadian license; many of them continued to give help without displaying a sign or collecting a fee. The usual charge for a doctor's visit was five dollars in town and for a trip into the countryside as much as five hundred dollars. St. Mary's, the first hospital in Dawson, was constructed through the efforts of Jesuit Father William Judge. This veteran of the Yukon opened a fifty-bed building which was soon so filled that many patients were sleeping on pallets on the floor. Of those in trouble he asked not what their faith was but how he could aid them. At first he worked alone, then in the summer of 1897 was joined by the Sisters of the Order of St. Anne, who served as nurses. He enlarged the hospital to three stories and also added a wing. When Father Judge died on January 10, 1899, he was beyond dispute the best-loved man in Dawson.

In August, 1898, a second hospital, the Good Samaritan, opened. Those no doctor could cure, if death came in winter, were placed in a rude spruce coffin, carried in a hearse drawn by dogs, and buried in a grave burned out of the ground by the same method used to thaw earth for mining.

For the destitute, such benevolent organizations as the Masons and the Odd Fellows provided aid. In the chaotic society of the Klondike it was inevitable that the police should have at Dawson a large list of missing people of whom no trace could now be discovered despite the prodding of anxious relatives.

The churches were not strongly supported in Yukon. The Catholics, Presbyterians, and Episcopalians all had church buildings. Even more poorly supported were laundries, whose charge for washing was almost the price of the new article.

An important place of recreation was the theater.[13] Of the four which offered vaudeville and local sketches, changing the program weekly, the Combination was in a wooden building and the other three—the Monte Carlo, the Mascot, and the Pavilion—were in tents. The admission price of fifty cents at the three and a dollar at the Combination included one cigar or one drink. Entering through the bar, the patron usually seated himself on boards supported by stools; if he entered the boxes, there was no extra charge but he was expected to buy champagne for his lady friends or for female members of the troupe. Some of the performers, veterans of the stage before coming north, were quite good. There was an overabundance of women singers, often with more beauty than talent, and some lacked both; Anna Kane was the best of them. The most popular dancers were Polly and Lottie Oatley. Ordinary actors and actresses earned $150 a week; orchestra musicians received $20 a day.

A variety of stage plays was presented in gold-rush Dawson, from *Uncle Tom's Cabin,* with Malemutes for bloodhounds, to *Camille.* There were also rodeos, circus freaks, acrobats, "Lady Godiva," "Little Egypt," minstrels, primitive motion pictures, and magicians. Hardly entertainment were wandering street bands, who took up a collection from anybody willing to pay for music produced by disappointed miners on instruments they were "pitiless enough to tackle."

Every second or third door downtown was a place to buy a drink. The best liquor available was much diluted; the worst was indeed bad. When whiskey was in short supply, "hootch" was made locally from sour dough, brown sugar, or both and flavored with blueberries or dried peaches; home-brewed beer was also sold. At a saloon a man

13 Adney, *Stampede,* 315, 337–42, 357, 426–28; Allan, *Gold, Men and Dogs,* 6–7; Bankson, *Nugget,* 184, 203, 207, 291; Berton, *Fever,* 374, 377, 387–89; Black, *My Seventy Years,* 132; Heilprin, *Alaska and the Klondike,* 53–54; Lung, *Gold,* 103; Lynch, *Three Years,* 56–57, 182–83; O'Connor, *High Jinks,* 84, 141–42, 147–48; Palmer, *In the Klondyke,* 176; Walden, *Dog-Puncher,* 113–14, 155–56; Winslow, *Big Pan-Out,* 193–97, 236.

dead broke appeared as welcome as a big spender; an abstainer was free to use the dipper in the water barrel at the end of the bar. The patrons, with almost no class lines drawn, were all friendly and good natured; some laughed and talked, while others looked on in silent enjoyment. Occasionally a prospector who had struck it rich would buy drinks for the whole roomful. Constantly to be seen in the various saloons was the mule Wise Mike, curled up near the stove. When some inebriated newcomer literally attempted to kick him out, he would rear up on his hind legs, snap his teeth ferociously, and wrestle with the befuddled drunk.

Some saloons were also gambling houses. To play, a man gave his poke of gold to the dealer, who simply by lifting it called its weight and value accurately, then deposited it in a drawer. When the player stopped he got his poke back, sometimes with his losses extracted, sometimes with his winnings in chips to be cashed at the teller's cage. To discourage dishonesty, lookouts armed with rifles surveyed the tables. One reason these houses were profitable was that a man who had set out to win a specified sum of money, such as the cost of a dinner, generally stopped when he got what he wanted, but if his luck was bad, he continued to play for a long time in the hope that a reversal might restore some of his losses. Gambling in Dawson was orderly, well conducted, and honest, thanks to the frequent presence of the Mounties. In the biggest game played in the gold-rush city, Sam Bonnifield lost a $150,000 poker pot to Louis Golden; both were professional gamblers.

And some saloons had dance halls. The girls there were not backward about asking a man to be their partner. When he did, the couple circled the room five or six times until the music stopped abruptly, then rushed to the bar. Sometimes the man paid in advance for several dances—a natural thing to do when there were about 125 of them in an average evening. The girls received about $125 a week as basic pay, to which were added commissions on such extras as champagne, which industrious, good-looking girls might make amount to $25 more pay per night. These dance-hall girls "lived private." Mostly they were plain, hefty, and so honest they would protect the gold of a drunken customer. Once when a girl in a dance hall publicly refused to marry a rich claim owner because he drank too much, the crowd egged him on until he promised her her weight in gold if she would change her mind. She did; she was immediately weighed and her cost proved to be $25,000. Reportedly she saved him from a drunkard's grave and raised a wonderful family.

Inevitably, houses of prostitution throve. These were in the red-light district of Dawson and also were among the chief business establishments of Lousetown. Hardly different in morals from the prostitutes was the girl who said that for the winter of 1897–98 she would serve as wife in every respect to the highest bidder. She stipulated that the money was to be deposited with a trading company and not paid to her until the end of the season. Both were to show courtesy and treat the other well; if matters proved unsatisfactory, the one breaking the agreement forfeited the money. On the day of the auction, a large crowd watched as she walked up and down the length of a bar, dressed in the latest Parisian fashion. After a sharp round of bidding, the successful purchaser paid about five thousand dollars for her.

Gradually, more respectable women came into the area. In the winter of 1899–1900, they formed a "vigilance committee" to make sure that only acceptable ladies were admitted to the high-class dances. The committee quickly learned the past and present of each woman in town, including the one who was not married to the man she called her husband and the one who had bribed her legal spouse to go away, leaving her to her pleasures.

Considerably rarer in Dawson than a wife was a baby. Mrs. George Black found in the winter of 1898–99 that her boy attracted many visitors who wished to feel his tiny fingers curl in their rough hands, to see him gurgling joyfully in his bath, to tell her with tears in their eyes of their own babies so far away.

Mail service to the Klondike was at first inadequate.[14] In the spring of 1898, the transport was simply dog-team outfits, making a trip between Dawson and Skagway anyhow, which as a public service generously carried as many letters as they could. Sorting the mail was a duty which the Mounties undertook, but they were so inexperienced that it occasionally took them a week to do it. Regular Canadian postal service began at Dawson in March, 1898.

Reading matter was at first in short supply.[15] Old magazines and newspapers were read to tatters. In the spring of 1898, on June 6 to be

14 Adney, *Stampede*, 357, 433–34; Steele, *Forty Years*, 324.
15 Adney, *Stampede*, 422–25; Bankson, *Nugget*, 90–109; Winslow, *Big Pan-Out*, 151, 209, 234.

exact, the first newspaper arrived in Dawson; a lawyer named Miller bought it for $160, charged admission to a public reading, and made $1,000. Eventually the boats brought in considerable quantities of important publications; the magazines sold for about a dollar each and the newspapers for twenty-five cents. It must have seemed strange to hear a news vendor going down the street calling "All the daily papers! *Kansas City Star, Chicago Times-Herald, Omaha Bee, Detroit Free Press, Springfield Republican.*"

The first newspaper to be published in Dawson was the *Yukon Midnight Sun,* initially appearing on June 11, 1898; a four-page, seven-column weekly, it cost fifty cents a copy or fifteen dollars a year. Five days later, the first issue of a rival, *The Klondike Nugget,* hit the streets. Classified advertisements in it cost a dollar a line and regular ones ten dollars an inch. The *Nugget* paid its compositors fifteen dollars a day and the average pay of other staff members was four hundred dollars a month. Both before and after the newspapers began appearing, a large number of notices were posted about town. Some were advertisements of all sorts and others were messages for particular individuals.

Dawson, like most gold-rush towns, had trouble with fires.[16] The first major one struck in December, 1897, and burned, among other things, the town's only sawmill. In all rebuilding, nails were salvaged from the ashes, since few new ones were available. A second major fire broke out on October 14, 1898, on the second floor of the Green Tree Hotel and did not stop until it had destroyed downtown Dawson. By this time the town had two fire engines but, unfortunately, had not paid for them and so had not been allowed to uncrate them. In the emergency the task of removing each part from the frozen tallow and assembling the machines began under the supervision of the former fire chief of Seattle. While some men worked frantically at this, others roped cabins and pulled them out of the way of the flames; still others dynamited larger places. To encourage these men a saloon owner put out a bucket filled with liquor and soon others did, too. Not all the drinking was done by the fire fighters; indeed, the occasion developed into Dawson's first major celebration. Finally the fire engines were put together, started pumping, and almost at once the water froze in the hose. The fire eventually burned itself out. The third conflagration came on April 26, 1899, and again great damage was caused.

16 Berton, *Fever,* 409; Walden, *Dog-Puncher,* 111; Winslow, *Big Pan-Out,* 230–33.

As that traditional American holiday the Fourth of July approached in 1898, the Mounties' Colonel Steele proclaimed it Dawson's first joint celebration for both Americans and Canadians. It was a great success, starting with a roar of guns and revolvers discharging just after midnight. This made all the dogs in town rush around in great distraction, with their ears lying straight back and their tails tucked between their legs.[17]

Branches of the Canadian Bank of Commerce and the Bank of British North America opened in Dawson in June, 1898.[18] The first quarters of the former were in a building fifteen feet by eighteen with no windows and a single door, in front of which was a counter. The "vaults" were two wooden, tin-lined boxes, four feet long, three feet wide, and three feet deep, protected by a lid. Nobody semed to think it unusual the day these vaults contained about a million dollars in gold dust, with no guard and the clerk at the counter issuing paper money from a stack a foot high. One of the chief functions of these banks was to purchase gold with paper money. The actual value of what was found on the various creeks varied from $15.00 to $18.50 an ounce. In the purchase of it, sometimes an accurate assay was made, but as often it was simply classified as "town dust," worth $17.00 an ounce originally but later reduced to $16.00 and less because of adulteration. The banks loaned money, primarily on mines and on Dawson property, at a fee of 2 per cent a month; private sources often charged 8 or 10 per cent.

Many miners visited Dawson only on the rare occasions when they could not stand the isolated life at their claims.[19] An ordinary cabin was twelve feet by fourteen, with sides made out of nine or ten logs, each eight to nine inches thick and chinked with moss. The roof, almost flat, was made from small poles covered with moss and surmounted by six inches of dirt. There was at least one window on the sunny side, if possible with double sashes to prevent frosting. With sashes costing twenty dollars apiece, white flour sacking or ginger ale bottles were often substituted. The floor was of poles, hewn flat on

17 Adney, *Stampede*, 425–26; Walden, *Dog-Puncher*, 148.

18 Adney, *Stampede*, 416–18; Bankson, *Nugget*, 202; Berton, *Fever*, 60–61, 299, 380; Heilprin, *Alaska and the Klondike*, 178; Lynch, *Three Years*, 34; Winslow, *Big Pan-Out*, 218.

19 Adney, *Stampede*, 197–201; Winslow, *Big Pan-Out*, 63, 225–30; Haskell, *Two Years*, 222; Tollemache, *Reminiscences*, 43–44.

the top, or of lumber. For heat there was the Yukon stove, selling for sixty-five dollars at a Dawson tinsmith's. It was shaped like a half-barrel and divided into two compartments: one for the fire and one for an oven. On even the coldest days it could keep a properly chinked and roofed cabin uncomfortably warm. The stove sat on four posts and its pipe went up through a square oil can on the roof. Ventilation came from a small box, located on the roof, which had a door that could be opened or closed. Light came from oil lamps and candles when available, otherwise from a "bitch," a milk or meat can with a wick to burn bacon grease. The bunks were simply poles and boards, with spruce boughs for a mattress and flour-sack-encased socks or moccasins for a pillow.

When the fire burned out in a cabin during the wintertime, everything froze. It was not uncommon for the occupant to wake up in the morning and find that icicles had formed around the top of his blankets during the night. On the ceiling and sides of the cabin, tremendous icicles, commonly called "glaciers," formed from the steam of cooking; these were a handy source of water for drinking and washing. Since an ax was dull and likely to crack if frozen, it was kept under the oven. When the owner left the cabin, he did not lock it, so that any traveler could enter it in an emergency; if one did, it was unforgivable not to replace shavings and kindling when failure to get an instant blaze might cost a man his life. Each cabin had some sort of a cache for food, for protection was absolutely necessary from the naturally thieving dogs who roamed everywhere.

In winter, the most common meal of a miner on his claim was coffee, boiled beans, and pancakes. Few miners had canned vegetables, dried fruits, or citric acid and so were in danger of scurvy. Their bread, if they baked it, was made of baking powder dough rather than the yeast variety.

Traveling between his claim and Dawson, a prospector frequently made the trip in a day.[20] If not, he stopped at one of the roadhouses, usually a rough log cabin with wooden bunks in tiers around the sides and a stove and sometimes a wooden bench in the center. The proprietor usually provided blankets and was always ready to sell food and liquor. The trails from Dawson to the mines were not kept in

[20] Adney, *Stampede,* 353; Bankson, *Nugget,* 222–23, 235; Haskell, *Two Years,* 75–76, 311; Heilprin, *Alaska and the Klondike,* 130; Tollemache, *Reminiscences,* 67, 95; Winslow, *Big Pan-Out,* 158–59.

good repair. Thus going up the lower part of Bonanza Creek in summer, a miner had to wade in mud above the ankles or else with fairly long strides try to keep his balance while walking on the wet, slippery tops of "niggerheads," rounded tufts of grass and moss projecting above the water. Most prospectors were carrying so heavy a load that they exaggerated the poor state of the roads and complained bitterly. When in the fall of 1898 the government gave Tom O'Brien the right to build a tramroad from Dawson up Bonanza Creek to Grand Forks, he instead simply leveled off an adequate winter sled road and started collecting a toll of one dollar per one hundred pounds. Violent objections caused the courts to rule his grant invalid in February of the following year.

Traveling in winter, a man had to take special care to protect his hands, feet, and face. Generally he wore a parka of blue denim or overall cloth, with a bit of fur around the opening of the hood. Like a big shirt, with no opening front or back, the parka stretched down to the knees and slipped on over the head. When the traveler came indoors, he took off his parka and it thawed; when he put it on again and went out, it promptly froze but kept the clothing underneath in good condition. If he camped along the trail, he was careful to brush the snow off his tent just before going to sleep; otherwise the tent cloth would freeze.

To haul freight overland in the Yukon area the traditional method was to use a dog team.[21] In gold-rush days a few St. Bernards, mastiffs, and collies were used; other breeds imported seldom could be induced to pull anything. Policeman Steele reported that in the spring of 1898 at Lake Bennett, where men sometimes tugged at a sled along with several dogs, the animals would almost always be wagging their tails with enjoyment at being in the same team as their masters. The use of such animals was not common. The Yukon-born Malamute, a native Eskimo dog, could endure more hunger and cold than any import. About as large as a collie, he was white, white-gray or white-black in color, in general appearance was quite wolflike, carried his tail tightly curled over his back, and had a very dismal howl. In harness he took pride in his work; unleashed, he was a natural-born thief and nobody expected him to be a watchdog. A Malamute raised by Eskimos was al-

21 Adney, *Stampede*, 208–33; Lynch, *Three Years*, 141; Steele, *Forty Years*, 301; Tollemache, *Reminiscences*, 108; Walden, *Dog-Puncher*, 34–38; Winslow, *Big Pan-Out*, 46, 109, 176.

ways roughly treated; if he was sold to a white man who showed him kindness, once he had recovered from his surprise he was capable of affection. To be worked effectively, most dogs needed patience from their owners. A few needed to be shown who was master, and this was done by using a fist on their thick-hair sides or, what sounds cruel but wasn't, by using a dog chain; a club or stick was used only by the ignorant. A Malamute did not need to be tied, like a horse, when at work on the trail, for he would simply lie down in the snow and wait for his master—except that when obviously headed home he might become impatient and abruptly start off on his own. He was fed all he could eat once a day, typically, a cup of rice, a pound of bacon, and a half-pound of fish. In 1898, a good sled dog cost $350. He could go at a good trot all day, pulling three or four hundred pounds of freight, if he had a man to help him over the difficult spots. Among the members of a team a natural leader would arise, gaining his place over his rivals by a series of encounters so fierce that they certainly would have been very painful had not the animals been so well protected by their dense fur.

A typical team for freighting was six or seven dogs, two of which, if possible, could lead so that one could break trail while the other rested. The harness of a dog was something like a horse collar, with side traces hitched back from dog to dog up to the animal just in front of the sled, called the sled dog, then past him to a small whiffletree. The sled dog, also attached to the whiffletree, had separate traces so that he could jump out and pull at right angles when needed. From the whiffletree about five feet of rope ran back to the nearest sled. At one side of the lead sled a so-called gee pole extended out from the front at an angle of forty-five degrees; it was six feet long and three inches thick at the butt. The driver walked astride the rope from the whiffletree and held the gee pole in one hand, steering the sled accurately and ready to put his weight to the pole should the sled start to slip in either direction. (If he were using only one sled and not several hitched together, instead of the gee pole there might be at the rear two handles, like those on a plow, for steering and preventing upsets.) Down steep hills the driver unsnapped the team and rode the gee pole, leaning far back with legs stuck out in front. An ordinary freight outfit consisted of three full-sized sleds chained together to follow in the same track. The lead sled had a load of six hundred pounds, the middle four hundred, and the rear two hundred. Using three sleds distributed the load over twenty-one feet of bearing surface; if all three tipped over, they could be righted one by one.

A genuine Yukon freight sled had a light frame of hickory, oak, or white birch lashed with rawhide. The runners were six inches high and sixteen inches apart. The sides extended a foot above the bed in front, two feet in the rear. The sled was loaded by putting a tarpaulin on the bed, piling the goods on it so that the heaviest weight came about one-third of the way back, then folding the cover over the top and lashing it down tight so that nothing could spill out. The dogs pulled the load at about three miles per hour; when returning with the sled light, they often went six or seven miles an hour. In Dawson during the winter of 1898–99, virtually every shop kept at least two dogs, hitched to a sled and ready to deliver goods locally.

At first only a few horses were used in the Klondike area, and they were killed in the fall because nobody believed they could live until spring.[22] In 1898–99, the Northwest Mounted Police tried the experiment of turning some loose and they fended for themselves successfully during the cold period, digging through the snow to the vegetation beneath. The next season, more than a thousand horses wintered in the Dawson area. The price of one animal was $500. Formed into pack trains, they transported freight between Dawson and the mines, carried two hundred pounds each, lived off the country, and made a one-way trip in a day. With the freight rate at forty-five cents a pound, by making about fifty round trips a season each horse earned his master about $4,500. With two men handling a train of five to thirty animals, the profits were enormous, despite the high rate of equine mortality. Most of those running trains were veterans at the task who had come in from many areas. So successful were the pack trains that men hitched horses to sleds in winter: experience had proved that they could pull a ton of goods over smooth, icy trails. By the fall of 1899, horses almost superseded dogs as animals to haul freight.

A special problem was transportation of gold dust from the mines. Sometimes it was carried by men, although not for long distances.[23] They would put five to eight hundred ounces in a moose-hide sack as a back pack. More commonly a pack train transported the gold to Dawson, the cargo being distributed about 125 pounds to each horse;

22 Lynch, *Three Years*, 143; Walden, *Dog-Puncher*, 169; Winslow, *Big Pan-Out*, 152–53.

23 Adney, *Stampede*, 413–14; Bankson, *Nugget*, 320–46; Steele, *Forty Years*, 333.

occasionally dogs brought it out. Whatever the mode, no special precautions were taken against robbery. When gold was shipped out of Dawson to Seattle, it went by river and ocean steamer with an escort of policemen. These Mounties drew their usual pay of $1.25 a day; often they received a small present from the banks in the United States.

For a time the Nuggett Express Company, organized by Eugene C. Allen, served the Klondike area. Among other functions it picked up mail in Dawson at fifty cents a letter and delivered it to customers on the creeks. It bought for them almost any item they desired from some Dawson merchant or another, collected a commission from the store, and charged the customer the regular retail price plus a minimum delivery charge of fifty cents a pound. As the business prospered, it extended its scope and performed such services as picking up for a Dawson dance-hall girl her diamonds in pawn at San Francisco. In 1900, the company went bankrupt.

Of the writers whose fame is connected with the Klondike, the most popular was English-born Robert Service.[24] He took no part in the gold rush. He was fortunate enough to begin writing after memory had healed the wounds of those who had hurried to the Yukon and they were now ready to recall their adventures in sentimental fashion; they made Service their poet laureate.

At the age of thirty (in 1906), Service found himself a clerk in the Whitehorse branch of the Canadian Bank of Commerce; he was also an amateur reciter of such verses as "Casey at the Bat." When one of the churches was organizing an entertainment, the editor of the local paper suggested that he write a poem for the occasion. Since Service had already scribbled at one time or another a fair amount of verse, he undertook the assignment, returned to the bank that evening, and started to work. The night watchman, hearing a noise, saw a figure bending over a desk, shut his eyes, and fired a shot, fortunately missing. Service went on that night to write a raw, rollicking dramatic monologue called "The Shooting of Dan McGrew." A month later, he composed another ballad, "The Cremation of Sam McGee," then wrote almost steadily for two months. He submitted his manuscript, called *Songs of a Sourdough* in Canada and *The Spell of the Yukon*

[24] Laura B. Berton, *I Married the Klondike*, 75; Robert Service, *Ploughman of the Moon*, 323–56; O'Connor, *High Jinks*, 136–37; Winslow, *Big Pan-Out*, 245; "The Yukon Troubadour," *Time*, Vol. LXXII (September 22, 1958), 30–32.

in the United States, to a Toronto publisher of church hymnals, expecting to pay the publication costs himself. As the printing was in progress, however, the press foreman noticed how quickly the type was being set and showed the proofs around the office. The employees were so impressed that the company became more interested and took the volume over as a commercial venture. Eventually the book sold a million copies.

After three years in Whitehorse, the bank transferred Service to Dawson, then a city of four thousand with less than a third of its dwellings occupied. He heard many yarns from old-timers. Living at the dormitory for bank employees, he wrote in the quiet hours between midnight and three in the morning. In four months of such labor he produced *Ballads of a Cheechako* (1909). His original publishers said they would be delighted to have the book if Service would omit one poem about the red-light district. He replied that he would be happy to do so if the company would increase his royalty from 10 per cent to 15 per cent; it agreed. The new volume succeeded, Service wrote years later, because it was steeped in the spirit of the Klondike and reeked with reality.

Service wrote his first novel, *The Trail of '98,* in a large hand, using a carpenter's pencil, on huge rolls of wallpaper, wrapping paper, and building paper, all of which were less expensive at the time in Dawson than ordinary writing paper. When he had finished a draft, he would pin it to the wall of his cabin and stare at it to see if it were satisfactory. None of Service's work could be classed as literature or as a fully rounded picture of Klondike life, but it was fun to read and the verses were very popular.

Rex Beach set out for the Klondike but only got as far up the Yukon River as Fort Yukon and Rampart City. He later went to Nome. None of his novels about the Northland, which enjoyed great success, were about the Klondike or the rush there.[25]

Joaquin Miller, a well-known poet of the time whom critics now consider a minor figure in the history of American literature, was sent north in 1897 as a correspondent of the Hearst newspapers.[26] He hiked over Chilkoot Pass with a small outfit because he expected to get the facts promptly and leave. He stayed too long in Dawson, sought to walk out to Circle City when the food shortage threatened, was

25 Rex Beach, *Personal Exposures,* 47.
26 Winslow, *Big Pan-Out,* 51, 116, 147–49, 245–46.

driven back by winter storms, ran out of provisions, and had to crawl the last miles back to town. Hospitalized, he recovered, except for a frozen ear and toe. Miller was not liked because his glowing, sentimental accounts about the beautiful scenery and his silence about the hardships of the trail were thought misleading. In 1899, he made a vaudeville tour of the United States, coming on stage in Yukon winter garb to tell of his experiences. He was well received by his audiences, except for the few people who had actually been to the Klondike.

In the fall of 1897, Jack London went over Chilkoot Pass and got to within about seventy-five miles of Dawson, spending the winter in an abandoned cabin at Stewart River.[27] In the enforced idleness of the long cold season he talked with the various men there a great deal and learned much about the country. Without planning it, he stored away scenes and incidents for scores of short stories and several novels. Here he met Elam Harnish, who was to be the hero of *Burning Daylight*. London went on to Dawson, there meeting the dog who was to be the central character in *The Call of the Wild* and Emil Jensen, who as the Malemute Kid was to be the chief figure in several short stories. As a result of his winter at Stewart River, London was so severely afflicted with scurvy that he had to leave the Klondike. With his dream of gold shattered, he thought for the first time of turning his Yukon experiences into a literary asset. His first ambition was to publish in *Outing Magazine* and *Youth's Companion;* he sold his first story of the Klondike to the *Overland Monthly* for five dollars. Between 1889 and 1903, London published two novels and three books of short stories dealing with the Yukon. One of these, *The Call of the Wild,* the story of a dog, imported into the Northland, who became the leader of a wolf pack, is generally considered to be the best of all his books. As a writer of adventure, he was a master of swift, vivid action narrated in a highly colored, sometimes violent style.

The Klondike gold rush had many characteristics similar to those described in earlier chapters: the great excitement aroused by the discovery, the mad rush to the mines, inadequate supplies at first, gradual improvement in means of transportation, robust recreation, and feverish life in a boom town. Among the differences were the rise of two gold-rush settlements, Skagway and Dyea, so far from the mines themselves; the restrictions on transportation, the methods of mining,

[27] Charmian London, *The Book of Jack London,* 222–57; Joan London, *Jack London and His Times,* 143–202; O'Connor, *High Jinks,* 124–26.

and the ordinary routines of living determined by the severe climate; the action of the Canadian government in taking control of the situation so much more quickly than the United States had ever done; the royalty tax on the proceeds of the mines; and the outstanding work of the Northwest Mounted Police. How long the Klondike fever would have lasted had not the Spanish-American War cut it short and the discovery of gold at Nome, Alaska, finally squelched it is an interesting problem on which to speculate.

17

"GOLD is where you find it." This old saying is true, as the many accidental or providential discoveries of metals related in this book amply demonstrate. Once an initial find became known, a horde of prospectors hurried to examine the region with great care for possible additional riches. Some of them had enough practical experience to know exactly what they were looking for and how to find it; others were quite ignorant when they began searching, but occasionally uncovered a major deposit. Specialized knowledge was not always transferable, as California's experts in gold discovered to their sorrow when they started seeking silver in Nevada. Occasionally, trained men were confused at places like Cripple Creek, where the gold formations were so unsuual that expert geologists could find nothing but amateurs looking everywhere located the treasure.

News of the discoveries which precipitated major rushes was usually slow to spread at first because of the wilderness isolation, but once it had reached civilization, it was disseminated rapidly. There was generally a fair amount of truth in the reports; seldom were they as accurate as those published by President Polk on California or as exaggerated as the rumors about the first finds in Colorado. If the region was as isolated as California in 1848 or as the Klondike, those already in the general neighborhood arrived at the site distinctly ahead of most people rushing there. The easiest place of all to reach was Cripple Creek, about forty-five miles away from the railroads serving Colorado Springs. Guidebooks to the gold fields were published, especially about early California and Colorado; with a few exceptions they were so vague and inaccurate that they were of no value to their purchasers and indeed sometimes were so wrong they were injurious.

Most treasure seekers financed themselves from their own savings or from the sale of their property. Quite a few, however, borrowed all or part of the necessary money to go on a rush, often from somebody who had to remain behind but wanted a chance to win part of a fortune. For those already in a mining region but short of funds, a grubstake could usually be arranged. Those making a mining rush westward most commonly traveled overland, in the 1850's probably in a fair-sized wagon train but by the seventies likely in a small group or alone. Some people sailed the ocean to California or the Klondike; others used the rivers to reach the mining areas of California, the Klondike, Montana, or Idaho. Men along the eastern seaboard formed co-operative associations to get their members to California, to afford mutual protection, to engage in business there, and to find gold; these organizations dissolved in the West, where the possibility of a lucky miner's making a fortune far outweighed any advantages of a socialistic group. Prospectors going to the Klondike almost invariably had at least one partner. In general, however, those taking part in a rush were, more likely than not, free of any partnership or sharing agreement.

When something valuable was found in a placer deposit, extracting the gold or silver was comparatively simple and usually relatively inexpensive. The techniques were crevicing, the pan, the rocker, the long tom, the sluice, the hydraulic hose, the boom, river mining, and coyoting. On the Klondike special methods were devised for frozen ground. If the mineral was in a quartz deposit, securing the treasure was difficult and costly. In extracting the ore the two greatest improvements made during the period discussed in this book were Nevada's square-set system of mine timbering and Colorado's Burleigh drill. The refining techniques for removing the precious metal from the surrounding waste rock were constantly being improved. Among the devices and processes used were the arrastra, the stamp mill, the bumping table, roasting, amalgamation, chlorination, and cyanidation.

Each major rush seemed a fine opportunity for a lucky individual to find a rich deposit and work it until there was nothing left valuable enough to remove. In actual fact one could do this in many placer areas, unless earlier he simply wished to sell out. In other placer regions and in all quartz countries, however, he had to market his claim to some partnership or company which had sufficient money to finance the difficult, expensive development work necessary to convert a promising prospect into a productive, profitable mine. The transition from individualistic to capitalistic enterprise came more quickly in some places than in others, but it was inevitable if mineral production was long sustained. A corporation having a mine might also own a water supply, a means of transportation, and a refinery. If its deposit was unusually valuable, a rival claimant might try to assert ownership. Such corporate strife was usually settled in the courts, like the spectacular cases at Virginia City (Nevada) but occasionally was fought out in such armed conflicts as those at Silver City (Idaho) and Leadville; at Butte both methods were used. The most common ground for legal action was the law of the apex, but for the variety of principles mentioned in the statute books there were at first no established precedents or interpretations to guide judges in making decisions. This made the task a hard one for a conscientious official but presented a golden opportunity if he was as corrupt as the early court bench at Virginia City (Nevada).

In the early days a miner had only a right of occupancy to his property; technically he was a trespasser on land belonging to the United States government. He preferred this status, since he did not wish to share his treasure and wanted maximum flexibility to operate in the way that would bring him the most money. The situation continued until the Civil War, when threat of confiscation alarmed the partnerships and corporations in Nevada. They forced through federal legislation enabling placer or quartz miners to get title to their claims from the government at very little expense. In areas where the mines promised to be enduring, such as Nevada or Montana, the problem of territorial or state taxation was usually solved by making the mineral charge too low and placing an undue burden on other sources of government support. In the Klondike there was no charge for title to a claim if a prospector had the required "Free Miner's Certificate," but there was a royalty on the yield; in practice this was no more satisfactory than tax methods in the United States because there was so much evasion. Occasionally labor disputes in mining regions reached major proportions; the best examples concerned the Leadville, Cripple Creek, and Coeur d'Alene areas.

Law and order were usually a problem for a new mining region in the United States. The territorial government gave little or no assistance to the local community. Its inefficient administration lacked the funds, the mobility, and the information to take effective action, confronted as it often was with long distances, poor communications, and winter weather. Governments left the solution to the people in each area, who improvised, just as western pioneers had always done since Colonial times. The legal methods which the prospectors developed in California were used on the later mining frontiers. The men organized a district to regulate the holding of mineral claims. To handle property disputes, they established a board of arbitrators or provided for a trial by a small jury; the latter also sat on minor criminal cases. In parts of California these tasks were at first performed by one man, the alcalde. Major crimes were heard by the miners' court, which included everybody in the area who had time to attend. These methods of controlling lawlessness usually worked well; if they proved ineffective, vigilantes arose. Those in California and Montana were quite active; those in Nevada, Colorado and the Black Hills did comparatively little. Eventually, all of these informal methods were replaced by regular territorial, county, and city governments as the area stabilized. In the Klondike, by contrast, the Northwest Mounted Police vigorously maintained law and order from the start, the national authorities quickly established an effective territorial government, the gold commissioner supposedly prevented all disputes about claims (but actually didn't because he was weak and had some unscrupulous assistants), and each prospector had to purchase a Free Miner's Certificate.

To help haul freight, every region, except the frozen north at first, used pack animals. A variant, the saddle train for passengers, apparently developed only in Idaho. As quickly as roads were opened, wagon and stage services started operating. Passenger and freight businesses were separate everywhere except in the Black Hills, where passengers with slim purses could either purchase seat space in a freight wagon or arrange to walk alongside while it carried their baggage. Only in Colorado were the mountain grades so steep that in some places a second team, pushing on a pole from the rear, was necessary. Another unique practice there was the self-returning horse, used to carry a man far up the hillside to a mine entrance. Occasionally federal troops gave some protection to wagon trains of emigrants moving westward, but only for a series of special expeditions from Minnesota to Montana did the United States give financial aid to the guide. Steamships were used considerably, especially in the earlier days, to serve the Black Hills, Klondike, Montana, and California mines. Eventually railroads were built to all enduring mineral centers except the Klondike.

Mining-rush towns were usually ugly in appearance and regarded by their inhabitants as quite temporary. Obviously most of them were at the site of a discovery, but San Francisco and Denver were somewhat removed, while Skagway and Dyea, ports of entry, were quite far away from any gold. Among the cities founded in mining days which became permanently important were San Francisco, Sacramento, Stockton, Denver, Butte, Helena, and Lewiston (Idaho). In most towns the value of lots during the mining excitement rose steadily; in Leadville and Creede there was much difficulty with lot jumping. Virtually every settlement suffered at least one major fire because the wooden buildings were so flimsy and dry. There was often a shortage of food during the early months of a rush or in the first winter; the most serious of these difficulties were at Dawson, Virginia City, Nevada, and Virginia City, Montana. The demand for food usually led farmers and ranchers to take up acreages adjacent to any town giving promise of permanence; they generally made considerable profit. Water contamination was a problem only in early Virginia City, Nevada, and Dawson. The demand for lumber was usually greater than the supply in the first two or three years of a town's life.

Prices and wages were always comparatively high in a new major area; sometimes they came down only gradually. Occasionally in the 1850's and 1860's, there were shortages of coins so serious that the volume of business transactions was curtailed. This was temporarily solved in California and Colorado by the minting of private money, which served until an adequate volume of that issued by the federal government was available. During the early days gold dust circulated freely, but it was awkward to handle and could be adulterated in ways not quickly or easily detected. Only in Idaho is there clear record of a criminal ring to distribute bogus gold dust, but individuals and perhaps less-obvious groups did it in every area.

Since all mining is a gamble, it is not surprising that there was considerable speculative buying and selling of claims. Stock-market operations in mineral-company shares, a variant of this, were extensive for Virginia City (Nevada), Leadville, and Cripple Creek properties. In gambling, which abounded everywhere, the games where the action was quick were more popular than those which were slow and demanded real skill.

Saloons were numerous and well patronized. At the dance halls a man could hire a hurdy-gurdy as his partner there, but she "lived private"; for a more co-operative female, he had to go to a special house. Mining-town theaters presented a variety of entertainment, from the best in drama to shows of a decidedly dubious nature; in variety houses of the lower sort, drinking was vigorously promoted. On the mineral frontiers of the Black Hills, Colorado, and Montana, John S. Langrishe, a gifted actor, presented excellent dramas for twenty years. Amateur thespians, musicians, and debaters held forth in most communities.

The average prospector neglected religion. He thought of Sunday as a day for relaxation or for doing chores inconvenient to the usual daily routine; on rare occasions he might wander into a Divine Service if it was available. There was no limitation in the things a man could do on Sunday except on the Klondike, where the police enforced a relatively Puritan type of Sabbath. As a region developed enough for married miners to bring their families west, a private school was usually established initially and later a tax-supported one evolved. Before the first school started, the first newspaper appeared. Health was a problem in a region's early days because of overexposure, overexertion, undernourishment, improper sanitation, inadequate hospitals (if, indeed, there were any), and too few doctors. To give mutual help in time of illness was just one of the many functions of the various flourishing fraternal organizations.

Some mining rushes, like that to California, brought in people from all over the world; others, like the Black Hills, chiefly attracted those already living in the United States. Against the Chinese there was strong prejudice and discriminatory action everywhere, except in the Black Hills and the Klondike. In many regions where mines gave promise of real permanence, Cornishmen in considerable numbers found employment. Indians in California were at first allowed to mine just like any other race but were shortly excluded. Elsewhere they were looked down upon, their property rights were disregarded, and they were at times mistreated. Understandably the red men were usually un-co-operative and frequently were provoked into hostile acts. In the Black Hills, only partly because of the rush, the Sioux made unusually effective warfare but eventually were crushed. The California tribes at first and the Nez Percés of Idaho always were helpful to the whites; the various natives in the Klondike area helped move freight.

The striking thing about the various mining frontiers is how similar conditions were. Special problems, however, were posed by the cold on the Klondike, by the high elevation at Leadville, and by the Indian reservation in the Black Hills. Some of the people made famous by mining activities who quickly come to mind are Sutter of California; Tabor of Colorado; Ralston, Sharon, and the Bonanza Four of Nevada; Clark, Daly, and Heinze of Montana; and Calamity Jane and the fictional Deadwood Dick of the Black Hills. Gold-rush writers most commonly remembered are Mark Twain, Jack London, Robert Service, and Bret Harte. On some of the mining frontiers, such as California, there began an economic development which continued long after mineral activities became insignificant; on others, such as the Klondike, once the wealth was extracted the area reverted almost to wilderness again. Whether more money was taken out of all the various mining frontiers than was spent in treasure seeking is a good question to ask, but there is insufficient evidence on which to base an answer. Certainly the funds realized did found some notable individual fortunes and help to finance important economic expansion.

GENERAL WORKS

Bancroft, Hubert H. *History of Nevada, Colorado and Wyoming, 1540–1888.* San Francisco, 1890.
——. *History of Washington, Idaho and Montana, 1845–1889.* San Francisco, 1890.
Quiett, Glenn C. *Pay Dirt: A Panorama of American Gold Rushes.* New York, 1936.
Rickard, T. A. *A History of American Mining.* New York, 1932.
Spence, Clark C. *British Investment and the American Mining Frontier, 1860–1901.* Ithaca, 1958.
Wolle, Muriel S. *The Bonanza Trail: Ghost Towns and Mining Camps of the West.* Bloomington, 1953.

CALIFORNIA

Bancroft, Hubert H. *California Inter Pocula.* San Francisco, 1888.
——. *History of California.* 7 vols. San Francisco, 1888.
Bari, Valeaka (ed.). *The Course of Empire.* New York, 1931.
Bieber, Ralph P. *Southern Trails to California in 1849.* Glendale, 1937.
Buck, Franklin A. *A Yankee Trader in the Gold Rush.* Boston, 1930.
Caughey, John W. *Gold Is the Cornerstone.* Berkeley, 1948.
——. "Shaping a Literary Tradition," *Pacific Historical Review,* Vol. VIII (1939), 201–14.
——. "Their Majesties the Mob," *Pacific Historical Review,* Vol. XXVI (1957), 217–34.
—— (ed.). *Rushing for Gold.* Berkeley, 1949.
Clappe, Louise A. K. S. *The Shirley Letters from the California Mines in 1851–52.* San Francisco, 1922.
Coy, Owen C. *Gold Days.* Los Angeles, 1929.

——. *The Great Trek*. Los Angeles, 1931.

Ellison, William H. *A Self-Governing Dominion: California, 1849–1860*. Berkeley, 1950.

Ferrier, William W. *Ninety Years of Education in California, 1846–1936*. Berkeley, 1937.

Harte, Geoffrey Bret. *The Letters of Bret Harte*. Boston, 1926.

Howe, Octavius T. *Argonauts of '49*. Cambridge, 1923.

Hutchison, Claude B. (ed.). *California Agriculture*. Berkeley, 1946.

Jackson, Joseph H. *Anybody's Gold: The Story of California's Mining Towns*. New York, 1941.

Jenkins, Olaf P. (ed.). *The Mother Lode Country*. State of California, Department of Natural Resources, Division of Mines, *Bulletin* No. 141. Sacramento, 1941.

Kemble, John H. *The Panama Route, 1848–1869*. Berkeley, 1943.

Lewis, Oscar. *Sea Routes to the Gold Fields*. New York, 1949.

Low, Garrett W. *Gold Rush by Sea*. Ed. by Kenneth Haney. Philadelphia, 1941.

MacMinn, George R. *The Theater of the Golden Era in California*. Caldwell, 1941.

MacMullen, Jerry. *Paddle-Wheel Days in California*. Stanford, 1944.

Nuhaus, Eugen. "Charles Christian Nahl: The Painter of California Pioneer Life," *California Historical Society Quarterly*, Vol. XV (1936), 295–305.

Paden, Irene D. *The Wake of the Prairie Schooner*. New York, 1943.

Paul, Rodman W. *California Gold: The Beginning of Mining in the Far West*. Cambridge, 1947.

Pomfret, John E. (ed.). *California Gold Rush Voyages, 1848–1849*. San Marino, 1954.

Read, Georgia W., and Ruth Gaines (eds.). *Gold Rush: The Journals, Drawings and Other Papers of J. Goldsborough Bruff*. New York, 1944.

Rydell, Raymond A. *Cape Horn to the Pacific: The Rise and Decline of an Ocean Highway*. Berkeley, 1952.

Shinn, Charles H. *Land Laws of Mining Districts*. Baltimore, 1884.

——. *Mining Camps: A Study in American Frontier Government*. New York, 1948. (Original ed. 1885.)

Stewart, George R., Jr. *Bret Harte: Argonaut and Exile*. Boston, 1931.

Taylor, Bayard. *Eldorado, or Adventures in the Path of Empire*. New York, 1949. (Original ed. 1850.)

Walker, Franklin. *San Francisco's Literary Frontier*. New York, 1939.

Wells, Evelyn, and Harry C. Peterson. *The 49ers*. Garden City, 1949.

Winther, Oscar O. *Express and Stagecoach Days in California.* Stanford, 1936.

———. "The Southern Overland Mail and Stagecoach Line, 1857–1861," *New Mexico Historical Review,* Vol. XXXII (1957), 81–106.

Wyman, Walker D. (ed.). *California Emigrant Letters.* New York, 1952.

Young, John P. *Journalism in California.* San Francisco, 1915.

Zollinger, James P. *Sutter: The Man and His Empire.* New York, 1939.

NEVADA

Adams, Romanzo. *Taxation in Nevada: A History.* Carson City, 1918.

Becker, George F. *Geology of the Comstock Lode and the Washoe District. Monographs* of the United States Geological Survey, Vol. III. Washington, 1882.

Beebe, Lucius, and Charles Clegg. *Legends of the Comstock Lode.* Oakland, 1950.

Benson, Ivan. *Mark Twain's Western Years.* Stanford, 1938.

Brooks, Van Wyck. *The Ordeal of Mark Twain.* New and rev. ed. New York, 1933.

Dana, Julian. *The Man Who Built San Francisco: A Study of Ralston's Journey with Banners.* New York, 1937.

DeQuille, Dan (pseudonym of William Wright). *The Big Bonanza.* New York, 1947. (Original ed. 1876.)

———. *A History of the Comstock Silver Lode and Mines.* Virginia City, 1889.

DeVoto, Bernard. *Mark Twain's America.* Boston, 1932.

Drury, Wells. *An Editor on the Comstock Lode.* Palo Alto, 1948.

Emrich, Duncan (ed.). *Comstock Bonanza.* New York, 1950.

Glasscock, C. B. *The Big Bonanza: The Story of the Comstock Lode.* Indianapolis, 1931.

Gorham, Harry M. *My Memories of the Comstock.* Los Angeles, 1939.

Hazlett, Mrs. Fanny G., and Gertrude Hazlett Randall. "Historical Sketch and Reminiscences of Dayton, Nevada," Nevada Historical Society *Papers,* Vol. III (1921–22), 12–93.

Hershiser, Beulah. "The Influence of Nevada on the National Mining Legislation of 1866," Nevada Historical Society, *Third Biennial Report* (1911–12), 126–67.

Kneiss, Gilbert H. *Bonanza Railroads.* Rev. ed. Stanford, 1946.

Lewis, Oscar. *Silver Kings: The Lives and Times of Mackay, Fair, Flood, and O'Brien, Lords of the Nevada Comstock Lode.* New York, 1947.

————. *The Town That Died Laughing.* Boston, 1955.
Lillard, Richard G. *Desert Challenge: An Interpretation of Nevada.* New York, 1942.
Lincoln, Francis C. *Mining Districts and Mineral Resources of Nevada.* Reno, 1923.
Lord, Eliot. *Comstock Mining and Miners. Monographs* of the United States Geological Survey, Vol. IV. Washington, 1883.
Lyman, George D. *Ralston's Ring.* New York, 1937.
————. *The Saga of the Comstock Lode: Boom Days in Virginia City.* New York, 1934.
Mack, Effie M. *Nevada: A History of the State from the Earliest Times Through the Civil War.* Glendale, 1936.
Michelson, Miriam. *The Wonderlode of Silver and Gold.* Boston, 1934.
Miller, Max. *Reno.* New York, 1941.
Shinn, Charles H. *The Story of the Mine, as Illustrated by the Great Comstock Lode of Nevada.* New York, 1896.
Smith, Grant H. *The History of the Comstock Lode, 1850–1920.* University of Nevada *Bulletin,* Vol. XXXVII, No. 3, Geology and Mining Series No. 37. Reno, 1943.
Smith, Henry Nash (ed.). *Mark Twain of the Enterprise.* Berkeley, 1957.
Trout, Alice F. "Religious Development in Nevada," Nevada Historical Society *Papers,* Vol. I (1913–16), 143–67.
Twain, Mark (pseudonym of Samuel L. Clemens). *Roughing It.* 2 vols. New York, 1904.
Wier, Jeanne E. "Mark Twain's Relation to Nevada and to the West," Nevada Historical Society *Papers,* Vol. I (1913–16), 99–104.
Works Progress Administration. *Nevada: A Guide to the Silver State.* Portland, 1940.

COLORADO

Bahmer, Robert H. "The Colorado Gold Rush and California," *Colorado Magazine,* Vol. VII (1930), 222–29.
Baker, James H., and LeRoy R. Hafen (eds.). *History of Colorado.* 5 vols. Denver, 1927.
Bancroft, Caroline. *Augusta Tabor: Her Side of the Scandal.* Denver, 1955.
————. "The Elusive Figure of John H. Gregory, Discoverer of the First Gold Lode in Colorado," *Colorado Magazine,* Vol. XX (1943), 121–35.
————. *Famous Aspen.* Denver, 1951.

————. *Gulch of Gold: A History of Central City, Colorado.* Denver, 1958.

————. *Historic Central City.* Denver, 1951.

————. *Silver Queen: The Fabulous Story of Baby Doe Tabor.* Denver, 1955.

Benn, Mary Lou. "Mary Hallock Foote, Early Leadville Writer," *Colorado Magazine,* Vol. XXXIII (1956), 93–108.

Burkey, Elmer R. "The Georgetown-Leadville Stage," *Colorado Magazine,* Vol. XIV (1937), 177–87.

Cooper, Ray H. "Early History of San Juan County," *Colorado Magazine,* Vol. XXII (1945), 205–12.

Cummins, D. H. "Toll Roads in Southwestern Colorado," *Colorado Magazine,* Vol. XXIX (1952), 98–104.

Degitz, Dorothy M. "History of the Tabor Opera House at Leadville," *Colorado Magazine,* Vol. XIII (1936), 81–89.

Dinkel, William M. "A Pioneer of the Roaring Fork," *Colorado Magazine,* Vol. XXI (1944), 133–40.

Ellis, Anne. *The Life of an Ordinary Woman.* Boston, 1929.

Ellis, Elmer. *Henry Moore Teller, Defender of the West.* Caldwell, 1941.

Espinosa, Fred. "Del Norte—Its Past and Present," *Colorado Magazine,* Vol. V (1928), 95–102.

Fritz, Percy S. *Colorado: The Centennial State.* New York, 1941.

Gandy, Lewis C. *The Tabors: A Footnote of Western History.* New York, 1934.

Gressley, Gene M. "Hotel de Paris and Its Creator," *Colorado Magazine,* Vol. XXXII (1955), 28–42.

Griswold, Don L. and Jean H. *The Carbonate Camp Called Leadville.* Denver, 1951.

Hafen, LeRoy. "Currency, Coinage and Banking in Pioneer Colorado," *Colorado Magazine,* Vol. X (1933), 81–90.

————. "Otto Mears, 'Pathfinder of the San Juan,' " *Colorado Magazine,* Vol. IX (1932), 71–74.

———— (ed.). *Colorado Gold Rush: Contemporary Letters and Reports 1858–1859.* Glendale, 1941.

————. *Overland Routes to the Gold Fields, 1859, from Contemporary Diaries.* Glendale, 1942.

————. *Pike's Peak Gold Rush Guidebooks of 1589.* Glendale, 1941.

Hagie, C. E. "Gunnison in Early Days," *Colorado Magazine,* Vol. VIII (1931), 121–29.

Hale, Jesse D. "The First Successful Smelter in Colorado," *Colorado Magazine,* Vol. XIII (1936), 161–67.

Hall, Frank. *History of the State of Colorado.* 4 vols. Chicago, 1889–90.

Harvey, Mrs. James R. "The Leadville Ice Palace of 1896," *Colorado Magazine,* Vol. XVII (1940), 94–101.

Henderson, Charles W. *Mining in Colorado: A History of Discovery, Development and Production.* United States Geological Survey *Professional Paper* No. 138. Washington, 1926.

Hill, Emma S. "Empire City in the Sixties," *Colorado Magazine,* Vol. V (1928), 23–32.

Horner, John W. *Silver Town.* Caldwell, 1950.

Kemp, Donald C. *Colorado's Little Kingdom.* Denver, 1949.

Kenna, Leo J. "Cripple Creek in 1900," *Colorado Magazine,* Vol. XXX (1953), 269–75.

Kingsbury, Joseph L. "The Pike's Peak Rush, 1859," *Colorado Magazine,* Vol. IV (1927), 1–6.

Kinkin, L. C. "Early Days in Telluride," *Colorado Magazine,* Vol. XXVI (1949), 14–26.

Lavender, David. *The Big Divide.* Garden City, 1948.

Lee, Mabel B. *Cripple Creek Days.* Garden City, 1958.

Major, Mrs. A. H. "Pioneer Days in Crestone and Creede," *Colorado Magazine,* Vol. XXI (1944), 212–17.

Mumey, Nolie. *Creede: History of a Colorado Silver Mining Town.* Denver, 1949.

Newton, Harry J. *Yellow Gold of Cripple Creek.* Denver, 1928.

Ourada, Patricia K. "The Chinese in Colorado," *Colorado Magazine,* Vol. XXIX (1952), 273–84.

Paul, Rodman W. "Colorado as a Pioneer of Science in the Mining West," *Mississippi Valley Historical Review,* Vol. XLVII (1960–61), 34–50.

Perrigo, Lynn I. "The Cornish Miners of Early Gilpin County," *Colorado Magazine,* Vol. XIV (1937), 92–101.

———. "The First Decade of Public Schools at Central City," *Colorado Magazine,* Vol. XII (1935), 81–91.

———. "The First Two Decades of Central City Theatricals," *Colorado Magazine,* Vol. XI (1934), 141–52.

———. "Law and Order in Early Colorado Mining Camps," *Mississippi Valley Historical Review,* Vol. XXVIII (1941–42), 41–62.

———. *The Little Kingdom: A Record Chiefly of Central City in the Early Days.* Boulder, 1934.

Pfeiffer, Emil W. "The Kingdom of Bull Hill," *Colorado Magazine,* Vol. XII (1935), 168–72.

Poet, S. E. "The Story of Tin Cup, Colorado," *Colorado Magazine,* Vol. IX (1932), 30–38.

Root, George A. "Gunnison in the Early Eighties," *Colorado Magazine*, Vol. IX (1932), 201–13.

Russell, James E. "Louis Dupuy and the Hotel de Paris of Georgetown," *Colorado Magazine*, Vol. XIII (1936), 210–15.

Sayre, Hal. "Early Central City Theatricals and Other Reminiscences," *Colorado Magazine*, Vol. VI (1929), 47–53.

Schoberlin, Melvin. *From Candles to Footlights: A Biography of the Pike's Peak Theatre, 1859–1876.* Denver, 1941.

Settle, Raymond W. and Mary L. *Empire on Wheels.* Stanford, 1949.

Shoemaker, Len. *Roaring Fork Valley.* Denver, 1958.

Spence, Clark C. "The British and Colorado Mining Bureau," *Colorado Magazine*, Vol. XXXIII (1956), 81–92.

Sprague, Marshall. *Money Mountain: The Story of Cripple Creek.* Boston, 1953.

Stone, Wilbur F. (ed.). *History of Colorado.* 3 vols. Chicago, 1918.

Tabor, Mrs. H. A. W. "Cabin Life in Colorado," *Colorado Magazine*, Vol. IV (1927), 71–75.

Taylor, Bayard. *Colorado: A Summer Trip.* New York, 1867.

Thomas, Chauncey. "Ouray, The Opal of America," *Colorado Magazine*, Vol. XI (1934), 17–22.

Thomas, C. S. "An Argonaut of the Roaring Fork," *Colorado Magazine*, Vol. VII (1930), 205–16.

Tischendorf, Alfred P. "British Investment in Colorado Mines" *Colorado Magazine*, Vol. XXX (1953), 241–46.

Villard, Henry. *The Past and Present of the Pike's Peak Gold Rush.* Ed. by LeRoy R. Hafen. Princeton, 1932. (Original ed. 1860.)

Waters, Frank. *Midas of the Rockies: The Story of Stratton and Cripple Creek.* New York, 1937.

Waters, L. L. *Steel Trails to Santa Fe.* Lawrence, 1950.

Wentworth, Frank L. *Aspen on the Roaring Fork.* Lakewood, 1950.

Willard, James F. "Sidelights on the Pike's Peak Gold Rush, 1858–59," *Colorado Magazine*, Vol. XII (1935), 3–13.

———. "Spreading the News of the Early Discoveries of Gold in Colorado," *Colorado Magazine*, Vol. VI (1929), 98–104.

Williams, Francis S. "The Influence of California Upon the Placer Mining Methods of Colorado," *Colorado Magazine*, Vol. XXVI (1949), 127–43.

———. "Trials and Judgments of the People's Courts of Denver," *Colorado Magazine*, Vol. XXVII (1950), 294–302.

Willison, George F. *Here They Dug Gold.* New York, 1931.

Wolle, Muriel S. "Adventure Into the Past, A Search for Colorado's Mining Camps," *Colorado Magazine*, Vol. XXVII (1950), 11–23.

———. *Stampede to Timberline: The Ghost Towns and Mining Camps of Colorado.* Boulder, 1949.

Works Progress Administration. *Colorado: A Guide to the Highest State.* New York, 1941.

MONTANA

Barrett, Martin. "Holding Up a Territorial Legislature," *Contributions to the Historical Society of Montana,* Vol. VIII (1917), 93–98.

Beal, Merrill D. *The Story of Man in Yellowstone.* Caxton, 1949.

Blake, Henry N. "The First Newpaper of Montana," *Contributions to the Historical Society of Montana,* Vol. V (1904), 253–64.

———. "Historical Sketch of Madison County, Montana Territory," *Contributions to the Historical Society of Montana,* Vol. II (1896), 76–87.

Briggs, Harold E. *Frontiers of the Northwest.* New York, 1940.

Burkhart, J. A. "The Frontier Merchant and Social History," *Montana Magazine of History,* Vol. II (October, 1952), 5–15.

Burlingame, Merrill G. "John M. Bozeman, Montana Trailmaker," *Mississippi Valley Historical Review,* Vol. XXVII (1940–41), 542–53.

———. *The Montana Frontier.* Helena, 1942.

———, and K. Ross Toole (eds.). *A History of Montana.* 3 vols. New York, 1957.

Chittenden, Hiram M. *The Yellowstone National Park: Historical and Descriptive.* New and enlarged ed., entirely rev. Cincinnati, 1918.

Clark, Archie L. "John Maguire: Butte's 'Belasco,' " *Montana Magazine of History,* Vol. II (January 1952), 33–40.

Clark, W. A. "The Origin, Growth and Resources of Montana," *Contributions to the Historical Society of Montana,* Vol. II (1896), 45–60.

Connolly, Christopher P. *The Devil Learns to Vote: The Story of Montana.* New York, 1938.

Dimsdale, Thomas J. *The Vigilantes of Montana.* Norman, 1953. (Original ed. 1866.)

Edwards, George. "Presbyterian Church History," *Contributions to the Historical Society of Montana,* Vol. VI (1907), 290–444.

Foor, Forrest L. "The Senatorial Aspiration of William A. Clark, 1898–1901: A Study in Montana Politics." Unpublished Ph.D. thesis, University of California. Berkeley, 1941.

Glasscock, C. B. *The War of the Copper Kings.* New York, 1935.

Hamilton, James M. *From Wilderness to Statehood.* Ed. by Merrill G. Burlingame. Portland, 1957.

Hedges, Cornelius. "Centennial Address on Lewis and Clarke County," *Contributions to the Historical Society of Montana,* Vol. II (1896), 107–18.

Herndon, Sarah R. "The Pioneer Public School of Montana," *Contributions to the Historical Society of Montana,* Vol. V (1904), 198–99.

Holter, A. M. "Pioneer Lumbering in Montana," *Contributions to the Historical Society of Montana,* Vol. VIII (1917), 251–81.

Housman, Robert L. "The First Territorial Legislature in Montana," *Pacific Historical Review,* Vol. IV (1935), 376–85.

Howard, Joseph K. *Montana: High, Wide and Handsome.* New Haven, 1943.

"Journal of Henry Edgar—1863," *Contributions to the Historical Society of Montana,* Vol. III (1900), 124–42.

Langford, Nathaniel P. *Vigilante Days and Ways.* Missoula, 1957. (Original ed. 1890.)

Levine, Louis. *The Taxation of Mines in Montana.* New York, 1919.

MacKnight, James A. *Mines of Montana.* Helena, 1892.

McNelis, Sarah. "F. Augustus Heinze: An Early Chapter in the Life of a Copper King," *Montana Magazine of History,* Vol. II (October, 1952), 25–32.

Mangam, William D. *The Clarks: An American Phenomenon.* New York, 1941.

Marcosson, Issac F. *Anaconda.* New York, 1957.

Mills, James H. "Reminiscences of an Editor," *Contributions to the Historical Society of Montana,* Vol. V (1904), 273–88.

Montana Writers' Program. *Copper Camp.* New York, 1944.

Munson, Edward L. "Lyman Ezra Munson," *Contributions to the Historical Society of Montana,* Vol. VII (1910), 199–202.

Murphy, Jerre C. *The Comical History of Montana.* San Diego, 1912.

Park, S. W. "The First School in Montana," *Contributions to the Historical Society of Montana,* Vol. V (1904), 187–97.

Pemberton, W. Y. "Montana's Pioneer Courts," *Contributions to the Historical Society of Montana,* Vol. VIII (1917), 99–104.

Phillips, Paul C., and H. A. Trexler. "Notes on the Discovery of Gold in the Northwest," *Mississippi Valley Historical Review,* Vol. IV (1917–18), 89–97.

Richter, F. E. "The Amalgamated Copper Company: A Closed Chapter in Corporate Finance," *Quarterly Journal of Economics,* Vol. XXX (1915–16), 387–407.

Ronan, Peter. "Discovery of Alder Gulch," *Contributions to the Historical Society of Montana*, Vol. III (1900), 143–52.

Sanders, Helen F. *A History of Montana*. 3 vols. Chicago, 1913.

——— (ed.). *X Beidler: Vigilante*. Norman, 1957.

Schreiner, M. Murray. "Last Chance Gulch Becomes the Mountain City of Helena," *Montana Magazine of History*, Vol. II (October, 1952), 33–42.

Smurr, J. W. "Afterthoughts on the Vigilantes," *Montana: The Magazine of Western History*, Vol. VIII (Spring, 1958), 8–20.

———. "The Montana 'Tax Conspiracy' of 1899," *Montana: The Magazine of Western History*, Vol. V (Spring and Summer, 1955), 46–53, 47–56.

"Steamboat Arrivals at Fort Benton and Vicinity," *Contributions to the Historical Society of Montana*, Vol. I (1876), 317–25; Vol. III (1900), 351–58.

Stone, Arthur L. *Following Old Trails*. Missoula, 1913.

Stout, Tom. *Montana: Its Story and Biography*. 3 vols. Chicago, 1921.

Stuart, Granville. *Forty Years on the Frontier*. Ed. by Paul C. Phillips. 2 vols. Cleveland, 1925.

———. "A Memoir of the Life of James Stuart," *Contributions to the Historical Society of Montana*, Vol. I (1876), 36–79.

Stuart, James. "The Yellowstone Expedition of 1863," *Contributions to the Historical Society of Montana*, Vol. I (1876), 149–233.

Toole, K. Ross. "The Anaconda Mining Company: A Price War and a Copper Corner," *Pacific Northwest Quarterly*, Vol. XXXXI (1950), 312–29.

———. "The Genesis of the Clark-Daly Feud," *Montana Magazine of History*, Vol. I (April, 1951), 21–33.

———. *Montana: An Uncommon Land*. Norman, 1959.

———. "When Big Money Came to Butte," *Pacific Northwest Quarterly*, Vol. XXXXIV (1953), 23–29.

Trimble, William J. *The Mining Advance into the Inland Empire*. Madison, 1914.

———. "A Reconsideration of Gold Discoveries in the Northwest," *Mississippi Valley Historical Review*, Vol. V (1918–19), 70–77.

Tuttle, Daniel S. "Early History of the Episcopal Church in Montana," *Contributions to the Historical Society of Montana*, Vol. V (1904), 289–324.

Vaughn, Robert. *Then and Now*. Minneapolis, 1900.

Wall, C. James. "Gold Dust and Greenbacks," *Montana: The Magazine of Western History*, Vol. VII (Spring, 1957), 24–31.

Warren, Charles S. "The Territory of Montana," *Contributions to the Historical Society of Montana,* Vol. II (1896), 61–75.
Weaver, David B. "Early Days in Emigrant Gulch," *Contributions to the Historical Society of Montana,* Vol. VII (1910), 73–96.
Winner, Dorothy. "Rationing During the Montana Gold Rush," *Pacific Northwest Quarterly,* Vol. XXXVI (1945), 115–20.
Works Progress Administration. *Montana: A State Guide Book.* New York, 1939.

IDAHO

Averill, Harry B., John M. Henderson, and William S. Shiach, *An Illustrated History of North Idaho.* N.p., 1903.
Beal, Merrill D., and Merle W. Wells. *History of Idaho.* 3 vols. New York, 1959.
Bird, Annie L. *Boise, the Peace Valley.* Caldwell, 1934.
Bristol, Sherlock. *The Pioneer Preacher.* Chicago, 1887.
Burcham, Ralph, Jr. "Elias Davidson Pierce, Discoverer of Gold in Idaho: A Biographical Sketch." Unpublished M.A. thesis, University of Idaho. Moscow, 1950.
———. "Reminiscences of E. D. Pierce, Discoverer of Gold in Idaho." Unpublished Ph.D. thesis, Washington State University. Pullman, 1957.
Clark, Barzilla W. *Bonneville County in the Making.* Idaho Falls, 1941.
Defenbach, Byron. *Idaho: The Place and Its People.* 3 vols. Chicago, 1933.
Donaldson, Thomas. *Idaho of Yesterday.* Caldwell, 1941.
Elsensohn, M. Alfreda. *Pioneer Days in Idaho County.* 2 vols. Caldwell, 1947–51.
French, Hiram T. *History of Idaho.* 3 vols. Chicago, 1914.
Goulder, W. A. *Reminiscences: Incidents in the Life of a Pioneer in Oregon and Idaho.* Boise, 1909.
Greenough, W. Earl. *First 100 Years of the Coeur d'Alene Mining Region.* Mullan, 1947.
Hailey, John. *The History of Idaho.* Boise, 1910.
Hawley, James H. (ed.). *History of Idaho, the Gem of the Mountains.* 4 vols. Chicago, 1920.
Holbrook, Stewart H. *The Rocky Mountain Revolution.* New York, 1956.
Jensen, Vernon H. *Heritage of Conflict.* Ithaca, 1950.
Johnson, Claudius O. *Borah of Idaho.* New York, 1936.

Kissane, Leedice. "Steve Adams, the Speechless Witness," *Idaho Yesterdays,* Vol. IV (1960), 18–21.

MacLane, John F. *A Sagebrush Lawyer.* New York, 1953.

McConnell, W. J. *Early History of Idaho.* Caldwell, 1913.

———. "The Idaho Inferno." MS in Bancroft Library, University of California. N.p., 1879.

McKenna, Marian C. *Borah.* Ann Arbor, 1961.

McLeod, George A. *History of Alturas and Blaine Counties, Idaho.* Rev. ed. Hailey, 1938.

Romig, Robert L. "The South Boise Quartz Mines, 1865–1892: A Study in Western Mining Industry and Finance." Unpublished M.A. thesis, University of California. Berkeley, 1951.

Scheinberg, Stephen. "Theodore Roosevelt's 'Undesirable Citizens,'" *Idaho Yesterdays,* Vol. IV (1960), 10–15.

Smith, Robert W. *The Coeur d'Alene Mining War of 1892: A Case Study of an Industrial Dispute.* Corvallis, 1961.

———. "A History of Placer and Quartz Gold Mining in the Coeur d'Alene District." Unpublished M.A. thesis, University of Idaho. Moscow, 1932.

Stoll, William T. *Silver Strike.* Boston, 1932.

Stone, Irving. *Clarence Darrow for the Defense.* Garden City, 1941. 13 *Pacific Reporter* 350.

Wardner, Jim. *Jim Wardner of Wardner, Idaho.* New York, 1900.

Weinberg, Arthur. *Attorney for the Damned.* New York, 1957.

THE BLACK HILLS

Aikman, Duncan. *Calamity Jane and the Lady Wildcats.* New York, 1927.

Bennett, Estelline. *Old Deadwood Days.* New York, 1928.

Briggs, Harold E. "The Black Hills Gold Rush," *North Dakota Historical Quarterly,* Vol. V (1930–31), 71–99.

———. "Early Freight and Stage Lines in Dakota," *North Dakota Historical Quarterly,* Vol. III (1928–29), 229–61.

Brown, Jesse, and A .M. Willard. *The Black Hills Trails.* Rapid City, 1924.

Casey, Robert J. *The Black Hills and Their Incredible Characters.* Indianapolis, 1949.

Hughes, Richard B. *Pioneer Years in the Black Hills.* Ed. by Agnes Wright Spring. Glendale, 1957.

Hyde, George E. *Red Cloud's Folk: A History of the Oglala Sioux Indians.* Norman, 1937.

Irving, J. D. *Economic Resources of the Northern Black Hills*. United States Geological Survey *Professional Paper* No. 26. Washington, 1904.

Jenney, Walter P. *The Mineral Wealth, Climate and Rain-fall and Natural Resources of the Black Hills of Dakota*. Senate Executive Document No. 51, 44th Cong., 1st sess.

Johannsen, Albert. *The House of Beadle and Adams and Its Dime and Nickel Novels: The Story of a Vanished Literature*. 2 vols. Norman, 1950.

Kingsbury, George W. *History of Dakota Territory*. Chicago, 1915.

Lamar, Howard R. *Dakota Territory 1861–1899: A Study of Frontier Politics*. New Haven, 1956.

Ludlow, William. *Report of a Reconnaissance of the Black Hills Made in the Summer of 1874*. Washington, 1875.

McClintock, John S. *Pioneer Days in the Black Hills*. Deadwood, 1939.

Pearson, Edmund. *Dime Novels; or, Following An Old Trail in Popular Literature*. Boston, 1929.

Peattie, Roderick (ed.). *The Black Hills*. New York, 1952.

Robinson, Doane. *Doane Robinson's Encyclopedia of South Dakota*. Pierre, 1925.

Smith, George M. *South Dakota: Its History and Its People*. 5 vols. Chicago, 1915.

Spring, Agnes W. *The Cheyenne and Black Hills Stage and Express Routes*. Glendale, 1949.

Stewart, Edgar I. *Custer's Luck*. Norman, 1955.

Tallent, Annie D. *The Black Hills*. St. Louis, 1899.

Works Progress Administration. *South Dakota: A Guide to the State*. 2nd ed., completely rev. by M. Lisle Reese. New York, 1952.

The Klondike

Adney, Tappan. *The Klondike Stampede*. New York, 1899.

Allan, A. A. *Gold, Men and Dogs*. New York, 1931.

Bankson, Russell A. *The Klondike Nugget*. Caldwell, 1935.

Beach, Rex. *Personal Exposures*. New York, 1941.

Berton, Laura B. *I Married the Klondike*. Boston, 1955.

Berton, Pierre. *The Klondike Fever*. New York, 1958.

Black, Mrs. George. *My Seventy Years*. New York, 1938.

Collier, William R., and Edwin V. Westrate. *The Reign of Soapy Smith*. Garden City, 1935.

Haskell, William B. *Two Years in the Klondike and Alaskan Gold-Fields.* Hartford, 1898.

Heilprin, Angelo. *Alaska and the Klondike.* New York, 1899.

London, Charmian. *The Book of Jack London.* New York, 1921.

London, Joan. *Jack London and His Times.* New York, 1939.

Lung, Edward B. *Black Sand and Gold.* New York, 1956.

Lynch, Jeremiah. *Three Years in the Klondike.* London, 1904.

O'Connor, Richard. *High Jinks on the Klondike.* Indianapolis, 1954.

Ogilvie, William. *Early Days on the Yukon and the Story of Its Gold Finds.* New York, 1913.

Palmer, Frederick. *In the Klondyke.* New York, 1899.

Rickard, T. A. *Through the Yukon and Alaska.* San Francisco, 1909.

Robertson, W. N. *Yukon Memories.* Toronto, 1930.

Service, Robert. *Ploughman of the Moon.* New York, 1945.

Shortt, Adams, and Arthur G. Doughty (eds.). *Canada and Its Provinces.* 25 vols. Toronto, 1914.

Steele, S. B. *Forty Years in Canada.* London, 1915.

Tollemache, Stratford. *Reminiscences of the Yukon.* Toronto, 1912.

Walden, Arthur T. *A. Dog-Puncher on the Yukon.* Boston, 1931.

Winslow, Kathryn. *Big Pan-Out.* New York, 1951.

"The Yukon Troubadour," *Time,* Vol. LXII (September 22, 1958), 30–32.

Gambling: California, 12, 22, 25, 61–62, 79, 84; Nevada, 91, 138; Colorado, 169, 171, 175, 185, 190, 205–206, 212; Montana, 231, 253–54; Idaho, 267, 277; Black Hills, 318, 320, 322, 324, 327; Klondike, 346, 348, 367; see also Speculation
Garr, H. H.: 248
Garretson, Fannie: 326
Garrett, Frank: 220
Gem, Idaho: 277, 279–80
Gem mine (Idaho): 278–80
Gem Theater: 319
Genoa, Nevada: 101
Geology: Comstock Lode, 96–97, 103, 112; White Pine District (Nevada), 154; California Gulch (Colorado), 166; Leadville, Colorado, 188, 194; Spencer, Colorado, 195; Cripple Creek, Colorado, 207; Lead, South Dakota, 306
George, Henry: 138
Georgetown, Colorado: 168, 176–79, 201–202
Georgetown Miner: 176
Georgia: 6, 157, 158
Georgia Gulch, Colorado: 172
Germany and Germans: 37, 47, 72, 94, 152
Gibbon, John: 297
Gihon, John H.: 68
Gila River (Arizona): 20
Gilmer, Salisbury and Patrick: 310–12, 314–15
Gilpin, William: 179
Gilpin County, Colorado: 176
Gilpin County Bumping Table: 199
Gilson, Horace C.: 273
Glengarry mine (Montana): 242
Glenwood Springs, Colorado: 197
Glorieta Pass (New Mexico): 179
Goddard, Luther M.: 283
Goetz, Jacob "Dutch Jake": 275
Gold Bottom Creek (Klondike): 333–35, 358
Gold Canyon (Nevada): 87–90; see also Comstock Lode
Gold commissioners: 358, 363–66
Gold Creek (Montana): 216
Gold Cup mine (Colorado): 195
Golden, Colorado: 170, 198
Golden, Louis: 372

Golden, Tom: 161
Golden Age, The: 261
Golden Chariot mine (Idaho): 271
Golden Era: 67
Golden Fleece mine (Colorado): 180
Golden Gate: see San Francisco, California
Golden Star mine (Black Hills): 307
Golden Terra mine (Black Hills): 307
Gold Hill, Colorado: 163
Gold Hill, Nevada: 91, 93, 137, 151; see also Virginia City, Nevada
Gold Hill News: 140
Goldrich, O. J.: 169–70
Gold Run (Black Hills): 300, 306–307
Gold Run (Colorado): 163
Good Samaritan Hospital: 370
Good Templars: 231
Goode, William H.: 169
Goodman, Joseph: 140–41
Goodrich Trail: 270
Goodwin, C. C.: 87
Goose Lake: 19
Gordon, John: 289–90
Gorgona, Panama: 33
Gould and Curry mine (Nevada): 94, 97, 112, 115, 121, 143
Government, Canadian national: 335, 359–61, 363
Government, City: California, 8, 38–39, 40–41, 83; Colorado, 178–79, 184–85; Montana, 221, 239; Black Hills, 317, 327; see also Vigilantes
Government, County: 328–29
Government, State: California, 84–85; Nevada, 102–104; Colorado, 179; Montana, 236–37, 245–50; Black Hills, 329
Government, Territorial: California, 83–84; Nevada, 102–104, 143; Colorado, 178–79; Idaho, 229; Montana, 229–30; Idaho, 273; Black Hills, 304, 328–29; Klondike, 361, 364–66
Government, U.S. national: see Army, U.S.; Arthur, Chester A.; Buchanan, James; Customs duty; Grant, U. S.; Lincoln, Abraham; Navy, U.S.; Senate, U.S.; and Supreme Court, U.S.
Grand Forks, Yukon Territory: 377
Granite Creek (Idaho): 264
Grant, Orvil: 297

231, 239, 253–55, 266–67, 274; Black
Hills, 312–14, 317, 319–20, 321–22,
324–25; Klondike, 346, 371–73, 380
Wood, Alvinus B.: 183, 187
Wood, Fremont: 284
Wood River Mining District (Idaho):
272
Woods, W. W.: 276
Woodville, South Dakota: 315
Woodward, Joseph: 92
Wool, John W.: 80
Wrangell, Alaska: 355–56
Wright, G. W.: 52
Wright, William: see DeQuille, Dan
Writers: California, 67–69; Nevada,
141–45; Colorado, 171, 193–94; Black
Hills, 323; Klondike, 380–82
Wyoming: 158, 168, 273, 290–91, 296

Yager, Erastus "Red": 228
Yakutat Bay (Klondike): 355
Yale University: 101
Yankton, South Dakota: 288, 314

Yellow Bird: 68
Yellow Jacket mine (Idaho): 272
Yellow Jacket mine (Nevada): 97, 114,
118, 126, 133
Yellowstone Expedition of 1863: 217–18
Yellowstone National Park: 219
Yellowstone River (Montana): 236, 287
300
Young, Brigham: 4
Young-Man-Afraid-of-His-Horses: 294
Yount, Jack: 90
Youth's Companion: 382
Yuba County, California: 45
Yuba River (California): 8
Yukon Midnight Sun: 374
Yukon River (Klondike): 331–32, 336,
338–42, 351, 353–56, 361, 369, 381
Yukon Territory: see Klondike, The,
and Government, Territorial

Zinc: 275
Zoller's Bar (Montana): 217